# Opportunities and Challenges of AI in Micro, Small, and Medium-Sized Enterprises

Rafael Ignacio Pérez-Uribe
https://orcid.org/0000-0001-9924-6657
*La Salle University, Colombia*

David Ocampo -Guzmán
https://orcid.org/0000-0002-6497-5646
*Universidad EAN, Colombia*

Maria Teresa Ramírez-Garzón
https://orcid.org/0000-0002-6319-3386
*University of Celaya, Colombia*

Luz Janeth Lozano-Correa
*Santo Tomas University, Colombia*

IGI Global
Scientific Publishing
Publishing Tomorrow's Research Today

| | |
|---|---|
| Vice President of Editorial | Melissa Wagner |
| Director of Acquisitions | Mikaela Felty |
| Director of Book Development | Jocelynn Hessler |
| Production Manager | Mike Brehm |
| Cover Design | Jose Rosado |

Published in the United States of America by
IGI Global Scientific Publishing
701 East Chocolate Avenue
Hershey, PA, 17033, USA
Tel: 717-533-8845 | Fax: 717-533-7115
Website: https://www.igi-global.com E-mail: cust@igi-global.com



Library of Congress Cataloging-in-Publication Data

Names: Pérez Uribe, Rafael Ignacio editor
http://id.loc.gov/rwo/agents/n2001102818
Title: Opportunities and challenges of AI in micro, small, and medium-sized enterprises / edited by Rafael Ignacio Pérez-Uribe, David Ocampo-Guzmán, Maria Teresa Ramírez-Garzón and Luz Janeth Lozano-Correa.
Description: Hershey, PA : IGI Global Scientific Publishing, [2026] | Includes bibliographical references and index. | Summary: "The general objective of this book is to clarify to the academic, business and government community the importance of Artificial Intelligence in business management"-- Provided by publisher.
Identifiers: LCCN 2025009775 (print) | LCCN 2025009776 (ebook) | ISBN 9798337328171 hardcover | ISBN 9798337328188 paperback | ISBN 9798337328195 ebook
Subjects: LCSH: Small business http://id.loc.gov/authorities/subjects/sh85123568 | Industrial management http://id.loc.gov/authorities/subjects/sh85065889 | Artificial intelligence http://id.loc.gov/authorities/subjects/sh85008180
Classification: LCC HD2341 .O47 2026 (print) | LCC HD2341 (ebook) | DDC 338.6/420285--dc23/eng/20250519
LC record available at https://lccn.loc.gov/2025009775
LC ebook record available at https://lccn.loc.gov/2025009776

British Cataloguing in Publication Data
A Cataloguing in Publication record for this book is available from the British Library.

# Editorial Advisory Board

# Table of Contents

# Detailed Table of Contents

The rapid advancement of Artificial Intelligence (AI) is transforming business operations, particularly in Micro, Small, and Medium Enterprises (MSMEs). This chapter reviews existing literature on AI's role in MSME management and decision-making, emphasizing its potential to enhance productivity, automate operations, and support data-driven strategies. AI tools such as predictive analytics, customer relationship management systems, and financial forecasting software strengthen operational efficiency and promote innovation. By enabling real-time decision-making and strategic planning, AI empowers MSMEs to improve competitiveness and achieve sustainable growth. The integration of AI fosters innovation, enhances customer engagement, and contributes significantly to the modernization of MSME business practices. This chapter provides a theoretical foundation for understanding AI's transformative impact on MSME business management and decision-making processes.



AI in MSMEs is transforming worldwide business by boosting operational efficiency, creativity, and inclusive economic growth. AI technologies, including machine learning, natural language processing, and predictive analytics, assist MSMEs in automating processes, simplifying value chains, customising customer interactions, and leveraging alternative financing. AIaaS, subscription-based, and data-driven business models are developed to enable resource-constrained MSMEs to compete in the digital economy. The chapter notes budget constraints, lack of digital infrastructure, human resource skill gaps, and organisational aversion to technology despite its revolutionary promise. Theories like TOE and DOI identify leadership, policy support, and innovation ecosystems as AI preparedness success factors. Case studies in India, Indonesia, and Jordan recommend digital literacy, localised AI technologies, ethical data governance, and cooperative tactics to boost MSME AI deployments.

Artificial Intelligence (AI) is revolutionizing the operational framework of Micro, Small, and Medium-Sized Enterprises (MSMEs) by improving efficiency, fostering innovation, and promoting sustainability. AI adoption in MSMEs encounters considerable obstacles, such as budgetary limitations, skill deficiencies, and regulatory hurdles. This book examines the opportunities and problems associated with AI application in MSMEs, emphasizing AI-enhanced operational efficiency, customer interaction, financial management, and sustainable business practices. Furthermore, it analyzes governmental regulations, AI support initiatives, collaborative approaches, and AI-as-a-Service (AIaaS) solutions that facilitate the surmounting of adoption obstacles. The discourse encompasses the function of AI in green marketing and the circular economy, highlighting AI's impact on sustainable corporate development. By strategically leveraging AI, MSMEs may augment competitiveness, refine decision-making, and promote long-term sustainability in a dynamic digital economy



This study investigates the intricate relationship between AI innovations, human capital development, and competitive advantage within Ethiopian small and medium-sized enterprises (SMEs). Utilizing a mixed-methods approach, the research reveals that AI technologies significantly enhance competitive advantage by improving operational efficiencies and decision-making processes. Furthermore, the findings underscore the mediating role of human capital, indicating that organizations that invest in employee training and skills development can better leverage AI tools. This dual focus on technological advancement and workforce development is essential for SMEs striving to thrive in an increasingly competitive landscape. The study emphasizes the importance of fostering a culture of continuous learning and collaboration between technology and human resource departments.

Colombia is the most biodiverse country in bird species and one of the top 5 in overall biodiversity in the world. Despite this, its economy has been historically focused on mineral extraction and agricultural products, despising unique and high-demand opportunities in nature-based tourism. Birdwatching offers significant potential for the strongest rural development and community well-being. This chapter applies strategic foresight to project the long-term impact of artificial intelligence (AI) on Micro, Small, and Medium-Sized Enterprises engaged in birdwatching in the Quindío region. Using qualitative methods including indexed literature review, expert interviews, and PESTEL analysis—it identifies emerging challenges and opportunities for sustainable birdwatching supported by AI. The study provides recommendations for each stakeholder involved in a birdwatching governance model, prioritizing the roles of academics, policymakers, MSME leaders, and community actors. The findings offer a replicable framework for aligning AI innovation with conservation and tourism development



Artificial Intelligence (AI) offers significant potential for the Micro, Small and Medium Enterprises (MSMEs) that drive economies in the Global South, yet its adoption remains low due to systemic barriers. This study explores how AI can be used effectively by these enterprises. Through qualitative analysis of 15 MSMEs across diverse sectors, key adoption strategies, challenges and opportunities were identified. The study's primary contribution is the AI Preparedness and Provision (AIPP) Framework. This model posits that successful adoption hinges on the synergy between two dimensions: a firm's internal AI Preparedness (strategic intent, capacity building, agile adoption, and collaboration) and the Ecosystem Provision of external support (financial, knowledge, contextual, regulations, and infrastructure). The AIPP framework provides a practical guide for both MSMEs and policymakers to bridge the gap between aspiration and action, enabling sustainable AI-driven growth across the Global South.

# Preface

## INTRODUCTION

This book *"Opportunities and Challenges of AI in Micro, Small, and Medium-Sized Enterprises"* stems from an urgent and shared question: how to transform the technological drive of artificial intelligence (AI) into a real force for prosperity for micro, small, and medium-sized enterprises. Here, voices, experiences, and analyses are brought together to offer a practical and critical roadmap that allows entrepreneurs, public managers, advisors, and communities to understand the concrete opportunities that AI opens up and, at the same time, recognize the risks and limitations that must be addressed responsibly.

This document explores the most immediate opportunities: automation of repetitive processes, improved customer service, optimized supply chains, access to data analytics previously only available to large corporations, and possibilities for personalizing products and services. These applications not only increase efficiency but can redefine business models, open market niches, and strengthen resilience to economic shocks.

The challenges that accompany AI adoption are also addressed: technological and capital barriers, skills gaps, governance and data governance gaps, risks of labor exclusion, and algorithmic biases that can reproduce inequalities. This book does not present technology as a panacea; it understands it as a tool that, when well designed and regulated, can enhance human capabilities, and when poorly managed, exacerbate preexisting vulnerabilities.

Throughout the chapters, conceptual frameworks, case studies, and practical guides for the ethical and sustainable implementation of AI solutions in local contexts are combined. Special attention is paid to phased adoption strategies, participatory governance, ongoing team building, and partnerships between businesses, governments, and academia. An approach is proposed that prioritizes economic and social well-being as much as technical efficiency.

This text invites deliberate action: to experiment with pilot projects, measure relevant results beyond technical performance, and adapt technologies according to real needs and local values. Its purpose is to offer each reader tools to make informed decisions, reduce risks, and articulate policies and practices that favor the inclusive and humane development of artificial intelligence in the productive base.

If AI transforms the way we produce and interact with the market, may that transformation serve to expand opportunities, dignify work, and strengthen communities. This document is a contribution to that end, a critical and practical guide for those who want technological innovation supported by artificial intelligence to go hand in hand with economic justice and sustainability.

## ORGANIZATION OF THE BOOK

### Chapter 1: Strategic Integration of Artificial Intelligence in MSME Decision-Making Processes: Bridging Capacity Gaps for Inclusive Digital Transformation

Artificial Intelligence (AI) adoption among micro, small, and medium-sized enterprises (MSMEs) has become a pivotal issue in the digital economy, where strategic decision-making is increasingly data-driven. Against this backdrop, this chapter explores the organizational, infrastructural, and policy-related factors that shape AI integration in MSMEs. Drawing on global policy frameworks and empirical insights, it examines how leadership orientation, digital infrastructure, and intermediary institutions influence adoption dynamics. Emphasis is placed on the need to contextualize support tools for resource-constrained environments. Promising innovations such as AI voucher schemes, regulatory sandboxes, and modular training systems are discussed as pathways to responsible and scalable implementation. Framing AI as a strategic enabler rather than a mere technical upgrade, the discussion contributes to ongoing debates on inclusive and sustainable digital transformation in small organizations.

### Chapter 2: AI-Driven Transformation in MSMEs Unlocking Opportunities, Overcoming Challenges, and Shaping the Future of Business Management

Micro, small and medium enterprises (MSMEs) make up the backbone of India's economy, contribute about 30% to the national GDP and provide employment to over

110 million people. However, in front of global digital changes and post-pandemic reorganisation, MSMEs must develop beyond traditional business models to remain competitive, flexible and durable. The emergence of Artificial Intelligence (AI) presents a paradigm change that offers tools that are able to make increased productivity, customer-focused innovation and data-driven decisions. This chapter seriously examines the transformational role of AI in the MSME region, focusing on India's socio-economic scenario, checking how AI can unlock new opportunities, address long-standing obstacles, and shape the future of business management.

## Chapter 3: Strategies and Impact of AI's Triad on Micro-enterprises and SMEs

In the early 21st century, the triad formed by the European Union, China, and the United States emerged as a key player in the development of artificial intelligence (AI). This chapter examines the characteristics of AI within each of these regions, as well as the commercial, technological, and economic relationships among them related to AI. It highlights their strengths and advantages in various categories, with a focus on microenterprises and small to medium-sized enterprises (SMEs). The chapter concludes with assessments and recommendations for implementing AI in these businesses.

## Chapter 4: Cost and Accessibility of AI - Breaking Barriers for MSMEs

This chapter explores the barriers to AI adoption faced by Micro, Small, and Medium Enterprises (MSMEs) due to cost and accessibility challenges. While AI presents significant opportunities for enhancing productivity, customer experience, and competitiveness, MSMEs often struggle with the financial burden of implementation, lack of technical infrastructure, and a shortage of skilled labor. The chapter provides a detailed analysis of the cost factors involved in AI adoption, including initial investment, ongoing maintenance, and hidden expenses. It also outlines strategies to overcome these barriers, such as leveraging cloud-based solutions, AI-as-a-Service, government support, and open-source tools. Financial models, such as subscription-based pricing and co-investment opportunities, are also explored to make AI more accessible and affordable. The chapter concludes with a look at future trends, emphasizing technological advancements that will further reduce the cost and complexity of AI for micro and small enterprises (MSMEs).

## Chapter 5: Role of Artificial Intelligence (AI) in MSMEs Sector A Paradigm Shift with Usage of AI in the Business Management and Decision Making

The rapid advancement of Artificial Intelligence (AI) is transforming business operations, particularly in Micro, Small, and Medium Enterprises (MSMEs). This chapter reviews existing literature on AI's role in MSME management and decision-making, emphasizing its potential to enhance productivity, automate operations, and support data-driven strategies. AI tools such as predictive analytics, customer relationship management systems, and financial forecasting software strengthen operational efficiency and promote innovation. By enabling real-time decision-making and strategic planning, AI empowers MSMEs to improve competitiveness and achieve sustainable growth. The integration of AI fosters innovation, enhances customer engagement, and contributes significantly to the modernization of MSME business practices. This chapter provides a theoretical foundation for understanding AI's transformative impact on MSME business management and decision-making processes.

## Chapter 6: AI-Powered Growth- Unlocking Opportunities and Navigating Challenges for Micro, Small, and Medium Enterprises

AI in MSMEs is transforming worldwide business by boosting operational efficiency, creativity, and inclusive economic growth. AI technologies, including machine learning, natural language processing, and predictive analytics, assist MSMEs in automating processes, simplifying value chains, customising customer interactions, and leveraging alternative financing. AIaaS, subscription-based, and data-driven business models are developed to enable resource-constrained MSMEs to compete in the digital economy. The chapter notes budget constraints, lack of digital infrastructure, human resource skill gaps, and organisational aversion to technology despite its revolutionary promise. Theories like TOE and DOI identify leadership, policy support, and innovation ecosystems as AI preparedness success factors. Case studies in India, Indonesia, and Jordan recommend digital literacy, localised AI technologies, ethical data governance, and cooperative tactics to boost MSME AI deployments.

## Chapter 7: Competitiveness and Productivity in Smes: Guided by AI

Artificial Intelligence (AI) is revolutionizing the operational framework of Micro, Small, and Medium-Sized Enterprises (MSMEs) by improving efficiency, fostering innovation, and promoting sustainability. AI adoption in MSMEs encounters considerable obstacles, such as budgetary limitations, skill deficiencies, and regulatory hurdles. This book examines the opportunities and problems associated with AI application in MSMEs, emphasizing AI-enhanced operational efficiency, customer interaction, financial management, and sustainable business practices. Furthermore, it analyzes governmental regulations, AI support initiatives, collaborative approaches, and AI-as-a-Service (AIaaS) solutions that facilitate the surmounting of adoption obstacles. The discourse encompasses the function of AI in green marketing and the circular economy, highlighting AI's impact on sustainable corporate development. By strategically leveraging AI, MSMEs may augment competitiveness, refine decision-making, and promote long-term sustainability in a dynamic digital economy

## Chapter 8: Does AI innovation improve competitive advantage of SMEs through human capital in Ethiopia?

This study investigates the intricate relationship between AI innovations, human capital development, and competitive advantage within Ethiopian small and medium-sized enterprises (SMEs). Utilizing a mixed-methods approach, the research reveals that AI technologies significantly enhance competitive advantage by improving operational efficiencies and decision-making processes. Furthermore, the findings underscore the mediating role of human capital, indicating that organizations that invest in employee training and skills development can better leverage AI tools. This dual focus on technological advancement and workforce development is essential for SMEs striving to thrive in an increasingly competitive landscape. The study emphasizes the importance of fostering a culture of continuous learning and collaboration between technology and human resource departments.

## Chapter 9: Emerging Opportunities and Challenges MSMEs in Birdwatching: An Approach Based on Artificial Intelligence and Strategic Foresight

Colombia is the most biodiverse country in bird species and one of the top 5 in overall biodiversity in the world. Despite this, its economy has been historically focused on mineral extraction and agricultural products, despising unique and high-demand opportunities in nature-based tourism. Birdwatching offers significant potential for the strongest rural development and community well-being. This chapter applies strategic foresight to project the long-term impact of artificial intelligence (AI) on Micro, Small, and Medium-Sized Enterprises engaged in birdwatching in the Quindío region. Using qualitative methods including indexed literature review, expert interviews, and PESTEL analysis—it identifies emerging challenges and opportunities for sustainable birdwatching supported by AI. The study provides recommendations for each stakeholder involved in a birdwatching governance model, prioritizing the roles of academics, policymakers, MSME leaders, and community actors. The findings offer a replicable framework for aligning AI innovation with conservation and tourism development.

## Chapter 10: Application Cases of Artificial Intelligence (AI) in Micro, Small and Medium Sized Enterprises: A Critical Analysis of Selected Industries in the Global South

Artificial Intelligence (AI) offers significant potential for the Micro, Small and Medium Enterprises (MSMEs) that drive economies in the Global South, yet its adoption remains low due to systemic barriers. This study explores how AI can be used effectively by these enterprises. Through qualitative analysis of 15 MSMEs across diverse sectors, key adoption strategies, challenges and opportunities were identified. The study's primary contribution is the AI Preparedness and Provision (AIPP) Framework. This model posits that successful adoption hinges on the synergy between two dimensions: a firm's internal AI Preparedness (strategic intent, capacity building, agile adoption, and collaboration) and the Ecosystem Provision of external support (financial, knowledge, contextual, regulations, and infrastructure). The AIPP framework provides a practical guide for both MSMEs and policymakers to bridge the gap between aspiration and action, enabling sustainable AI-driven growth across the Global South.

## Chapter 11: Leveraging AI to Scale SMMES, Opportunities for Sustainable Local Economic Development in South Africa

The study explored the use of Artificial Intelligence (AI) in South Africa to scale Small, Medium and Micro Enterprises (SMMEs) and promote sustainable local economic development. It used a qualitative research approach, analyzing AI integration, challenges, and outcomes. The results indicated that AI improved business efficiency, customer engagement, and market access, especially in urban and semi-urban areas. However, barriers such as limited digital infrastructure, skills shortages, and inadequate policy support persisted. To fully benefit from AI-driven growth, SMMEs require inclusive strategies and targeted interventions.

## IN CONCLUSION

As editors of *"Opportunities and Challenges of AI in Micro, Small, and Medium-Sized Enterprises"*, we are proud to present this comprehensive examination of the factors that shape the Opportunities and Challenges of AI of micro, small and medium- sized enterprises (MSMEs) in a rapidly evolving global market. The diverse perspectives offered in the chapters of this book highlight the complexity of the challenges faced by MSMEs with the use of artificial intelligence for resource optimization, both in emerging and developed economies. These types of companies, considered the backbone of local economies, are crucial players in the pursuit of national and regional economic growth.

Artificial intelligence offers micro, small, and medium-sized enterprises (MSMEs) a decisive lever for increasing productivity, improving customer service, and accessing markets, while posing structural challenges in terms of capacity, governance, and equity that require public policies, training, and adoption models tailored to local contexts.

Several key opportunities for AI in MSMEs are described throughout the book: automation of repetitive tasks and process optimization that reduce operating costs and response times; personalization, 24/7 support, and sentiment analytics that increase customer retention and lifetime value; accessible tools that enable data-driven decision-making and scale business strategies; data-driven services, platforms, and microservices that transform offerings and create additional revenue; and digital capabilities that facilitate exporting, outsourcing, and international collaboration.

We hope that the insights, cases, models, and strategies presented in this book will serve as valuable resources for academics, policymakers, and practitioners alike. By addressing the critical elements of MSME´s AI, we believe that this collection contributes meaningfully to the broader discourse on economic productivity, resilience, and innovation.

In conclusion, we invite readers to reflect on the lessons shared in these pages and apply them to their own projects, whether in academia, research, business, or policymaking. As MSMEs continue to navigate the complexities of the global marketplace, we trust that the knowledge contained in this book will provide them with essential methods and tools for managing Artificial Intelligence to drive long-term growth and success.

**Rafael Pérez-Uribe**
*La Salle University, Colombia*

**David Ocampo Guzmán**
*Universidad EAN, Colombia*

**María Teresa Ramírez-Garzón**
*University of Celaya, Colombia*

**Janeth Lozano Correa**
*Santo Tomas University, Colombia*

# Acknowledgment

First, as an act of humility and contrition, we would like first to express our sentiment of gratitude to the Creator. We are truly grateful for yet another opportunity to learn, to write, to evaluate, to revise and to share and disseminate knowledge. In this case, about artificial intelligence and its use in MSMEs.

Secondly, it is our honour and our privilege to share "the stage" with colleagues from different countries and cultures. It will always be an enrichening experience to read your work, and for you to read and evaluate ours.

A very loud and special THANK YOU for our panel of peer reviewers, who so selflessly have taken time out of their busy schedules to revise every chapter of this book. They are the cornerstone of this project and without their invaluable collaboration this book would have never seen the light of day.

Last, but not least, we strongly hope this book will contribute to the academic and organizational world to develop different types of approaches, methodologies, strategies, and management techniques to face the phenomenon of "Opportunities and Challenges of AI in Micro, Small, and Medium-Sized Enterprises" from different points of view and different contexts.

Sincerely yours,

The Editors.

# Chapter 1
# Strategic Integration of Artificial Intelligence in MSME Decision-Making Processes:
## Bridging Capacity Gaps for Inclusive Digital Transformation

**Fatma Ince**
http://orcid.org/0000-0002-0628-5858
*Mersin University, Turkey*

## ABSTRACT

*Artificial Intelligence (AI) adoption among micro, small, and medium-sized enterprises (MSMEs) has become a pivotal issue in the digital economy, where strategic decision-making is increasingly data-driven. Against this backdrop, this chapter explores the organizational, infrastructural, and policy-related factors that shape AI integration in MSMEs. Drawing on global policy frameworks and empirical insights, it examines how leadership orientation, digital infrastructure, and intermediary institutions influence adoption dynamics. Emphasis is placed on the need to contextualize support tools for resource-constrained environments. Promising innovations such as AI voucher schemes, regulatory sandboxes, and modular training systems are discussed as pathways to responsible and scalable implementation. Framing AI as a strategic enabler rather than a mere technical upgrade, the discussion contributes to ongoing debates on inclusive and sustainable digital transformation in small organizations.*

DOI: 10.4018/979-8-3373-2817-1.ch001

## INTRODUCTION

Artificial intelligence has rapidly gained prominence across organizations of all sizes, offering transformative potential in strategic decision-making. In particular, micro, small, and medium-sized enterprises are beginning to leverage AI to enhance efficiency, responsiveness, and innovation, enabled through scalable and cost-effective cloud-based AI and analytics solutions increasingly adopted by MSMEs (Organisation for Economic Co-operation and Development [OECD], 2021). This trend marks a shift from traditional barriers that once confined AI usage to larger corporations.

MSMEs account for over 90 percent of global businesses and provide more than 50 percent of employment worldwide, yet they continue to face structural constraints such as limited financial resources, insufficient digital infrastructure, and a lack of specialized expertise (The United Nations Conference on Trade and Development [UNCTAD], 2025a; World Bank, 2023). Research shows these challenges are especially relevant when integrating AI into decision-making processes, as small organizations often struggle with adoption due to cost, skills gaps, and organizational readiness issues (Oldemeyer et al., 2024). The emerging AI ecosystem aims to reduce these gaps. For instance, UNCTAD (2025b) projects the global AI market will reach USD 4.8 trillion by 2033, spotlighting the importance of inclusive AI strategies, particularly for smaller economies and enterprises.

Recent empirical and systematic studies offer crucial insights into the organizational, technological, and contextual dynamics shaping AI adoption in MSMEs. For instance, Ayinaddis (2025) identifies key determinants such as technology readiness, managerial engagement, and external collaboration, while Oldemeyer, Jede, and Teuteberg (2024) highlight recurring challenges including knowledge deficits, infrastructure constraints, and cost-related barriers. Together, these studies emphasize the importance of aligning AI integration strategies with the unique structural conditions and resource limitations of small enterprises.

This chapter explores how the integration of AI strategically aligns with MSME decision-making processes. It synthesizes interdisciplinary research from information systems, management science, and entrepreneurship to identify key enablers and barriers, examine organizational dynamics, and propose conceptual frameworks that support AI-driven decision-making in resource-constrained environments. Through a theoretical and literature-based analysis, the discussion advances a deeper understanding of the strategic role of AI in MSMEs and offers insights into how small enterprises position themselves within the evolving digital ecosystem.

## BACKGROUND

This chapter adopts a conceptual and theoretical approach that relies on the analysis of secondary sources. Rather than employing primary data collection or empirical techniques, it draws upon a wide range of existing academic literature, policy reports, and institutional documents that address the intersection of artificial intelligence and managerial decision-making in MSMEs. The methodology focuses on identifying relevant contributions from peer-reviewed journals and authoritative sources published within the past decade. These materials are selected for their conceptual relevance, disciplinary diversity, and contribution to understanding the digital transformation processes in micro, small, and medium-sized enterprises. While no empirical data is gathered, the literature-based method enables a structured synthesis of current knowledge and theoretical insights. This approach supports a critical reflection on the implications of AI adoption for managerial practices and allows for the development of evidence-informed suggestions for future research and practice.

Artificial intelligence is no longer a peripheral tool in organizational operations; it has become a core component of decision-making within micro, small, and medium-sized enterprises. Yet, this integration does not occur in isolation. It is shaped by digital readiness, structural capacities, leadership vision, and broader market conditions. Understanding the organizational pathways through which AI becomes embedded in MSME decision-making requires a comprehensive perspective that bridges internal structures and external ecosystems. The following discussion delves into this transformation by examining how MSMEs navigate the digital environment, develop strategic orientations for AI adoption, and apply intelligent technologies across functional areas. This analysis provides a clearer understanding of the key factors that facilitate or hinder AI-enabled decision making in resource constrained settings.

### The Evolving Digital Ecosystem and MSMEs

The digital transformation of the global economy increasingly shapes how micro, small, and medium-sized enterprises operate and compete. Technological advances in cloud computing, artificial intelligence-as-a-*service* (AIaaS), and digital platforms have reduced the cost and complexity of deploying intelligent systems. These developments allow MSMEs to access capabilities that were once exclusive to large corporations. However, despite these opportunities, MSMEs remain vulnerable to digital exclusion due to persistent challenges such as poor infrastructure, limited digital literacy, and uneven regulatory support (OECD, 2021). This evolving landscape reflects both an expansion of potential and a replication of existing inequalities.

Another dimension of the digital ecosystem transformation is the rise of modular and customizable AI tools tailored to small business needs. Low-code platforms, sector-specific analytics kits, and open-source machine learning libraries now enable incremental adoption and experimentation without requiring significant capital investment (World Bank, 2023). These tools facilitate learning-by-doing and reduce the perceived risk of adopting advanced technologies. As such, MSMEs can increasingly align AI integration with their operational realities rather than retrofitting technologies designed for large-scale enterprises. Nonetheless, the adoption remains uneven across regions, particularly in emerging markets where MSMEs face compounded constraints (UNCTAD, 2025a).

Moreover, the ecosystem shift is not purely technological. Institutional dynamics, public–private partnerships, and policy innovation also significantly shape the inclusiveness of AI adoption. For example, national AI ecosystems such as Singapore's AI Grand Challenge, include public–private research consortia that target sectors like healthcare and education, facilitating research commercialization and SME engagement (Organisation for Economic Co-operation and Development [OECD], 2025). Such collaborative mechanisms enhance MSMEs' strategic positioning by providing both technical and institutional support in evolving environments. Still, the impact of these measures varies widely depending on governance quality, local market structure, and the adaptive capacity of organizations. These structural disparities indicate that access to technology alone is not enough. Meaningful integration depends on context-sensitive strategies, well-designed support systems, and an in-depth understanding of MSMEs' constraints and motivational dynamics.

## Why a Strategic Approach to AI in MSMEs Is Needed

While the availability of AI tools has increased, many MSMEs still lack a coherent strategy for integrating these technologies into their core decision-making processes. Without a structured approach, organizations often engage in fragmented adoption that implementing isolated tools without alignment to business goals or capacity. This can lead to wasted resources, poor user uptake, and underutilization of AI capabilities (Oldemeyer et al., 2024). Strategic integration, on the other hand, ensures that AI implementation is purpose-driven, sustainable, and aligned with organizational objectives. It also promotes better planning for change management, workforce reskilling, and operational redesign.

A strategic orientation is particularly crucial for resource-constrained organizations. MSMEs frequently face trade-offs between short-term survival and long-term innovation, making it essential to prioritize AI investments that deliver tangible value. Studies suggest that strategic AI adoption in MSMEs is positively associated with performance gains, particularly when guided by high level managerial commitment and external collaboration (Ayinaddis, 2025). Moreover, organizations that develop clear AI roadmaps are better positioned to integrate these technologies incrementally, learn from implementation outcomes, and iterate in ways that align with both business needs and technological evolution.

In addition, strategic alignment allows MSMEs to embed AI into organizational routines rather than treating it as an external or experimental add-on. This is especially important given the rapid pace of technological change and the increasing complexity of AI tools. A strategic perspective helps smaller organizations manage uncertainty, build absorptive capacity, and create feedback loops that support continuous improvement (OECD, 2025). As the digital landscape continues to evolve, MSMEs that adopt a structured and intentional approach to AI are more likely to remain competitive, resilient, and adaptive in the long term.

## The Strategic Importance of AI in Business Management

Artificial intelligence has evolved from a niche technological tool into a critical strategic resource within modern business environments. This evolution is not merely technological but also conceptual, as organizations increasingly recognize AI as integral to long-term planning, competitive positioning, and innovation management. The transition from task specific automation to strategic decision support highlights a broader shift in how organizations perceive value creation through digital means. No longer confined to operational back-ends, AI systems are now embedded across departments, from finance and marketing to supply chain and executive planning, where they inform core decisions with precision and scale (Machucho & Ortiz, 2025).

The growing relevance of AI in business is closely tied to its capacity to process vast and complex datasets in real time. Traditional decision-making approaches, particularly in smaller organizations, often depend on managerial intuition and historical experience. These methods, while valuable, are limited in their ability to adapt to rapidly shifting market dynamics. AI offers a counterpoint by enabling managers to simulate future scenarios, forecast market trends, and evaluate risks using predictive analytics and machine learning models. The difference is not only one of speed or scale, but also of reliability. Data-informed decisions tend to produce more consistent outcomes in volatile environments, particularly when orgaizations must make choices with incomplete information (Davenport & Ronanki, 2018).

Recent studies confirm this strategic pivot and highlight the importance of change. According to Salesforce (2024), 91 percent of small and medium-sized enterprises that adopted AI technologies reported a noticeable improvement in revenue growth. This figure is particularly relevant for resource-constrained organizations, which often lack the financial and organizational flexibility of larger competitors. When applied strategically, AI functions not only as a support mechanism but as a catalyst for growth. Predictive tools optimize inventory management, customer relationship systems refine targeting strategies, and AI-driven dashboards offer executives real-time oversight over performance indicators. Such applications contribute directly to competitive advantage and long-term positioning in the market (Chui et al., 2018; Csaszar et al., 2024).

Beyond its technical benefits, AI also enhances the organization's capacity for learning and adaptation. When organizations integrate AI into their daily routines, they begin to institutionalize knowledge in a way that is dynamic and cumulative. Systems are continuously trained with new data, and the feedback loop between action and insight becomes shorter and more effective. This accelerates organizational learning and encourages experimentation. Organizations can test multiple strategic hypotheses, measure outcomes more accurately, and recalibrate their approaches in an evidence-based manner. In this sense, AI contributes not only to immediate efficiency, but to long-term strategic resilience (Ransbotham et al., 2021; Sánchez et al., 2025).

One of the most critical strategic contributions of AI is its role in proactive rather than reactive management. While traditional models often rely on post-event analysis, AI enables organizations to engage in forward-looking planning. Whether forecasting customer demand, anticipating supply chain disruptions, or detecting early signs of financial distress, AI tools allow decision-makers to act before problems become critical. This shift from retrospective to anticipatory management is transformative, particularly in sectors characterized by uncertainty and rapid change. Strategic agility, once considered a luxury for large organizations, becomes achievable even for smaller players when AI tools are properly leveraged (Brynjolfsson & McElheran, 2016; Bughin et al., 2018).

The stakes are particularly high for SMEs, making transitional phases harder to manage. These enterprises operate with limited room for error and often lack the deep reserves that buffer large corporations from external shocks. The strategic integration of AI therefore represents not just a competitive edge but a structural necessity. However, successful adoption requires more than technology. It demands alignment between digital systems and business objectives, the presence of digital leadership, and an organizational culture that supports experimentation and data-based thinking. Without these conditions, AI investments may fail to deliver strategic value, regardless of their technical sophistication (OECD, 2021).

The contemporary business ecosystem is experiencing a significant transformation that increasingly favors micro, small, and medium-sized organizations. This shift is driven by a combination of technological, policy, and market developments that collectively reduce historical scale-related disadvantages. The democratization of technology that most notably through cloud computing, software-as-a-service (SaaS) models, and digital marketplaces, has made advanced tools more affordable, scalable, and user-friendly, allowing smaller organizations to access capabilities that were previously exclusive to large corporations. For example, modular AI solutions, such as AI-as-a-service platforms, low-code development tools, and sector-specific analytics kits, now enable businesses to experiment incrementally without incurring high upfront infrastructure costs. This gradual implementation approach supports continuous learning, minimizes disruption risk, and encourages innovation within constrained operational settings (Pandey, 2025; Syed et al., 2025).

In parallel, recent public policy initiatives are actively supporting inclusive digital transformation through SME targeted funding programs, tax incentives, and streamlined regulatory compliance processes. These frameworks contribute to a more equitable competitive landscape by lowering institutional barriers and encouraging adoption of intelligent technologies across all business sizes. Furthermore, evolving market dynamics now favor characteristics commonly found in smaller organizations, such as niche customization, localized production, and agile responsiveness. Consumer preferences are increasingly oriented toward personalized, rapidly delivered, and ethically produced goods and services that domains in which MSMEs tend to thrive. Additionally, the decentralization of global supply chains and the rise of digital digital business-to-business (B2B) platforms have further eroded traditional procurement and distribution advantages once tied to large-scale operations (Wieland, A., & Durach, 2021; World Bank. 2023). These developments suggest that organizational adaptability and digital integration, rather than size alone, are becoming decisive factors for sustained competitiveness in the current business environment.

Therefore, understanding AI not just as a tool but as a strategic framework is essential for MSMEs navigating the digital economy. Strategic integration involves more than buying software; it requires new capabilities, new mindsets, and new structures. Organizations must think holistically about how data flows through their organization, how insights are generated and acted upon, and how AI interacts with human judgment. This holistic orientation transforms AI from a cost center into a value generator and allows even the smallest organizations to compete in complex markets.

## MAIN FOCUS OF THE CHAPTER

### AI Applications in Managerial Decision-Making

Artificial intelligence technologies are being increasingly integrated into managerial decision-making processes across business types and sectors. In the context of micro, small, and medium-sized organizations, the application of AI extends beyond automation to more sophisticated roles such as data interpretation, predictive modeling, and strategic simulation. As AI tools become more accessible and context-aware, their relevance for managerial decision-making grows rapidly. This chapter presents a thematic review of key application areas in which AI contributes to decision-making, particularly within the constraints and priorities of smaller businesses.

One of the most mature and widely adopted uses of AI in decision-making lies in customer analytics. AI enables organizations to track, segment, and analyze customer behaviors in real time, drawing insights from transactional data, website interactions, and social media activity. Machine learning algorithms cluster customer types, identify churn patterns, and suggest targeted interventions to improve retention and satisfaction. For resource-constrained organizations, such insights are essential to personalize offerings and prioritize customer relationship management with precision. Research highlights that AI-driven customer intelligence not only improves marketing efficiency but also supports higher-level strategic decisions related to pricing, positioning, and brand development (Akter et al., 2025; Peretz-Andersson et al., 2024).

Another critical domain is financial forecasting and planning. AI-powered tools can analyze historical financial data, detect anomalies, and simulate cash flow scenarios under different market conditions. These tools support budget planning, investment analysis, and early-warning systems for financial distress. Particularly for organizations operating on tight margins, predictive financial tools serve as essential safeguards against liquidity crises and inform long-term financial sustainability. In recent years, fintech solutions specifically targeting MSMEs have incorporated AI modules for credit risk evaluation, invoice factoring decisions, and tax optimization, often with cloud-based delivery models that reduce deployment costs (OECD, 2021; Subramanyam, 2025; UNCTAD, 2025a).

Operational optimization represents a third major application area. AI enhances supply chain visibility, demand forecasting, inventory control, and scheduling through the use of predictive analytics and real-time sensor data. For example, AI systems may detect inventory depletion patterns and automatically adjust procurement timing, reducing stockouts or overstock situations. These systems also support capacity planning, logistics routing, and maintenance scheduling that decisions that directly impact efficiency and cost. For small businesses, which often operate without dedicated operations analysts, these capabilities allow for data-driven management that scales with demand fluctuations (Salesforce, 2024; Su et al., 2025).

Risk management and crisis response are additional domains where AI plays an increasingly strategic role. Organizations use AI to detect fraud, assess cybersecurity threats, and anticipate regulatory compliance risks. In uncertain environments, AI tools help managers prepare contingency plans by modeling best-case and worst-case scenarios using probabilistic algorithms. During global disruptions such as the COVID-19 pandemic, AI applications helped organizations make rapid operational adjustments and simulate alternative strategies for workforce reallocation, remote service delivery, or financial restructuring (Mahmud, 2025; Ransbotham et al., 2022).

In human resource management, AI contributes to more structured and data-supported decision-making in recruitment, performance evaluation, and workforce planning. Algorithms can screen job applicants based on predefined skill sets, analyze team performance metrics, and even suggest internal mobility pathways for talent retention. However, the ethical and legal challenges surrounding fairness, transparency, and bias in algorithmic HR tools are particularly relevant for small organizations lacking internal compliance departments. As such, the adoption of AI in human capital management requires careful governance and context-specific implementation (Machucho & Ortiz, 2025). Institutional frameworks and well-being resources available to decision-makers have a substantial impact on how organizations adapt to AI-enabled planning and simulation processes (İnce, 2023).

Strategic decision-making is also increasingly influenced by AI-based scenario planning and simulation tools. Executives and managers use these systems to test hypotheses, compare outcomes, and allocate resources in a simulated environment. These applications are particularly valuable for MSMEs operating in volatile markets or with limited strategic foresight capacity. They allow leaders to identify long-term opportunities or vulnerabilities and make adaptive choices before committing scarce resources. In some cases, AI tools are integrated into digital dashboards that consolidate financial, operational, and customer data into a single decision-support interface (Aguinis et al., 2024; Brynjolfsson & McElheran, 2016; Saranya et al., 2025).

AI applications also play a growing role in regulatory decision-making. As compliance frameworks become more complex, AI tools help organizations track legal updates, flag risks, and generate audit-ready documentation. For small businesses, which often lack dedicated legal teams, these tools reduce administrative burden and ensure alignment with sectoral requirements. This function is particularly important in highly regulated sectors such as finance, healthcare, and food production, where compliance failures can lead to severe operational or reputational damage (Katz, 2025; OECD, 2021).

A cross-cutting theme across all these domains is the increasing modularity and interoperability of AI tools. Instead of requiring full-scale enterprise systems, many AI solutions come in lightweight, plug-and-play formats that integrate with existing workflows. This flexibility allows small organizations to adopt AI incrementally, testing value in one area before scaling to others. It also lowers the risk of disruption and creates a feedback loop through which decision-makers build trust in the technology over time (UNCTAD, 2025a).

Overall, AI applications in managerial decision-making are expanding not only in scope but also in accessibility. While larger organizations have traditionally led adoption, MSMEs are rapidly catching up, driven by declining technology costs, improved user interfaces, and more tailored implementation models. As this thematic review illustrates, AI is no longer limited to operational automation but is embedded in the strategic, financial, and human dimensions of organizational management.

## Challenges and Enablers of AI Adoption in MSMEs

While artificial intelligence holds significant promise for micro, small, and medium-sized businesses, its adoption remains uneven across industries and regions. Many organizations continue to encounter structural, financial, technical, and cultural challenges that limit their ability to integrate AI into core business functions. At the same time, a growing ecosystem of public support mechanisms, technological innovations, and implementation models is beginning to lower entry barriers. This section explores both the persistent obstacles and emerging enablers that shape AI adoption in smaller organizations.

One of the most prominent challenges is the lack of digital infrastructure. Many MSMEs still operate with outdated hardware, inconsistent internet connectivity, and fragmented information systems. Without a stable technological foundation, AI tools cannot be deployed or integrated effectively into daily operations. Even when digital infrastructure exists, it may not be compatible with advanced software or cloud-based solutions, leading to high switching costs or workflow disruptions (Baabdullah et al., 2021; Mugisha et al., 2025). Furthermore, cybersecurity concerns and data storage limitations deter many businesses from investing in AI systems that rely heavily on sensitive internal and customer data.

Financial constraints represent another significant barrier. AI implementation typically requires up-front investments not only in software but also in training, process redesign, and maintenance. For businesses with limited working capital, these costs can be prohibitive. Even when low-cost or freemium AI tools are available, many decision-makers hesitate to invest due to uncertainty about return on investment or concerns about hidden technical complexity. A lack of access to affordable credit or innovation grants further exacerbates the problem, particularly in low and middle income economies (Jain et al., 2025).

Human capital limitations also slow AI adoption. Many organizations report a shortage of staff with the technical skills required to operate, maintain, or interpret AI systems. This includes not only programmers and data scientists but also mid-level managers who are expected to make data-informed decisions using AI-generated insights. Digital literacy gaps, especially among older workers or traditional business owners, often translate into resistance or misuse of available technologies (Mohib et al., 2025; Peretz-Andersson et al., 2024). Moreover, in organizations where digital transformation is not embedded into long-term planning, AI tends to be treated as an experimental add-on rather than a strategic tool.

Organizational culture and leadership orientation further influence the pace of AI adoption. In many small businesses, there is an ingrained preference for routine, hands-on management styles and reliance on intuition. This mindset may resist algorithmic recommendations or automation processes that reduce human oversight. Leaders who lack digital vision may also underestimate the long-term benefits of AI integration or may perceive it as a trend relevant only to larger, tech-intensive organizations. In such cases, digital innovation is often delayed not by a lack of tools, but by a lack of conviction (Dipoatmodjo, 2025).

Despite these challenges, several enablers are emerging that support AI adoption in MSMEs. One of the most important is the rise of AI-as-a-Service models. These platforms offer subscription-based access to AI tools without requiring significant infrastructure investment. Organizations can integrate features such as chatbots, recommendation engines, or predictive analytics modules through user-friendly interfaces, often with minimal technical support. This modularity and scalability allow businesses to adopt AI incrementally, reducing perceived risk and promoting gradual digital maturation (Mugisha et al., 2025).

Governmental and multilateral policy initiatives also play a crucial role in enabling adoption. Programs that offer funding, tax incentives, or capacity-building workshops targeted specifically at small businesses have been shown to increase digital uptake. *A case in point is* national strategies that incorporate digital transformation vouchers, cloud adoption subsidies, and AI literacy campaigns targeting business owners and employees. These initiatives not only lower the financial barrier but also help to create a supportive ecosystem that fosters experimentation and learning (OECD, 2021; UNCTAD, 2025a).

Another enabling factor is the development of context-sensitive AI solutions. Rather than offering generic platforms, technology providers are increasingly designing sector-specific or region-specific tools that reflect the realities of MSMEs. These include AI systems that support agriculture, retail, logistics, or local service delivery, often using local languages and simplified user interfaces. By aligning product design with operational constraints, these solutions improve adoption rates and ensure higher value generation from AI implementation (Pandey, 2025).

Peer learning and ecosystem engagement also facilitate AI diffusion. Business networks, local chambers of commerce, and innovation hubs offer MSMEs opportunities to observe pilot projects, share lessons learned, and build informal support communities. Participation in such networks reduces perceived complexity and provides social proof of AI's value. When small business owners see successful examples of AI use in comparable contexts, their willingness to experiment with similar tools increases significantly (Ayinaddis, 2025).

Finally, AI is increasingly embedded within widely used business platforms such as accounting software, customer relationship management systems, and e-commerce applications. Even when not explicitly adopted as standalone solutions, AI functionalities become accessible through integrated features like automated invoicing, dynamic pricing suggestions, and customer segmentation dashboards. This form of "invisible adoption" enables gradual digital transformation without necessitating significant behavioral or structural changes. Over time, such passive exposure facilitates organizational familiarity and lays the groundwork for more intentional and strategic AI integration.

## SOLUTIONS AND RECOMMENDATIONS

Public policy and institutional frameworks play a crucial role in shaping the trajectory of AI adoption among micro, small, and medium-sized enterprises. While the strategic integration of AI depends heavily on organizational readiness and resource availability, external enablers such as infrastructure development, legal clarity, financial support, and intermediary engagement significantly influence outcomes. This overview examines the key policy areas where targeted interventions can help bridge existing gaps, foster inclusive digital transformation, and enable MSMEs to derive long-term value from AI technologies.

### Strengthening Digital Foundations for AI Adoption

Robust and accessible digital infrastructure is a fundamental prerequisite for effective AI adoption among MSMEs. In many low and middle income countries, digital divides persist in the form of unreliable internet access, insufficient bandwidth, and geographic disparities, especially in rural and peri-urban regions. These barriers hinder the effective utilization of AI tools, which increasingly rely on cloud-based architectures and real-time data processing. Without adequate connectivity, even the most user friendly AI systems remain inaccessible, exacerbating existing inequalities between large organizations and MSMEs (World Bank, 2025).

Governments have a central role in correcting these disparities through investment in broadband infrastructure and national digitalization strategies that explicitly include MSME-focused objectives. For example, the European Union's "Digital Europe Programme" allocates substantial funding to support high-capacity networks, cybersecurity infrastructure, and data interoperability, which are all critical for successful AI implementation (European Commission, 2025). Similar efforts can be seen in Southeast Asia, where initiatives led by the Association of Southeast Asian Nations [ASEAN] Digital Masterplan 2025 aim to strengthen regional digital readiness, including targeted infrastructure upgrades for small enterprises (ASEAN, 2025). Given that regional disparities in digital infrastructure and institutional capacity shape how organizations benefit from public innovation support mechanisms (İnce, 2024).

However, infrastructure investments alone are insufficient. Policies must be complemented with capacity-building mechanisms that ensure MSMEs can meaningfully engage with the technologies provided. This includes technical support hotlines, regional AI implementation centers, and digital help desks within existing public-private partnerships. The World Economic Forum (2025) emphasizes that inclusive access to infrastructure must be accompanied by inclusive access to knowledge, or else the digital transformation risks deepening structural inequality rather than alleviating it.

Traditional digital training models, which often focus narrowly on basic computer use or general digital awareness, no longer align with the complexity of AI-enabled management. As AI technologies become more embedded in everyday business operations, training content must evolve to reflect emerging demands in data analysis, model interpretation, and strategic decision-making (OECD, 2025). Previous research has emphasized the importance of modular and context-sensitive training programs to foster long-term digital engagement among smaller organizations (İnce, 2021). MSMEs, in particular, need capacity-building programs that are both modular and customized to their operational realities.

A promising development is the emergence of tiered training systems that differentiate between strategic, operational, and technical learning needs. For instance, managers may require scenario-based workshops on evaluating AI vendors or forecasting return on investment, while operational staff benefit more from hands-on exercises using sector-specific tools (UNCTAD, 2025a). These training layers not only build technical literacy but also foster internal alignment across roles, which is essential for long-term AI integration.

To maximize outreach and impact, delivery channels should leverage existing business ecosystems such as local chambers of commerce, entrepreneurship centers, and university-business partnerships. These institutions often enjoy high trust among MSMEs and can contextualize training to local market conditions. Furthermore, embedding digital literacy into vocational education and lifelong learning programs ensures that the next generation of workers and entrepreneurs enter the labor market with a basic understanding of AI principles (International Labour Organization [ILO], 2021).

## Incentivizing Responsible AI Integration in MSMEs

Financial incentives remain a powerful policy tool to promote AI experimentation among MSMEs, particularly those that face liquidity constraints or perceive innovation as risky. However, many current subsidy schemes are overly broad, often failing to address the unique needs of AI deployment. MSMEs require more targeted instruments such as innovation vouchers, AI-specific grant programs, and outcome-based co-financing models that reward long-term integration rather than one-off procurement (OECD, 2021).

In Germany, for example, the "go-digital" initiative offers consultancy and implementation grants specifically for AI use cases in small businesses, reducing barriers to initial experimentation (Perspektiven schaffen, 2024). Similarly, South Korea's AI Voucher Program allows eligible MSMEs to receive funding to procure AI services, emphasizing scalability and sustainability (Government of the Republic of Korea, 2020). These models indicate that well-designed incentives can both stimulate demand and guide businesses toward responsible technology use.

To prevent misuse or superficial applications, incentive programs must incorporate transparent evaluation metrics. These can include benchmarks such as improved productivity, enhanced decision-making capabilities, or measurable customer satisfaction. Furthermore, linking financial support to ethical standards such as fairness, transparency, and explainability, helps ensure that AI adoption aligns with broader societal goals and business ethics frameworks (Radanliev, 2025).

AI regulation is rapidly becoming a defining issue in the digital economy, with implications for privacy, accountability, and competition. However, MSMEs often lack the legal capacity or compliance infrastructure to navigate complex regulatory landscapes. This regulatory uncertainty can deter AI adoption, especially when businesses fear legal penalties or reputational damage from unintended misuse (Ransbotham et al., 2022).

To address these challenges, policymakers should design legal frameworks that are scalable to the capacities of MSMEs. In the U.K., the Information Commissioner's Office provides a regulatory sandbox that enables businesses, including MSMEs, to test AI applications under regulatory supervision. Such sandboxes promote innovation while ensuring compliance with legal standards, including data protection, algorithmic transparency, and consumer consent. Simplified guidelines and sector-specific adaptations can further demystify complex regulatory requirements and encourage responsible AI deployment tailored to the needs of smaller enterprises (UK Information Commissioner's Office, 2025).

Furthermore, legal accessibility must be paired with institutional support. Help desks, online toolkits, and multilingual documentation enable broader engagement with AI laws, especially in diverse business environments. Creating regional ombuds services or legal aid programs specifically for MSMEs using digital technologies could further reduce compliance gaps. Ultimately, regulations must strike a balance between safeguarding public interest and empowering innovation in small business ecosystems.

MSMEs often operate in isolation, lacking the resources and strategic networks that larger organizations use to adapt to technological change. In this context, intermediary organizations such as business associations, cooperatives, and incubators can serve as vital conduits for AI-related support. These actors understand the unique challenges of their constituencies and are positioned to bridge the gap between top-down policy and grassroots practice (Ayinaddis, 2025).

Empowering intermediaries involves equipping them with the tools, funding, and knowledge to act as AI multipliers. For example, chambers of commerce could organize sector-specific AI demonstration days, while cooperatives may offer shared access to AI systems through pooled infrastructure models. The Inter-American Development Bank (2024) has piloted such models in Latin America, enabling MSMEs to access advanced technologies collectively rather than individually.

Moreover, intermediaries can play a key role in monitoring the real-world impact of AI policy and practice. Their feedback loops help refine public interventions and ensure that programs remain aligned with business realities. As trusted voices within the community, they also facilitate peer-to-peer learning and foster a culture of experimentation. Strengthening these networks is essential for achieving inclusive and context-sensitive digital transformation.

## FUTURE RESEARCH DIRECTIONS

Although this chapter provides a theoretical and literature-driven exploration of AI adoption in MSMEs, several research gaps remain that warrant future empirical investigation. First, longitudinal studies examining the sustained impact of AI adoption on organizational performance in MSMEs are still limited. Most available studies provide cross-sectional snapshots, which fail to capture the dynamic nature of AI integration over time. Future research should prioritize long-term impact assessments, particularly regarding the relationship between AI capabilities and strategic adaptability in volatile markets. Moreover, there is a growing need to explore sector-specific patterns of adoption, especially in industries where MSMEs constitute a dominant share of economic activity, such as agriculture, retail, and creative services (Ayinaddis, 2025; UNCTAD, 2025a).

Second, comparative international research is needed to assess how regional policy ecosystems shape the success of AI implementation in resource-constrained environments. As policy interventions and digital infrastructure vary significantly between developed and developing economies, research should investigate how different institutional conditions affect AI-related decision-making outcomes. Additionally, future studies could evaluate the role of intermediaries such as business associations, incubators, and public private innovation networks, in facilitating AI access for MSMEs. Interdisciplinary approaches combining insights from organizational behavior, digital transformation, and development economics may also offer a more comprehensive understanding of the multifaceted nature of AI integration (Peretz-Andersson et al., 2024; World Bank, 2023). Advancing this research agenda will help design evidence-based frameworks that not only support adoption but also promote equitable and sustainable digital transformation for small businesses.

## CONCLUSION

The strategic integration of artificial intelligence into business decision-making represents a key dimension of organizational transformation in the contemporary digital economy. For micro, small, and medium-sized enterprises, adopting AI is not only about introducing technological tools but also about redefining how strategic capabilities are developed and applied in constrained environments. This chapter demonstrates that AI enables these organizations to strengthen their agility, optimize processes, and gain insights that improve both operational and strategic outcomes.

While the benefits are increasingly clear, MSMEs encounter persistent barriers that hinder their ability to fully leverage AI. These include limited infrastructure, restricted access to capital, skill shortages, and institutional fragmentation. However, recent advancements in cloud technologies, open-source AI frameworks, and modular software-as-a-service offerings contribute to reducing these constraints. Moreover, global policy initiatives and development programs increasingly recognize the role of MSMEs in inclusive economic growth, and accordingly design support instruments that enhance digital readiness and foster innovation in small organizations.

This discussion contributes to the broader literature by framing AI as a strategic enabler rather than merely a technical upgrade. The analysis emphasizes that successful AI adoption in MSMEs depends on organizational readiness, leadership commitment, and the presence of supportive external ecosystems. It also shows that context matters. The unique needs, limitations, and market positions of MSMEs require tailored frameworks rather than one-size-fits-all approaches commonly designed for larger enterprises.

For policymakers and support institutions, this analysis underscores the importance of building comprehensive ecosystems that promote AI awareness, provide relevant training, support experimentation, and offer incentives that reduce perceived risk. Regulatory clarity, infrastructure investment, and partnerships between public and private actors are all crucial to this process. Intermediary institutions such as chambers of commerce and local innovation hubs play a vital role in translating high-level strategies into practical solutions for MSMEs on the ground.

In summary, the future of AI adoption in MSMEs rests on coordinated actions that bridge the gap between potential and practice. By aligning technological solutions with organizational capacity and environmental support, AI can serve as a catalyst for resilience, competitiveness, and sustainable growth. The strategic integration of AI in small enterprises is no longer a speculative proposition but a necessary step in ensuring their relevance and contribution in a rapidly evolving digital world.

## REFERENCES


Aguinis, H., Beltran, J. R., & Cope, A. (2024). How to use generative AI as a human resource management assistant. *Organizational Dynamics*, *53*(1), 101029. DOI: 10.1016/j.orgdyn.2024.101029

Akter, J., Roy, A., Rahman, S., Mohona, S., & Ara, J. (2025). Artificial intelligence-driven customer lifetime value (CLV) forecasting: Integrating RFM analysis with machine learning for strategic customer retention. *Journal of Computer Science and Technology Studies*, *7*(1), 249–257. DOI: 10.32996/jcsts.2025.7.1.18

Association of Southeast Asian Nations [ASEAN]. (2025). *ASEAN Digital Masterplan 2025*. https://asean.org/book/asean-digital-masterplan-2025/

Ayinaddis, S. G. (2025). Artificial intelligence adoption dynamics and knowledge in SMEs and large firms: A systematic review and bibliometric analysis. *Journal of Innovation & Knowledge*, *10*(3), 100682. Advance online publication. DOI: 10.1016/j.jik.2025.100682

Baabdullah, A. M., Alalwan, A. A., Slade, E. L., Raman, R., & Khatatneh, K. F. (2021). SMEs and artificial intelligence (AI): Antecedents and consequences of AI-based B2B practices. *Industrial Marketing Management*, *98*, 255–270. DOI: 10.1016/j.indmarman.2021.09.003

Brynjolfsson, E., & McElheran, K. (2016). The rapid adoption of data-driven decision-making. *The American Economic Review*, *106*(5), 133–139. DOI: 10.1257/aer.p20161016

Bughin, J., Seong, J., Manyika, J., Chui, M., & Joshi, R. (2018). *Notes from the AI frontier: Modeling the impact of AI on the world economy*. McKinsey Global Institute. *4*(1), 2-61. https://www.mckinsey.com/featured-insights/artificial-intelligence/notes-from-the-ai-frontier-modeling-the-impact-of-ai-on-the-world-economy

Chui, M., Harryson, M., Manyika, J., Roberts, R., Chung, R., & van Heteren, A. (2018). *Applying artificial intelligence for social good*. McKinsey Global Institute. 1-22. https://www.mckinsey.com/featured-insights/artificial-intelligence/applying-artificial-intelligence-for-social-good

Csaszar, F. A., Ketkar, H., & Kim, H. (2024). Artificial intelligence and strategic decision-making: Evidence from entrepreneurs and investors. *Strategy Science*, *9*(4), 322–345. DOI: 10.1287/stsc.2024.0190

Davenport, T. H., & Ronanki, R. (2018). Artificial intelligence for the real world. *Harvard Business Review, 96*(1), 108–116. https://hbr.org/2018/01/artificial-intelligence-for-the-real-world

Dipoatmodjo, T. S. P. (2025). Experiencing Change: A Phenomenological Study of Employee Adaptation to AI-Driven Digital Transformation in a Tech Company. International Journal of Humanity Advance [IJHABS]. *Business & Sciences, 3*(1), 25–34. DOI: 10.59971/ijhabs.v3i1.448

European Commission. (2025). *Digital Europe Programme.* https://commission.europa.eu/funding-tenders/find-funding/eu-funding-programmes/digital-europe-programme_en

Government of the Republic of Korea. (2020). *AI voucher program to help SMEs adopt artificial intelligence.* Korea.net. https://www.korea.net/Government/Briefing-Room/Press-Releases/view?articleId=4933&type=O

İnce, F. (2021). Opportunities and Challenges of E-Learning in Turkey. In Khan, B., Affouneh, S., Hussein Salha, S., & Najee Khlaif, Z. (Eds.), *Challenges and Opportunities for the Global Implementation of E-Learning Frameworks* (pp. 202–226). IGI Global Scientific Publishing., DOI: 10.4018/978-1-7998-7607-6.ch013

İnce, F. (2023). Comparison of Japan and OECD Countries in Terms of Well-Being Resources. *Problemy Ekorozwoju, 18*(2), 78–85. DOI: 10.35784/preko.3945

İnce, F. (2024). Comparison of National Well-being of Mediterranean Countries in terms of EU: Turkey, Italy, Spain. *Acta Scientiarum. Health Sciences, 46*(1), e65161. DOI: 10.4025/actascihealthsci.v46i1.65161

Inter-American Development Bank. (2024). *Responsible artificial intelligence for growth in Latin America and the Caribbean (RAI 4 Growth)* (Project No. RG-T4463). https://www.iadb.org/en/project/RG-T4463

International Labour Organization [ILO]. (2021). *Digitalisation of TVET and skills development: Leveraging technology to support lifelong learning.* International Labour Organization. https://www.skillsforemployment.org/sites/default/files/2024-01/WEB-Digitalisation%20of%20TVET.pdf

Jain, A., Kakade, K. S., & Vispute, S. A. (2025). The role of artificial intelligence (AI) in the transformation of small- and medium-sized businesses: Challenges and opportunities. In Dixit, S., Maurya, M., Jain, V., & Subramaniam, G. (Eds.), *Artificial intelligence-enabled businesses: How to develop strategies for innovation* (pp. 209–226). Wiley., DOI: 10.1002/9781394234028.ch12

Katz, Y. (2025). Shaping the future of AI governance in agriculture and related industries. *SunText Review of Economics & Business*, *6*(1), 223. DOI: 10.51737/2766-4775.2025.123

Machucho, R., & Ortiz, D. (2025). The impacts of artificial intelligence on business innovation: A comprehensive review of applications, organizational challenges, and ethical considerations. *Systems*, *13*(4), 264. DOI: 10.3390/systems13040264

Mahmud, D. (2025). Building AI-driven economic resilience systems to support stability during future pandemic lockdowns. *Review of Applied Science and Technology*, *4*(2), 1–32. DOI: 10.63125/adyfcg48

Mohib, M., Khan, F. K., El Burari, E. R., & Ali, S. (2025). The Challenges and Limitations of Artificial Intelligence Adoption in Small and Medium-Sized Enterprises. *Review Journal of Social Psychology & Social Works*, *3*(1), 292–303. DOI: 10.71145/rjsp.v3i1.99

Mugisha, J., Adyanga, A. F., & Ocan, J. (2025). The Role of Artificial Intelligence (AI) in Transforming Small and Medium Enterprises (SMEs): A Narrative Review. *Applied Data Science and Analysis*, *2025*, 112–117. DOI: 10.58496/ADSA/2025/007

Oldemeyer, L., Jede, A., & Teuteberg, F. (2024). *Investigation of artificial intelligence in SMEs: A systematic review of the state of the art and the main implementation challenges.* Management Review Quarterly., DOI: 10.1007/s11301-024-00405-4

Organisation for Economic Co-operation and Development [OECD]. (2021). *The digital transformation of SMEs.* OECD Publishing. https://doi.org/DOI: 10.1787/bdb9256a-en

Organisation for Economic Co-operation and Development [OECD]. (2025). *The Adoption of Artificial Intelligence in Firms: New Evidence for Policymaking.* OECD Publishing. https://doi.org/DOI: 10.1787/f9ef33c3-en

Pandey, A. (2025). *Big Tech has AI, but Indian MSMEs need something more—Desi AI. The Economic Times.* https://economictimes.indiatimes.com/small-biz/sme-sector/big-tech-has-ai-but-indian-msmes-need-something-moredesi-ai/articleshow/122015182.cms

Peretz-Andersson, E., Tabares, S., Mikalef, P., & Parida, V. (2024). Artificial intelligence implementation in manufacturing SMEs: A resource orchestration approach. *International Journal of Information Management*, *77*, 102781. DOI: 10.1016/j.ijinfomgt.2024.102781

Perspektiven schaffen. (2024). *Förderprogramm "go-digital" bis 2024 verlängert.* Bundesministerium für Bildung, Familie, Senioren, Frauen und Jugend. https://www.perspektiven-schaffen.de/ps-de/unternehmen-arbeitgeber/tipps-fuer-kleine-und-mittlere-unternehmen-kmu-/-foerderprogramm-go-digital-bis-2024-verlaengert-194698

Radanliev, P. (2025). AI ethics: Integrating transparency, fairness, and privacy in AI development. *Applied Artificial Intelligence, 39*(1), e2463722. Advance online publication. DOI: 10.1080/08839514.2025.2463722

Ransbotham, S., Khodabandeh, S., Kiron, D., LaFountain, B., & Kiron, D. (2022). *The cultural benefits of artificial intelligence in organizations.* MIT Sloan Management Review and Boston Consulting Group. 63270, 1-21. https://web-assets.bcg.com/85/90/95939185404cbd901aba0d54f1d7/the-cultural-benefits-of-artificial-intelligence-in-the-enterprise-r.pdf

Salesforce. (2024, December 4). *New research reveals SMBs with AI adoption see stronger revenue growth.* https://www.salesforce.com/news/stories/smbs-ai-trends-2025/

Sánchez, E., Calderón, R., & Herrera, F. (2025). Artificial Intelligence Adoption in SMEs: Survey Based on TOE–DOI Framework, Primary Methodology and Challenges. *Applied Sciences (Basel, Switzerland), 15*(12), 6465. DOI: 10.3390/app15126465

Saranya, T. S., Babhuti, K., Jyoti, D., Kaur, H., & Kapoor, T. (2025). The Evolving Role of Artificial Intelligence (AI) in Human Resource Management (HRM). In Kapoor, T., Singh, A., Sahay, K., Kaur, H., & Verma, R. (Eds.), *Sustainable Management Practices for Employee Retention and Recruitment* (pp. 301–310). IGI Global Scientific Publishing., DOI: 10.4018/979-8-3693-8679-8.ch015

Su, X., Zeng, L., Shao, B., & Lin, B. (2025). Data-driven optimization for production planning with multiple demand features. *Kybernetes, 54*(1), 110–133. DOI: 10.1108/K-04-2023-0690

Subramanyam, S. V.Sasikiran Vepanambattu Subramanyam. (2025). Cloud-based enterprise systems: Bridging scalability and security in healthcare and finance. *IJSAT-International Journal on Science and Technology, 16*(1), 2305. Advance online publication. DOI: 10.71097/IJSAT.v16.i1.2305

Syed, N., Anwar, A., Baig, Z., & Zeadally, S. (2025). Artificial intelligence as a service (AIaaS) for cloud, fog and the edge: State-of-the-art practices. *ACM Computing Surveys, 57*(8), 211. DOI: 10.1145/3712016

The United Nations Conference on Trade and Development [UNCTAD]. (2025a). *Technology and Innovation Report 2025: Inclusive artificial intelligence for development.* United Nations Conference on Trade and Development. https://unctad.org/publication/technology-and-innovation-report-2025

The United Nations Conference on Trade and Development [UNCTAD]. (2025b). *AI market projected to hit $4.8 trillion by 2033.* https://unctad.org/news/ai-market-projected-hit-48-trillion-2033-emerging-dominant-frontier-technology

UK Information Commissioner's Office. (2025). *ICO regulatory sandbox: Enabling innovation in the public interest.* https://ico.org.uk/for-organisations/regulatory-sandbox/

Wieland, A., & Durach, C. F. (2021). Two perspectives on supply chain resilience. *Journal of Business Logistics, 42*(3), 315–322. DOI: 10.1111/jbl.12271

World Bank. (2023). *SME finance policy guide: Creating an enabling environment for small businesses.* International Finance Corporation. https://www.ifc.org/smefinance

World Bank. (2025). *Financial inclusion overview.* https://www.worldbank.org/en/topic/financialinclusion/overview

World Economic Forum. (2025). *Global risks report 2025.* World Economic Forum. https://reports.weforum.org/docs/WEF_Global_Risks_Report_2025.pdf

## KEY TERMS AND DEFINITIONS

**AI:** Artificial Intelligence refers to computer systems or algorithms designed to perform tasks that typically require human cognitive functions, including learning, reasoning, and problem-solving.

**AIaaS:** AI-as-a-Service is a model for delivering artificial intelligence capabilities such as machine learning or natural language processing, through cloud-based platforms without requiring local installation or development.

**B2B:** Business-to-Business refers to commercial interactions and transactions that take place between two or more businesses, rather than between a business and individual consumers.

**Digital Infrastructure:** Digital infrastructure consists of the foundational digital systems and services, such as broadband internet, data storage, and cybersecurity, that enable the functioning of information and communication technologies.

**Digital Transformation:** Digital transformation is the process of integrating digital technologies into core organizational operations, changing how value is delivered to stakeholders.

**Inclusive Innovation:** Inclusive innovation is the development and implementation of technologies that are designed to be accessible and usable by a broad range of users, including those in resource-constrained environments.

**MSMEs:** Micro, Small, and Medium-Sized Enterprises are businesses defined by national or international thresholds related to employee numbers, annual revenue, or asset size.

**Organizational Readiness:** Organizational readiness refers to the internal capacity of a business to implement new tools or systems, encompassing leadership alignment, employee engagement, and procedural integration.

**Policy Intervention:** Policy intervention refers to deliberate actions taken by public authorities or institutions to influence outcomes in a particular domain through measures such as funding, training, or regulation.

**SaaS:** Software-as-a-Service is a cloud-based delivery model in which software applications are accessed remotely via the internet, typically through a subscription-based service.

**Strategic Decision-Making:** Strategic decision-making involves planning and executing long-term organizational goals through the evaluation of internal and external factors.

**Technology Readiness:** Technology readiness describes the extent to which an organization is prepared to adopt and utilize new technologies, including infrastructure, workforce capabilities, and operational systems.

**UNCTAD:** United Nations Conference on Trade and Development is a United Nations body that conducts research and provides policy recommendations in areas such as trade, investment, and technology, with a focus on supporting economic development, especially in developing countries.

# Chapter 2
# AI-Driven Transformation in MSMEs: Unlocking Opportunities, Overcoming Challenges, and Shaping the Future of Business Management

**Shatabdi Chandramani Nannaware**
http://orcid.org/0009-0008-8510-623X
*Pune Institute of Business Management, India*

**Parvathy Nair**
http://orcid.org/0000-0003-2233-7897
*Pune Institute of Business Management, India*

**M. Rajalaxmi**
*Pune Institute of Business Management, India*

## ABSTRACT

*Micro, small and medium enterprises (MSMEs) make up the backbone of India's economy, contribute about 30% to the national GDP and provide employment to over 110 million people. However, in front of global digital changes and post-pandemic reorganisation, MSMEs must develop beyond traditional business models to remain competitive, flexible and durable. The emergence of Artificial Intelligence (AI) presents a paradigm change that offers tools that are able to make increased productivity, customer-focused innovation and data-driven decisions. This chapter*

DOI: 10.4018/979-8-3373-2817-1.ch002

*seriously examines the transformational role of AI in the MSME region, focusing on India's socio-economic scenario, checking how AI can unlock new opportunities, address long-standing obstacles, and shape the future of business management.*

## 1 INTRODUCTION

Rapid progress in AI has revolutionised industries globally, yet MSME often struggle to keep pace with such changes due to resource loss and limited technical expertise. Integration of artificial intelligence in subtle, small and medium enterprises is not only a technological upgradation, but a deep change that is re-shaping business management (Khan, 2024). This fusion of AI and traditional trade strategies promotes innovation in diverse fields. it is necessary that future leaders understand and benefit AI's ability within the established trade model (Farayola et al., 2023). AI offers solutions that can help SMEs to overcome challenges, improve interactions with customers and suppliers and promote productivity (Peretz-Andersson et al., 2024) . Micro, Small and Medium Enterprises (MSME) are the cornerstone of India's economic structure, which contributes about 30% to the country's GDP and employs over 110 million people (Ministry of Electronics and Information Technology [MEIT], 2024). In a rapid digital economy, Artificial Intelligence (AI) is emerging as a transformative force capable of re-shaping the financial and strategic outlines of MSME. While large corporations have rapidly adopted AI solutions, Indian MSME are gradually embracing AI-operated equipment to remain competitive, agile and innovative in a global business environment. Adopting AI in MSME can lead to analysis and AI-powered personalisation in marketing (Lu et al., 2022), from automatic customer service to inventory. For example, Indian companies such as Lenskart are using AI for facial mapping and individual eyewear recommendations, while Zoho Corporation provides AI-integrated SAAS equipment to suit small businesses (ET Bureau, 2024). In addition, the Ministry of Electronics and Information Technology (MEIT) shows the government's commitment to integrating AI in AI (MEIT, 2024), such as Udyog Bharat 4.0 and AI, capable of the MSME Scheme by MEIT. However, with the rise of inexpensive AI-operated equipment, MSME has the opportunity to automate processes, increase customer engagement, optimize supply chains, and make data-powered decisions. This chapter offers an observation of AI's role in MSME and determines the stage for intensive discussion on its effects, opportunities, challenges, and future prospects.

The McKinsey Global Institute (MGI) has developed a comprehensive and wide data set occupying MSME productivity in many regions and sub-sectors in 16 countries, representing more than 50% of the global GDP simultaneously. These countries include ten advanced economies - such as the United States, Germany and

Japan - and six emerging economies, including India, Brazil and Nigeria. The data is particularly granulated; in the manufacturing sector alone, it includes 24 level-two and 95 level-three sub-regions, providing a fine understanding of productivity patterns. This depth of analysis is responsible for the variation of enterprise size, degree of formalisation, and sectoral dynamics. Taking advantage of this unique cross-country and cross-sectoral perspective, research highlights the difference in MSME productivity relative to large firms(Madgavkar et al., 2024). This highlights how productivity interval manifests in industries and geography and provides information about how MSME can cooperate with big companies or adopt serial strategies to unlock the potential value. This micro-level analysis is particularly valuable to identify reference-specific liver of development, such as targeted technology adoption, supply chain integration, or upskilling initiatives, which can greatly increase MSME performance within diverse economic settings. The purpose of this chapter is to examine the current status of AI adoption among Indian MSME. it is highlighted how small and medium enterprises are beginning to integrate intelligent technologies in their main operations. It wants to identify major opportunities that are present in AI productivity, improving scalability and promoting innovation within these enterprises. In doing so, it analyses major challenges and obstacles, such as infrastructure boundaries, digital illiteracy, and financial obstacles, which obstruct extensive AI integration. In addition, the chapter examines the government's initiative and the role of policy interventions, such as the AI for MSME scheme and the Digital India Program, which aim to intensify the AI deployment in the MSME region. Finally, it provides real-world examples and practical strategic structures to guide successful AI implementation, both for emerging startups and established small businesses in diverse industries.

## 2. UNDERSTANDING AI IN THE MSME CONTEXT

Artificial intelligence (AI) refers to the simulation of human cognitive processes-from learning, argument and decision-making by masters. Major AI technologies include machine learning, natural language processing, computer vision and generic models, specific business requirements of each (OECD, 2023). In the MSME context, AI includes user-friendly, scalable solutions such as cloud-based chatbots, AI-operated invoices, voice-based assistants and fraud detection systems, available on payment-use models such as AI-as-a-Service (AIaaS) (Deloitte, 2025).

Platforms such as Google Cloud AI, AWS AI, and Zoho AI have especially sewed a low-code/no-code tool for MSME, which enables rapid deployment without large capital investment. It also makes the scope of AI accessible to micro-entertainment, democratizes innovation in the business levels(Madgavkar et al., 2024).

## 2.1 Relevance of AI for MSME

AI is a strategic promoter for MSME trying to increase productivity, privatisation and efficiency. According to the Ministry of MSME (2023), India's MSME sector faces acute competition and high operating costs - AI integration is not only beneficial but also necessary. AI equipment can automate repetitive processes, improve sales forecasts, and provide customer insight by reducing operating costs(McKinsey, 2025). For example, StyleDotMe, a startup in India, uses AI-operated enrichment reality to offer virtual tried-on experiences, greatly improving customer engagement(Codingmart, 2024). In Agritech, companies such as Fasal and Crude are equipped with AI-managed crop consultants and weather forecasts, improving the yield by reducing input waste (NITI Aayog, 2025). Similarly, small manufacturers now deploy AI-based future maintenance and quality control devices to avoid downtime and reduce production errors, a practice once only for large enterprises (MIT Technology Review, 2025).AI's relevance is also extending to professional services, such as legal and accounting firms, now using AI platforms for document analysis, tax compliance, and automatic legal research PWC 2025)

## 2.2 Current State of AI Adoption in Indian MSME

The Indian MSME region, including more than 63 million enterprises, plays an important role in the country's economic structure, contributing about 30% to GDP, and more than 110 million people (MSME Ministry, 2023) have been appointed. As the global economy moves towards data-operated models, Indian MSME are gradually embracing artificial intelligence (AI) to be competitive, agile and ready for the future. However, with differences marked in industries, regions and enterprise sizes, the speed and nature of AI adoption in this region are uneven.

### Trends and Sectoral Insights

Retail and E-Commerce MSME: Rapidly deploying AI for personal marketing, inventory adaptation and customer engagement. With devices such as chatbots, recommended engines and AI-based CRM platforms, businesses can now increase user experiences and improve retention. Startups like SNITCH and BlissClub use AI to curate personal shopping trip and automate their content marketing, enabling scalability without big teams.

Healthcare-focused MSME: AIs are integrated into clinical equipment, telemedicine and patient engagement platforms. For example, a health-tech startup uses image analysis and automated patient use AI to diagnose diseases through triaging and virtual health assistants. Post-pandemic, AI-competent symptom checkers and chatbot-powered pre-diagnosis tools have spread in urban health MSME ecosystems.

Manufacturing MSME: The future has started using AI for maintenance, detection of defects and quality control. The use of low-cost sensors combined with AI analytics has enabled these businesses to reduce downtime and production losses. Platforms such as Zestiot and Detect Technology worked with small-scale manufacturers to deploy such solutions.

Education and Skilling MSME: AI has been adopted to personalise learning routes, automate administrative functions and give multilingual materials. Tier-2 and Tier-3 integrate platform AI, such as Teachmint, to offer real-time responses to students and teachers in cities and to offer customised teaching modules.

## 3. OPPORTUNITIES OFFERED BY AI FOR MSME GROWTH

Integration of Artificial Intelligence (AI) presents Indian MSME with unprecedented opportunities for scale, competition and innovation in today's digital economy. By reducing the operational burden, customising customer experiences, and guiding data-informed strategies, AI is not only a technological upgradation but also a business environment. These benefits are particularly valuable for MSME, which often face financial and resource deficiencies. With cheap AI solutions available through cloud platforms and via SaaS models, small businesses can tap into transformational capacity without a large upfront investment (Deloitte, 2024).

Enhanced Operational Efficiency and Automation: One of the most immediate benefits of AI for MSME lies in automatic operations. AI-operated enterprise resource planning (ERP) systems, inventory control systems, and process automation tools help reduce human error and improve turnaround time. For example, platforms such as Zoho and Teleprime integrate AI to automate to automatic - GST compliance and cash flow predictions, especially useful for small retailers and service providers(Zoho Creator, 2025)

AI for Strategic Decision-Making and Risk Mitigation: AI strengthens MSME with real-time data-powered insights that were previously accessible to large corporations with dedicated analytics teams. With equipment such as Power BI, Zoho Analytics, and Google Looker Studio, MSME can analyse trends, predict demand and assess financial performance without intensive technical expertise. In the financial domain, AI is helping MSME with credit risk scoring, fraud detection and loan repayment forecast. Fintech platform AIs such as Lendingkart and NeoGrowth use borrowers of small enterprises to assess them quickly and accurately, enabling rapid debt dispensing with low risk.

## 3.1Emerging AI Trends with Immediate MSME Relevance and Applicability

### AI-Enabled Predictive Maintenance for Small Manufacturers

Small and medium manufacturing units often face costly downtime due to machine breakdown and a lack of preventive mechanisms. Trend Insight: Affordable IoT and AI-based predictive maintenance systems are now being adopted even by small factories. These systems collect vibration, temperature, and power-consumption data to predict machine malfunction and failure in advance. Example: Tata Power's MSME digital cluster initiative in Maharashtra has introduced low-cost AI sensors developed by Altizone Systems, allowing small tool-and-die manufacturers to predict equipment failure 20-30% earlier, reducing downtime and maintenance costs by 25%. Relevance: MSME can now adopt open-source AI maintenance platforms (e.g., TensorFlow Lite, Azure IoT Edge) that integrate with existing legacy machinery while reducing cost barriers.

## 4. CHALLENGES AND BARRIERS IN AI ADOPTION AMONG INDIAN MSME

Despite the increasing recognition of Artificial Intelligence (AI) as a strategic environment for micro, small and medium enterprises (MSME), it adoption is uneven of widely adopted due to many structural and systemic challenges. These obstacles - the basis of financial, technical, legal and operating dimensions - often disrupt MSME ability to effectively deploy AI. Understanding these obstacles is important for India's MSME ecosystem to develop inclusive, scalable AI policies.

## 4.1 Financial, Technical, and Talent Gaps

Despite the increasing availability of AI devices, a major obstacle to MSME in India is the high cost of integration and efficient manpower. The AI system often requires adequate investment in infrastructure, data processing capabilities and adaptation, which find most small businesses financially unattainable. A recent report by (Razorpay, 2024)has shown that 72% of MSME in India cite as the primary reasons for adoption and vague ROI as the primary reasons.

Additionally, the lack of AI-ready talent affects MSME. While large firm data can attract scientists and machine learning engineers, MSME often struggle to find basic technical support. According to a report by the Indian Mission and NIELIT (2024), only 12% MSME has access to trained employees at AI Fundamental, even in Tier 1 cities.

An example is Fabheads, a Chennai-based MSME developing carbon fibre 3D printing. While its main operations are technology-operated, its founders reported challenges in the recruitment of AI engineers locally due to a skill gap and competition with better-paid technical startups(Entrepreneur India, 2025)

## 4.2 Integration with Legacy Systems

Many Indian MSME rely on heritage software, Excel sheets, or even manual documentation for their daily operations. Such an environment requires not only a software upgrade to integrate AI solutions, but also a complete overhaul of data practices and operational workflows - a process that is both expensive and disruptive. According to a 2023 study by India SME Forum, about 65% of MSME in India still use a standalone accounting software without any API, making it difficult to integrate the AI-managed analytics tool. Companies such as a logistics tech firm, Ezyhaul, a logistics tech firm working with small Indian fleet operators, found that integrating AI for route adaptation was possible only after digitising the data collection in partners, often separate onboarding and training sessions were required. (Khan, 2024).This fusion of AI and traditional trade strategies promotes innovation in diverse fields. it is necessary that future leaders understand and benefit from AI's ability within the established trade model (Farayola et al., 2023).

In addition, even cloud migration - a condition for several AI services - Remains Limited. An (IDC global, 2024) .The report shows that only 18% of Indian MSME have adopted a full cloud-based enterprise resource planning (ERP) system, limiting the scalability of AI deployment.

## 4.3 Ethical, Legal, and Data Privacy Concerns

The data collection with AI has emerged as important issues with much rely on data confidentiality, consent and compliance. The rollout of the Digital Personal Data Protection Act (DPDPA), 2023 has increased regulatory probes on the way of collecting, stores and using customer data. MSME, dedicated legal and compliance is a shortage of teams, often find themselves unknown or sick to handle these developed requirements. For example, the credit-landing MSMS can inadvertently break the consent norms or inappropriately handle individual data to process the borrower applications, using the third-party AI tool to unknowingly, expose them to legal punishment. The Telecom Regulatory Authority of India (TRAI) warned in early 2024 that several small firms using AI-operated call centres were violating unwanted communication norms and data storage rules.

Additionally, algorithmic bias and opacity present reputational and ethical risks. A 2024 MIT-Sloan study analysing AI deployments in Indian education startups showed that AI-based screening tools for student assessments disproportionately underperformed in vernacular language settings, leading to unfair grading in rural schools.

Moreover, the lack of explainability in AI models makes it difficult for MSME to justify automated decisions, especially in sectors like recruitment or finance. Without human-in-the-loop validation mechanisms, MSME risk making flawed or legally questionable decisions.

## 5. SUSTAINABLE BUSINESS TRANSFORMATION THROUGH AI

Stability has become a commercial imperative rather than a corporate option. For Indian MSME, which often encounter pressure to reduce operating costs while meeting environmental criteria, artificial intelligence (AI) provides tangible pathways to increase energy efficiency and reduce environmental impact. AI-operated solutions can help MSME monitor energy consumption in real time, predict maintenance needs, and adapt resource usage, which can reduce both emissions and utility expenses. For example, the Bangalore-based clean-tech firm, accurates, uses AI to monitor the use of energy in industrial machines.

Through future insight, it helps small-scale factories to reduce energy wastage and adapt motor operations, causing a decrease of 15–20% in power consumption over time (Cleantech Insights, 2024). AI algorithms in platforms such as EcoEnergy Insights assess the HVAC and refrigeration system, helping retail and manufacturing MSME to accommodate operations to stay within stability thresholds. In urban settings, AI-enabled Building energy management systems (BEMS) is helping commercial MSME installations in the real estate and hospitality sectors, which reduce carbon footprints. These systems track real-time energy loads, occupancy patterns, and weather data to control light and cooling dynamically, contributing to climate goals without renouncing productivity.

## 5.1 Sustainable Product Innovation using AI

AI plays an important role in enabling MSME to design and manufacture environmentally durable products. With devices such as AI-based material simulation, lifestyle assessment (LCA), and generative designs, MSME can create products that comply with energy-skilled, recycled and green standards from the designing phase. For example, a Gujarat-based construction(Rematerials) technique uses the AI-powered adaptation algorithm to develop MSME. Their AI models test thermal conductivity, durability and content compatibility, reduce the requirement of physical prototypes and enable rapidly, low-illuminated production cycles.

In the segment of consumer goods, an MSME from Delhi uses AI to convert carbon emissions from Graviky Labs, vehicles and chimneys to ink and other usable products. Their machine-learning models help customise carbon capture and predict polluting efficiency, converting industrial pollution into environmentally friendly goods. This indicates how AI can support circular economy practices by enabling upscaling on a large scale. In addition, AI is used for permanent agricultural techniques in smart agriculture. The new products launched in 2024 help to adapt the use of fertilisers and pesticides to platforms such as crown AIs, small agricultural traders with soil health, rainfall and crop phase, thus reducing ecological damage by improving yields by improving yield.

## 5.2 Aligning AI Strategies with UN SDGs and ESG Goals

The application of AI in MSME can contribute significantly to the global stability structure, especially the United Nations Sustainable Development Goals (UN SDGs) and Environment, Social and Governance (ESG) targets. AI enables MSME to monitor and report progress on metrics such as carbon footprint, water use, labour status and governance practices - components in stability ratings and compliance reports. For example, a data working with Indian MSME offers an intelligence firm, a sustainable, AI-operated dashboard that tracks ESG KPI such as energy intensity, emission rate and real-time compliance records.

AI also supports social and governance goals by ensuring supply chain transparency. Tools such as Blockchain-Employed AI are being operated by MSME in apparel and leather groups in Kanpur and Kolkata to track labour status and moral sourcing practices. It supports SDG 8 (decent work and economic development) and SDG 9 (industry, innovation and infrastructure). In addition, AI enables stability assessment to investors and regulators through automatic ESG scoring. MSME, targeting green financing or procurement contracts, are fast adopting these devices to improve the credibility of their stability and attract conscious customers and partners towards the environment.

What is important moving is an assistant ecosystem that includes government-supported incentives, stability training programs and partnership with AI solution providers. MSME who embedded AI into their stability strategies will not only prove their operations, but also make a greenery, a more just contribution to a more just economy.

## 6. FUTURE OUTLOOK AND EMERGING TRENDS

Mature, Indian Micro, Small and Medium Enterprises (MSME) in the form of Artificial Intelligence (AI) are at the tail of a transformative leap. Beyond the operational efficiency, AI is redefining how small businesses look at the approach to innovation, inclusion and stability. The future of AI in MSME will be operated by emerging models such as AI-as-a-Service (AIaaS), decentralised systems, such as adopting moral structure and promoting local innovation. Together, these trends are shaping a more inclusive and intelligent MSME ecosystem, aligning with national and global goals.

### 6.1 AI-as-a-Service (AIaaS) for MSME

One of the most game-changing trends for MSME is the rapid development of the AI-A-Service (AIAAS), where businesses can use powerful AI tools based on membership or payments without making a high capital investment. Cloud providers and startups are providing modular AI equipment for equal marketing, sales, accounting and even legal compliance. For example, a intellectual AI platform located in Bengaluru, lely.ai, now provides no-code chat and voice bots designed for small businesses, especially for small businesses. These bots automate customer engagement on WhatsApp, Instagram and websites, freeing human resources by improving customer service (Shetty, 2024.)

### 6.2 Ethical AI and Responsible Innovation

Since AI has become mainstream in MSME, moral deployment, prejudice mitigation and transparency are being emphasised. Small businesses relying on algorithm decision-making must ensure that their AI systems do not discriminate or operate in a black box. A recent initiative by Delhi-based legal-technical MSME IndusLawTech includes an AI policy checklist for small businesses to assess fairness in AI use during recruitment, loan approval or customer division (Abhishek

Sharma, 2025). This ensures that the AI systems also follow fairness and inclusive guidelines at the microenterprise level.

In Rural Healthcare, DocBot India, a Medtech in Pune, uses a clear AI (XAI) model to diagnose conditions based on MSME, X-rays and pathology images. The company creates transparency in its clinical equipment by incorporating confidence scores and reference visuals, which can be reviewed by healthcare workers in non-urban clinics-promoting both confidence and accountability.

### 6.3 The Role of Decentralised AI and Local Innovation

Decentralised AI refers to systems where data and decision-making are distributed instead of being centralised. For Indian MSME, especially working in rural or semi-urban areas, decentralised AI enables innovation to innovation without high-end server or constant internet access, an important feature in areas with limited infrastructure.

An example is a Shikshalokam ed-tech non-profit organisation working with education-focused MSME .It appoints Edge-AI tools that run on low-power equipment in rural schools to assess teaching quality and student learning without sending sensitive data to the Cloud. These devices allow localised insight and privacy-protection analytics for analytics.

## 7. CASE STUDY ECO-AI TEXTILES – INTEGRATING AI FOR SUSTAINABLE MANUFACTURING IN TIRUPPUR'S MSME SECTOR

The same textiles, a subtle enterprise established in Tiruppur in Tamil Nadu in 2021, is part of the rich knitwear export Cluster in India (Textile Magazine, 2024). It focuses on the production of environmentally friendly clothing using MSME organic cotton and natural colours. In 2023, founders began an AI integration journey to reduce water and chemical use, improve supply chain stability and meet ESG compliance demands from global buyers(Bhavan, 2023)

### Problem Statement

MSME of Tiruppur are under increasing pressure:

- Reduce wastewater discharge, as the city has faced environmental sanctions in the past.
- Less carbon emissions from production processes.

- Meet the traceability and compliance demands of environment-conscious global buyers (eg, H&M, Decathlon, Zara). However, younger players often have the infrastructure and skills to apply real-time monitoring or future stability tools.

## AI-Driven Sustainable Solutions

### Water and Energy Optimisation

EcoAI Textiles deployed an AI-enabled sensor system to monitor:

Water consumption in dyeing units. Boiler temperature and energy use pattern. By applying machine learning models, they adapted the dye cycles, reduced the use of water by 35% and energy consumption is 22% per batch

### AI for Waste Reduction in Fabric Cutting

Using a low-cost AI pattern layout tool (developed with a local IIT-incubated startup), a single optimised fabric cutting to reduce textile waste.

As a result, East-consumer waste reduction by 18%. Automatic scrap.

## ESG Traceability via AI Dashboards

The company created a visual dashboard for emissions, water use and staff welfare matrix. It was shared with European buyers in real time, seeking transparency under Scope 3 reporting and green deal alignment.

## Outcomes

The Tamil Nadu Pollution Control Board was compliant with the ZLD (zero liquid discharge) mandate. Three new export customers were placed on the ship due to AI-enabled ESG reporting. Green innovation in manufacturing is recognised under the MSME Champions Scheme (2024). Making local technical abilities to 20+ women employed and trained in digital stability tracking roles.

## Key Insights

Even small MSME in traditional regions can lead to stability with inexpensive, decentralised AI solutions. Partnership with local AI startups and public plans can find digital differences for MSME. The AI applications in stability reporting and compliance are rapidly becoming market discrimination.

## 7.1 AgroSense Foods – AI-Powered Quality Assurance for Small-Scale Food Processors in Nashik

Agrosense Foods, an MSME specialising in dehydrated fruits and organic snacks in Nashik, Maharashtra, faced challenges in maintaining consistent quality, early detection of spoilage and meeting export-grade safety standards. In 2023, the enterprise adopted an affordable AI-based visual inspection system integrated with IoT temperature sensors to automate quality checks and predict product shelf life.

*AI Integration and Outcomes:* AI visual analytics: The firm deployed a low-cost camera module trained through the open-source TensorFlow model to detect discolouration or contamination in batches of fruits. Predictive shelf-life modelling: IoT sensors track humidity and temperature during storage, feeding real-time data into AI algorithms that predict the likelihood of spoilage.

### Analytical Insights

Defect Detection Accuracy: The AI model achieved 91% accuracy in identifying substandard products while reducing manual inspection time.

Waste Reduction: By predicting spoilage early, waste was reduced by 17%, translating into higher operating margins.

Export Readiness and Compliance: The system enabled compliance with FSSAI and EU safety standards, thereby facilitating entry into export markets.

This case emphasises how democratisation of AI – through open-source tools and cloud-based analytics – can empower MSMEs in the food processing sector to match large-scale manufacturers in efficiency, sustainability and market access.

# 8. ROLE OF WOMEN ENTREPRENEURS IN AI-ENABLED MSME

Women entrepreneurs are rapidly emerging as drivers of innovation and stability in the MSME region of India. In recent years, many women-led enterprises have adopted artificial intelligence (AI) to improve commercial operations, increase customer access and align with ESG goals. A remarkable example is Vistar Farms, co-established by Hyderabad-based MSME Biotech Entrepreneur Nilima Dhameja. The company uses AI-competent sensors to monitor soil health and irrigation patterns, which helps female farmers to increase yield and reduce water use. Another case is LoomAI, which is a Delhi-based moral fashion brand, established by Shreya Patil which uses AI-powered inventory forecasts to reduce textile waste and customise production batches for export orders.

The rise of AI in MSME also calls for deliberate and inclusive efforts to close the gender digital divide. We have introduced AI and tech-centred skilling modules such as Hub Telangana, Google's Women-Will, and Niti Aayog's female entrepreneurship platforms that specially aspire to women entrepreneurs and digital leaders.

In collaboration with technology firms and government departments, the purpose of these initiatives is to ensure that AI adoption does not exclude women from the skills prepared for the future. In addition, state-level MSME support schemes in Kerala and Karnataka now provide bonus points in grant approval for women-led businesses using emerging technologies.

### Challenges and Prospects for Women in AI-Driven Enterprises

Digital infrastructure intervals in rural and peri-urban areas where many female entrepreneurs operate. Limited access to funding, especially for technology-intensive enterprises. Gender bias in AI Equipment, Algorithms and Investment Decisions: Socio-cultural obstacles.

However, possibilities are developing. With increasing focus on inclusive innovation and ESG-linked investments, female-deeds integrated into the AI-linked enterprises are being seen as fast, flexible, scalable and socially impressive. Platforms such as the United Nations Women's Women Empowerment Principle (WEPS) and G20 Digital Integration initiative are emphasising the policies of intersection that encourage women to adopt technology among entrepreneurs.

With the right policy encouragement and access to AI-competent ecosystems, female entrepreneurs can play an important role in shaping a permanent, inclusive MSME economy that thrives on both digital and human intelligence.

## 9. PLATFORMIZATION AND AI-DRIVEN MARKETPLACES FOR MSME

The rapid growth of digital platforms has revolutionised the manner of operating MSME in India, making them infection in AI-enabled marketplaces, data-managed from physical stores. The platform refers to the embedding of MSME in a large-scale digital ecosystem- B2B or B2C-where Artificial Intelligence (AI) plays a central role in streamlining operations, enhancing visibility and is capable of making real-time decisions.

AI-operated platforms such as Udaan (B2B), Meesho (B2C), and Industry buying have integrated the machine learning algorithms to facilitate intelligent inventory, real-time price search, automated logistics coordination and fraud. For example, Meesho, which enables millions of small home-based entrepreneurs to sell online, uses AI to personalise the recommendations of the product and optimise advertising placements(Ghosh, 2025). Its AI algorithms analyse user behaviour in areas to suggest trending products and pricing strategies, which helps MSME to adapt to hyper-local market preferences.

### 9.1 The Role of ONDC and E-Commerce Aggregators

The open network for Digital Commerce (ONDC) launched by the Government of India in 2022 represents a groundbreaking shift towards democratic to digital commerce for MSME. The ONDC aims to break the monopoly of platform giants by offering an open, inter -operational network that allows small vendors to reach customers in any compatible buyer app, regardless of the platform they originate. AI plays a central role in the infrastructure of ONDC - especially in catalogue standardisation, intelligent matchmaking, logistics routing and dynamic pricing. It uses AI models for auto-tag products, resolves the data mismatch, and provides anticipatory insight on demand trends for small businesses.

An emerging example, an ONDC participant in Bangalore, is Sellerapp, which has developed AI-powered equipment that allows MSME to list products, create customised titles and details and analyse sales trends in ONDC channels. It is particularly impressive for MSME that lack branding or digital marketing capabilities. E-commerce aggregators like Bharat E-Mart and eSamudaay are also joining ONDCs to onboard rural MSME, offering vernacular interfaces and AI-operated onboarding support. These devices simplify travel to unskilled entrepreneurs, digitally preserving their autonomy and bringing them into formal digital commerce.

## 10. EVALUATING ROI AND SCALABILITY OF AI IN MSME CONTEXTS

For MSME with limited resources and risk hunger, it is important to evaluate the return on investment (ROI) for AI adoption. Unlike large corporations, MSME should focus on lean implementation models where cost savings, operational efficiency and strategic benefits are of average and quick feel. A practical cost-profit structure should be considered:

-Initial investment (software, hardware, training), Implementation time and interruption risk

-Short-term vs. long-term payment (eg, automation vs. customer retention)
Abstract advantage, such as brand reliability or digital visibility

For example, AI equipment used in customer service or supply chain plans can reduce manual workload and error margin within months. However, generic AI may offer long-term strategic leverage for material creation or pricing strategies. A modular and scalable approach - starting with a business function - is often most effective for MSME.

## 10.1 Metrics to Assess Success Productivity, Revenue, Emissions

The AI performance in the MSME context should be measured in both tangible and abstract metrics. Traditional ROI models must be expanded to incorporate stability and productivity dimensions. Suggested performances are included in the matrix.

Operations productivity benefits: short time per function, increase in throughput, reduction in errors in manual processes
Revenue uplift: Average sequence price increase, high lead conversion. customer lifetime value, Cost Savings: Reduction in hours of manpower, cost of carrying inventory
Use of energy Stability Matrix: Carbon footprint due to AI-operated adaptation Lack of material wastage.
Customer Impact: Improves satisfaction rating, reduces response time, and increases repeat purchase rates.

By integrating financial KPI with performance indicators related to ESG, MSME can display values not only for their lower line but also for investors and green-funding institutes.

In addition, MSME should prioritize solutions that offer incremental scalability- they should allow more features or data layers instead of investing in high-capacity solutions, instead of investing in high-capacity solutions.

# 11. CYBERSECURITY AND RISK MANAGEMENT IN AI-DRIVEN MSME

As MSME adopt Artificial Intelligence (AI) to automate operations, process customer data and engage in digital commerce, their cybersecurity risk also increases significantly. The irony is that AI can introduce both new weaknesses and provide solutions to detect and respond to them. The AI-enhanced Detection Systems use machine learning to monitor unusual patterns in real-time network, endpoints and digital transactions. These devices can identify those discrepancies, such as irregular login efforts, suspicious access spaces, or abnormal data transfer, are often missed by traditional security systems. For MSME, deploying light AI-powered cybersecurity equipment, without the need for in-house cybersecurity teams, enables future danger analysis and rapid event response.

Additionally, some cloud-based solutions now offer safe file sharing, malware detection and embedded AI features for fishing safety. These devices are particularly suited for small enterprises with limited infrastructure, as they reduce dependence on manual monitoring and reduce the cost of continuous security management.

## 11.1 MSME Vulnerability to Cyber-Attacks

MSME are rapidly targeted by cyber criminal due to their relatively weak security control, fragmented IT systems and limited awareness. General attack vectors include ransomware, Business Email Compromise (BEC), data violations and supply chain infiltration. Unlike large firms, MSME often lack dedicated security officers or event response protocols. As they integrate AI tools in customer-support and back-end systems, their digital surface area expands-they make them more susceptible to identity theft, algorithm manipulation and data poisoning attacks. This vulnerability is particularly important for sensitive customer data, proprietary designs or MSME handling financial transactions.

### - Compliance with Data Governance Standards like the DPDP Act, 2023

The Digital Personal Data Protection (DPDP) Act, 2023, introduces legal obligations for all data users, including the collection of personal data, processing and storage. With AI systems often relying on large amounts of data, ensuring compliance becomes both a technical and strategic priority. Under the Act, MSME requires: Get clear consent for data collection, ensure objective limits and data minimisation. Provide a mechanism for data subjects, correct and eradicate their data. Inform officials and users of data violations within a specified time limit. Apply proportional proper security safety measures to the quantity and sensitivity of processed data.Top of Form

The AI model, especially people used for profiling or personalisation, should now be developed and deployed with privacy-by-design principles. For MSME, it means choosing vendors and equipment that provide underlying consent tracking, safe data storage and transparent algorithm logic. Failure in compliance with the

DPDP Act can result in reputational damage and financial punishment. Therefore, active alignment with the emerging data governance framework is essential not only for legal compliance but also to build confidence with loyal customers digitally.

## 12. GLOBAL POLICIES PROMOTING AI IN MSME

As AI adoption becomes an important driver of economic competition, many countries have launched targeted policies and programs to integrate AI in the operation of micro, small and medium enterprises (MSME). These global policy frameworks are not only designed to increase digital readiness, but also to ensure that AI is accessible, moral and scalable for small businesses. Below are the three important initiatives of the European Union, Singapore and Canada that provide valuable lessons for emerging economies like India.

### 12.1 EU's Digital Europe Programme Supporting AI Access for SMEs

The Digital Europe Program (DEP) launched by the European Union in 2021 is aimed at intensifying the digital change of European economies by investing € 7.5 billion between 2021 and 2027. A major pillar of this program is supporting the upliftment of artificial intelligence through grants, training, and access to weaving.

SMEs can reach the European Digital Innovation Hub, which provides an AI testing environment, technical support and networking opportunities with researchers and technical providers. The program offers the AI-on-demand platform, open-source tools, datasets and pre-trained models, which are suited for areas such as manufacturing, health and logistics. Special provisions exist for cross-border cooperation, which enable SMEs to co-develop or pilot AI applications from various European Union countries(European Commission, 2024)

### Canada's Pan-Canadian AI Strategy and SME Empowerment

Canada began the Pan-Canadian Artificial Intelligence Strategy in 2017, which became one of the first countries to implement the National AI policy. The strategy focuses on advancing research, talent and commercialisation with several provisions to support SMEs.

This global policy initiative shows how governments can democratise AI by reducing admission obstacles for MSME, promoting the use of moral AI and aligning public funds with sector-specific needs. For countries like India, adapting to the elements of these programs the regional AI hub, co-finance for the AI tool, and the sector-tailored onboarding of huge MSME can accelerate the adoption of AI among the MSME base.

## 13. AI AND THE GIG ECONOMY'S INTERSECTION WITH MSME

The convergence of Artificial Intelligence (AI), Gig Economy, and Micro, Small and Medium Enterprises (MSME) is shaping new employment models and operating capacity. Since MSMMs adopt digital platforms to manage fast commercial functions, AI is playing an important role in connecting them to a flexible, on-demand workforce, which enables agility, scalability and cost adaptation.

AI-operated gig platforms such as *Taskmo*, *Awign*, and *GigIndia* in India are changing how MSME reach human resources. These platform profiles use AI algorithms for matching, predicting demand and real-time availability analysis, allowing small businesses to appoint efficient or semi-skilled workers on short notice. For example, a small D2C brand in Jaipur can use AI-Enabled Platforms to hire freelance delivery partners during seasonal peaks, while MSME AI-based personality and language evaluation in Mumbai can make part-time customer support agents using the agents using AI-based personality and language evaluation devices. These platform workers streamline recruitment by being fit in history, rating, geography and jobs - faster than traditional human resource processes.

### 13.1 MSME as Micro-Platforms for Gig-Based Services

Interestingly, some MSME are developing themselves in micro-platforms from gig-gig-works consumers, offering services such as freelance training, niche logistics, digital content and repair services through app-based channels. For example, Tier-2 cities are launching MSME hyper-local platforms, connecting beauticians, electricians, or tuition teachers to customers through hyper-localised gig models with the help of AI tools for resulting planning and customer response. This model is expanding economic participation not only to users, but by enabling very small enterprises to become a platform manufacturer. With AI service remittance, reputation management and assistance in customer relationship equipment, these MSME can score largely without overheads.

Integration of AI with the Gig economy opens powerful possibilities to reduce flexibility for MSME, reduce HR costs and enter new service-based business models. However, it also demands a responsible approach for workforce management, algorithm fairness and gig activists safety. As India's MSME and Gig Ecosystems are mature, AI will be in the centre of shaping a new type of digital labour-market equipment-which the machine mixes with human flexibility with intelligence.

## 14. CROWDSOURCED AI MODELS AND OPEN INNOVATION IN MSME

The traditional model of centralised AI development is being complemented by gradually decentralised, community-operated approaches by the traditional model-big corporations and global research hubs. In this developed scenario, MSME are no longer consumers of AI, they are emerging as co-compulsions and contributors, which are to open, localise and democratise the AI ecosystem. Crowdsource AI and Open Innovation MSME are adapted to solutions, reduce cost barriers and strengthen co-development technologies that align with their unique needs.

Crowdsource refers to AI machine learning models that are trained using decentralised data contributions from a community of users or organisations. In the MSME context, this approach is especially useful in areas such as agriculture, handloom, logistics and manufacturing, where standardised global models are often reduced by relevant accuracy.

### 14.1 Collaborative AI Across Decentralised MSME Networks

Beyond the isolated innovation, a new frontier is AI development in the MSME network, capable of digital clusters, co-commented innovation hubs and government-led digital commons. In this setup, small businesses shared in AI infrastructure, co-invest data lakes, labelling platforms, and model training pipelines-without relying on the same seller.

Emerging examples include: Industrial MSME groups using AI to explore forecast maintenance or defects in accurate construction, Fisherfolk Cooperative Societies applying AI models to catch forecasts and maritime security. Decentralised logistics providers pooling data using AI and Blockchain-AI hybrids are being piloted in artisan supply chains to ensure product traceability and proper compensation.

The rise of congestion and open innovation structure in AI indicates a powerful change of how MSME interacts with technology. Instead of staying in the circumference, MSME can now help shape AI devices that they use, ensuring relevant relevance, cultural alignment and strength. With appropriate policy assistance, training, and moral rule, community-AI ecosystems can become the cornerstone of similar digital changes for MSME worldwide.

## 15. CONCLUSION AND RECOMMENDATIONS

The integration of artificial intelligence (AI) within India's subtle, small and medium enterprises (AI) represents a significant range in running productivity, stability and innovation. This chapter has investigated how AI is re-shaping operations by automating the supply chains and supporting the customer privatisation to support and support the green transformation and inform decision making. The evidence prepared from the industry insight, regional trends, and case studies, such as agriculture and such garments, shows that AI is no longer exclusive to big corporations. With the availability of government initiatives such as low-cost platforms, cloud-based analytics and Digital India and Samarth, AI has become increasingly accessible to small businesses-even in rural and underprivileged contexts. However, challenges persist as limited digital literacy, old infrastructure, lack of talent and privacy concerns.

At the same time, AI adoption is catalysing a permanent change in the MSME landscape, aligning several enterprises along with the United Nations Sustainable Development Goals (SDG) and Environment, Social and Governance (ESG) structure. It highlights the role of AI not only in economic development but also to promote inclusive, responsible and climate-flexible development.

## 15.1 Actionable Recommendations for Stakeholders

Start small, scale smart: Start with AI in high-impact, low-risk functions (inventory, marketing, or CRM)

Invest in AI literacy: Encourage data interpretation, moral AI use and cybersecurity awareness.

Leverage Government Program: Explore support under MSME Champion, Startup India.

## 15.2 For Policymakers

Give a subsidy to the AI toolkit for micro and rural enterprises.

Develop regional AI laboratories and incubators that are focused on vernacular and low-resources models.

Ensure regulator clarity on data protection and AI morality for MSME operations.

## 15.3 For Technology Providers and Startups

Co-construction with MSME: Construct reference-inconvenience, inexpensive AI equipment with offline functionality.

Offer an AI-as-a-Service (AIaaS) model for non-technical service businesses.

Promote transparency through an explainable AI dashboard and multilingual interfaces.

## 15.4 For Academia and Researchers

Foster collaborative pilot projects in rural MSME groups.
Documents and published field-specific AI use cases to guide policy and practice.
Encourage interdisciplinary research on informal economies and stability on stability.

# 16. VISION FOR THE FUTURE OF AI-ENABLED MSME

Further, Indian MSME has the ability to develop AI in their origin and develop in enterprises led by innovation globally. The future is contained in the Democratized AI ecosystem-where decentralised data, community-made models, and the next wave of human-focused design power change. As technologies such as AIAS, Edge Computing and Mature of Ethical AI Governance, MSME will no longer adopt late, but are torchbearers of inclusive digital change. With correct partnership, policies and digital visions, AI-competent MSME can run technical sovereignty not only in business development but also in social equity, environmental stability and India's next development phase.

# 17. CONCLUSION

The chapter begins by defining the scope of AI technologies - including generative AI, intelligent automation and machine learning - and gives them space within the MSME context. The relevance of AI is not limited to large corporations; With cloud-based AI platforms, vernacular interfaces, and edge computing, even rural and micro-entertainment can reach its benefits. The chapter then introduces regional insights into textiles, logistics, agriculture and retail on the current position of AI adoption in Indian MSME. Drawing from recent data and government reports, it highlights the increasing trend of digital adoption among MSME, especially in Tier-2 and Tier-3 cities, while also underlining regional inequalities in infrastructure and readiness. The study of the case of the real world serves as the foundation stone of this work. The case of Krishi, a Bolngir-based startup, offers an AI-manual permanent agricultural solution to tribal farmers, examples of hyper-local AI deployment, green logistics and climate-flexible agriculture. However, the chapter also accepts important challenges in MSME's AI travel. Financial obstacles, lack of technical talent, and limited digital literacy are the major obstacles, especially between micro and informal enterprises. Additionally, integration with the absence of heritage systems, data safety concerns and standardized AI policies causes severe risk. This chapter examines the developed landscape of AI-operated changes in MSME, providing a holistic analysis of opportunities, challenges and strategic directions with both Indian and global approaches. The chapter begins with a groundwork laid with an understanding of AI in the MSME context. It defines relevant AI technologies relevant to small businesses, including machine learning, natural language processing, computer vision and most recently, generic AI and intelligent automation. MSME are using these devices for tasks such as fast customer engagement, future planning analysis, product privatisation and operation adaptation. The relevance of AI increases in areas such as logistics, retail, agriculture and manufacturing, where the cost-effectiveness and agility is paramount. In addition, Chapter AI presents a basis of MSME facing challenges and obstacles in adoption. Financial obstacles, lack of technical skills, integration with heritage systems, and concerns on data privacy and morality are the main issues. Along with implementing India's Digital Personal Data Protection (DPDP) Act, 2023, MSME should now prioritise safe and responsible AI usage even with limited resources. A special focus is on permanent trade change through AI, where MSME are adopting AI tools for energy optimisation, permanent product design and green logistics. These efforts align with the United Nations Sustainable Development Goals (SDG) and global structures such as Environment, Social and Governance (ESG) benchmarks. Examples of the real world show how AI can support climate flexibility, water efficiency and physical protection, especially in areas such as agricultural technology and textile manufacturing. The chapter also includes a special segment on evaluating the scalability of ROI and AI, which introduces specific cost-profit outlines for MSME references. Metrics such as increase in productivity, revenue growth, time saved, reduction in carbon emissions, and customer acquisition costs have been exposed as a practical KPI for MSME adopting AI. The importance of measuring the total cost (TCO) of ownership - the emphasis is to include the hidden costs such as integration, training and updates, allowing MSME to make better investment decisions.

Ethical AI, and decentralised AI infrastructure are shaping the future of MSME innovation. Low-code/no-code platforms, cloud-based sins, and associates are also capable of participating in the AI network AI economy. The rise of platforms also discussed in the chapter, where MSME benefit from ONDCs such as B2B/B2C Marketplace, using algorithm rankings and individuality and personalisation for individuality and sale.

Unique additions for the chapter include congested AI models and innovation ecosystems, where MSME co-develop the AI solutions friendly to local references. In contributing to open-source AI platforms or creating a cooperative AI cluster, small businesses is making equipment owned by the community that promotes digital freedom and strength. Cybersecurity and risk management receive attention as AI expands the digital footprint of MSME. AI-enhanced threat Detection tools, compliance with new data laws, and employee awareness programs are necessary to protect against cyber threats and create a digital trust. The chapter ends with a forward-looking view, emphasising that AI can serve as a symbiotic if MSME are empowered with correct equipment, training and policies. Strategic recommendations are made to create inclusive, scalable and moral AI

## REFERENCES


Aayog, N. I. T. I. (2025). *Artificial Intelligence revolutionising Agriculture*. https://www.niti.gov.in/artificial-intelligence-revolutionising-agriculture

Abhishek Sharma. (2025). *Experts Flag DPDP Rules As Hurdle For MSMEs & Digital-first Businesses - BW Businessworld*. https://www.businessworld.in/article/experts-flag-dpdp-rules-as-hurdle-for-msmes-digital-first-businesses-554002

Bhavan, U. (2023). *Ministry of Micro, Small and Medium Enterprises*. www.msme.gov.in

Cleantech Insights. (2024). *From Buzz to Impact_AI's Role in Accelerating the Clean Economy _ Cleantech Group*. https://www.cleantech.com/from-buzz-to-impact-ais-role-in-accelerating-the-clean-economy/

Codingmart. (2024). *StyleDotMe MirrAr_ AR for Jewelry & Fashion - Try On Virtually!* https://codingmart.com/styledotme-mirrar-ar-for-jewelry-fashion-try-on-virtually/

Deloitte. (2024). *ai-adoption-in-India-driven-by-transformative-potential-balanced-by-cost-sensitivity*. https://www.deloitte.com/mu/en/about/press-room/ai-adoption-in-India-driven-by-transformative-potential-balanced-by-cost-sensitivity.html

Deloitte. (2025). *ai-adoption-in-India-driven-by-transformative-potential-balanced-by-cost-sensitivity*.

Entrepreneur India. (2025). *News and Trends*. https://www.entrepreneur.com/en-in/news-and-trends/how-one-entrepreneur-is-shaping-the-ai-narrative-for-a/494394

European Commission. (2024). *Shaping Europe's digital future*. https://digital-strategy.ec.europa.eu/en/activities/digital-programme

Farayola, O. A., Abdul, A. A., Irabor, B. O., & Okeleke, E. C. (2023). Innovative business models driven by AI technologies: A review. *Computer Science & IT Research Journal*, *4*(2), 85–110. DOI: 10.51594/csitrj.v4i2.608

Ghosh, A. R. (2025). *AI for the masses: Inside Meesho's bold leap with BharatMLStack*. Retrieved from ETCIO. https://cio.economictimes.indiatimes.com/news/artificial-intelligence/revolutionizing-e-commerce-meeshos-bharatmlstack-makes-ai-accessible-for-all/122205234

IDC global. (2024). *Navigate your next move with confidence*. https://www.idc.com/

Khan, M. A. (2024). Understanding the Impact of Artificial Intelligence (AI) on Traditional Businesses in Indonesia. *Journal of Management Studies and Development, 3*(02), 146–158. DOI: 10.56741/jmsd.v3i02.584

Lu, X., Wijayaratna, K., Huang, Y., & Qiu, A. (2022). AI-Enabled Opportunities and Transformation Challenges for SMEs in the Post-pandemic Era: A Review and Research Agenda. In *Frontiers in Public Health* (Vol. 10). Frontiers Media S.A., DOI: 10.3389/fpubh.2022.885067

Madgavkar, A., Piccitto, M., White, O., Ramírez, M. J., Mischke, J., Chockalingam, K., & Bush, J. (2024). *A microscope on small businesses Spotting opportunities to boost productivity*. McKinsey Global Institute.

McKinsey. (2025). *A*. https://www.mckinsey.com/capabilities/quantumblack/our-insights/the-state-of-ai-in-2022-and-a-half-decade-in-review#/

Ministry of Electronics and Information Technology [MEIT]. (2024). *10fcadec-462c330211502fed3d24ea83*.

Peretz-Andersson, E., Tabares, S., Mikalef, P., & Parida, V. (2024). Artificial intelligence implementation in manufacturing SMEs: A resource orchestration approach. *International Journal of Information Management, 77*, 102781. https://doi.org/https://doi.org/10.1016/j.ijinfomgt.2024.102781. DOI: 10.1016/j.ijinfomgt.2024.102781

PWC. (2025). 54% of the companies have implemented AI for business_ PwC India survey.

Razorpay. (2024). *MSME Full From & Definition_ Latest MSME Turnover Limit & Classification in 2025*. https://razorpay.com/learn/new-msme-definition-turnover-2020/

Shetty, A. (n.d.). *What is conversational AI?-Benefits and Examples*. https://yellow.ai/conversational-ai/

Technology Review, M. I. T. (2025). Inside India's scramble for AI independence _. *MIT Technology Review*.

Textile Magazine. (2024). *Tirupur's Journey Towards Becoming a Global Hub for Sustainable Textile and Apparel Manufacturing - The Textile Magazine*. https://www.indiantextilemagazine.in/tirupurs-journey-towards-becoming-a-global-hub-for-sustainable-textile-and-apparel-manufacturing/

Zoho Creator. (2025). *AI-powered low-code application development platform _ Zoho Creator*. https://www.zoho.com/creator/ai-software-development-platform/

# Chapter 3
# Strategies and Impact of AI's Triad on Micro-Enterprises and SMEs

**Jose Manuel Saiz-Alvarez**
http://orcid.org/0000-0001-6435-9600
*Catholic University of Santiago de Guayaquil, Ecuador & National Autonomous University of Honduras, Honduras & Catholic University of Avila, Spain*

## ABSTRACT

*In the early 21st century, the triad formed by the European Union, China, and the United States emerged as a key player in the development of artificial intelligence (AI). This chapter examines the characteristics of AI within each of these regions, as well as the commercial, technological, and economic relationships among them related to AI. It highlights their strengths and advantages in various categories, with a focus on microenterprises and small to medium-sized enterprises (SMEs). The chapter concludes with assessments and recommendations for implementing AI in these businesses.*

## INTRODUCTION

The term "Artificial Intelligence" (AI) was born in 1955 within the Dartmouth Summer Research Project on Artificial Intelligence (McCarthy et al., 1955), whose proposal, presented at a conference held at Dartmouth College in 1956, explored how to make machines use language, form abstractions and concepts, solve problems hitherto reserved for humans and improve themselves. As a result of this conference, the first work that laid the foundations on how machines can simulate the logical functioning of the brain, the basis for the development of neural networks, is the

DOI: 10.4018/979-8-3373-2817-1.ch003

seminal paper by McCulloch and Pitts (1943) who proposed a mathematical and logical model in which, inspired by the human brain, they introduced the concept of an artificial neuron (known as the McCulloch-Pitts neuron) that could perform simple logical operations (such as AND, OR, NOT) which, when interconnected, formed networks capable of computing any computable function. This fact was a crucial step in linking computational logic with neural activity, laying the foundation for the development of artificial neural networks, a fundamental pillar of today's AI.

This chapter aims to analyze how AI is evolving in the three primary global business and trade blocs that are most advanced in AI: China, the European Union, and the United States. To this end, we will analyze the key elements and main milestones in each block and propose corporate strategies based on AI to enhance the daily operations of micro, small, and medium-sized enterprises (SMEs).

## BACKGROUND

AI is transforming the operational strategy of organizations, regardless of their legal form, and is impacting the human resources working within them, who also benefit from its application in the workplace to achieve greater productivity and efficiency. This impact will transform the labor market, where those who can effectively incorporate it into their daily operations will be favored.

There is no single AI. The classification of AI varies according to the criteria used, with two of the most common classifications:

a) By Capability or Intelligence Level, being the most widespread classification. It is based on the level of intelligence and capabilities that AI possesses, ranging from the most basic to the most advanced, and in some cases, even hypothetical, as a future aspiration. As a result, a distinction is made between:
    - Artificial Narrow Intelligence (ANI) or Weak AI: This is the most common type, designed and trained to perform a specific and well-defined task. It lacks consciousness, emotions, and the ability to apply its knowledge to other areas, so it simulates intelligence in a minimal environment. Examples of ANI are voice assistants (Siri, Google Assistant, Alexa, among the best known), recommendation systems (e.g., Netflix, Amazon, Temu, AliExpress and Spotify), spam filters (e.g., in Gmail, Proton Mail, Yahoo and Hotmail, among others), facial recognition, automatic translators and game systems, such as Deep Blue in chess.
    - Artificial General Intelligence (AGI) or Strong AI: It is capable of understanding, learning, and applying its intelligence to a wide range of tasks, like a human being, so it learns from experience, reasons, solves

problems, and understands complex concepts in different domains. Today, it is still under development, although significant advances are being made in this type of intelligence across various fields and areas of knowledge, where AI «engages in the full process of gathering visual information, processing that information, learning, and acting» (Zook, 2017, p. 464) in interactions with the user.

   - Artificial Super Intelligence (ASI): Represents a level of intelligence that far exceeds human cognitive capacity in creativity, problem solving, and social skills. This type of AI is the future, raising ethical and philosophical dilemmas about the future of humanity.

b) By Functionality, classified according to how the AI operates and the level of complexity of its capabilities. According to Hintze (2016), it is classified into:
   - Reactive Machines: These are the most basic AI systems. They have no memory, nor the ability to learn from past experiences. They react to current inputs with predefined outputs.
   - Limited Memory Machines: They store and utilize past experiences (short-term memory) to make present decisions, but this memory is temporary and does not accumulate overtime (e.g., autonomous vehicles).
   - Theory of Mind (under development): Able to understand emotions, beliefs, intentions, and desires of other entities (humans or machines), so they could interact socially in a more sophisticated way and anticipate behaviors (e.g., humanoids that can interpret expressions and thus adapt their behavior in their interaction with humans).
   - Self-awareness (under development): Able to understand the world and be aware of itself, its existence, its internal states, and its feelings (if any).

Both narrow AI (ANI) and general AI (AGI) are already used in microenterprises and SMEs in developed countries. Thanks to the Internet, there is a growing deployment in developing countries, opening new business and growth opportunities for these nations. Those who master AI will hold global leadership. This impact can be seen not only in the economy, due to the positive synergies generated in planning and management with the massive use of AI, but also in business, with the growing efficiency and productivity achieved with its application in numerous areas of knowledge and the power of obtaining and synthesizing large volumes of information for their benefit, as «information, in general, is a deterministic abstract quantity rather than a probability-based property of the nature, so information is a general form of abstract objects represented by symbolical, mathematical, communication, computing, and cognitive systems» (Wang, 2017, p. 122) to ground AI.

## MAIN FOCUS OF THE CHAPTER

This struggle for leadership in AI, particularly in generative AI (GenAI), is being waged by the triad comprising the European Union, China, and the United States. This innovative technology, based on GenAI, empowers users to generate state-of-the-art content by leveraging the vast amount of data at their disposal (Nagar, Afaq, & Narula, 2025, p. 144). As far as Europe is concerned, the EU is actively shaping its AI strategy, founded on the principles of excellence in AI development, reliable AI systems, and responsible innovation based on ethical values and data protection. European companies present a strong collaboration with the United States, driven by a mutual commitment to trusted AI, focusing on joint research, standards and risk management through platforms such as the Trade and Technology Council (TTC), a high-level forum established between the EU and the United States in June 2021 to strengthen transatlantic cooperation on key issues related to trade, technology and security, based on shared values. In contrast, the EU's relationship with China in the field of AI is more complex. While there are areas of potential cooperation, such as AI ethics, sustainable development, and global governance, significant challenges remain due to divergent values on data privacy, human rights, and national security.

ASI represents a hypothetical concept of the future where AI not only matches human intelligence in all aspects, but far surpasses it in virtually all cognitive abilities, including creativity, general problem solving, and social skills, the latter being the most dangerous and challenging aspect for humans because it can influence an individual's decision making. Unlike ANI and AGI, an ASI would be capable of recursive self-improvement, leading to an explosion of intelligence that could radically transform society and our understanding of all that exists. The implications of ASI are profound, ranging from unprecedented advances in science and technology to existential concerns about control and the alignment of its goals with human values. Its development, although still distant, is a central theme in the ethics and philosophy of futuristic AI, particularly in extreme cases.

The ethics and philosophy of AI lead to controversies about the depth and convenience (or lack thereof) of its implementation in macroeconomic environments and business environments at the micro level, particularly in competitive and globalized contexts. These issues will be discussed in the following section.

### A Three-Fold Controversy Related to AI

One of the main problems with AI is the acceptance of its implementation by the primary stakeholders: the human team, especially those who perform repetitive tasks, as they are aware that a machine can easily replace them. This situation is perceived as a danger to these workers, who form lobbies in collusion with trade unions, primarily in countries where trade unionism is not influenced by political interests, to secure their jobs.

However, this desire to preserve jobs to avoid the digitization and automation of processes, mainly productive but also commercial processes and sales of the product or service marketed in the market, although not entirely, is not exempt. This resistance to change is especially pronounced in SMEs, regardless of the nation or the level of economic development in which the organization is located.

However, a strong resistance to change, especially in the implementation of technological processes, is detrimental to the company in the medium to long term, as it gradually becomes uncompetitive, particularly in global environments. The company must innovate at all times of its existence, especially if it wishes to achieve, or if necessary, maintain leadership positions within its sector. Without innovation, technological obsolescence arises in the medium term, which in turn accelerates the maturity of the product or service marketed in the market. This issue is a serious problem for the organization, since the product or service loses its appeal to the market.

A second controversy related to the implementation of AI-based production and commercial processes concerns the ethical and moral implications of their use. From an ethical point of view, it is immoral to dispense with human resources committed to the organization, perhaps in many cases for an extended time, which makes it unfair (and ungrateful) to discard human talent that has contributed value to the organization for years, and even decades. AI is not the solution to eliminate a problem; rather, AI should be one more tool on which the organization can rely to solve a given problem. Thus, AI achieves its maximum impact when it collaborates with the company's human team in a network. This collaboration is essential when a company is small (for example, in microenterprises) or when competition is intense, as they often compete with a limited number of products or services offered to the market, which increases the commercial risk in business operations. Unity is strength, especially in a highly 'glocalized' business world (think globally, act locally), so collaboration between companies creates synergies that benefit everyone and allows new market niches to be opened or existing ones to be expanded.

Finally, a third controversy arises from the interaction between public administrations and micro-enterprises and SMEs in their relationship with AI. Most visibly in the European Union, public regulation of AI is of great importance, which contrasts with China and the United States, for example, where administrative regulation is much smaller, thus encouraging entrepreneurship policies from the private sector, including the development of AI.

These three controversies give rise to the idea among microentrepreneurs and SMEs that AI is more of a problem than a solution to the challenges faced by organizations worldwide. These problems and challenges mean that, in general, microenterprises and SMEs tend to reject AI as a system to be implemented as part of the corporate strategy in the medium and long term, which makes these organizations more risk-averse, as well as more cautious and conservative in their investments and in the development of their business plan in the medium and long term.

These business controversies, which tend to generate a specific rejection of AI, are countered by government policies that encourage the implementation of AI. As a result, public decision-makers have a fundamental role to play in introducing public policies to promote the implementation of AI in microenterprises and SMEs, as more than 90% of the business fabric of almost all countries in the world, including the most advanced countries on the planet, is made up of microenterprises and SMEs.

## The EU's AI strategy

As a result, the EU is pursuing a path of strategic autonomy, investing heavily in innovation, infrastructure, and talent development at the European level to foster competitive and self-sufficient AI ecosystems within its borders. While the EU lags behind the U.S. and China in terms of volume of AI research investment and output, its focus on regulatory leadership and ethical AI gives the EU a distinct strategic advantage in shaping the future of responsible AI globally, to which end the EU is striving to put in place the planet's first comprehensive legal framework for AI with the adoption of Regulation (EU) 2024/1689 of the European Parliament and of the Council of 13 June 2024, laying down harmonized rules on AI and amending Regulations (EC) 300/2008, (EU) 167/2013, (EU) 168/2013, (EU) 2018/858, (EU) 2018/1139 and (EU) 2019/2144 and Directives 2014/90/EU, (EU) 2016/797 and (EU) 2020/1828. Thus, the Act explicitly prohibits certain AI practices deemed to be of unacceptable risk, including harmful AI-based manipulation of human behavior, exploitation of vulnerabilities (e.g., targeting children or the elderly), social scoring systems, individual assessment of crime risk, untargeted internet tracking for facial recognition databases, and emotion recognition in workplaces and educational institutions.

Thus, to achieve the goal of responsible AI, the EU plans to invest €20 billion per year from public and private sources over the next decade, with the Horizon Europe and Digital Europe programs being key in this process in which at least €1 billion per year is already being invested in AI between 2021 and 2027, as well as the launch in April 2025 of the AI Continent Action Plan which includes the development of so-called AI Factories and Gigafactories aimed at advanced AI computing and massive data storage, with plans to procure millions of cutting-edge, European-produced AI chips. The European Commission has already received 76 proposals for these gigafactories, although it is still significantly behind the United States in terms of investment (Table 1).

*Table 1. Pillars of the EU's AI strategy.*

| Pillar | Description |
|---|---|
| Investment in AI | 20 billion euros/year (public and private) in the next decade<br>1 billion/years from Horizon Europe and Digital Europe (2021-2027)<br>AI Factories and Gigafactories |
| Collaboration in AI | Quadruple helix models (Business - Government - NGO - Universities)<br>Increase funding for startups |
| Talent retention | Synergies and best practice policies for talent retention<br>Funding for master's and doctoral degrees in AI. |
| Data Protection Law for AI | User protection and the creation of common European data spaces, as well as the pooling of resources for supercomputers. |
| Ethics and security in AI | Development of an ethical framework for AI<br>Increased protection against cyber threats. |

Source: Author.

The construction of giga factories involves establishing large-scale supercomputing centers dedicated to the development and training of advanced AI models. This initiative aims to enhance the European Union's technological autonomy and allow it to compete with the United States and China. Each gigafactory will be equipped with tens of thousands of cutting-edge graphics processing units (GPUs), AI-optimized supercomputers, and support services for businesses, startups, and research institutions.

The development of EuroHPC JU aims to create a world-class, federated, and secure supercomputing infrastructure that is accessible to a diverse range of users. EuroHPC JU not only acquires and deploys high-performance supercomputers, including pre-exascale and exascale systems capable of executing over a billion operations per second, but also promotes research and development of innovative technologies and applications. Its activities include supporting the European HPC supply chain, which encompasses processor and software development, as well as providing computing services for industry, scientific research, and public administration.

Additionally, EuroHPC JU invests in AI giga factories to integrate artificial intelligence into supercomputing and to train the next generation of experts. Through these initiatives, it contributes to Europe's digital sovereignty by driving scientific progress, enhancing industrial competitiveness, and addressing societal challenges in areas such as medicine, climate, and security.

Implementation of the AI Act is phased, with prohibitions taking effect on 2 February 2025, rules for general-purpose AI on 2 August 2025, and high-risk AI systems on 2 August 2026—non-compliance results in heavy penalties. The extraterritorial application of the EU AI Law and its strict prohibitions reflect a proactive attempt to impose European values globally, which could generate compliance burdens, but also foster a trust premium for EU-aligned AI.

The EU is forging a distinct path in AI development by prioritizing strategic autonomy through investment processes involving the 27 countries that currently comprise the EU, the establishment of a unified regulatory framework, and the development of homegrown human talent. This approach seeks to reduce technological dependence on the outside and ensure that AI develops in line with European values by driving a concerted effort to build a unified and robust domestic ecosystem, emphasizing the synergies created through the use of shared infrastructure by removing barriers, improving financing with the development of Mutual Guarantee Societies, and developing ecosystems with increasing interregional cooperation with the formation of European joint stock companies working in cross-border collaboration in industrial clusters.

Related to AI, the EU aims to create common European data spaces and pool resources to build the next generation of supercomputers used for training AI. The so-called 'AI Continent Action Plan' is a crucial step in strengthening Europe's AI ecosystem, supported by significant investments in big data infrastructure, supercomputing, and targeted funding mechanisms. This plan includes the creation of AI Factories and Gigafactories, with EU funding of €20 billion (InvestAI Initiative) for the construction of gigafactories designed for advanced AI computing and data warehousing (Table 2).

*Table 2. Location of AI gigafactories in the EU (planned or operational)*

| Country | Gigafactory | Country | Gigafactory |
|---|---|---|---|
| Germany | HammeHAI<br>JAIF | Luxembourg | Meluxin-AI |
| Spain | Barcelona Supercomputing Center AIF | Sweden | MIMER |
| Finland | LUMI AI Factory | Austria | AIF Austria |
| Italy | IT4LIA Bologna | Bulgaria | BRAIN++ |
| Greece | Pharos | France | AIF2 |
| Poland | PIAST AIF | Slovenia | SLAIF |

Source: Adapted from Eurostat data and European Commission information.

Throughout this process, STEM (Science, Technology, Engineering, and Mathematics) professions are of fundamental importance for the development and implementation of GenIA. Thus, EU Member States share the best practices on how to retain human talent by funding master's and PhDs in AI, complemented by initiatives to advance digital skills and talent, such as the AI Skills Academy and the CLAIRE (Confederation of Laboratories for Artificial Intelligence Research in

Europe) initiative to strengthen European excellence in AI R&D and innovation. CLAIRE is one of the largest networks of AI research groups and institutes in the world and aims to help European AI researchers to engage in research activities and collaborations across Europe through global networking, application for EU-funded projects, innovation and industrial cooperation, joined by the Horizon 2020-funded AI4EU project, aims to mobilize the entire European AI community to realize the promise of AI for European society and economy, and create a leading AI collaboration platform to foster economic growth. The program also plans to increase public and private investments in AI, build the necessary competence, and address ethical issues. These efforts demonstrate a clear understanding that technological leadership depends on human capital—the emphasis on excellence in AI research and academic funding points to a long-term strategy.

Alongside this, the EU has established an ethical framework for AI. The AI Law, as the cornerstone of the strategy, is the world's first comprehensive legal framework for AI, establishing standards for the responsible and safe development of AI. It also regulates general-purpose AI models, including popular GenAI tools like DALL-E, RunwayML, DeepArt, and GANPaint, to ensure proper oversight and control. The AI Compact, a voluntary initiative, invites AI developers and users to begin aligning themselves with the Act's obligations before its full implementation, encouraging early compliance and cooperation across sectors. In addition, complementary legal frameworks on AI-adapted civil liability and sector-specific safety regulations complement this effort.

The extraterritorial application of the AI Act, which extends to providers and users outside the EU if their AI systems are used within the EU, is a crucial element. This issue requires non-EU entities to appoint authorized representatives in the EU to coordinate their compliance efforts. The fact that the AI Act is the world's first comprehensive legal framework and its risk-based approach, along with explicit prohibitions, demonstrates a clear intent to lead governance. Extraterritorial application is key: it is not just about domestic rules but about influencing global practices. The existence of the European AI and Society Fund to empower civil society groups in shaping AI policy for justice, inclusive and sustainable societies further underlines the EU's commitment to a values-based approach to avoid malicious applications in cybercrimes, such as automated hacking, phishing attacks, malware, creation of attack payloads, and social engineering tactics, cryptographic manipulation (Sharma, Chopra, & Singh, 2025). This strategy distinguishes itself from U.S. market-driven innovation and China's state-led implementation, positioning the EU as a global leader in responsible AI development, which it sees as a form of strategic autonomy.

## EU's collaboration in AI

### EU-USA relationship in AI

The Trade and Technology Council (TTC), established during the EU-U.S. Summit in Brussels on 15 June 2021, has consistently been a strong partner committed to driving digital transformation and cooperating on new technologies based on shared values. TTC serves as a crucial forum for both sides to coordinate approaches on key global trade, economic, and technology issues and to deepen transatlantic trade and economic relations based on shared values. Both entities recognize that AI technologies offer powerful advances but can also threaten fundamental values and freedoms if not developed and deployed responsibly or if misused. They, therefore, affirm their willingness to develop and deploy innovative and trustworthy AI systems. In this regard, the explicit mention of implementing the OECD Recommendation on AI and the AI Bill of Rights suggests a deliberate effort to co-create a Western model of AI governance and development. This model contrasts with, for example, China's state-driven and surveillance-oriented approach.

Within the TTC, the EU and the United States have agreed on several specific AI cooperation initiatives. At the Sixth TTC Ministerial Meeting in April 2024, they reaffirmed their commitment to a risk-based approach to AI. They announced a new dialogue between the EU AI Office and the U.S. AI Security Institute. They also agreed to advance transatlantic cooperation on AI, 6G, and critical technologies and emerging technologies, and extended administrative arrangements to build resilient semiconductor supply chains.

In addition, both sides seek to explore cooperation on AI technologies designed to enhance privacy protection, in full compliance with their respective standards and regulations. A joint economic study has been conducted to examine the impact of AI on the future of the workforce. A significant step was the publication of the first Joint Roadmap on Assessment and Measurement Tools for Trusted AI and Risk Management (AI Roadmap) in December 2022, as well as the synthesis of U.S.-EU AI cooperation initiatives in Table 3. The coming to power of the current administration, led by President Trump, has led to a slowdown in the implementation of these agreements.

*Table 3. AI Cooperation Initiatives between the EU and the USA.*

| Area of Cooperation | Specific Initiatives |
|---|---|
| Cooperation on AI | Commitment to a risk-based approach; support for safe and trusted AI technologies; dialogue between the EU AI Office and the U.S. AI Security Institute. |
| Critical and emerging technologies | Transatlantic cooperation on AI, 6G, emerging technologies, resilient semiconductor supply chains, and digital identity mapping |
| Trust standards and frameworks | Joint Roadmap on Assessment and Measurement Tools for Trusted AI and Risk Management; cooperation on privacy-enhancing AI technologies; development of a shared repository of metrics for trust in AI |
| AI Impact | Joint economic study on the impact of AI on the labor market; collaboration in areas such as climate, health, and agriculture; working group to analyze AI misuse (arbitrary surveillance and social scoring systems) |

Source: Adapted from CTT.

## EU-China collaboration in AI

The volume and application of AI research and deployment in China represent a competitive challenge and a potential area for collaboration with the EU, despite the EU's concerns in its relationship with China on issues related to data privacy. Despite this fact, the European interest to collaborate with China is given because since 2016 the Asian nation leads the research papers on AI (40% of the world) and patents in GenAI (70% of the world) that are six times higher than patents on AI in the United States (Table 4), as well as by the increasingly closer trade relations between the EU and China thanks to the different Silk Roads linking Europe with Asia. As a result, further collaboration between the EU and China is to be expected, as seen, for example, in the Asian Infrastructure Investment Bank, whose beginnings were driven by senior Chinese and European managers.

*Table 4. Comparison of key AI metrics*

| Key Metrics | China | United States | European Union |
|---|---|---|---|
| Research papers on AI | 155,487 | 81,130 | 101,455 |
| Patents in GenAI (2014-2023) | >38,000 (70% worldwide) | >6,000 | nd |
| Investment in AI (mM USD) | 98 | 605 | 210 |
| AI market value (mM USD) | 60 | 87 | 35 |
| Public Expenditure on AI (mM USD) | 55,000 | 750 | 23,000 |
| AI adoption in manufacturing | 77% | 46% | nd |
| Public confidence in AI | High (>70%) | Low (35%) | Very low (19%) |

Legend: MM USD (billions of dollars/year), nd (no data)

China has positioned itself as a global leader in artificial intelligence (AI), driven by a robust government strategy, substantial investments, and an innovative ecosystem. The country is making rapid progress in various areas, including language models, autonomous vehicles, and industrial applications. The Chinese government prioritizes AI development to become the world's leading center for innovation by 2030. To support this ambition, national plans have been introduced that provide subsidies for startups, promote the development of specialized chips (such as those produced by Huawei), and encourage collaboration between companies and universities. Major companies like Baidu, Alibaba, Tencent (collectively known as BAT), and Huawei are at the forefront of this progress. Baidu has developed Ernie, a competitor to GPT-4, while firms like SenseTime excel in facial recognition technologies. Xiaomi and DJI are leading innovations in robotics and autonomous drones.

Thanks to existing public-private collaboration in China, especially in Special Economic Zones, along with government-led investment initiatives and growing links between higher education institutions (HEIs) and industry, Chinese generative AI models are closing the performance gap with U.S. models, with some Chinese models outperforming their U.S. counterparts. Thus, for example, the Chinese open-source LLM (Large Language Model) ecosystem is advancing rapidly, with models such as Alibaba's Qwen 1.5 and Zhipu AI's ChatGLM3 outperforming their U.S. counterparts.

DeepSeek, which developed its R1 model at a cost of just $5.6 million — much lower than comparable U.S. models — is accelerating global AI adoption and has led to increased AI investments by Chinese tech giants such as Alibaba and Tencent. China is at the forefront of AI application globally, driving productivity and transforming its traditional industries, while also boasting a vast consumer market and numerous industrial application scenarios. As a result, Chinese companies hold 74.7% of global AI patents and aim to make China the world leader in AI by 2030, with an industry valued at more than $150 billion, driven by government initiatives and growing, diversified cooperation with the EU (Table 5).

*Table 5. EU-China AI Cooperation: Areas and Challenges*

| AREAS OF COOPERATION | |
|---|---|
| **Complementarity in R&D and Innovation** | The EU is strong in fundamental research, while China excels in adapting AI in industry, so there is potential for synergy between theoretical and applied innovation. |
| Sustainable Development | Shared interests in sustainable growth (EU Green Pact, China's innovation strategy); potential for collaboration in healthcare, elderly care, and Social Security efficiency. |
| **CHALLENGES FOR COOPERATION** | |
| Data Privacy Compliance | The EU has concerns about compliance with the General Data Protection Regulation, which has been in force in the EU since 2018, regarding Chinese AI products, transparency in training data, user consent, and data transfer outside the EU. |
| Strategic Autonomy *vs.* Security | A contradiction arises between the EU's quest for autonomy and its reliance on security, leading to increased scrutiny of Chinese AI products on national security grounds. |
| Ethics | Concern that Chinese models may incorporate preferences not aligned with EU ethical standards, including the use of AI for digital surveillance and control. |

*Source:* Author.

## Perception of Spain microenterprises and SMEs in AI.

As the fourth-largest economy in the EU by size, surpassed only by Germany, France, and Italy, Spain is making significant advances in the field of AI, with a clear vision of boosting technological development, innovation, and its ethical application in various sectors. The main initiatives are articulated around the National Artificial Intelligence Strategy (ENIA), which has been updated to the AI 2024 Strategy which, endowed with 760 million euros per year, presents three main lines of action: a) Strengthening the key levers for AI development: This includes boosting investment in supercomputing (such as MareNostrum 5 and the Spanish Supercomputing Network - RES), generating sustainable data storage capabilities, developing models and data that constitute a public AI infrastructure, and fostering specialized AI talent through grants and training; b) Facilitate the expansion of AI in the public and private sector, by incorporating AI into government processes to improve services to the population, and catalyze change in the private sector, with special emphasis on SMEs through programs such as Kit Consulting and Kit Digital. Pilot projects and innovative solutions that benefit microenterprises are also promoted. Additionally, c) Promote transparent, ethical, and humanistic AI:

The aim is to ensure the responsible development and use of AI, respecting human rights, equality, privacy, and non-discrimination.

Along with this, the Spanish Agency for the Oversight of Artificial Intelligence (AESIA) was established in August 2023 to lead the debate on the use of AI, define best practices, ensure the evaluation of models, and build a relationship of trust with this technology. Its role is fundamental in ensuring the ethical and responsible use of AI in Spain. This creation has been complemented by the development of the ALIA language model, which is open source and accessible both in Spanish and in the co-official Spanish languages (Galician, Catalan and Basque), to strengthen Spain's technological sovereignty in AI, improve the quality of natural language processing in Spanish and incorporate the linguistic and cultural context of Spain. The ICO joins this program - Next Tech fund, a joint initiative of Spain's Official Credit Institute (ICO) and the Secretary of State for Digitalization and Artificial Intelligence (under the Ministry of Digital Transformation and Public Function of the Government of Spain), is also fostering the development of innovative digital projects, including AI, intending to mobilize up to €8 billion in public-private collaboration. Finally, programs are being implemented to attract and train AI experts, creating collaborative networks between universities, research centers, and Spanish companies. The ATRAE 2025 program stands out, with a budget of 45 million euros, to attract international leaders in research areas with high social impact, including AI.

As a result, Spanish microenterprises and SMEs are adopting AI-based strategies. According to ONTSI (2024), the most frequent uses of AI among Spanish companies are flow automation and decision support. In micro companies, the use of AI grew from 4.6% in 2021 to 5.8% in 2023. However, in small companies, the decline is from 9.4% to 6.6% over the same period, suggesting that this segment faces specific challenges due to intense competition. Finally, Spanish microenterprises primarily use AI for: converting spoken language into text (44.8%), generating written or spoken language (39.8%), Administrative processes (21.4%), Financial management (18.4%), and Marketing and sales (15.8%).

According to IONOS (2023), although Spanish SMEs are the ones that value the use of AI the most within the EU, 25% of SMEs in Spain would be willing to use AI if its cost were less than 1% of their monthly turnover. This issue underlines that the initial investment is a significant concern. In addition, Spanish SMEs have a positive perception (60%) about the quality of AI-generated content for their needs, suggesting confidence in its capabilities. However, 73% of SMEs are aware that AI poses a moderate to high risk of job loss, and 71% believe the government should regulate its use.

Due to this risk and the lack of specialized AI training, according to the 2025 Barometer of Artificial Intelligence Adoption in Spanish SMEs (IndesIA/Autónomos y Emprendedores), 97% of SMEs have not yet incorporated AI into their businesses.

Better training in AI would lead, as Brynjolfsson, Li, & Raymond (2025) show, to an increase in productivity of 15% on average, with considerable heterogeneity among workers, the improvement being greater in employees with little training and experience, while the most experienced and qualified employees experience minor relative improvements, with these improvements being very high when the problem to be solved is complex. Thus, Aisa and Cabeza (2025) show that those who do not use AI in their work maintain a traditional retirement pattern, and the most trained and/or healthy among them prolong their working lives because AI compensates for the skills that tend to deteriorate with age, allowing them to remain longer in the labor market. Moreover, Minniti, Prettner, and Venturini (2025) find that AI reduces the labor share in Europe by 0.5% to 1.6%, having a particularly negative impact on low-skilled and medium-skilled workers, while for high-skilled workers, there is job expansion.

The following section will outline solutions and recommendations for implementing AI successfully in the most reluctant sectors and industries.

## SOLUTIONS AND RECOMMENDATIONS

Microenterprises and SMEs view AI as a promising tool to enhance their competitiveness, but the actual implementation faces significant challenges related to resources, knowledge, and change management. R&D and innovation are complementary, where the EU excels in fundamental research but struggles with large-scale commercialization. In contrast, Chinese technology companies excel in rapid deployment and iteration of models, leading to companies with strong industry-specific adaptability, greater contextual awareness, and the generation of robust system-level integration capabilities. This synergy between theoretical (EU) and applied (China) innovation creates a solid foundation for achieving an efficient and shared technology ecosystem.

Thus, the implementation of AI in microenterprises and SMEs presents a landscape of great opportunities, but also significant challenges:

### Opportunities for microenterprise and SMEs in AI

#### Process optimization and efficiency gains

AI automates repetitive tasks, increasing labor productivity and, in turn, improving the company's economic performance. In addition, AI optimizes inventory management, which lowers the cost of storage and enables the implementation of JIT (Just in Time) policies, which in turn improve business results. In addition, the increased automation achieved with AI enhances logistics, enabling the optimization of production and marketing processes both domestically and internationally. This fact, in turn, facilitates entry into new market niches and the expansion of existing ones. Finally, the incorporation of AI in the organization facilitates the prediction of machinery failures, a fact that is fundamental in the manufacturing industry, which cannot afford stoppages in the production chain. All this translates into greater operational efficiency and a significant reduction in costs, resulting in a net profit increase for the company.

### Personalization of customer experience

With AI, micro and SMEs can analyze customer data to provide personalized recommendations, given the greater amount of information available. In addition, customer service is improved through chatbots, which tend to solve problems and complaints more easily and effectively, with GPT-3.5, GPT-4, Gemini 1.0, Llama 2, and Claude being the most used today (Kamalov et al., 2025). Ultimately, AI facilitates the development of more effective marketing campaigns, thereby enhancing customer satisfaction and loyalty.

### Advanced data analytics for decision-making

AI enables microenterprises and SMEs to process large volumes of data, identify patterns, and gain valuable insights about the market, consumer behavior, and business performance, facilitating more informed and strategic decisions.

### Access to new markets and business models

AI can help microenterprises and SMEs identify untapped market niches, develop innovative products and services, and explore new business models based on data or customization on scale.

### Improved competitiveness and innovation

By adopting AI, microenterprises and SMEs can innovate more quickly, differentiate themselves from the competition, and remain relevant in an increasingly digitized marketplace, thereby driving their long-term growth and sustainability.

## Challenges for microenterprises and SMEs in AI

### Lack of knowledge and training

Many microenterprises and SMEs lack the technical expertise and skilled personnel needed to implement and manage AI solutions, including difficulty in understanding which technologies are relevant and how to apply them to their operations. In this regard, Cheng et al. (2025) show that as the SME becomes stronger in the market, it stops seeking new knowledge from the market and instead develops it mainly within the organization, which incentivizes the implementation of AI-based strategies. As a result, experience and job stability are key employment factors that favor the implementation of AI strategies and strengthen the existing skills within the organization.

### Initial cost and access to funding

The initial investment in AI software, hardware, and specialized talent can be prohibitive for many SMEs with limited budgets, making it challenging to access these new technologies.

### Data quality and availability

AI relies heavily on high-quality data. However, microenterprises and SMEs often have their data structured, incomplete, or scattered, making it challenging to train AI models and obtain reliable results effectively.

### Resistance to change and cultural adaptation

AI implementation implies changes in work processes and employee responsibilities. Internal resistance, fear of job automation, and lack of a culture of innovation can hinder adoption. Thus, in this regard, Han and Huang (2025) demonstrate that companies with higher AI implementation tend to have a greater surplus of human resources, especially in the manufacturing industry and in sectors where the company has a low market share, particularly among workforces with low levels of education. Therefore, it is necessary to train the organization's human resources to adapt to the opportunities for increased productivity offered by AI, as well as to enhance the SME's ability to meet its development needs and balance technology and human capital.

## Regulatory and ethical frameworks

Regulation surrounding the use of AI, data privacy, cybersecurity, and ethics in algorithmic decision-making is still in development. SMEs may face legal uncertainty and the need to comply with complex regulations that may vary by region. Thus, as shown by Jin and Yu (2025), the implementation of AI in enterprises increases digital liability risk for companies, leading to greater corporate awareness of end-consumer care through easier access to quality information in real-time. As a result, it is necessary to strengthen the regulatory framework so that the State has greater control over the activity carried out by microenterprises and SMEs regarding AI practices.

# Towards greater Eurasian cooperation on AI

This collaboration process will mainly take place between China and the EU, given the growing isolationism that the United States will face following the implementation of the current administration's tariff policy.

Thus, the current AI landscape is defined as the driving force behind the next industrial and technological revolution, in which, with US leadership in decline, new economic players are emerging and leading the world toward a new geopolitical reality. This new reality will be led by China, characterized by the creation of ecosystems of innovation and entrepreneurship based on state capitalism defined by the use of large amounts of money for investment, the training of highly specialized human resources in AI, and growing international collaboration between Chinese and foreign companies, especially those located in Special Economic Zones (SEZs), mainly Shenzhen, defined as a global center for high technology, finance, and innovation, which is why it is known as the Chinese Silicon Valley; Xiamen, defined as specializing in high-tech industries, manufacturing, and services; and Hainan, whose importance lies in its service economy and the promotion of a free trade port to attract global investment. As a result, China has emerged as a leader in investment, infrastructure development, and large-scale AI applications, driven by vast amounts of data and a pragmatic approach. This is compounded by the recent application in China of semiconductors made from selenium compounds instead of silicon, which increases performance, reduces energy requirements, and accelerates transmission speeds.

The EU is characterized by its emphasis on fundamental research, ethical regulation (such as the General Data Protection Regulation - GDPR), and the development of human-centered AI, given the social market economy that characterizes European economic policy, with respective adaptations in each European country according to the ideology and economic model prevailing at the time. Hence, collaboration between these two giants offers immense potential, but also presents profound challenges due to their fundamental differences in values, governance, and geopolitical strategy.

## Positive aspects of the collaboration

### *Acceleration of Innovation and Technological Development*

Given their complementary nature, there is a synergy of strengths between the two blocs, with the EU contributing its excellence in research and its focus on ethics and security. In contrast, China contributes its capacity for scaling up and its speed and effectiveness in commercial implementation. However, the recent push for the current US tariff policy has prompted the EU and China to face a "common enemy" in the commercial and technological arena, which has had a direct impact on the development of AI. This has created a need to find solutions to mitigate the impact of these tariff restrictions, which in turn has influenced foreign direct investment in this area. However, the EU has not opted for an unconditional rapprochement with China. Instead, it has focused on its strategic autonomy strategy, which means that it seeks to reduce its dependence on both superpowers, the US and China, in critical technological areas such as AI.

However, such a reduction in dependence, both on the EU and on China, can only happen in the medium to long term, so in the short term, collaboration is expected to continue on joint projects in AI research, the development of new AI-assisted materials, and the implementation of solutions for climate change, in which the United States is no longer interested, at least at the federal government level.

### *Benefits of collaboration*

The greater degree of collaboration resulting from the opening of the Chinese market has given European companies access to the vast Chinese market and its supply chains. In contrast, Chinese companies, mainly through Huawei, have gained access to large databases of EU customers, particularly in Spain. Huawei is a crucial player in the global AI ecosystem, despite trade restrictions imposed by the United States. Its importance can be summarized as follows:

- **Massive investment in R&D:** Huawei invests a significant amount of its revenue in research and development of cutting-edge technologies, including AI. This has enabled it to develop its own AI platforms, such as the "ModelArts" platform, which makes it easier for companies to create and deploy AI models.
- **Computing infrastructure:** The company is a global leader in telecommunications infrastructure (such as 5G and 6G) and data centers. AI requires high computing power and fast networks, and Huawei provides the key hard-

ware and software components for this. The company has developed its own AI chips, such as the Ascend series, to reduce its dependence on foreign suppliers and enhance its solutions.

- **Vision of "AI for all scenarios":** Huawei has an ambitious strategy to integrate AI across its entire ecosystem, from the cloud (Huawei Cloud) and IoT (Internet of Things) devices to consumer devices and 6G networks. Its goal is to democratize AI, making it more accessible to businesses of all sizes and across various industries.
- **Impact on industrial digitalization:** Huawei focuses on applying AI to transform entire industries, such as smart manufacturing, energy, and healthcare. Its expertise in these fields enables it to develop practical and scalable solutions that have a real impact on productivity and efficiency.

In addition, collaboration enables the establishment of new global standards that improve existing ones. Thus, collaboration to create technical and interoperability standards in AI could prevent global market fragmentation and promote smoother trade between all countries.

Collaboration between the EU and China exists on AI-related issues, although it is selective and takes place in an environment of growing caution. The dynamics are complex and based on complementary strengths and the need for both sides to remain competitive.

- **Collaboration in research and development (R&D):** Collaboration between universities and research institutes on both sides is well established. Chinese and European researchers co-author thousands of articles on AI every year. China has surpassed the United States in the production and publication of articles on AI. This collaboration, however, has come under scrutiny, especially in areas with potential military or surveillance applications.

• *Alliances in industrial sectors:*

o **Smart manufacturing:** German companies such as Siemens and Bosch are collaborating with Chinese partners to develop AI-based automation and innovative factory solutions. The EU's expertise in precision engineering is combined with China's production capacity and scale. Siemens' collaboration with China began in 1985, shortly after China opened up to foreign investment, with the signing of a trade and technology investment agreement between the German multinational and the then Ministry of Machinery, Electricity and Electronic Industries of China (in operation until 1988), which was first replaced by the Ministry of Machinery and Electronics and then by the current Ministry of Industry and Information Technology (MIIT).

- o **Automotive:** European automotive giants such as Volkswagen are collaborating with Chinese technology companies to integrate AI into autonomous driving and electric vehicles. This is compounded by the arrival of Chinese automotive giants in the EU, with Spain being their main port of entry, following the arrival of Chery, in a strategic alliance with Spanish company Ebro-EV Motors, which has begun building SUVs at the former Nissan plant in Barcelona's Zona Franca (Spain). The Omoda and Jaecoo brands have also joined the fray.
- o **Cloud services:** Chinese companies such as Alibaba and its Alibaba Cloud are establishing a presence in the European Union, offering cloud services and AI solutions to European companies, which encourages a form of commercial cooperation. This growing presence of Chinese companies in the EU in sensitive and strategic sectors is displacing the United States in key areas. This process has been accelerating in the second decade of the current century.

• *Challenges in collaboration:*

- o **Data privacy:** The main barrier is the conflict between the EU's strict General Data Protection Regulation (GDPR) and data management practices in China. Any AI collaboration involving the handling of personal data must comply with EU regulations, which may slow down the development of AI in China.
- o **Security and ethics:** European companies are aware of the security risks and ethical implications of partnering with Chinese companies, especially in technologies that may have dual uses (civil and military). The EU actively seeks to ensure that AI is developed ethically and transparently. This is sometimes difficult to achieve given the Chinese government's opacity on this sensitive and strategic issue for its national interests. However, AI can be used to address global challenges in areas such as health (e.g., cooperation in the development of AI-assisted medical diagnostics, drug discovery, and pandemic management) and the environment (e.g., the joint use of AI for environmental monitoring, energy optimization, and the development of smart grids).

### *Negative aspects and challenges of collaboration*

The central negative aspect of such collaboration between the EU and China for the development and application of AI is the difference in values and the emergence of risks related to the handling of data characterized by its business confidentiality and the need to protect European consumer privacy. While the EU prioritizes privacy, transparency, and individual rights, the Chinese model focuses on social control and state security. This difference means that the adoption of Chinese AI technologies in the EU could erode data protection, which is highly regulated in the EU to protect citizens, thereby affecting trust in institutions.

Furthermore, excessive collaboration could lead to the EU becoming dependent on Chinese technology, which would limit its digital sovereignty and make it vulnerable to external geopolitical pressures. Added to this is the risk of unfair trade practices, particularly with the risk that collaboration could be used by China for forced technology transfer to its Special Economic Zones, intellectual property theft, especially if European companies outsource internal knowledge and manufacturing processes. These factors would distort the market in China's favor, primarily if the Asian nation engages in economic dumping using state subsidies for manufacturing. This would harm European companies by preventing them from competing with prices below manufacturing costs.

Despite these security risks, in which the integration of foreign systems from leading AI countries opens the door to cyberattacks and espionage, and legal and regulatory fragmentation in which differences in data protection legislation create complex and risky legal environments for companies, technological collaboration is necessary, as is the case in other scientific and academic environments, to develop AI properly. However, although the planet is moving towards a multipolar world due to the growing economic, social, and political importance of the BRICS+ countries, in AI-related matters, the number of players will be much smaller. The financial and geopolitical gains are much greater, so a fierce battle is expected in this area of knowledge in the coming years.

Thus, one of the keys to the success of AI in microenterprises and SMEs lies in proactively addressing these challenges, taking advantage of opportunities to boost their growth and transformation in the digital era. The second key is specialized training in AI, where international collaboration and cooperation are essential for its successful development and implementation in quadruple helix technology ecosystems (comprising Public Administration, Business, NGOs, and Universities) to maximize its impact on society.

## FUTURE RESEARCH DIRECTIONS

Future research directions related to AI would be to analyze how developing countries are implementing it and the impact it can have on their economies to overcome poverty. A second avenue of research is to investigate the key success factors for international collaborative educational systems based on STEM-related technical specialties to accelerate the development of AI. Finally, a third research direction would be to study the impact of AI on how the level and specialty of training influence the labor market regarding AI.

## CONCLUSION

The EU's position in the global AI race is multifaceted, characterized by a strong focus on governance and ethics, while facing challenges in research volume and investment scale compared to the United States and China. The Stanford AI Index Report 2025 indicates that the U.S. leads in the production of major AI models; however, China is rapidly closing the performance gap, reaching near parity by 2024 in several key benchmarks. In addition, the U.S. dominates global AI investment, driven by massive private equity and venture capital funding, while China is leveraging substantial state-backed initiatives along with private investment to accelerate its AI industry. The EU, despite its public investment targets, lags significantly behind in terms of overall funding, relying more on strategic public funding and regulatory frameworks to guide its ecosystem.

The EU is targeting EUR 20 billion per year in investment from the EU, public and private sectors over the next decade, with programs such as Horizon Europe and Digital Europe investing at least EUR 1 billion per year. However, these figures, while significant for a coordinated public effort, appear modest compared to the scale of private investment in the United States and combined public-private spending in China. The main difference lies in the divergent funding models: the market-driven dynamism of the United States, the state-led strategic thrust of China, and the EU's attempt to foster a continental-scale ecosystem with a combination of public funding and regulatory guidance, recognizing its investment gap.

For its part, China demonstrates strong leadership in the scale and speed of AI adoption and commercialization across diverse industries, driven by state policy, a vast market, and increased public confidence in AI, positioning it for significant productivity gains and economic growth. The U.S. excels in translating fundamental research into innovative products, particularly in enterprise solutions and financial services, but faces lower public trust. EU adoption rates are not explicitly detailed comparatively, suggesting that it lags in widespread commercialization, focusing more on regulatory compliance.

China is at the forefront of AI application globally, driving productivity and transforming its traditional industries. The country serves as a testing ground for the enterprise adoption of AI at scale, with a vast consumer market of 1.4 billion people and numerous industrial application scenarios. Chinese tech companies are applying AI on a large scale in everyday life, from facial recognition payment systems to AI-powered medical diagnostics in hospitals, personalized recommendations in e-commerce platforms. Supply chain optimization, making it so that, in manufacturing, 77% of Chinese companies use AI in multiple processes, compared with 46% in the United States. China's AI investments are expected to generate a 52% return on invested capital by 2030 and are anticipated to drive China's GDP growth. Confidence in AI is high in China (over 70%), in contrast to low confidence in the United States and the Western world (35%).

Finally, the United States excels in translating cutting-edge research into real-world products, driven by its private sector companies. U.S. companies have the edge in AI software and enterprise solutions. The U.S. financial sector is at the forefront of AI adoption, with 62% of firms using AI to a moderate or large degree, and 58% testing or implementing generative AI. Between 72% and 78% of firms in the U.S. financial sector are actively using or experimenting with AI solutions.

The creation and launch in 2021 of the Trade and Technology Council (TTC) by the U.S. and EU as a high-level forum to strengthen cooperation on key global technology, economic, and trade issues, promoting shared prosperity, competitiveness, and market-oriented democratic values, is an example of collaboration leading to a win-win strategy for both parties. Hence, collaboration between the triad is necessary to make AI more inclusive and humane. Despite this business and technological success in terms of AI, the current aggressive tariff policy initiated by the United States affects countries around the world. It undermines the effectiveness of technological collaboration agreements among companies, universities, and research centers. While supporters of these policies argue that they are necessary to protect jobs and domestic industries, historical evidence and economic analysis indicate that such measures often lead to escalating tensions, a loss of trust, and a weakening of the multilateral trading system. As a result, cooperation agreements become less effective and, in some cases, entirely ineffective.

## REFERENCES


Aísa, R., & Cabeza, J. (2025). Artificial intelligence: Redefining the retirement pattern. *Research in Economics, 79*(3), 101062. DOI: 10.1016/j.rie.2025.101062

Brynjolfsson, E., Li, D., & Raymond, L. (2025). Generative AI at Work. *The Quarterly Journal of Economics, 140*(2), 889–942. DOI: 10.1093/qje/qjae044

Cheng, Y., Yang, Z., Cheng, Y., Ge, Y., & Zhu, H. (2025). Evolutionary modeling reveals that value-oriented knowledge creation behaviors reinvent jobs. *Humanities & Social Sciences Communications, 12*(1), 385. DOI: 10.1057/s41599-025-04706-1

Han, Y., & Huang, Y. (2025). Does artificial intelligence lead to human resource slack? Evidence from China. *Finance Research Letters, 84*, 107803. DOI: 10.1016/j.frl.2025.107803

Hintze, A. (2016, 14 November). From reactive robots to sentient machines: The four types of AI. Live Science. https://www.livescience.com/56858-4-types-artificial-intelligence.html

Jin, C.-X., & Yu, J.-Q. (2025). Does the popularization of artificial intelligence increase the risk of corporate digital responsibility? *Finance Research Letters, 80*, 107375. DOI: 10.1016/j.frl.2025.107375

Kamalov, F., Calonge, D. S., Hultberg, P. T., Smail, L., & Jamali, D. (2025). Comparative analysis of leading artificial intelligence chatbots in the context of entrepreneurship. *Journal of Innovation and Entrepreneurship, 14*(1), 58. DOI: 10.1186/s13731-025-00527-3

McCarthy, J., Minsky, M. L., Rochester, N., & Shannon, C. E. (1955). *A Proposal for the Dartmouth Summer Research Project on Artificial Intelligence*. Dartmouth College.

McCulloch, W. S., & Pitts, W. (1943). A Logical Calculus of Ideas Immanent in Nervous Activity. *The Bulletin of Mathematical Biophysics, 5*(4), 115–133. DOI: 10.1007/BF02478259

Nagar, S., Afaq, A., & Narula, S. (2025). Shaping the Future of Emerging Economies. In Gaur, L. (Ed.), *Generative Artificial Intelligence and Ethics: Standards, Guidelines, and Best Practices* (pp. 143–168). IGI Global., https://doi.org/, DOI: 10.4018/979-8-3693-3691-5.ch007

National Observatory of Technology and Society (ONTSI)(2024). *Brújula | Indicadores de uso de inteligencia artificial en las empresas españolas 2023*. Red.es

Sharma, G., Chopra, P., & Singh, S. (2025). Unveiling Security Vulnerabilities in Generative AI. In Gaur, L. (Ed.), *Generative Artificial Intelligence and Ethics: Standards* (pp. 267–286). Guidelines, and Best Practices., DOI: 10.4018/979-8-3693-3691-5.ch012

Wang, Y. (2017). On the Mathematical Theories and Cognitive Foundations of Information. In IRMA (Information Resources Management Association)(Ed.) *Artificial Intelligence: Concepts, Methodologies, Tools, and Applications* (pp. 122-144), Hershey, PA (USA): IGI Global. https://doi.org/DOI: 10.4018/978-1-5225-1759-7.ch005

Zook, A. (2017). Game AGI Beyond Characters. In IRMA (Information Resources Management Association) (Ed.) *Artificial Intelligence: Concepts, Methodologies, Tools, and Applications* (pp. 463-484), Hershey, PA (USA): IGI Global. https://doi.org/DOI: 10.4018/978-1-5225-1759-7.ch020

## ADDITIONAL READING

IRMA (Information Resources Management Association) (Ed.). *Artificial Intelligence: Concepts, Methodologies, Tools, and Applications*, Hershey, PA (USA): IGI Global. https://doi.org/ DOI: DOI: 10.4018/978-1-5225-1759-7

Jaber, W. (2024). *Artificial Intelligence in the Age of Nanotechnology*. IGI Global., DOI: 10.4018/979-8-3693-0368-9

Monteiro, J., Rodrigues, M. A., & Carvalho, M. A. (2026). *Artificial Intelligence of Things (AIoT) for Retail and Services Management*. IGI Global., DOI: 10.4018/979-8-3693-8512-8

Pérez-Uribe, R. I., Ocampo-Guzmán, D., & Lozano-Correa, L. J. (2025). *Models, Strategies, and Tools for Competitive SMEs*. IGI Global., https://www.doi.org/10.4018/979-8-3693-4046-2

Pérez-Uribe, R. I., Salcedo-Pérez, C., Muñoz-Maya, C. M., & Ramírez-Salazar, M. P. (2026). Variables That Explain the Way of Innovating in Colombian Companies: A Perspective Under the Rise Model. In Leal Jamil, G., Carvalho Jamil, L., Geada, N., & Pinho Vieira, A. A. (Eds.), *Innovation Management for Disruptive Maturity in Competitive Scenarios*. IGI Global., https://www.doi.org/10.4018/979-8-3693-4030-1.ch019

Saiz-Alvarez, J. M., & Castillo-Nazareno, U. H. (2025). ICT-Related Crowdsourcing and Best Practices in Public-Private Partnerships for Economic Development. In Baporikar, N. (Ed.), *Public Private Partnership Dynamics for Economic Development* (pp. 243–266). IGI Global., DOI: 10.4018/979-8-3693-9153-2.ch012

Singh, B., Kaunert, C., Lal, S., Arora, M. K., & Raghav, A. (2025). *Developing Smart Sustainability with Artificial Intelligence*. IGI Global., DOI: 10.4018/979-8-3693-8684-2

Srivastava, G. (2023). Analyzing Artificial Intelligence from Social Science Perspectives: Artificial Intelligence and Human Intelligence. In Anubha & Sharma, H. (Eds.) Data-Driven Approaches for Effective Managerial Decision Making (pp. 143-154). Hershey, PA (USA): IGI Global. https://doi.org/DOI: 10.4018/978-1-6684-7568-3.ch007

## KEY TERMS AND DEFINITIONS

**AESIA:** Acronym of the Spanish Agency for the Oversight of Artificial Intelligence, this public organization, established in 2023, focuses on leading the debate and the best practices to be applied in the use of AI, to ensure quality evaluation, and build a relationship of trust with partners.

**Artificial General Intelligence (AGI):** Also known as Strong AI, it is a theoretical type of AI that can perform any intellectual task that a human can do. This includes abilities such as learning, reasoning, and adapting to new situations. Unlike current AI, which is designed for specific tasks, AGI would possess human-like understanding and cognitive abilities across various domains.

**Artificial Narrow Intelligence (ANI):** Often referred to as Weak AI, it describes AI systems that are specifically designed and trained to perform a particular task or a limited range of functions. This is currently the only type of AI that exists. Examples include voice assistants, recommendation engines, and chess programs.

**Artificial Super Intelligence (ASI):** It is a hypothetical form of AI that not only matches human intelligence in every aspect but also significantly surpasses it in all cognitive areas, including creativity, problem-solving, and learning capacity. It represents the most advanced level of AI, which is currently only theoretical, and has the potential to transform and enhance itself.

**Large Language Models (LLM):** Artificial intelligence programs are trained on large amounts of text data to understand, generate, and respond to natural language. They serve as the foundation for many applications, such as chatbots and writing tools.

**The McCulloch-Pitts Neuron:** Initially proposed in 1943 and essential for the development of artificial neural networks, this concept involves processing multiple binary inputs. If the sum of these inputs exceeds a predefined threshold, it produces a value of 1; otherwise, it results in a value of 0.

**The Trade and Technology Council (TTC):** It is a high-level forum established between the EU and the United States in June 2021 to strengthen transatlantic cooperation on key issues related to trade, technology, and security, based on shared values.

# Chapter 4
# Cost and Accessibility of AI:
## Breaking Barriers for MSMEs

**N Sathyanarayana**
http://orcid.org/0000-0002-4185-7751
*Jain University, India*

**Varanasi Rahul**
http://orcid.org/0000-0003-2407-7654
*Jain University, India*

**Y. Fathima**
http://orcid.org/0000-0002-0045-1421
*Jain University, India*

**R. Arun**
http://orcid.org/0009-0001-1571-3201
*Jain University, India*

**V. Lava Kumar**
http://orcid.org/0000-0002-3539-9280
*GITAM University, India*

## ABSTRACT

*This chapter explores the barriers to AI adoption faced by Micro, Small, and Medium Enterprises (MSMEs) due to cost and accessibility challenges. While AI presents significant opportunities for enhancing productivity, customer experience, and competitiveness, MSMEs often struggle with the financial burden of implementation, lack of technical infrastructure, and a shortage of skilled labor. The chapter provides a detailed analysis of the cost factors involved in AI adoption, including*

DOI: 10.4018/979-8-3373-2817-1.ch004

*initial investment, ongoing maintenance, and hidden expenses. It also outlines strategies to overcome these barriers, such as leveraging cloud-based solutions, AI-as-a-Service, government support, and open-source tools. Financial models, such as subscription-based pricing and co-investment opportunities, are also explored to make AI more accessible and affordable. The chapter concludes with a look at future trends, emphasizing technological advancements that will further reduce the cost and complexity of AI for micro and small enterprises (MSMEs).*

## INTRODUCTION

Capabilities & Artificial Intelligence benefits offered by AI can increase operational efficiency to an extent that business disruptions can occur. While large companies have incorporated AI into their business strategies, they use SMMEs and write them in full face financial constraints, a lack of infrastructure, and insufficient human expertise required (Gupta et al., 2022). One such challenge is the expense of deploying AI, which can be prohibitive for cash-strapped small businesses. It cannot be used for AI software and hardware, and it requires an initial investment in training, without which further reconfiguration will not succeed (Bussmann et al., 2020).

AI brings many opportunities (How do you know, please statistics) for MSMEs, such as automation of repetitive jobs, improved customer service, and market insights from analytics-based data. AI offers MSMEs significant advantages—such as 20–35% productivity gains and up to 44% revenue growth through automation, 77% improved work quality and $5,000+ cost savings via enhanced customer service, and data-driven decision-making that boosts forecasting accuracy and innovation—with adoption rates reaching 43% in Europe and 67% in Asia-Pacific (Brynjolfsson et al., 2024). Such benefits reinforce Small businesses' productivity, operational costs, and customer satisfaction to be competitive in the digital Market. Nevertheless, the complexity of AI, infrastructure, and expertise in MSMEs impede technology use (Suryani et al., 2023).

The chapter focuses on the expenditure and accessibility of AIML for MSMEs that encounter AI adoption, considering the investment and technological capability of small businesses. It also discusses approaches that might be used to meet the challenges by utilising cloud-based AI, AI-as-a-Service, and government backing. The chapter examines new financing mechanisms like subscription pricing and co-investment vehicles to facilitate AI for small firms (Prasetyo & Andrilla, 2025).

Another major trend enabling non-technical users to access AI is the rising use of low-code and no-code platforms. It allows smaller companies to get value from AI while not requiring experts (Kok et al., 2024). Also, new technologies such as 5G networks and edge computing are likely to lower the cost and complexity of

AI integration, making it progressively easier for MSMEs to integrate disruptive technology (Satyam et al., 2023).

Hence, in the following chapter, a close examination will be taken to identify obstacles and solutions to it, and an attempt is made to provide some recommendations on how to work with and use AI for MSMEs so that they can benefit from this exhibit of an enthralling technology and its merits.

Several methodological approaches are commonly employed in studying the adoption of AI by MSMEs. Qualitative research, such as interviews and case studies, accumulates data that can be used for future reference. For example, "Among small business owners who have worked for less than two years, 55% say they both far exceed expectations in terms of their lives." At the same time, quantitative methods (including surveys and statistical analyses) can provide broader views of AI trends, adoption rates, and economic effects on MSMEs. At the same time, researchers feel it is important to back up such arguments with circumstantial evidence from a real-world context that would bear out that such stories do not exist. Geographic factors can play a significant role. For example, MSMEs with good information infrastructure and government backing are likelier to adopt AI than those in less developed regions. Cultural and temporal factors also shape the pace and success of AI adoption. For example, while adoption rates for AI are high throughout regions such as Asia-Pacific (67%), countries in Africa or Latin America may meet greater obstacles as they lack access to funding and technical resources. These contextual influences must be considered if one wishes to grasp the changing dynamic of AI adoption in MSMEs fully.

## BACKGROUND

This chapter examines the barriers to adopting Artificial Intelligence (AI) in MSMEs, particularly the challenges of cost and accessibility. Although AI has great potential to drive productivity, customer experiences, and competitiveness, MSMEs typically encounter challenges when adopting AI into their businesses. These barriers include the high cost of AI deployment, insufficient technical architecture, and a shortage of expertise.

The cost-related aspects of adopting AI are evaluated in the chapter (direct and indirect costs: initial investment, maintenance, and hidden, marginal costs). It also covers financial models and AI, making it accessible to smaller businesses (cloud-based, AI-as-a-Service, government incentives). The chapter also discusses how AI can optimise operations, support informed decision-making, and lower costs for MSMEs. It ends with a review of key trends and the impact of technology development, such as 5G and edge computing, on lowering the cost of AI and technology complexity, enabling more SMBs to use AI.

## Conceptualising AI in the context of MSMES

AI could transform business today, creating new possibilities for MSMEs. The potential for efficiency gains and better decision-making is also huge, even at small companies. However, high cost, technical difficulties, and the unavailability of expert resources frequently jeopardise MSMEs' deployment. In this section, the use of AI in MSMEs is discussed. Based on understanding the use case, potential, and challenges for acceptance and implementation of technology are identified, and the approach to MSMEs in their work style by AI is reviewed.

## Theoretical Framework and Methodological Approaches in AI Adoption for MSMEs

To improve the depth and clarity of this chapter, a theoretical framework that delineates key concepts and principles relating to AI adoption, especially in the unique context of Micro, Small and Medium Enterprises (MSMEs), is necessary. One such model is the Technology-Organisation-Environment (TOE) framework. It tells us how technological, organisational and environmental factors all play a role in adopting new technologies, such as AI. According to this framework, manufacturers must consider the financial investment and technical infrastructure for introducing AI and internally lay organisational groundwork and external environmental variables such as government policy pressures and market competition forces. Moreover, DOI (Diffusion of Innovations Theory) offers ways to examine how innovation diffuses through organisations and sectors, which could help explain why some MSMEs in certain regions are slow while others rapidly adopt new technologies (Rogers, 2003).

## Defining AI and Its Relevance to MSMEs

AI stands for artificial Intelligence and includes technologies and systems that mimic human mental functions like learning and problem solving (McCarthy, 1956). In machine learning, there are areas such as natural language processing, RPA, etc.. It can be a game-changer for MSMEs, enabling them to automate processes, enhance customer experience, and make more informed decisions. Even resource-strapped small businesses can leverage AI to streamline mundane tasks, improve efficiencies, and personalise customer experiences without building complex infrastructure or huge teams from the ground up. For MSMEs specifically, the application of AI would be to level the playing field against stronger competitors, using automation and data-based insights to scale and operate cost-effectively. The advent of inexpensive AI tools that are cloud-based and open-source platforms has eased the adoption of AI by micro and small businesses.

## Opportunities and Challenges of AI Integration in Small Enterprises

AI also provides opportunities for MSMEs since, with AI, routine tasks can be automated, customer-facing functions can be enhanced, and decisions based on data can be made. Automation lowers hype expenses, increases efficiency, and reduces errors. AI-driven tools (e.g., chatbots, predictive analytics) can allow for personalised customer experiences, and in turn, you can keep your customers happy and loyal. Other uses AI provides for MSMEs include: AI (turning them into cost-effective competitors in rapidly changing marketplaces, improving their supply chain management, providing them with competitive marketing solutions, and product development).

While implementing AI in MSME is plausible, it is not easy. Artificial intelligence solutions generally require heavy investment in software and hardware, on top of the expense of teaching workers to use such systems. As AI requires advanced expertise to install and maintain, MSMEs also accumulate technical complexity. Few operators are trained for AI, which means many smaller companies depend on consultants or vendors, and the pain. One reason the incorporation of AIs into business operations will encounter resistance is that it disrupts existing business models. Breaking these barriers requires good planning, inexpensive innovations, and a flexible culture.

Gupta et al., (2022) underscore the significant upfront costs of AI implementation, including such investments as software and hardware, along with ongoing maintenance and training, which are prohibitively expensive for small businesses. Besides, MSMEs have significant infrastructure challenges. Many are running old systems that will not work with AI technology (Bussmann et al., 2020). Lack of personnel with requisite professional qualifications adds yet another layer of difficulty. The AI implementation requires expertise in machine learning, data science and systems integration (Lomas & Reeta 2024).

AI-as-a-service gives MSMEs access to AI capabilities on a subscription basis, thereby reducing the need for the significant initial investment that might be better spent on other projects (Prasetyo & Andrilla, 2025). At the same time, the arrival of low-code/no-code platforms means that someone who is not a technical person can do AI, so a lack of specialised knowledge democratises their whole operation (Kok et al., 2024). Capitalising on these developments will require producing specific local case studies on strengths and weaknesses for different regions later. Such differences in different regions of the world to AG adoption as this April-May- book global statistics show is significantly HIGHER in regions that include Asia-Pacific - a whopping 67%, WHILE IN Europe, it is only 43%.

## Empirical Evidence of AI Adoption in MSMEs and Use Cases of Success

There are noticeable differences in the rate of AI adoption among micro, small, and medium-sized enterprises (MSMEs). This study shows that 43% of such companies adopt AI. The adoption rate of Asia-Pacific MSMEs is far more impressive: 67% shows that this region is skewed toward AI. Other than that, primary barriers include the high cost of initial technology investments and later operating expenses. In these respects, businesses of all sizes generally find it challenging to take on board AI as a force that strengthens their labour relations (Gupta et al., 2022).

One study by Kok et al shows that introducing AI and automation led to 20-35% improvements in productivity for MSMEs, and created a revenue increase ranging from 20 to 44%. However, customer service solutions like chatbots and predictive analytics in MSME customer service have been responsible for cost savings as high as $5,000. Many small businesses that used these services also noted significant improvements in customer satisfaction ratings and customer service efficiency (Gupta et al., 2022). These findings show the potential for AI to provide MSMEs with valuable tools to increase their operational efficiency, lower costs, and be more competitive.

## How AI Can Enhance Productivity and Growth for MSMEs

AI could boost the productivity of micro and small enterprises (MSMEs) by as much as 15-20% and unlock additional revenue opportunities of around US$380-450 billion, enabling them to automate most of the 'mundane' work that eats into their time. AI automation in customer service captures this essence — chatbots tend to answer most simple questions, freeing up people to take on high-value activities. Predictive analytics can streamline inventory management so businesses are never overstocked or understocked of important products.

AI helps with data-driven decisions with insights, helping MSMEs decide on product development, prices, entry into the market, etc. Leveraging AI will also increase a competitive edge for MSMEs locally and globally. AI can also digest a variety of data, allowing SMB owners to recognise trends and market opportunities that they otherwise would have overlooked, enabling them to draw ahead of competitors, save money, and increase their company's revenue. In summary, AI helps MSMEs scale up and achieve sustainable growth.

## Cost Factors in AI Adoption

It is costly for any Micro, Small and Medium Enterprise (MSME) to invest in Artificial Intelligence (AI). While AI solutions will improve efficiency and competition, they are just an expensive gamble to play for smaller businesses with hardly any room in their budget to manoeuvre. Below, we will discuss the price tag on using AI, from initial investments to maintaining and operating it, and how to ensure getting the best ROI. A sound understanding of these cost components is a fundamental prerequisite for MSMEs to evaluate the potential viability of any AI and its offsetting value if implemented.

### Statistical Evidence on AI Cost Barriers and Sectoral/Regional Differences in MSMEs

A significant percentage of MSMEs cite high costs as a primary barrier to AI adoption. A recent survey by Gupta et al. (2022) reveals that 58% of MSMEs in Europe and 67% in Asia-Pacific are hindered by the high upfront investment required for AI technologies, including software, hardware, and skilled labor. However, these challenges vary greatly across sectors. For instance, manufacturing MSMEs face higher costs for infrastructure upgrades to integrate AI, while service-based businesses often struggle with the expense of software solutions and customer data analysis tools (Bussmann et al., 2020). Regional disparities also come into play, with MSMEs in emerging economies facing even greater financial hurdles due to limited access to capital and inadequate digital infrastructure. These sectoral and regional differences must be considered when discussing the financial barriers to AI adoption, as they demonstrate that AI challenges are not uniform across all MSMEs.

### Understanding the Financial Implications of AI Adoption for MSMEs

The initial investment to implement AI technologies can be significant, including expenses for purchasing AI software, modernising existing systems, and recruiting experienced agents or consultants. AI's power quickly becomes the right thing without sacrificing quality or decision-making. However, to use this power, people must bear the cost burden first, which does not fit smaller businesses. In addition, recurring costs such as maintenance, software updates, staff training, and integration into existing systems must be considered, as well as hidden costs, such as data storage and security efforts to protect business-sensitive data. Although the aforementioned financial woes led to massive layoffs within the sector, AI has the potential to provide significant returns in the form of increased operational efficiency, cost reduction and enhanced customer experience.

## Initial Investment and Ongoing Costs of AI Integration

The first cost of integrating AI in the case of the different MSMEs could be very high, such as when considering the equipment costs and paying the implementation experts or consultants. In addition, the infrastructure needed for Artificial Intelligence (AI) technologies like machine learning systems, natural language processing tools, and automated workflows skyrockets the cost. Meanwhile, for small enterprises, such expenses might range from entry systems that provide solutions to even AI-as-a-Service systems in monthly or annual fees.

After implementing AI into a business, costs keep coming. Continuous maintenance, software updates, and new AI capabilities are necessary to ensure the technology is valuable and current. Moreover, companies may also have to spend money on training employees to operate and handle AI systems. Existing processes may need to be changed for integration, which will likely require business downtime and/or technical support. The other aspect is continuous; these expenses can loom large on MSMEs, which can only ponder the advantages of AI in juxtaposition to the price paid to ensure its preservation.

## Maximising ROI from AI Adoption in Small Enterprises

MSMEs can ensure that the benefits of such implementation outweigh the costs and maximise their ROI from AI adoption by careful planning and strategic implementation of AI technologies. One way of doing this is by making sure that repetitive tasks that take up precious time and resources are automated. Even automation: examples include: AI-driven inventory management, chatbots for customer support and AI tools for financial forecasting that will facilitate operations, reduce human errors and increase efficiency, saving costs.

AI tools, scaled correctly, can drive even higher ROI and provide opportunities for cost-effectiveness. Cloud-based, subscription-based AI solutions help MSMEs avoid enormous, upfront costs and pay as you use resources, making it easy to scale when the business scales. On top of that, using data analytics and predictive models can empower small businesses to make informed decisions about attracting the right audience or maximising pricing strategies, which is crucial in increasing wealth.

Lastly, building internal AI expertise through training can reduce dependency on expensive external consultants and ensure long-term cost savings. MSMEs can improve their competitive position and enhance overall business performance by making intelligent, strategic investments.

## Challenges to AI Accessibility for Msmes

The lack of AI-ready infrastructure for AI solutions to plug into is one technology challenge for MSMEs in implementing AI in their workplace. The world's biggest companies are overwhelmingly tech firms. However, most small companies run on outdated technology or equipment that cannot keep pace with AI systems, which are typically power hungry. For instance, many AI models require powerful servers, state-of-the-art storage systems, and network bandwidth to combine publishing with unavailable output for most MSMEs. In addition, the new AI solution needs to work with current enterprise processes and legacy systems, which can be complex and expensive. Small business owners cannot replace or upgrade weaving machines as they are too expensive (Sinuhaji, F. G., Sibarani, H. J., & Pakpahan, V. M. 2024).

## The Role of Training in Empowering MSMEs

While the chapter effectively addresses the cost barriers to AI adoption by MSMEs, it is crucial to emphasize the availability of practical solutions and the importance of training in overcoming these challenges. MSMEs can access advanced AI technologies without making huge initial investments with cloud-based AI solutions and AI-as-a-Service platforms. The solutions offer not only scalability and flexibility, but also their provision to small businesses, which means they pay only for what they use. This all reduces the financial pressure (Prasetyo & Andrilla, 2025). In addition, training and up-skilling employees is necessary for MSMEs to utilise AI successfully. For example, in Indonesia, an initiative by the Government organised training in the use of AI for small business people. This led to a 40% increase in productivity over those companies that participated without such help (Kok et al., 2024). In addition, partnerships with universities and AI-focused organisations can provide ongoing support for MSMEs, encouraging them to develop their internal capacity while reducing dependency on external consultants.

## Technological Barriers to AI Accessibility for MSMEs

One of the most essential technology barriers for MSMEs developing AI within their working environment is the lack of infrastructure for AI solutions to converge. Most small businesses operate on old or limited technology that cannot keep pace with AI systems, which demand much processing. For instance, many AI models require powerful and moderate-range servers, high-level storage systems, and networking technologies to publish with output inaccessible to numerous MSMEs. Moreover, the new AI solution must work with current business workflows and legacy solutions;

these might be complex and create too much waste. Small business owners cannot replace or upgrade the weaving machines, as they are costly (Sinuhaji et al., 2024).

Despite the advances, the very same technological barriers exist. A massive amount of capital is required to invest in infrastructure and data management systems, which are economically unviable for most small businesses (Bussmann et al., 2020).

## Financial Constraints and the High Cost of AI Solutions

While it is important to understand that AI does not need to be expensive, when investing in companies such as AI to finance their software and infrastructure needs, it would be an expensive way of financing. Moreover, it is even pricier if you factor in recurring costs, such as maintenance, software updates, and staff retraining. None of these costs has a guarantee of ROI (Gupta et al., 2022), making the visible benefits of AI less favourable for some MSMEs. As a result, the costs associated with AI could outweigh the benefits of AI for many MSMEs.

The relatively low cost of adopting AI-as-a-Service and cloud-based subscription model seems (a) to offset the capital investment and the overhead savings; (b) it to continue to constitute a financial bridgehead for micro, small and medium scale enterprises (MSMEs) that have less funding capacity available (Sinuhaji et al., 2024). Hence, AI presents financial risks to business while knowing that AI potentially hold opportunities for new efficiencies and new growth (Gupta et al., 2022).

## The Skills Gap: Addressing the Shortage of AI Professionals in Small Businesses

Writing AI code requires specialisation in areas such as machine learning, data science and algorithm building, and most small businesses do not have experts on their payroll to take on the challenge. This is further complicated by the trend toward an increased demand for AI skills, in which the bigger players could recruit experienced AI staff from smaller ones because of their resource advantage (Lomas & Reeta 2024).

Small businesses, in addition, tend to be unable to provide ongoing employee training and so are unable to build the internal capacity required to govern and maintain AI systems (Lomas & Reeta 2024).

The path to the success of MSMEs in breaking these barriers may lie in collaboration with universities or AI-specialised training programs to train and upgrade the available resources while filling the special skills gap. Moreover, easy-to-use AI tools, such as low or no-code platforms, can reduce the need for deep tech skills and help less technically sophisticated firms do AI (Bussmann et al., 2020).

## MAIN FOCUS OF THE CHAPTER

### Strategies to overcome cost and accessibility barriers

Overcoming cost and accessibility barriers is essential for healthcare, education, and technology equity. These barriers disproportionately affect marginalised populations, including individuals with disabilities, those in low-income areas, and people in rural regions. Effective solutions must be multifaceted, addressing systemic limitations and individual needs through policy, technology, and community-based approaches.

#### Leveraging AI and Assistive Technologies

AI transforms access through cost-effective and scalable solutions. AI-based technologies like chatbots and adaptive learning systems for personalised assistance can empower users with disabilities. Such advances empower independence and circumvent structural access problems within industries such as health and education (Ferebee, 2025). Similarly, tools such as the Easy Reading platform allow users with cognitive impairments to adapt webpage interfaces to their needs and preferences, promoting digital inclusion in multiple segments of users (Wüst et al., 2023).

#### Policy and Structural Reforms

Inclusive policy reforms can mitigate structural inequities. In Indigenous communities in Canada, improved access to healthcare was achieved through localised infrastructure investments, enhanced Indigenous representation in medical professions, and community-led health planning (Nguyen et al., 2020). In Nigeria, reforms at tertiary institutions helped overcome attitudinal, physical, and logistical barriers for students with disabilities. Implementing resilience-based approaches, improved support systems, and policy enforcement significantly enhanced accessibility (Ahmed, 2017).

#### Inclusive Digital Literacy and Education

Studies show that many individuals struggle with digital tools due to a lack of training, reinforcing existing inequalities. Recommendations include investing in digital literacy programs, raising awareness, and building user confidence (Tapp, 2023). In Pakistan, disparities in digital education among marginalised students were addressed through interventions that combined infrastructure development with targeted educational reforms (Amjad et al., 2024).

## Technology-Focused Interventions

Cost-effective technology can significantly reduce access barriers. For example, low-cost mobile learning platforms that utilise packet-based technologies have proven successful among university students, especially in high smartphone ownership (Dyson et al., 2009). Virtual Reality (VR) technology is another promising tool. It can train managers to understand and address environmental and attitudinal barriers faced by individuals with autism, thereby fostering more inclusive workplaces (O'Sullivan & Kearney, 2018).

## Community-Based and Patient-Centred Approaches:

Enhancing healthcare for individuals with disabilities necessitates a shift toward patient-centred care Communication barriers, inadequate personalisation, and poor provider-patient interaction are significant obstacles. Effective patient education using accessible content has improved understanding and outcomes (Hart, 2015). Similarly, tailored communication strategies with patients with intellectual disabilities help ensure accurate diagnoses and effective treatment plans (Teo, 2023).

## Universal Design and Accessibility Standards

Universal design principles ensure systems are accessible to the broadest range of users. For example, in university settings, neurodivergent students face diverse barriers, from physical access to institutional stigma. Implementing inclusive technologies and redesigning organisational practices based on user feedback enhances access (Borsotti et al., 2024). In education, ensuring that platforms meet accessibility standards is essential. Strategies include training educators, using inclusive teaching materials, and leveraging AI for adaptive learning (Dembitska & Sivert, 2024).

## Localising Solutions in Contextual Settings

Contextual cognisance is imperative, especially in rural contexts. Healthcare barriers, such as a lack of transportation and digital access, are major hurdles for older adults in low-income areas. Intervention schemes such as telehealth training programs, community health kiosks, and trained staff have indicated potential (Bella et al., 2025)

Second, designing pedagogical interventions for underserved college students, such as those in Pakistan's remote areas, bridges the digital divide and improves fairness in the long run (Amjad et al., 2024).

# FINANCIAL MODELS TO SUPPORT AI ADOPTION IN MSMES

Artificial Intelligence (AI) holds great promise for Micro, Small and Medium Enterprises (MSMEs), particularly when it comes to becoming more efficient, achieving better decision-making support and engaging more customer-oriented. Nevertheless, the implementation of AI in MSMEs is limited due to financial obstacles such as high initial investment, difficult access to finance, and unclear ROI. To tackle these obstacles, different financing models have surfaced to ensure the adoption of AI in MSME activities. This article discusses two successful utility models, namely (1) Government-Supported Incentive Models and (2) Fintech-Driven Microfinancing Models.

## Government-Supported Incentive Models

Artificial intelligence (AI) is a key driver in making micro, small, and medium enterprises (MSMEs) more competitive and productive. As a result, public funding is required to compensate for the lack of incentives through subsidies, grants and financial incentives to encourage the use of AI by MSMEs. These government-led efforts offset the high upfront costs of adopting leading technologies among small businesses and enable them to effectively compete in an AI-enabled global economy (Abaddi, 2024).

Under government-supported incentive schemes, governments provide a range of direct financial assistance and adopt enabling mechanisms that help MSMEs to adopt AI:

### AI Innovation Grants

These grants offer funding to support the building or augmentation of AI solutions to boost MSMEs. By lessening the large initial costs of developing or buying new AI systems, such grants induce MSMEs to innovate and deploy AI solutions within their operations (Abaddi, 2024).

### Tax deductions or rebates

Some jurisdictions offer R&D or digital transformation investment tax credits. Such tax credits motivate MSMEs to adopt AI technologies by reducing the cost of R&D. This prompts organisations to consider new AI use cases that can spur growth and efficiency (Abaddi, 2024).

## Infrastructure

Creating AI training nodes and sharing digital platforms contribute to capacity building in technology and expertise required directly or indirectly by MSMEs. These investments facilitate the ability of small businesses to access the tools, resources, and knowledge necessary to successfully integrate and use AI systems (Abaddi, 2024).

These initiatives mitigate upfront financial risks to AI adoption and reduce the cost of AI experimentation for MSMEs. For instance, Jordanian government support was identified to have a significant moderating effect on facilitating conditions' influence on MSMEs' intention towards AI adoption, particularly where such support had a fusion of innovative firm and supportive context (Abaddi, 2024). This case is indicative of how public policy can help to create an environment where MSMEs can experiment with AI technologies without the potentially crippling financial risks that are typically assumed when adopting new solutions.

## Evidence and Impact

The importance of finance to support businesses is important under the special context: the financial model should help small and micro enterprises to relieve pressure of finance, financing, and financing cost as well as other financial problems; and to let AI technology in the scope of financial support and tax incentives and support for public infrastructure. The governments, realising that AI can be a strategic enabler for economic growth, have begun to provide incentives to drive digital transformation among MSMEs, particularly in emerging markets (Abaddi, 2024).

AI innovation grants are a part of these models, and these are designed to buy or develop AI-based solutions for MSMEs. This fund provides small businesses with finance for AI investments without the large initial outlays (Abaddi, 2024). In addition to the direct subsidies, the Government also offers tax incentives for R&D in the area of AI in the case of MSMEs to defray the experimentation and innovation costs associated with the deployment of AI (Prasetyo & Andrilla, 2025).

Government policies have successfully promoted AI adoption in many countries, such as Jordan, by enhancing the digital ecosystem and creating a conducive technological environment (Abaddi, 2024).

In light of the above, this incentive model clichédallows MSMEs to compete in an ever-more-digital world economy by lowering the perceived risk and enduring significant cost barriers to entry (Prasetyo & Andrilla, 2025).

## Fintech-Driven Microfinancing Models

The second financial model focuses on fintech-powered microfinancing solutions. It provides Micro, Small, and Medium Enterprises (MSMEs) access to small, AI-enabled loans tailored to their specific cash flow, credit history, and risk profile. These financing options are often unavailable through traditional banking systems, which typically impose strict collateral requirements and lengthy approval processes (Gupta et al., 2022). Fintech platforms use innovative AI technologies to assess creditworthiness and offer flexible loan terms, addressing the financial needs of MSMEs that are often excluded from conventional financial services.

### Description and Mechanism

Here is how Fintech platforms are using AI to provide MSMEs with several crucial advantages:

#### *1. Smart Credit Scoring*

Conventional credit scoring models are based on formal financial histories, which most MSMEs do not maintain. However, fintech rely on alternative data to assess the creditworthiness of companies that lack a formal credit history, including paying for utilities, mobile payment history, and even social media behaviour. State-of-the-art credit scoring using that data is on the horizon. (Omokhoa et al., 2024).

#### *2. Dynamic Loan Structuring*

As opposed to static loans, fintech platforms dynamically structure loans in real time according to the business's financial position. By tracking live financial information, AI-enabled systems can adapt payment plans in real time, which can make them more suitable for MSMEs with cash-flow issues (Bussmann et al., 2020).

#### *3. Automated Underwriting*

AI-enabled algorithms automate credit scoring and risk assessment, reducing the time taken to approve loans. This lowers the cost of administration and the calculation length and facilitates quicker credit disbursal to MSMEs with potentially less conventional forms of collateral (Sinuhaji et al., 2024). These platforms eliminate the requirement of physical collateral and also reduce the complexity of loan terms to make it easier for MSMEs to get loans for growth and innovation (Sinuhaji et al., 2024).

*4. Evidence and Impact*

AI-driven fintech models in Southeast Asia have demonstrated potential to scale impact towards increased MSME sustainability and operational efficiency. Fintech also contributed significantly to the sustainability of firms in Indonesia, through widened access to finance services that help micro, small, and medium enterprises (MSMEs) to manage cash flow and sales more effectively. With applied predictive analysis and customer categorisation, GZI initiated marketing and financial profiling to realise effectiveness (Khaq et al., 2024).

Indian MSMEs have enjoyed reduced interest rates, enhanced credit access, and even personalised financial services through fintech solutions. As a result, Fintech has emerged as an important enabler of financial inclusion, especially for firms that rely on access to informal credit networks without recourse to formal financial intermediaries (Gupta et al., 2022).

The cloud infrastructure, combined with machine learning algorithms, helps fintech platforms to spread their wings to the underserved and rural MSME segments, by providing them with innovative, affordable, flexible and scalable solutions (Gupta et al., 2022). Such platforms allow equal access to funding, thus empowering MSMEs to grow even in a low-resource environment.

## Challenges and Considerations

Fintech-driven microfinancing models are promising, but they have challenges to address. Government-supported models face the threat of bureaucracy and fund misallocation that may undermine effectiveness. These models are successful because they are executed well, are transparent, and have an easy capacity-building mechanism to ensure that the funds flow effectively (Lomas & Reeta 2024).

While with the fintech models, like in the case of data governance, regulators will be adaptable and support fintech models, digital literacy needs to be addressed. Especially in emerging economies, however, many MSME owners do not possess the required digital competencies to take full advantage of fintech platforms, and hence may face limited effects (Lomas & Reeta 2024). Moreover, ensuring fairness and inclusivity in AI systems has become crucial, since algorithmic bias and data privacy are ancient and new challenges to avoid the reproduction of inequalities (Lomas & Reeta 2024).

The benefits of fintech-based microfinancing will be maximised if these platforms are embedded in the broader ecosystem that deals with regulation, capacity building, and digital infrastructure investment. This will ensure that fintech solutions are accessible, equitable, and sustainable for MSMEs in varied sectors and geographies.

### Practical Solutions, Successful Adoption Models, and Overcoming Barriers

While financial barriers are significant, MSMEs are increasingly finding practical solutions to overcome these challenges. Modular and affordable AI tools, cloud-based platforms, and government collaborations are emerging as key enablers for AI adoption among small businesses. For example, AI-as-a-Service models allow MSMEs to access AI tools on a subscription basis, bypassing the need for hefty upfront investments (Prasetyo & Andrilla, 2025).

In Indonesia, retail MSMEs have successfully implemented AI for inventory management using low-cost, cloud-based predictive analytics tools, resulting in a 30% reduction in operational costs (Satyam et al., 2023). Similarly, government-backed AI innovation grants have enabled small businesses to experiment with AI without bearing the full financial risk, as seen in Jordan, where MSMEs have used government incentives to implement AI solutions that enhance customer service and operational efficiency (Abaddi, 2024).

## SOLUTIONS AND RECOMMENDATIONS

### Future outlook and trends in AI accessibility for MSMES

The potential for AI access for MSMEs is bright because technological advances have made AI solutions more affordable and less complex. 5G and edge computing will facilitate the deployment of an AI system, and companies across a wide range of industries will adopt AI to reduce the cost of data processing and data latency.

As AI gains traction, there are also new financing models that are making it possible for MSMEs to get funds to invest in technology, including AI, for which there are platforms where you can mortgage your intellectual property or business to get loans. This paper will analyse those trends and predict the future accessibility of AI to MSMEs during the next decade.

### The Impact of 5G and Edge Computing on AI Accessibility for MSMEs

Making AI accessible to MSMEs: There is new technology on the horizon, like the potential of 5G and the rise of edge computing, which will open new doors for AI, as small and medium enterprises will use AI that will transform their businesses.

With ultra-high speed data transmission, very low latency, and superior reliability, the rapid deployment of 5G networks can promote new business models.

Particular interest is how edge computing is accelerating much of this transformation, processing data on the edge and at the point of collection to eliminate the latency that would be added for shipping the data to the cloud for processing.

Edge computing is where AI models run on a local server or device, allowing MSMEs to use AI-based tools like predictive maintenance and inventory management (Bourechak et al., 2023). Given the low data security requirements, MSMEs will have access to AI capabilities, making AI solutions more relevant and less risky for small businesses. The low-latency 5G offers the delay-free functioning of AI-based applications, which is important for MSMEs to gain a competitive advantage in the fast-changing digital market (Ahsan et al., 2024).

## Advancements in AI Algorithms and Hardware: Reducing Costs and Complexity

Improvements in AI algorithms and hardware are fundamental in lowering the costs and complexity of AI solutions, especially for resource-constrained small and medium-sized enterprises (SMEs). AI hardware has also changed as the hardware has advanced, enabling the use of accelerators explicitly designed for executing AI workloads running a broader class of models, at a more affordable price in a more efficient way (Li, 2023).

An important one is optimising AI algorithms. This would include AI algorithms such as gradient descent and genetic algorithms that are tailored and optimised to remove computational overhead and be efficient in training and inference (Meng, 2024). Enhancing these algorithms enables organisations to run big AI models on cheaper hardware, saving a company's infrastructure costs and reducing the overall cost of AI implementation.

Dedicated AI hardware (including GPUs, FPGAs, AI-specific processors and the rest) is designed with scaling interest into the beneficial computational requirements of AI models (Li, 2023). Such hardware solutions empower faster data processing and lower power consumption, and, more importantly, offer a cheaper option for organisations that wish to leverage the benefits of AI but are not willing to invest heavily in cloud infrastructure.

Furthermore, optimised AI models and hardware (hardware-aware AI model optimisation) push businesses one step further to deploy AI models better (Li, 2023) and play a less complex game, allowing them to be more reachable to small businesses and deploy AI models on weak devices, such as adopting IoT and edge devices.

AI methods and infrastructure are evolving rapidly and continue to remove barriers to SMEs' adoption of AI.

## Low-Code and No-Code Platforms: Democratizing AI for Small Businesses

The realisation of this AI dream is primarily driven by low-code and no-code (LCNC) platforms, which are making it possible for small businesses and organisations to harness artificial intelligence-powered solutions with little to no technical prowess. They provide visual interfaces, drag-and-drop components, and automation tools that enable non-technical users to quickly and economically design and implement AI applications. Small businesses can use AI-based solutions to optimise business processes, improve customer experiences, and spur innovation (Elshan et al., 2023).

What are likely the most significant advantages of LCNC platforms? Their ability to speed up development cycles and reduce costs is a massive boon to startups and SMBs attempting to build web and mobile apps without much capital. AutoML solutions such as Microsoft Power Platform, Google AutoML or Amazon SageMaker offer a simple interface for users to build and deploy machine learning models with minimal coding (Kok, 2024). These platforms are applied in AI solutions, including image classification, natural language understanding and predictive analytics, resulting in the broad availability to small business owners.

Furthermore, LCNC platforms support business agility by allowing employees to create and oversee AI applications to respond to new business needs. This makes innovation relatively low and empowers small organisations to adopt innovation fast and more agile without being structured by depending upon an in-house software development group (Bhattacharyya & Kumar, 2021).

## Emerging Financial Models: AI-Powered Lending Platforms for MSMEs

As MSMEs are a niche category, and it is not easy to get finance through traditional sources because of the high interest, high collateral, and long timelines in getting the funds, AI-backed lending platforms can play a critical role. This use case leverages advanced technologies like Machine learning algorithms, Big Data and Alternative credit scoring models to offer MSMEs easy and flexible lending options. In this section, we will explore the disruptions that new AI models in lending can bring in accelerating, diversifying, and enhancing MSME credit.

### AI in Credit Scoring for MSMEs

One big game changer for these AI-based lending platforms: the use of alternative credit scores data. In the traditional lending models, lenders tend to use a minimal dataset, which may consist of considering the formal credit scores and financial history, for instance. In the case of AI models, however, a wide variety of data points are involved, from mobile payment activity to utility bill payments and even social media postings. However, the reliability of financial statements would be demonstrated based on other references (Omokhoa et al., 2024).

Leveraging alternative data, AI models will more efficiently and soundly analyse MSMEs' creditworthiness and provide an opportunity for businesses with nominal or no support from traditional banks to acquire a loan. Emerging markets have a high demand for financial services for SMMEs since many operate in the informal sector without formal financial services (Omokhoa et al., 2024).

## Dynamic Loan Structuring and Risk Management

Traditionally, loans do not adjust, meaning that if you agree to pay back a certain amount each month, you will pay that amount whether or not your business profits or struggles are going. However, AI-based platforms "watch" the borrower's solvency and edit the schedule and the terms of the loan with business development in mind, as per business cash flow, with the help of machine learning (Bussmann et al., 2020). That helps those MSMEs pay their debt more responsibly, lowering the risk of default and upping the chances of successful repayment.

Furthermore, AI models also help with more sophisticated risk management, which analyses behaviours and patterns often overlooked in other, more traditional models. For instance, AI is leveraged to detect early warning signs of financial distress in an MSME, allowing creditors to respond by providing restructuring support before a business enters distress. (Bussmann et al., 2020).

## AI in Peer-to-Peer (P2P) Lending for MSMEs

Peer-to-peer (P2P) lending platforms have also risen to prominence, backed significantly by AI, that effectively connects small businesses to individual investors or groups of investors, doing away with intermediaries such as banks. Using AI, such platforms match borrowers with suitable lenders for different factors, such as type of business, financial status, and their level of risk taking(Sinuhaji et al., 2024).

This could have a particularly significant impact on MSMEs in emerging markets as AI in P2P lending will solve the challenges of these businesses in getting finance from banks, either because they need significant collateral or are not instructive enough. The presence of P2P platforms featuring AI usage (counterparty, party-to-party) makes it easier to access funds, and funding is fast for MSMEs (Sinuhaji et al, 2024).

## Scalability and Cost Efficiency

Leveraging AI, such lending platforms can operate at scale, offering lower-cost financing to an ever-greater pool of MSMEs. Conventional borrowing procedures often require significant manual verification and review that can be expensive and time-consuming. On the contrary, AI systems automate the lending, or at least part of it, comprising credit scoring, loan approval, and repayment condition management, and enable cost mitigation (Gupta et al., 2022). By mitigating those operational costs, lending platforms can offer MSME borrowers lower rates and improved terms overall, which markedly lowers the cost of loans and increases access for small business owners and managers without a banking deposit to access credit as low as 10% APR.

Moreover, because AI systems can handle a large amount of data quickly and accurately, these platforms are building on this technology to scale by managing thousands of loans simultaneously without incurring any marginal cost. (Gupta et al., 2022).

## Challenges and Considerations

While AI-enabled lending platforms have many advantages for MSMEs, their adoption is not smooth. Major concerns such as data privacy and algorithmic bias are still at large. Lending platforms must make sure that whatever AI system they have is transparent, fair and unbiased in a way that would not prejudice any group of MSMEs (Lomas & Reeta 2024)

Also, credit facilities with AI's assistance have an excellent opportunity to expand with inclusive finance. However, they also need to depend on digital prowess and technology availability. The AI solutions being developed and deployed for lending purposes on the continent may fail to be effective where they may be most needed (Lomas & Reeta 2024), if, for example, access to smartphones, stable internet connections or even rudimentary financial literacy is in short supply. Investment in digital infrastructure to ensure these platforms work and in educational programs to ensure MSMEs can take advantage of them is a must.

# Future Trends: How AI Accessibility for MSMEs Will Evolve in the Next Decade

This technological advancement, coupled with businesses' changing needs, is likely to make AI even more accessible to MSMEs over the next decade or so. With the rapid development of AI technologies, small businesses will soon have high-quality, targeted, cost-effective solutions that allow them to consume AI capabilities without deep technical skills.

A prominent trend is the combination of AI and edge computing, allowing MSMEs to process data on-site and generate immediate insights and increased operational efficiency without dependence on far-off cloud servers (Satyam et al., 2023) Task-based AI systems are likely to become more common, and this transition will be fueled by 5G networks that allow faster and more reliable data transfer that is highly needed for real-time AI applications (Suryani et al., 2023).

In addition, low-code and no-code platforms will remain instrumental in democratizing AI, allowing even non-technical users in small businesses to create and implement AI solutions easily. This will lower the development cost and allow people with fewer resources to use AI (Omokhoa et al., 2024). MSMEs will generally have minimum technical expertise to leverage AI tools for functions like marketing, customer service, inventory management, and financial forecasting, as these tools will be user-friendly and customizable (Kouroupetroglou et al., 2012). The second trend that will dictate how accessible MSMEs can be to Al will also be an increased concentration on ethical AI, given that large businesses tend to deploy AI more quickly these days, and therefore can benefit more from it, it will be important to allow small businesses to deploy Al tools in an ethical manner, which takes into account privacy, fairness, and inclusivity (Fatima et al., 2024).

## Practical Implications

The impact of AI adoption is different in the context of MSME operations. First, AI could improve company efficiency by automating repetitive work, including data entry and customer and inventory management. This allows MSMEs to focus their resourcing on more strategic activities, delivering increased productivity and reduced operating costs. MSMEs can adopt AI-driven solutions with no significant upfront spend, given that matching grants and tax rebates are provided as Government-supported incentives., This facilitates faster AI Technology adoption and better competition between smaller and larger companies.

Moreover, AI-powered fintech ensures capital availability since MSMEs have been constantly denied traditional financial sources. On the flip side, these companies are using alternative data to underwrite loans so small businesses can get the loans they need to invest in AI and, ultimately, in a digitisation transformation.

## FUTURE RESEARCH DIRECTIONS

### AI for MSMEs: The Evolution of Accessibility of AI

Technology like 5G and edge computing provides MSMEs an exciting opportunity to use AI solutions that were too expensive or complex to install earlier. MSMEs may use 5G's ultra-fast data transfer, ultra-low latency, and ultra-high dependability to develop real-time AI-based apps. Edge computing reduces the need for an extensive infrastructure by processing data at the service or device level. This benefits MSMEs in manufacturing, logistics, and retail. Future research. The literature implies that future research should focus on how these technologies might help MSMEs integrate AI into their business strategies. A study of prices, efficiency, and scalability, especially for instantaneous data analysis, where the technologies mentioned above reside, seems to remain.

### Low-Code/No-Code Platforms

Our low-code and no-code (LCNC) platforms can even democratise AI so that non-technical MSME users can design and utilise AI apps without domain-specific knowledge. These drag-and-drop interfaces and automated technologies help small businesses adopt AI-based solutions rapidly and cheaply. However, such platforms' long-term viability and ability to handle more complex AI jobs need additional study. Further research is required to understand how these platforms perform in the real world, including user uptake, non-technical user difficulties, and security vulnerabilities. Second, the effects of LCNC platforms on MSMEs' decision-making and operational efficiency should be examined to determine their role in AI adoption.

### Financial Models and AI Adoption

Initial AI technology expenditure is a significant barrier to MSMEs adopting AI. Government-backed incentives and AI-driven fintech are the financing solutions recommended to address this. These models aim to democratise AI by reducing implementation costs. Government subsidies or grants help lower AI adoption costs. Fintech-based microfinance models offer MSMEs tailored financing. In future studies, similar economic models may be tested in different regions and in underdeveloped countries with little capital availability. These models' effects on AI adoption rates and long-term viability can help researchers identify the best trim company funding options.

## AI-Driven Decision Making and Personalisation

AI is transforming how organisations choose marketing strategies and manage inventory. AI could help MSMEs understand customer behaviour, optimise supply chains, and provide customer support without money. Small businesses may utilise data-driven insights to improve operations, customer experiences, and decision-making, making AI solutions more accessible. More research is needed to address MSMEs' practical concerns when using AI for decision making, such as how to incorporate AI into existing processes and organise and manage the huge data to be mined for customisation. Finally, understanding how AI affects customer satisfaction and retention is essential, especially in personalisation-driven markets.

## AI and Legacy System Integration

Most MSMEs run on legacy technology platforms that are unsuitable for integrating AI systems. As AI use gains adoption, MSMEs must find ways to overlay AI on top of the current legacy systems. That might include investing in infrastructure, switching to more cloud-based solutions, or adopting new modular AI tools that work with older systems. Further research is needed into the practical integration of AI with legacy systems, particularly hybrid models that integrate cloud-based AI with on-premise systems. Future research should explore the sustainable operation of MSMEs during the integration and compare the cost-effectiveness of these hybrid approaches.

## AI Ethics & Data Privacy & Security

Data privacy, security, and ethics are becoming more critical as MSMEs deploy AI. Small firms must employ AI properly, especially for consumer data management and decision-making. That entails following data protection laws, avoiding algorithmic bias, and making AI systems visible and fair. Future research should examine whether and how MSMEs might integrate ethical AI in compliance with data protection laws. Future research should also investigate how ethical frameworks may guide small firms ethically towards AI, including issues like discrimination, privacy breaches, and AI-driven decision misuse.

## Develop and Train the AI Workforce

MSMEs struggle to embrace AI due to a lack of expertise. Small business owners may need consultants to apply and maintain AI technologies. Future studies should focus on MSME-specific staff training programs to increase in-house AI skills and lessen dependency on pricey consultants. Academic-industry partnerships (tech businesses, MSMEs) may be crucial to practical training. Studying how MSMEs may create a continuous learning culture to adapt to fast-changing AI technology and stay competitive in the digital age would be fascinating.

### Evaluating the ROI of AI in MSMEs

The lack of AI professionals hinders MSMEs' AI deployment. AI system implementation and maintenance may require consultancy firms and additional costs for small businesses. Future studies should focus on MSME-specific staff training programs to increase in-house AI skills and reduce outside consultant costs. An effective training program may include partnerships between academic institutions (tech companies, MSMEs). It would be of interest to study how MSMEs can create a continuous learning culture to adapt to fast-changing AI technology and stay competitive in the digital age.

## CONCLUSION

Artificial Intelligence (AI) can increase efficiency, boost productivity and help MSMEs interact with customers better. However, the path to expanded AI use is riddled with obstacles, particularly for smaller companies that may not have the financial means, technical capabilities or workforce to experiment with AI. As discussed in this chapter, the significant initial investment cost of AI-related technologies and ongoing maintenance, training, and data security costs make AI technologies a barrier to MSMEs. All these bottlenecks often mean resistance or reluctance to AI, regardless of its advantages.

However, these barriers are not insurmountable. MSMEs can use low-entry options, like AI-as-a-Service, cloud-based platforms, and open-source tools, to adopt AI without substantial Capex investments. The Pay-per-use model uses specific programs, such as paid for over a subscription. Government incentives and fintech-based microfinancing offer more pathways for small businesses to mitigate the risk of investment in AI. These solutions enable MSMEs to gradually scale their AI projects and work on a pay-per-use model that better fits their budgets and long-term growth goals.

There is an additional problem for micro, small, and medium enterprises (MSMEs): they do not have well-trained workers for the AI job Market. However, education is known for helping through partnerships with academia, AI-level workforce programs, and providing customers with easy-to-use AI platforms that require minimal technical skills. In particular, the advent of low-code and no-code tools offers a way to mitigate this possible blocker, enabling business owners and staff to develop and run AI models without in-depth programming experience.

Looking beyond that, new tech will continue to move into the market – the spread of 5G networks, edge computing, or more specific AI hardware – and it could be expected that the cost and the effort of rolling out AI will continue to decline. This will continue to democratise access to AI technologies for small businesses as they will become more accessible, scalable, and easier to integrate into SME's day-to-day operations. This will provide MSMEs a better footing to benefit from AI as these trends unfold, helping them to stay ahead in an AI-led market.

In short, the future looks promising for incorporating AI in MSMEs despite their struggle. With the proper planning, tools, and financing, MSMEs can leverage AI to transform their businesses and accelerate growth.

## REFERENCES


Abaddi, S. (2024). AI's call: Jordan's MSMEs answer with intent. *Journal of Entrepreneurship in Emerging Economies*. DOI: 10.1108/JEEE-11-2023-0446

Ahmed, A. (2017). *Overcoming barriers to inclusive mobility: Experience of disabled people in Tertiary Institutions of Kano*. Nigeria / Ahmed Abubakar.

Ahsan, S. M. M., Dhungel, A., Chowdhury, M., Hasan, M. S., & Hoque, T. (2024). Hardware accelerators for artificial intelligence. *arXiv (Cornell University)*. https://doi.org//arxiv.2411.13717DOI: 10.48550

Amjad, A. I., Aslam, S., Tabassum, U., Sial, Z. A., & Shafqat, F. (2024). Digital equity and accessibility in higher education: Reaching the unreached. *European Journal of Education*, *59*(4), e12795. Advance online publication. DOI: 10.1111/ejed.12795

Bella, G., Borowski, E., & Stathopoulos, A. (2025). Examining healthcare access with physical vs. telehealth options: Promise and peril for socially vulnerable older adults. *Journal of Transport & Health*, *40*, 101940. Advance online publication. DOI: 10.1016/j.jth.2024.101940

Bhattacharyya, S. S., & Kumar, S. (2021). Study of deployment of "low code no code" applications toward improving the digitization of supply chain management. *Journal of Science and Technology Policy Management*, *14*(2), 271–287. DOI: 10.1108/JSTPM-06-2021-0084

Borsotti, V., Begel, A., & Bjørn, P. (2024). Neurodiversity and the accessible university: Exploring organizational barriers, access labor and opportunities for change. *Proceedings of the ACM on Human-Computer Interaction*, *8*(CSCW1), 1–27. DOI: 10.1145/3641011

Bourechak, A., Zedadra, O., Kouahla, M. N., Guerrieri, A., Seridi, H., & Fortino, G. (2023). At the Confluence of Artificial Intelligence and Edge Computing in IoT-Based Applications: A Review and New Perspectives. *Sensors (Basel)*, *23*(3), 1639. DOI: 10.3390/s23031639 PMID: 36772680

Brynjolfsson, E., Li, D., & Raymond, L. (2024). Generative AI at Work. November 7, 2024 https://arxiv.org/pdf/2304.11771

Bussmann, N., Giudici, P., Marinelli, D., & Papenbrock, J. (2020). Explainable AI in fintech risk management. *Frontiers in Artificial Intelligence*, *3*, 26. Advance online publication. DOI: 10.3389/frai.2020.00026 PMID: 33733145

Dembitska, S., & Sivert, I. (2024). *Digital accessibility in education: challenges and prospects*. Health and Safety Pedagogy.

Dyson, L., Raban, R., Litchfield, A., & Lawrence, E. (2009). Addressing the cost barriers to mobile learning in higher education. *International Journal of Mobile Learning Organisation, 3*(4), 381–398. DOI: 10.1504/IJMLO.2009.027455

Elshan, E., Dickhaut, E., & Ebel, P. A. (2023). Offense or defense? Digital Innovation strategy to face competitive position shifting in mobile app platform. *Proceedings of the . . . Annual Hawaii International Conference on System Sciences/Proceedings of the Annual Hawaii International Conference on System Sciences*. https://doi.org/DOI: 10.24251/HICSS.2023.746

Fatima, P., Haider, S., Ali, M. A., Abbas, M., Akhtar, I., Rasool, M., Maqbool, H., & Khan, N. (2024). AI Unleashed: Pioneering trends and future directions in artificial intelligence. *Saudi Journal of Engineering and Technology, 9*(08), 406–418. DOI: 10.36348/sjet.2024.v09i08.005

Ferebee, S. (2025). *AI and accessibility: Breaking barriers for people with disabilities*. Premier Journal of Artificial Intelligence., DOI: 10.70389/PJAI.100011

Gupta, U., Agarwal, B., & Nautiyal, N. (2022). Financial technology adoption – A case of Indian MSMEs. *Finance: Theory and Practice, 26*(6), 192–211. DOI: 10.26794/2587-5671-2022-26-6-192-211

Hart, S. (2015). Patient education accessibility. *Medical Writing, 24*(3), 190–194. DOI: 10.1179/2047480615Z.000000000321

Khaq, Z., Subroto, V. K., & Susanto, E. (2024). AI-Driven Strategies for Enhancing MSME Sales and Business Sustainability in the Digital Era. *Journal of Management and Informatics, 3*(2), 180–194. DOI: 10.51903/jmi.v3i2.28

Kok, C. L., Tan, H. R., Ho, C. K., Lee, C., Teo, T. H., & Tang, H. (2024). A comparative study of AI and low-code platforms for SMEs: Insights into Microsoft Power Platform, Google AutoML, and Amazon SageMaker. *2024 IEEE 17th International Symposium on Embedded Multicore/Many-core Systems-on-Chip (MCSoC)*, Kuala Lumpur, Malaysia, 50-53. https://doi.org/DOI: 10.1109/MCSoC64144.2024.00018

Kouroupetroglou, C., Tektonidis, D., Koumpis, A., & Ignatiadis, I. (2012). Exploring Accessibility Scenarios for 2020 in Relation with Future ICT Trends on Assistive Technology and Accessibility. [iJIM]. *International Journal of Interactive Mobile Technologies, 6*(1), 7. DOI: 10.3991/ijim.v6i1.1790

Li, X. (2023). Analysis of the designs and applications of AI chip. *Highlights in Science. Engineering and Technology, 76*, 168–180. DOI: 10.54097/k1p7yk27

Lomas & Reeta. (2024). "AI-Driven FinTech Solutions for Financial Inclusion: A Study on MSME Sector Empowerment," *2024 1st International Conference on Advances in Computing, Communication and Networking (ICAC2N)*, Greater Noida, India, pp. 1887-1891, DOI: 10.1109/ICAC2N63387.2024.10895674

McCarthy, J. (1956). Dartmouth Summer Research Project on Artificial Intelligence.

Meng, X. (2024). Optimization of algorithmic efficiency in AI: Addressing computational complexity and scalability challenges. *Applied and Computational Engineering*, *45*(1), 305–311. DOI: 10.54254/2755-2721/45/20241637

Nguyen, N., Subhan, F., Williams, K., & Chan, C. B. (2020). Barriers and mitigating strategies to healthcare access in Indigenous communities of Canada: A narrative review. *Health Care*, *8*(2), 112. Advance online publication. DOI: 10.3390/healthcare8020112 PMID: 32357396

O'Sullivan, M., & Kearney, G. (2018). Virtual Reality (VR) Technology: Empowering Managers to Reduce and Eliminate Accessibility Barriers for People with Autism Spectrum Disorders. *Studies in Health Technology and Informatics*, *256*, 253–261. DOI: 10.3233/978-1-61499-923-2-253 PMID: 30371482

Omokhoa, N. H. E., Odionu, N. C. S., Azubuike, N. C., & Sule, N. K. (2024). AI-Powered Fintech innovations for credit scoring, debt recovery, and financial access in Microfinance and SMEs. *Gulf Journal of Advanced Business Research*, *2*(6), 411–422. DOI: 10.51594/gjabr.v2i6.55

Prasetyo, R. J., & Andrilla, R. (2025). Balikpapan Micro, Small, and Medium Enterprises (MSMEs) and Artificial Intelligence Adoption: TOE Framework. *Jurnal GeoEkonomi*, *16*(1), 11–20. Advance online publication. DOI: 10.36277/geoekonomi.v16i1.540

Satyam, P., Geetha, K., Shashikala, K. S., & Kumar, N. A. (2023). AI-enabled edge computing models: Trends, developments, and future implications. *2023 2nd International Conference on Edge Computing and Applications (ICECAA)*, Namakkal, India, 63-67. https://doi.org/DOI: 10.1109

Sinuhaji, F. G., Sibarani, H. J., & Pakpahan, V. M. (2024). MSMEs and the Role of Technology in Achieving Business Sustainability. [JAIEA]. *Journal of Artificial Intelligence and Engineering Applications*, *4*(1), 588–593. DOI: 10.59934/jaiea.v4i1.724

Suryani, I. P., Suri, A. G., & Shafira, Z. (2023). How fintech peer-to-peer lending affected MSMEs' financial Access: Case Study Amartha. *InFestasi*, *19*(2), 166–181. DOI: 10.21107/infestasi.v19i2.22921

Tapp, F. W. (2023). Breaking barriers or widening divides? An examination of survey responses. *Journal of Innovations*. https://doi.org/DOI: 10.62470/4a253027

Teo, J. (2023). Overcoming communication barriers to facilitate healthcare access for people with intellectual disability. *The Singapore Family Physician, 48*(7), 18–21. Advance online publication. DOI: 10.33591/sfp.48.7.u3

Wüst, M., Maskut, N., Baumann, L., Heitplatz, V. N., Wilkens, L., Dirks, S., & Bühler, C. (2023). Easy reading – Keeping the user at the digital original: Assessment and potential use of Easy Reading for digital accessibility. In *Lecture Notes in Computer Science*. http://dx.doi.org/DOI: 10.1007/978-3-031-35897-5_34

## KEY TERMS AND DEFINITIONS

**AI-as-a-Service:** A cloud-based service model that allows businesses to access artificial intelligence tools and capabilities on a subscription basis, without heavy upfront investments in hardware or software.

**Cloud Computing:** The delivery of computing services—such as storage, processing, and software—over the internet, which enables businesses to scale their operations and access AI technologies without investing in physical infrastructure.

**Fintech (Financial Technology):** Technologies and innovations aimed at improving and automating financial services, such as payments, lending, and investment, often using AI-driven solutions.

**Low-Code/No-Code Platforms:** Software development platforms allow users to create applications with minimal coding or no coding, making it easier for non-technical users to deploy AI solutions in business operations.

**Machine Learning:** A subset of AI that enables systems to learn from data, identify patterns, and make decisions without being explicitly programmed, often used to improve business processes in MSMEs.

**Predictive Analytics:** Using statistical algorithms and machine learning techniques to analyse historical data and predict future outcomes, helping MSMEs make informed decisions based on data-driven insights.

**Supply Chain Optimisation:** The process of improving the efficiency and effectiveness of the supply chain, often using AI technologies to forecast demand, optimise inventory, and reduce operational costs.

**Technology Adoption:** The process through which businesses integrate and implement new technologies, such as AI, into their operations. This often involves overcoming barriers related to cost, infrastructure, and expertise.

# Chapter 5
# Role of Artificial Intelligence (AI) in the MSME Sector:
## A Paradigm Shift With Usage of AI in the Business Management and Decision Making

**Priyanka Koundal**
http://orcid.org/0000-0001-8885-4120
*Lovely Professional University, India*

**Rohit Koundal**
http://orcid.org/0009-0000-1550-0153
*Lovely Professional University, India*

## ABSTRACT

*The rapid advancement of Artificial Intelligence (AI) is transforming business operations, particularly in Micro, Small, and Medium Enterprises (MSMEs). This chapter reviews existing literature on AI's role in MSME management and decision-making, emphasizing its potential to enhance productivity, automate operations, and support data-driven strategies. AI tools such as predictive analytics, customer relationship management systems, and financial forecasting software strengthen operational efficiency and promote innovation. By enabling real-time decision-making and strategic planning, AI empowers MSMEs to improve competitiveness and achieve sustainable growth. The integration of AI fosters innovation, enhances customer engagement, and contributes significantly to the modernization of MSME*

DOI: 10.4018/979-8-3373-2817-1.ch005

*business practices. This chapter provides a theoretical foundation for understanding AI's transformative impact on MSME business management and decision-making processes.*

## INTRODUCTION

The business environment is undergoing rapid transformation driven by technological advancements that are reshaping industries, markets, and organizational strategies. Among these advancements, Artificial Intelligence (AI) has emerged as a pivotal force, offering innovative opportunities and solutions for enterprises across all scales. Micro, Small, and Medium Enterprises (MSMEs), which constitute the backbone of many economies worldwide, are increasingly recognizing the potential of AI to enhance their operational efficiency, decision-making processes, and innovation capacity(Farooq et al., 2024). This research explores the diverse roles AI-based models play in MSME business management and decision-making, providing a detailed overview of how these technologies integrate into the core functions of small and medium enterprises.

MSMEs are critical contributors to economic growth, employment, and innovation, representing approximately 90% of all businesses and over half of global employment according to the World Bank. In many developing economies, MSMEs serve as the primary livelihood source for large populations(Nandeeswariah & Ramana, 2021). Despite their importance, MSMEs face persistent challenges such as limited access to finance, intense competition, resource constraints, and difficulties adopting emerging technologies. The accelerating pace of digital transformation has further widened the gap between large corporations and smaller enterprises. However, the increasing accessibility of AI offers MSMEs a unique chance to bridge this divide and compete on a more equal footing.

Once confined to large organizations, AI technologies—including machine learning, natural language processing, computer vision, and predictive analytics—are becoming more affordable and accessible for MSMEs(Bhalla, 2025). These technologies enable automation of routine tasks, efficient data analysis, and generation of actionable insights previously unattainable for smaller businesses. The integration of AI is thus not merely a technological upgrade but a fundamental shift in business operations, competitiveness, and value delivery(Wamba-Taguimdje et al., 2020). Operating in dynamic and often unpredictable environments, MSMEs must swiftly respond to changing market conditions, customer demands, and competitive pressures. Traditional management approaches, reliant on manual processes and intuition, are insufficient in such contexts. AI-based models offer critical advantages by providing real-time insights, automating repetitive functions, and supporting more informed decision-making. This allows MSMEs to enhance operational efficiency, reduce costs, innovate continuously, and adapt rapidly.

AI's application within MSMEs is broad and impactful. It enables enhanced decision-making through data-driven analysis and predictive forecasting, thereby reducing guesswork and optimizing resource allocation(Ekrokpe et al., 2025). Automation of administrative tasks like data entry, invoicing, and customer service improves operational efficiency and frees human resources for strategic activities. AI also drives personalized customer engagement by tailoring marketing efforts and product recommendations, which fosters loyalty and boosts sales(Rane et al., 2024). Financially, AI supports credit assessment by leveraging alternative data and enhances risk management through fraud detection and real-time anomaly monitoring(P. Singh, 2025). Furthermore, AI-powered analytics assist MSMEs in identifying new market opportunities and refining product innovation strategies, helping them stay competitive and expand their reach.

In manufacturing contexts, AI-based predictive maintenance and quality control reduce downtime and maintain high product standards(Andrianandrianina Johanesa et al., 2024). Sales processes benefit from AI through improved lead generation and automated follow-ups, increasing conversion rates and supporting business growth. These diverse applications collectively enable MSMEs to compete more effectively with larger firms by providing access to sophisticated tools and insights that were once exclusive to big enterprises.

In conclusion, the integration of Artificial Intelligence (AI) into Small and Medium Enterprises (SMEs) is pivotal for enhancing their operational efficiency, decision-making capabilities, and competitive positioning in an increasingly dynamic market. AI technologies empower SMEs by providing advanced data analysis, which facilitates real-time decision-making and helps manage complexities associated with big data. Furthermore, AI optimizes supply chain and inventory management, leading to improved forecasting accuracy and reduced operational costs. The successful implementation of artificial intelligence is contingent upon various factors, including managerial support, competitive pressures, and organizational training, which collectively foster a culture of continuous learning and adaptability among employees. Additionally, a structured approach to AI adoption can help SMEs navigate challenges related to costs and technical skills, ensuring that they can leverage AI tools effectively. By addressing psychological barriers and promoting a balance between AI reliance and human judgment, Small and Medium Enterprises can maintain employee motivation and critical thinking. Ultimately, the strategic adoption of AI not only enhances operational performance but also contributes to the long-term sustainability and resilience of SMEs, positioning them favourably in a competitive landscape. As such, AI stands as a transformative force that can significantly shape the future of SMEs.

Despite these promising benefits, challenges persist. Many MSMEs encounter barriers such as limited technical expertise, high initial investment costs, and concerns related to data privacy and security. However, the growing availability of user-friendly AI platforms, cloud computing solutions, and supportive government initiatives are gradually mitigating these obstacles(Alzebda & Matar, 2025). Strategic adoption, focused on areas with the greatest impact potential, is essential for MSMEs to harness the full benefits of AI.

This study aims to provide a comprehensive understanding of how AI-based models transform MSME business management and decision-making. By synthesizing existing research, case studies, and best practices, it highlights AI's transformative potential and offers insights valuable for business owners, policymakers, and technology providers committed to supporting MSME growth and resilience in today's digital economy. The objectives of the study are stated as following-

- To assess the impact of Artificial intelligence through content analysis in the MSME sector.
- To explore the key roles of AI-based models in business management and decision-making for MSMEs.

## RESEARCH METHODOLOGY

This study used a qualitative research design to analyse the role of AI-based models in the MSME sector and their contribution to sustainability and Industry 4.0 and 5.0. The literature review includes existing empirical studies on artificial intelligence (AI) and sustainability in Industry 4.0 and 5.0. The research aims to evaluate the significance of AI-based systems in MSMEs for improved business operations, promoting sustainability by optimizing resource allocation and aligning AI adoption. The findings contribute to discussions on digital transformation, sustainable business growth, and the role of Industry 4.0 and 5.0 in MSME development. The study provides practical insights for policymakers, business leaders, and researchers on AI's impact on MSME management.

## BACKGROUND

### MSMEs sector contribution towards economic development

The Micro, Small, and Medium Enterprises (MSMEs) sector is crucial for India's economic development, significantly contributing to the nation's GDP, employment, and exports. This sector's decentralized structure promotes inclusive growth, reaching even the most remote areas of the country. MSMEs are a primary source of employment, accommodating a substantial portion of the workforce, including semi-skilled and unskilled labour, and play a vital role in fostering skill development and entrepreneurship, thereby cultivating a culture of self-reliance. Moreover, MSMEs are instrumental in regional development and in mitigating income disparities by establishing operations in tier-2 and tier-3 cities and rural regions, which generates local employment and stimulates economic activity outside metropolitan areas(Haji, 2021). They also play a critical role in global supply chains, significantly contributing to India's export capabilities across diverse sectors.

The sector's inherent agility and capacity for innovation enable MSMEs to swiftly adapt to market changes and adopt new technologies, creating a dynamic competitive landscape. Government initiatives like Make in India and Startup India further enhance the sector's growth by offering financial support, technological assistance, and market access. Overall, the MSME sector is indispensable for sustainable economic development in India, underscoring its strategic importance in shaping the nation's economic

MSMEs contributes to employment generation, regional development, export promotion, and innovation, driving inclusive and sustainable economic growth. MSMEs are the largest employment-generating segment, providing livelihoods to over 111 million individuals and playing a crucial role in reducing unemployment and underemployment(Kokilavizhi & Amsaveni, 2023). They also promote entrepreneurship by lowering entry barriers for new business ventures, fostering a culture of innovation. Regional and rural development is another significant aspect of the MSME sector. By establishing enterprises in remote and underdeveloped areas, MSMEs decentralize economic activity and mitigate the concentration of industries in urban centres(Muchie & Bekele, 2009). This geographical dispersion reduces regional disparities and empowers local communities by providing access to financial services, skill development, and market linkages.

MSMEs are significant contributors to India's export sector, accounting for 40-50% of total exports. Their ability to cater to niche markets and adapt to global demand patterns enhances the country's export competitiveness(Ahmed & Haseen, 2017). MSMEs operate across various sectors, reducing the economy's reliance on any single industry and enhancing its resilience to external shocks. The MSME sector's contribution to India's GDP is substantial, estimated at 29-30%(Martinravi & Krishnasamy, 2025; Sahoo & Ashwani, 2020). Its resilience and adaptability have enabled the Indian economy to withstand global economic shocks and maintain a trajectory of sustainable and inclusive growth. Continued policy support and investment in the sector are essential to unlocking its full potential and reinforcing its role as the backbone of the national economy.

## Importance of business management and decision-making of MSMEs

Effective business management and robust decision-making are paramount for the sustainability and growth of MSMEs. Unlike larger corporations with specialized departments and extensive resources, MSMEs often rely heavily on the capabilities of their owner-managers, who frequently wear multiple hats. This necessitates a comprehensive approach to management that encompasses strategic planning, resource optimization, and agile response to market dynamics.

Strategic decision-making is critical for MSMEs to define long-term objectives, allocate scarce resources efficiently, and gain a competitive edge. This involves a systematic process of observing market trends, analysing internal capabilities, evaluating risks, and formulating actionable plans. While larger firms may employ complex analytical tools, MSMEs often benefit from simpler, yet effective, frameworks that enable informed choices regarding product diversification, market expansion, or technology adoption. The ability to pivot quickly in response to unforeseen challenges, such as economic fluctuations or supply chain disruptions, is also heavily dependent on the quality of managerial decisions.

Furthermore, sound management practices translate into operational efficiency, cost reduction, and enhanced profitability for MSMEs. This includes effective financial management, human resource management, and marketing strategies. Studies indicate that managerial competence, particularly in decision-making, significantly correlates with MSME success. By fostering a culture of data-driven insights and continuous learning, MSMEs can mitigate common pitfalls such as cash flow issues or insufficient business planning, thereby ensuring their resilience and long-term viability in a competitive landscape.

Effective business management and decision-making are vital for the success of Micro, Small, and Medium Enterprises (MSMEs). By optimizing resources and making informed decisions, MSMEs can enhance their competitiveness, drive growth, and ensure sustainability in an ever-changing market landscape(Abdin, 2016). Given their resource constraints, the ability to manage efficiently and make strategic choices is crucial for their survival and long-term prosperity. Business management and decision-making are essential components that support the sustainable growth, efficiency, and competitiveness of MSMEs. In the context of a rapidly changing global economy, MSMEs must adopt strategic management practices and informed decision-making to foster adaptability, innovation, and value creation(Nandeeswariah & Ramana, 2021). Effective business management entails the systematic coordination of resources—human, financial, technological, and informational—to achieve organizational objectives. Well-managed MSMEs are more likely to attract investment and expand into new markets due to their operational transparency and growth potential(D. Singh et al., 2018).

Decision-making within MSMEs is characterized by its centralized, agile, and entrepreneurial nature, providing a competitive edge in dynamic markets(Koundal et al., 2024). Timely and informed decisions regarding product development, pricing, and market expansion are crucial for long-term sustainability(Martínez-Peláez et al., 2024). The use of modern management tools, such as cost-benefit analysis and financial modelling, further enhances decision-making accuracy and strategic planning(Koundal et al., 2025). Additionally, effective decision-making fosters innovation by enabling rapid experimentation and responsiveness to consumer preferences. Business management and decision-making are foundational to the success and resilience of MSMEs(Al-Hattami, 2022), With focusing on these areas, MSMEs can navigate complexities, seize opportunities, and contribute significantly to economic development, innovation, and inclusive growth.

## Industry 4.0 and Industry 5.0 promotes AI

The transition from Industry 4.0 to Industry 5.0 marks a significant evolution in industrial paradigms, primarily driven by the integration of Artificial Intelligence (AI). Industry 4.0, known as the Fourth Industrial Revolution, is characterized by the convergence of digital and physical technologies, leading to the establishment of cyber-physical systems. This era has fostered the promotion of AI through various mechanisms, including the generation and analysis of big data, advanced automation, the creation of digital twins, real-time decision-making, and predictive capabilities. The interconnected systems in Industry 4.0 produce vast amounts of data, which AI processes to enhance maintenance strategies, optimize production, and improve supply chain visibility.

In contrast, Industry 5.0 builds upon the technological advancements of its predecessor, shifting the focus toward human-centricity, resilience, and sustainability(Engelbrecht et al., 2024). In this new paradigm, AI's role evolves from merely optimizing processes to augmenting human capabilities and addressing broader societal objectives. Key features of Industry 5.0 include human-robot collaboration (cobots), which allows robots to work alongside humans safely and effectively, enhancing productivity and creativity(Leng et al., 2022, p. 5). AI also facilitates mass customization and personalization of products by analysing consumer preferences and market trends, enabling dynamic adjustments in production.

Furthermore, Industry 5.0 emphasizes resilience and adaptability in industrial systems, with AI enabling intelligent supply chain management and responsive production lines. Sustainability is another critical aspect, as AI optimizes resource use, minimizes waste, and supports circular economy models. Unlike the automation-centric approach of Industry 4.0, Industry 5.0 leverages AI to enhance human decision-making, providing workers with real-time insights and intelligent recommendations. Both Industry 4.0 and Industry 5.0 are fundamentally intertwined with AI's development and application. While Industry 4.0 established the foundation for AI-driven automation, Industry 5.0 utilizes AI to foster collaboration, sustainability, and resilience, positioning AI as a pivotal enabling technology in these transformative industrial revolutions.

Industry 4.0 refers to the fourth industrial revolution, characterized by the integration of advanced technologies such as artificial intelligence (AI), the Internet of Things (IoT), robotics, big data, and cloud computing into manufacturing and business processes(Golovianko et al., 2023). It focuses on automation, real-time data exchange, and smart systems to improve efficiency, reduce costs, and enhance productivity. Its relevance lies in enabling businesses, including MSMEs, to become more agile, competitive, and responsive to market demands. Industry 5.0 goes a step further by emphasizing the collaboration between humans and machines(Adel et al., 2024). It brings a human-centric approach to technology, where intelligent systems work alongside human intelligence to foster creativity, personalization, and sustainable innovation. The relevance of Industry 5.0 lies in its focus on social value, environmental responsibility, and the well-being of workers—creating a balance between technological advancement and human needs. This shift is especially significant in shaping future-ready, resilient, and inclusive business models.

The evolution of industrial paradigms, particularly from Industry 4.0 to Industry 5.0, has significantly reshaped global manufacturing and service sectors, with Artificial Intelligence (AI) playing a pivotal role in this transformation. Industry 4.0, characterized by the digitalization of manufacturing through the integration of cyber-physical systems, the Internet of Things, and advanced robotics, positions AI as a foundational enabler(Lewandowska et al., 2023). AI enhances operational efficiency by facilitating real-time monitoring, predictive maintenance, and adaptive control, thereby fostering the concept of the "smart factory" where decentralized decision-making and self-optimizing processes are paramount(Adel et al., 2024).

Additionally, AI supports personalized consumer experiences and promotes ethical decision-making through explainable AI models, aligning algorithmic outcomes with societal values. The transition from Industry 4.0 to 5.0 is characterized by a synergistic relationship rather than a straightforward replacement, with AI serving as a crucial link between operational and information technologies(Golovianko et al., 2023; Mourtzis et al., 2022). This convergence is reflected in the adoption of AI-powered edge computing and the integration of AI with blockchain technologies, which enhance operational transparency and efficiency.

The implications of these industrial shifts are profound, necessitating policy adjustments to foster innovation ecosystems and educational reforms to equip the workforce with interdisciplinary skills in AI and ethical technology. Industries, particularly micro, small, and medium enterprises (MSMEs), stand to benefit from the adoption of AI-driven practices, as Industry 4.0 provides the tools for automation while Industry 5.0 emphasizes ethical and inclusive growth(Santos & Sant'Anna, 2024). Both Industry 4.0 and Industry 5.0 significantly advance the role of AI, with the former focusing on automation and efficiency, and the latter on collaboration, ethics, and sustainability. Together, they represent a transformative continuum that redefines the future of industry, positioning AI as a partner in innovation and responsible progress.

## AI evolution

The evolution of artificial intelligence (AI) within industrial management has undergone significant transformation, characterized by conceptual advancements, technological breakthroughs, and evolving paradigms that have reshaped the operational and strategic frameworks of industries globally. This trajectory can be traced from the mid-20th century theoretical foundations to AI's current status as a pivotal element of contemporary industrial strategy(Farooq et al., 2024). The inception of AI as a scientific discipline is attributed to Alan Turing's foundational work in the 1950s, particularly his introduction of the Turing test, followed by John McCarthy's formalization of the term "artificial intelligence" at the Dartmouth Conference in 1956(Luger, 2025). Early AI research concentrated on developing algorithms capable of reasoning and problem-solving, aiming to replicate human cognitive functions.

The practical application of AI in industrial contexts began in the 1960s and 1970s, highlighted by the introduction of Unimate, the first industrial robot, which showcased automation's potential in manufacturing(Detesan & Moholea, 2024; Rahaman et al., 2025). However, challenges such as the complexity of industrial problems and limited computational capabilities led to periods of stagnation, known as "AI winters"(Fui-Hoon Nah et al., 2023).

The 1980s witnessed a resurgence in AI interest, driven by the development of expert systems that emulated human decision-making processes, enhancing operational efficiency in industrial settings. This period also saw the emergence of early autonomous systems, exemplified by the first self-driving car, indicating AI's applicability in complex industrial scenarios(Perrotta & Selwyn, 2020). The late 1990s and early 2000s marked a significant shift towards machine learning, propelled by increased computational power and data availability. This transition facilitated a move from rule-based systems to data-driven management approaches, enabling predictive analytics and optimization across various industrial domains.

The advent of deep learning in the 2010s, coupled with the rise of Industry 4.0, further revolutionized industrial management by integrating AI with cyber-physical systems, the Internet of Things (IoT), and big data analytics(Naidoo & Sibanda, 2024). AI systems now support real-time monitoring, predictive maintenance, and adaptive manufacturing, enhancing efficiency and resilience in industrial operations. The historical development of AI in industrial management illustrates a dynamic interplay between theoretical advancements and practical applications. From early automation to modern intelligent manufacturing, AI has fundamentally altered industrial management practices. As AI technologies continue to advance, their influence on efficiency, innovation, and competitiveness in industries is poised to grow, ushering in a new era of intelligent industrial management.

## Significance of AI adoption in the MSMEs sector

Micro, Small, and Medium Enterprises (MSMEs) play a crucial role in both developed and developing economies by driving employment, innovation, and inclusive growth. The integration of Artificial Intelligence (AI) within this sector is increasingly recognized as a transformative force, democratized by advancements in AI tools, cloud infrastructure, and data analytics, which have become more accessible to smaller firms(Van Der Vlist et al., 2024). The adoption of AI in MSMEs promises significant enhancements in productivity, decision-making, customer engagement, and sustainability.

AI facilitates operational efficiency by automating repetitive tasks and optimizing internal processes, thereby allowing human resources to focus on strategic functions. Tools such as chatbots and robotic process automation (RPA) streamline administrative tasks, while machine learning algorithms support predictive maintenance in manufacturing, reducing downtime and improving asset utilization(A. K. Singh et al., 2025). Moreover, AI shifts MSMEs from intuition-based to data-driven decision-making, enabling the analysis of historical data and market trends to generate actionable insights. This capability is particularly beneficial in volatile environments, where agile decision-making can confer a competitive advantage.

In terms of customer experience, AI enhances personalization and engagement through tools like natural language processing chatbots and predictive analytics for targeted marketing(Krishnan et al., 2022). These advancements enable MSMEs to compete effectively with larger firms in customer relationship management and market outreach. AI also fosters innovation by facilitating rapid prototyping and design optimization, thereby reducing the costs and risks associated with research and development(Aldoseri et al., 2024). This is particularly advantageous for MSMEs that often face funding and technical expertise constraints. Financially, AI improves financial planning, credit risk analysis, and fraud detection, enhancing access to finance for MSMEs by providing a more accurate assessment of creditworthiness.

Additionally, AI aids compliance with regulatory requirements, reducing administrative burdens.

The socio-economic implications of AI adoption in MSMEs are profound, as it promotes inclusivity and empowerment, particularly for marginalized groups and those in rural areas. AI tools can bridge digital divides and enhance participation in global value chains. In the context of post-pandemic recovery, AI adoption is critical for enhancing the resilience and adaptability of MSMEs, enabling them to navigate disruptions and transition to digital business models effectively(Carayannis et al., 2024; Sahu & Panda, 2024).

Operational efficiency and cost reduction are immediate advantages of AI for MSMEs, as they can automate repetitive tasks such as data entry, inventory management, customer service inquiries, and basic accounting. This automation reduces operational costs and frees up valuable human capital, allowing employees to focus on more strategic, creative, and value-added activities. AI empowers MSMEs with data-driven insights, enabling them to make more informed decisions regarding product development, pricing strategies, marketing campaigns, and market opportunities. AI-powered solutions facilitate personalized customer interactions, enhancing customer satisfaction and loyalty. Access to finance and risk management is a significant challenge for MSMEs, particularly in emerging economies. AI is revolutionizing the lending landscape by enabling faster and more inclusive credit assessment, reducing human bias, and accelerating loan approvals. AI-driven predictive analytics can help MSMEs manage financial risks and identify potential defaults. AI can also foster innovation and competitive advantage within the MSME sector by automating routine tasks and providing insightful data, freeing up resources and fostering an environment for MSMEs to explore new product and service offerings, enhance existing ones, and develop new business models. However, challenges such as high initial costs, lack of technical expertise, data quality issues, and resistance to change are diminishing.

## MAIN FOCUS OF THE CHAPTER

### Key Roles of AI based models in MSMEs business management and decision-making as per existing studies

*Table 1. Roles of AI based models*

| Role of AI based Models | Description and Impact on MSMEs | Sources |
|---|---|---|
| **Enhanced Decision-Making** | Artificial Intelligence (AI) significantly enhances decision-making processes within Micro, Small, and Medium Enterprises (MSMEs) by enabling the rapid analysis of large and complex datasets. Through data-driven insights, AI helps identify emerging market trends, customer preferences, and competitive dynamics, thereby supporting more informed and strategic decisions. Moreover, AI-powered predictive analytics facilitate demand forecasting, risk identification, and behavioural prediction, allowing MSMEs to proactively adapt to market changes. This integration of AI not only reduces reliance on intuition but also optimizes business strategies, ultimately contributing to improved operational efficiency and competitiveness. | (Ekrokpe et al., 2025; Kumar et al., 2024) |
| **Operational Efficiency** | Artificial Intelligence (AI) plays a pivotal role in enhancing operational efficiency and promoting automation within Micro, Small, and Medium Enterprises (MSMEs). By automating routine and repetitive tasks such as data entry, scheduling, payroll processing, and customer support, AI reduces the likelihood of human error, lowers operational costs, and reallocates human resources toward more strategic, value-added functions. Furthermore, AI-driven systems optimize core business processes, including inventory management, supply chain coordination, and quality assurance. These intelligent solutions enable real-time monitoring, predictive maintenance, and demand forecasting, resulting in improved productivity, cost-effectiveness, and overall organizational efficiency. | (Chotisarn & Phuthong, 2025) |
| **Customer Engagement** | Artificial Intelligence (AI) significantly contributes to improved customer engagement and personalization within Micro, Small, and Medium Enterprises (MSMEs). AI-powered tools such as chatbots and recommendation engines enable round-the-clock customer support and deliver personalized product or service suggestions based on individual preferences and behaviour. This enhances customer satisfaction, fosters loyalty, and strengthens long-term customer relationships. Additionally, AI facilitates targeted marketing by analysing customer data to segment audiences effectively and develop tailored marketing campaigns. Such data-driven personalization strategies lead to increased customer engagement, improved conversion rates, and higher overall sales performance. | (Jain et al., 2025) |

continued on following page

*Table 1. Continued*

| Role of AI based Models | Description and Impact on MSMEs | Sources |
|---|---|---|
| **Risk Management** | Artificial Intelligence (AI) enhances risk management and improves financial access for Micro, Small, and Medium Enterprises (MSMEs) by enabling more accurate and inclusive credit assessment and risk prediction. AI-driven credit scoring models utilize alternative data sources—such as transaction histories, utility bill payments, and even digital footprints like social media activity—to evaluate the creditworthiness of MSMEs that may lack formal credit records. This facilitates broader access to financing, especially for underserved or first-time borrowers. Furthermore, AI-powered predictive analytics assist financial institutions in assessing the probability of loan defaults, thereby mitigating credit risk, reducing the volume of non-performing assets, and enhancing the overall financial stability of both MSMEs and lenders. | (P. Singh, 2025) |
| **Market Expansion & Innovation** | Artificial Intelligence (AI) facilitates access to new markets and drives innovation within Micro, Small, and Medium Enterprises (MSMEs) by enabling data-informed strategic expansion and continuous product development. AI-driven analytics help identify emerging market opportunities, optimize digital presence, and customize offerings to meet the needs of diverse customer segments, thereby supporting effective market penetration and expansion. Additionally, AI supports innovation by assisting in competitor analysis, customer feedback interpretation, and the formulation of targeted marketing strategies. These capabilities empower MSMEs to develop new products and services, adapt rapidly to changing market demands, and maintain a competitive edge in dynamic business environments. | (Santos & Sant'Anna, 2024) |
| **Fraud Detection & Financial Security** | Artificial Intelligence (AI) plays a critical role in enhancing fraud detection and financial security for Micro, Small, and Medium Enterprises (MSMEs). By continuously analysing financial transactions and behavioural patterns, AI algorithms can detect anomalies and potentially fraudulent activities in real time. This proactive monitoring significantly reduces the risk of financial fraud, safeguards business assets, and enhances the overall integrity of financial operations. The implementation of AI-driven security measures not only minimizes financial losses but also fosters greater trust and confidence among stakeholders, including customers, partners, and financial institutions. | (Bhalla, 2025) |

continued on following page

*Table 1. Continued*

| Role of AI based Models | Description and Impact on MSMEs | Sources |
|---|---|---|
| **Real-Time Business Forecasting** | Artificial Intelligence (AI) enables real-time business forecasting by continuously analysing vast amounts of data to predict sales, demand fluctuations, and evolving market trends. For MSMEs, this capability allows for proactive strategic adjustments and greater operational agility in response to dynamic market conditions. By anticipating changes and identifying emerging opportunities, AI-driven forecasting supports timely decision-making, reduces uncertainty, and enhances the ability of MSMEs to remain competitive and resilient in rapidly changing business environments. | (Syeda Rafina Ahmed, 2025) |
| **Automated Bookkeeping & Financial Management** | Artificial Intelligence (AI) significantly contributes to automated bookkeeping and financial management within Micro, Small, and Medium Enterprises (MSMEs). AI-powered tools streamline routine financial tasks such as bookkeeping, invoice processing, and the generation of financial reports, thereby ensuring greater accuracy, consistency, and compliance with regulatory standards. By automating these labour-intensive processes, AI reduces the administrative burden on business owners and financial staff, allowing them to allocate more time and resources to strategic and growth-oriented activities. This enhances overall financial efficiency and supports more informed financial decision-making. | (Azman et al., 2021) |
| **Predictive Maintenance & Quality Control** | Artificial Intelligence (AI)-driven predictive maintenance and quality control systems play a vital role in optimizing operations, particularly within manufacturing-oriented Micro, Small, and Medium Enterprises (MSMEs). These systems continuously monitor equipment performance and production processes to forecast maintenance requirements before failures occur, thereby minimizing unplanned downtime. Additionally, AI facilitates consistent quality assurance by detecting deviations and defects in real time, ensuring that products meet established standards. This proactive approach reduces repair costs, enhances operational efficiency, and maintains high-quality output, ultimately supporting the competitiveness and sustainability of manufacturing MSMEs. | (Andrianandrianina Johanesa et al., 2024) |
| **Enhanced Lead Generation & Sales Automation** | Artificial Intelligence (AI)-powered lead generation and sales automation tools enhance the marketing and sales capabilities of Micro, Small, and Medium Enterprises (MSMEs) by systematically analysing customer data to identify high-potential leads. These tools automate follow-up communications and personalize outreach efforts, optimizing conversion strategies throughout the sales funnel. As a result, AI-driven solutions improve sales efficiency, accelerate customer acquisition, and support sustainable business growth for MSMEs. | (Justina Eweala Abubakar et al., 2025; Madanchian, 2024) |

Source: Own elaboration (2025).

Artificial Intelligence (AI) plays a transformative role in enhancing the operational and strategic capabilities of Micro, Small, and Medium Enterprises (MSMEs) across multiple dimensions. By automating routine tasks such as bookkeeping, invoice processing, payroll, and customer support, AI reduces manual errors, lowers administrative burdens, and allows human resources to focus on higher-value activities. AI-driven data analytics provide MSMEs with deep insights into market trends, customer preferences, and competitive dynamics, facilitating data-driven decision-making and strategic planning. Predictive models enable real-time forecasting of sales, demand, and risks, allowing businesses to remain agile and proactively adapt to changing market conditions. In manufacturing contexts, AI-powered predictive maintenance and quality control systems minimize downtime, reduce repair costs, and ensure consistent product standards.

Moreover, AI enhances customer engagement through personalized recommendations and 24/7 support, while targeted marketing campaigns improve conversion and sales efficiency. AI also expands financial access for MSMEs by automating credit assessments using alternative data and enabling lenders to better predict default risks, thereby fostering financial inclusion and stability. Additionally, AI supports market expansion and innovation by identifying new opportunities, optimizing online presence, and facilitating competitor analysis. In the realm of security, AI continuously monitors transactions to detect fraud in real time, safeguarding business assets and enhancing stakeholder trust. The integration of Artificial Intelligence into the operations of MSMEs is proving to be a transformative force that enhances decision-making, operational efficiency, and customer engagement. By leveraging AI's capabilities in data analysis, automation, and predictive analytics, MSMEs can streamline their processes, reduce errors, and focus on strategic initiatives that drive growth.

Furthermore, AI's role in risk management and market opportunity identification empowers these businesses to navigate challenges and innovate effectively. As MSMEs continue to adopt AI technologies, they are not only improving their competitive edge but also positioning themselves for sustainable success in an increasingly dynamic marketplace. The ongoing evolution of AI presents a significant opportunity for MSMEs to thrive, adapt, and lead in their respective industries. Finally, AI-driven lead generation and sales automation tools streamline customer acquisition processes, further driving growth and competitiveness. Collectively, these AI applications empower MSMEs to optimize operations, innovate, and sustain competitive advantage in dynamic business environments.

## FUTURE RESEARCH DIRECTION

While existing studies highlight the transformative potential of AI for MSMEs, several areas warrant further investigation to deepen understanding and support practical implementation. Future research should explore the barriers and facilitators influencing AI adoption within diverse MSME contexts, including technological readiness, cost constraints, and workforce skills. Longitudinal studies are needed to assess the long-term impact of AI integration on MSME performance, sustainability, and competitive advantage. Additionally, sector-specific analyses could provide tailored insights into how AI applications vary across industries such as manufacturing, retail, and services. Research should also examine the ethical, legal, and social implications of AI deployment in MSMEs, particularly regarding data privacy, algorithmic bias, and workforce displacement. Moreover, there is a need to develop and evaluate scalable, cost-effective AI solutions specifically designed for the resource limitations of MSMEs. Investigating the role of government policies, financial incentives, and ecosystem partnerships in accelerating AI adoption would further inform supportive frameworks. Finally, empirical research focusing on the user experience and change management processes within MSMEs can shed light on best practices for maximizing AI benefits while mitigating risks. Addressing these research gaps will contribute to creating an inclusive and sustainable AI-driven future for MSMEs globally.

## FINDINGS AND CONCLUSION

The analysis reveals that Artificial Intelligence (AI) substantially enhances the efficiency, agility, and competitiveness of Micro, Small, and Medium Enterprises (MSMEs) across a broad spectrum of business functions. AI-driven automation effectively reduces manual workloads and errors in routine administrative tasks such as bookkeeping, payroll, and customer service, allowing MSMEs to reallocate resources toward strategic priorities. Data analytics and predictive modelling empower MSMEs with actionable insights for informed decision-making, real-time forecasting, and proactive risk management. In manufacturing sectors, AI-based predictive maintenance and quality control contribute to reduced downtime and improved product consistency.

Enhanced customer engagement through AI-powered personalization and targeted marketing improves customer satisfaction and sales outcomes. Furthermore, AI facilitates greater financial inclusion by automating credit assessment and enabling more accurate risk prediction for lenders. AI also supports MSMEs in exploring new markets and fostering innovation through data-driven opportunity identification and competitive analysis. The integration of AI in fraud detection enhances financial security by providing real-time monitoring and anomaly detection. Finally, AI-enabled lead generation and sales automation optimize customer acquisition, thereby driving revenue growth. Collectively, these findings underscore the multifaceted value of AI adoption in transforming MSME operations and growth trajectories.

Artificial Intelligence represents a critical enabler for the sustainable development and competitive resilience of MSMEs in increasingly dynamic and complex market environments. By automating routine tasks, improving decision-making through data-driven insights, and enhancing customer and financial interactions, AI equips MSMEs with the tools necessary to optimize operations and innovate continuously. The adoption of AI not only addresses traditional constraints such as limited resources and access to finance but also opens new avenues for market expansion and value creation. However, to fully realize these benefits, MSMEs must invest in appropriate AI technologies and build organizational capabilities that support digital transformation. Policymakers and stakeholders should also facilitate AI adoption by providing targeted support, infrastructure, and capacity-building initiatives tailored to the specific needs of MSMEs. Ultimately, leveraging AI will be indispensable for MSMEs seeking to thrive in the competitive global economy.

A study by (Abaddi, 2025) investigated the factors influencing AI adoption among MSMEs in Jordan using the Technology-Organization-Environment (TOE) framework. The research found that business innovativeness, management support, perceived benefits, and technological infrastructure positively impacted AI adoption intentions. Additionally, the study highlighted that innovation culture, employee digital skills, and market competition moderated these relationships, emphasizing the importance of a conducive organizational environment for successful AI integration. (Panigrahi et al., 2023) explored the adoption of AI chatbots in Indian SMEs to enhance sustainable manufacturing supply chain performance. Their research demonstrated that AI chatbots could significantly improve communication efficiency, reduce response times, and streamline supply chain operations, leading to enhanced overall performance in the manufacturing sector.

(Santosa & Surgawati, 2024) examined the adoption of AI as marketing tools among MSMEs in Indonesia. The study identified key factors such as top management commitment, employee adaptability, perceived usefulness, and perceived ease of use as significant determinants influencing AI adoption. The research highlighted that AI tools could enhance marketing strategies, customer engagement, and competitive advantage for MSMEs in Indonesia. (Arroyabe et al., 2024) analyzed AI adoption in European SMEs, focusing on digital capabilities, innovation, and external environmental support. The findings indicated that internal capabilities, particularly digital and innovation capabilities, played a more significant role in AI adoption than external environmental support. This underscores the importance of developing internal competencies to leverage AI technologies effectively.

(Lim & Seng, 2024) investigated the determinants of AI adoption in accounting functions among Malaysian SMEs. The study found that perceived ease of use, management support, organizational readiness, government support, and external pressure positively influenced AI adoption in accounting practices. These factors were crucial in transforming traditional accounting processes into AI-supported systems, enhancing efficiency and accuracy. (Le Dinh et al., 2025) discussed the benefits of AI-powered process automation for SMEs, emphasizing increased efficiency, cost savings, improved accuracy, enhanced decision-making, scalability, and better customer experience. The article highlighted practical applications across various business functions, including customer service, marketing, sales, human resources, financial management, and supply chain management.

MSMEs operate across diverse sectors—from manufacturing and services to agriculture and technology—and constitute a major segment of both rural and urban economies. As these enterprises strive to remain competitive in an increasingly digital world, technological innovation becomes critical. Among emerging technologies, Artificial Intelligence (AI) has emerged as a transformative force, redefining the way MSMEs manage their operations and make decisions. It refers to systems or machines that mimic human intelligence to perform tasks and can iteratively improve themselves based on the information they collect. It includes a wide array of subfields such as machine learning (ML), natural language processing (NLP), robotics, image and speech recognition, and expert systems. The promise of AI lies in its capacity to analyze massive datasets, identify patterns, generate predictions, and enable intelligent automation. For MSMEs, which often operate with resource constraints, AI represents an opportunity to achieve greater efficiency, reduce costs, and gain strategic insights without the need for large-scale infrastructure or workforce expansion.

One of the core contributions of AI to MSME business management lies in its ability to streamline and optimize internal processes. Inventory management, supply chain logistics, procurement, and warehousing—all essential operational domains—can benefit from AI-powered predictive analytics and automation. For instance, AI systems can forecast demand with high accuracy, thereby reducing inventory carrying costs and minimizing the risks of stockouts or overstocking. Similarly, AI can be employed for route optimization in logistics, enabling timely deliveries and reduced fuel consumption. These operational enhancements directly translate into cost savings and improved service delivery. AI also empowers MSMEs with advanced tools for customer relationship management (CRM). Through chatbots and virtual assistants, enterprises can offer 24/7 customer service, instantly respond to queries, and guide users through product selections or service bookings.

Additionally, AI-driven sentiment analysis tools can gauge customer emotions based on reviews and feedback, helping businesses refine their offerings and communication strategies. Recommendation engines—widely used in e-commerce—leverage AI algorithms to personalize product suggestions based on user behavior, thereby increasing conversion rates and customer satisfaction.

Marketing strategies have seen a paradigm shift with AI integration. Traditional marketing relied heavily on assumptions and generalized data. In contrast, AI enables hyper-personalization through data analytics. MSMEs can now segment their customer base more effectively, target advertisements with precision, and assess campaign performance in real time. Tools such as predictive analytics, customer lifetime value models, and churn prediction help MSMEs tailor their marketing efforts to specific customer segments, optimizing their marketing budgets and boosting return on investment.

In the financial domain, AI contributes significantly to accounting, bookkeeping, fraud detection, and credit risk analysis. AI-enabled accounting software automates repetitive tasks such as invoice generation, payroll processing, and tax filing. This not only saves time but also enhances accuracy and compliance. Fraud detection systems powered by machine learning can monitor transactions for anomalies and alert businesses about suspicious activities in real-time. For MSMEs seeking credit, AI-based credit scoring models offer quicker and more reliable assessments, potentially improving access to finance for previously underserved enterprises.

AI also plays a crucial role in human resource management. From screening resumes to conducting initial interviews through AI chatbots, MSMEs can streamline recruitment processes. Moreover, AI-driven performance analytics tools provide insights into employee productivity, skill gaps, and training needs. These insights support informed HR decision-making and contribute to building a more skilled and motivated workforce. Learning management systems (LMS) integrated with AI can further offer personalized training modules based on employee performance and learning preferences. The integration of AI extends to strategic decision-making as well. Business intelligence tools powered by AI can generate dashboards that track key performance indicators, visualize data trends, and support scenario analysis. Such tools enable MSME managers to make informed, data-driven decisions rather than relying solely on intuition or limited data.

AI's impact on product development and innovation cannot be overlooked. AI-driven design tools assist in rapid prototyping, performance simulations, and customer-driven customization. MSMEs in manufacturing, fashion, or digital services can utilize AI to develop products that better meet consumer needs, thus enhancing market relevance and competitive advantage. Furthermore, feedback loops established through AI tools help continuously improve product quality and adapt to changing customer preferences. The advent of cloud-based AI platforms and software-as-a-service (SaaS) solutions has made these technologies accessible to MSMEs without requiring heavy upfront investments(Chitra et al., 2024). These platforms provide ready-to-use AI tools that can be integrated into existing business systems. Many offers scalable solutions that allow MSMEs to start small and expand as needed. Open-source AI frameworks and APIs further lower the entry barrier, encouraging experimentation and innovation at minimal cost.

Digital payment systems, another area transformed by AI, are particularly relevant for MSMEs operating in informal or semi-formal sectors(Jha & Dangwal, 2025). AI enhances these systems by detecting fraudulent transactions, optimizing payment routes, and providing insights into customer purchasing patterns. The integration of AI in mobile payment apps and digital wallets facilitates seamless transactions, financial inclusion, and data-driven business models. AI also contributes to improving the supply chain and vendor relationship management. MSMEs can leverage AI tools to evaluate supplier performance, manage procurement cycles, and predict price fluctuations in raw materials. Advanced forecasting models enable businesses to proactively manage disruptions, negotiate better contracts, and maintain reliable supply chains. These improvements enhance operational resilience and support long-term sustainability.

A key outcome of this study is the realization that AI serves not just as a tool for efficiency but also as a catalyst for growth, innovation, and competitiveness. MSMEs, traditionally seen as resource-constrained and technology-averse, are now at the forefront of adopting AI-driven transformations. Through the effective use of AI, these enterprises are reimagining their operations, customer interactions, product offerings, and market strategies. Another important insight drawn from this study is the collaborative potential AI offers. MSMEs can engage in partnerships with AI solution providers, academic institutions, and industry bodies to co-create customized solutions that address specific business challenges. Such collaborations foster knowledge exchange, build technical capacity, and ensure the relevance of AI applications. Moreover, AI facilitates a feedback-rich environment where continuous learning and adaptation become integral to business strategy.

Artificial Intelligence (AI) models are being increasingly used by Micro, Small, and Medium Enterprises (MSMEs) and business organizations to streamline business management and enhance decision-making processes. Predictive analytics models, such as ARIMA and Facebook Prophet, analyse historical data to forecast sales, predict customer demand, and identify emerging market trends. Decision Support Systems (DSS) synthesize vast amounts of business data to provide real-time insights and actionable recommendations(Ali, 2023). Natural Language Processing (NLP) models, such as OpenAI's GPT series, Google Dialog flow, and Microsoft Azure Language Services, interpret and analyse unstructured data from sources like customer feedback, emails, and social media(Halvoník & Kapusta, 2024). AI-powered chatbots and virtual assistants automate customer service, handle routine queries, and deliver consistent support around the clock, improving customer satisfaction. Machine Learning (ML) algorithms are used for process optimization, customer segmentation, recommendation systems, and fraud detection. Recommendation engines, such as Amazon Personalize and Google Recommendations AI, analyse user behaviour and preferences to suggest products or services, driving sales and customer engagement. AI-powered solutions like SAP Integrated Business Planning and Oracle SCM Cloud analyse procurement, sales, and logistics data to predict inventory needs, optimize stock levels, and enhance supply chain efficiency. AI-based credit assessment models evaluate the creditworthiness of MSMEs using alternative data sources, improving access to financing for businesses lacking traditional credit histories.

In conclusion, Artificial Intelligence holds immense promise in transforming the MSME landscape across all dimensions of business management and decision-making. From operational efficiency and customer engagement to financial management, marketing, HR, and innovation, AI introduces a level of intelligence and agility previously inaccessible to small and medium businesses. As MSMEs navigate the complexities of globalization, digital disruption, and shifting market demands, AI offers a reliable compass to steer through uncertainty and achieve sustained growth. The study reaffirms that the strategic adoption of AI is not merely a technological upgrade but a fundamental shift in business mindset. It encourages MSMEs to think big, act smart, and operate efficiently. With continued advancements in AI tools and increasing accessibility, MSMEs stand to benefit immensely by embracing AI-driven transformation. As they integrate AI into their core functions, MSMEs are not only enhancing their own competitiveness but also contributing to the broader goal of national economic development and technological progress.

The study investigates the pivotal role of AI-based models in the management and decision-making processes of Micro, Small, and Medium Enterprises (MSMEs), revealing several practical implications. Primarily, it emphasizes AI's transformative potential in enhancing operational efficiency, particularly for MSMEs that often grapple with limited resources and workforce constraints. AI-driven tools, such as demand forecasting systems and intelligent inventory management, can automate routine tasks, streamline operations, and reduce overhead costs, thereby allowing managers to focus on strategic initiatives.

Moreover, the study highlights the enhancement of decision-making through data-driven insights. Many MSMEs traditionally rely on intuition due to a lack of real-time data analysis. AI technologies address this gap by collecting and analysing business data, providing actionable insights that empower MSME owners to make informed decisions regarding pricing, procurement, and customer targeting, ultimately reducing uncertainty and improving responsiveness to market changes.

The research also underscores AI's potential in improving customer relationship management. AI-enabled Customer Relationship Management (CRM) platforms analyse customer behaviour and preferences, enabling MSMEs to create personalized marketing strategies and foster customer loyalty. This capability, previously a competitive advantage for larger corporations, is now accessible to MSMEs through affordable AI solutions. In financial management, AI applications enhance budgeting, forecasting, and fraud detection, supporting better cash flow management and financial planning for businesses lacking in-house expertise. The predictive accuracy and compliance features of these tools help maintain financial stability and transparency.

For policymakers, the findings advocate for supportive frameworks to encourage AI adoption among MSMEs, including financial subsidies and capacity-building initiatives. Technology developers are urged to create cost-effective, user-friendly AI tools tailored to MSME needs, while educational institutions should offer specialized training programs focusing on practical AI applications in various business functions. In conclusion, the study provides a comprehensive roadmap for translating AI research into actionable strategies for MSMEs, thereby contributing to their operational excellence, competitive agility, and long-term growth.

## REFERENCES


Abaddi, S. (2025). Factors and moderators influencing artificial intelligence adoption by Jordanian MSMEs. *Management & Sustainability: An Arab Review*, *4*(1), 47–73. DOI: 10.1108/MSAR-10-2023-0049

Abdin, M. D. (2016). Role of SMEs in Asian Economies. *Role of SMEs in Asian Economies (December 23, 2016)*. https://papers.ssrn.com/sol3/papers.cfm?abstract_id=2889166

Abubakar, J. E., Yusuf, S. O., & Yusuf, P. O.Justina Eweala AbubakarSamuel Omokhafe YusufProsper Onagie Yusuf. (2025). From branding to sales conversion: How AI-Powered CRM systems shape the customer journey for African SMEs. *International Journal of Science and Research Archive*, *14*(2), 494–506. DOI: 10.30574/ijsra.2025.14.2.0369

Adel, A., Alani, N. H., & Jan, T. (2024). Factories of the future in industry 5.0—Softwarization, Servitization, and Industrialization. *Internet ofThings : Engineering Cyber Physical Human Systems*, *28*, 101431. DOI: 10.1016/j.iot.2024.101431

Ahmed, I., & Haseen, S. (2017). Growth of MSME sector and its contribution to exports of India in post reform period. *ZENITH International Journal of Business Economics & Management Research*, *7*(12), 54–65.

Ahmed, S. R.Syeda Rafina Ahmed. (2025). The Future of Artificial Intelligence in Business Management: Exploring Opportunities, Overcoming Challenges, and Shaping the Next Era of Corporate Leadership. *Journal of Information Systems Engineering & Management*, *10*(30s), 559–566. DOI: 10.52783/jisem.v10i30s.4874

Al-Hattami, H. M. (2022). Impact of AIS success on decision-making effectiveness among SMEs in less developed countries. *Information Technology for Development*, •••, 1–21. DOI: 10.1080/02681102.2022.2073325

Aldoseri, A., Al-Khalifa, K. N., & Hamouda, A. M. (2024). AI-Powered Innovation in Digital Transformation: Key Pillars and Industry Impact. *Sustainability (Basel)*, *16*(5), 1790. DOI: 10.3390/su16051790

Ali, S. (2023). *Predictive Analytics Solutions: Harnessing Data for Proactive Business Strategies*. Open Science Framework. https://doi.org/DOI: 10.31219/osf.io/gy49q

Alzebda, S., & Matar, M. A. I. (2025). Factors affecting citizen intention toward AI acceptance and adoption: The moderating role of government regulations. *Competitiveness Review*, *35*(2), 434–455. DOI: 10.1108/CR-06-2023-0144

Andrianandrianina Johanesa, T. V., Equeter, L., & Mahmoudi, S. A. (2024). Survey on AI Applications for Product Quality Control and Predictive Maintenance in Industry 4.0. *Electronics (Basel)*, *13*(5), 976. DOI: 10.3390/electronics13050976

Arroyabe, M. F., Arranz, C. F. A., Fernandez De Arroyabe, I., & Fernandez De Arroyabe, J. C. (2024). Analyzing AI adoption in European SMEs: A study of digital capabilities, innovation, and external environment. *Technology in Society*, *79*, 102733. DOI: 10.1016/j.techsoc.2024.102733

Azman, N. A., Mohamed, A., & Jamil, A. M. (2021). Artificial intelligence in automated bookkeeping: A value-added function for small and medium enterprises. *JOIV: International Journal on Informatics Visualization*, *5*(3), 224–230. DOI: 10.30630/joiv.5.3.669

Bhalla, N. (2025). Role of AI in MSMEs and Its Impact on Financial Performance and Business Sustainability. In Margaretha Van Der Poll, H., Andrew Van Der Poll, J., & Ngwakwe, C. C. (Eds.), (pp. 323–336). Advances in Finance, Accounting, and Economics. IGI Global., DOI: 10.4018/979-8-3693-6011-8.ch013

Carayannis, E. G., Dumitrescu, R., Falkowski, T., & Zota, N.-R. (2024). Empowering SMEs "Harnessing the Potential of Gen AI for Resilience and Competitiveness.". *IEEE Transactions on Engineering Management*, *71*, 14754–14774. DOI: 10.1109/TEM.2024.3456820

Chitra, M., Surianarayanan, R., Mahamuni, V. S., Mohammed, S., Keno, M. T., & Boopathi, S. (2024). Study on Cloud Computing-Empowered Small and Medium Enterprises. In Patel, R. K. (Ed.), (pp. 189–220). Advances in Business Information Systems and Analytics. IGI Global., DOI: 10.4018/979-8-3693-4227-5.ch008

Chotisarn, N., & Phuthong, T. (2025). A bibliometric analysis insights into the intellectual dynamics of artificial intelligence for the micro, small, and medium enterprises. *Cogent Business & Management*, *12*(1), 2491684. DOI: 10.1080/23311975.2025.2491684

Detesan, O.-A., & Moholea, I. F. (2024). Unimate and Beyond: Exploring the Genesis of Industrial Robotics. In Pisla, D., Carbone, G., Condurache, D., & Vaida, C. (Eds.), *Advances in Service and Industrial Robotics* (Vol. 157, pp. 263–271). Springer Nature Switzerland., DOI: 10.1007/978-3-031-59257-7_27

Ekrokpe, O. P., Jayawickrama, U., & Butun, C. (2025). Exploring the Role of Artificial Intelligence in Small and Medium Enterprises for Improved Decision-Making: A Scoping Review. In Delibašić, B., Radovanović, S., Delias, P., Liu, S., & Duarte, S. P. (Eds.), *Decision Support Systems XIV. Human-Centric Group Decision, Negotiation and Decision Support Systems for Societal Transitions* (Vol. 546, pp. 89–109). Springer Nature Switzerland., DOI: 10.1007/978-3-031-90863-7_7

Engelbrecht, A., Yitmen, I., & Almusaed, A. (2024). *Industry 4.0 Transformation Towards Industry 5.0 Paradigm-Challenges, Opportunities and Practices: Challenges*. Opportunities and Practices.

Farooq, M., Ramzan, M., & Yen, Y. Y. (2024). *Transformative Impacts of AI in Management*. IGI Global., DOI: 10.4018/979-8-3693-4322-7

Fui-Hoon Nah, F., Zheng, R., Cai, J., Siau, K., & Chen, L. (2023). Generative AI and ChatGPT: Applications, challenges, and AI-human collaboration. *Journal of Information Technology Case and Application Research, 25*(3), 277–304. DOI: 10.1080/15228053.2023.2233814

Golovianko, M., Terziyan, V., Branytskyi, V., & Malyk, D. (2023). Industry 4.0 vs. Industry 5.0: Co-existence, Transition, or a Hybrid. *Procedia Computer Science, 217*, 102–113. DOI: 10.1016/j.procs.2022.12.206

Haji, K. (2021). E-commerce development in rural and remote areas of BRICS countries. *Journal of Integrative Agriculture, 20*(4), 979–997. DOI: 10.1016/S2095-3119(20)63451-7

Halvoník, D., & Kapusta, J. (2024). Large Language Models and Rule-Based Approaches in Domain-Specific Communication. *IEEE Access : Practical Innovations, Open Solutions, 12*, 107046–107058. DOI: 10.1109/ACCESS.2024.3436902

Jain, A., Kakade, K. S., & Vispute, S. A. (2025). The Role of Artificial Intelligence (AI) in the Transformation of Small- and Medium-Sized Businesses: Challenges and Opportunities. In Dixit, S., Maurya, M., Jain, V., & Subramaniam, G. (Eds.), *Artificial Intelligence-Enabled Businesses* (1st ed., pp. 209–226). Wiley., DOI: 10.1002/9781394234028.ch12

Jha, S., & Dangwal, R. C. (2025). Actual adoption of Fintech services among micro-entrepreneurs of urban slum area of Uttarakhand. *Journal of Science and Technology Policy Management*. DOI: 10.1108/JSTPM-08-2023-0144

Kokilavizhi, S., & Amsaveni, R. (2023). Role of MSME in economic self reliance. *Sustainable developments through MSMES: a pathway to self-reliant India, 25*, 97.

Koundal, P., Bhalla, M., & Bandna. (2024). The Role of AIS in Enhancing Small Business Agility and Sustainability in Industry 5.0: In T. O. Olubiyi, S. D. Suppiah, & C. Chidoko (Eds.), *Advances in Business Strategy and Competitive Advantage* (pp. 301–330). IGI Global. DOI: 10.4018/979-8-3693-7362-0.ch012

Koundal, P., Bhalla, M., & Kailay, M. (2025). Non-financial information as a mediator in the link between accounting information systems and decision-making outcomes in SMEs: A structural equation modelling study. *International Journal of Business and Systems Research*, *1*(1), 10071211. DOI: 10.1504/IJBSR.2025.10071211

Krishnan, C., Gupta, A., Gupta, A., & Singh, G. (2022). Impact of Artificial Intelligence-Based Chatbots on Customer Engagement and Business Growth. In Hong, T.-P., Serrano-Estrada, L., Saxena, A., & Biswas, A. (Eds.), *Deep Learning for Social Media Data Analytics* (Vol. 113, pp. 195–210). Springer International Publishing., DOI: 10.1007/978-3-031-10869-3_11

Kumar, M., Raut, R. D., Mangla, S. K., Ferraris, A., & Choubey, V. K. (2024). The adoption of artificial intelligence powered workforce management for effective revenue growth of micro, small, and medium scale enterprises (MSMEs). *Production Planning and Control*, *35*(13), 1639–1655. DOI: 10.1080/09537287.2022.2131620

Le Dinh, T., Vu, M.-C., & Tran, G. T. C. (2025). Artificial Intelligence in SMEs: Enhancing Business Functions Through Technologies and Applications. *Information (Basel)*, *16*(5), 415. DOI: 10.3390/info16050415

Leng, J., Sha, W., Wang, B., Zheng, P., Zhuang, C., Liu, Q., Wuest, T., Mourtzis, D., & Wang, L. (2022). Industry 5.0: Prospect and retrospect. *Journal of Manufacturing Systems*, *65*, 279–295. DOI: 10.1016/j.jmsy.2022.09.017

Lewandowska, A., Berniak-Woźny, J., & Ahmad, N. (2023). Competitiveness and innovation of small and medium enter-prises under Industry 4.0 and 5.0 challenges: A comprehensive bibliometric analysis. *Equilibrium. Quarterly Journal of Economics and Economic Policy*, *18*(4), 1045–1074. DOI: 10.24136/eq.2023.033

Lim, T. K., & Seng, L. W. (2024). Determinants Of Artificial Intelligence Adoption In Accounting Among Malaysia Small And Medium-Sized Enterprises. *Journal of Accounting* [JABM]. *Business and Management*, *32*(1), 90. DOI: 10.31966/jabminternational.v32i1.1456

Luger, G. F. (2025). Computing, Representations, and Definitions of Artificial Intelligence. In G. F. Luger, *Artificial Intelligence: Principles and Practice* (pp. 27–49). Springer Nature Switzerland. DOI: 10.1007/978-3-031-57437-5_2

Madanchian, M. (2024). The Impact of Artificial Intelligence Marketing on E-Commerce Sales. *Systems, 12*(10), 429. DOI: 10.3390/systems12100429

Martínez-Peláez, R., Escobar, M. A., Félix, V. G., Ostos, R., Parra-Michel, J., García, V., Ochoa-Brust, A., Velarde-Alvarado, P., Félix, R. A., Olivares-Bautista, S., Flores, V., & Mena, L. J. (2024). Sustainable Digital Transformation for SMEs: A Comprehensive Framework for Informed Decision-Making. *Sustainability (Basel), 16*(11), 4447. DOI: 10.3390/su16114447

Martinravi, C. P., & Krishnasamy, K. (2025). Unleashing the potential of MSMEs in India: A strategic analysis. *Journal of the International Council for Small Business, 6*(1), 123–143. DOI: 10.1080/26437015.2024.2397664

Mourtzis, D., Angelopoulos, J., & Panopoulos, N. (2022). A Literature Review of the Challenges and Opportunities of the Transition from Industry 4.0 to Society 5.0. *Energies, 15*(17), 6276. DOI: 10.3390/en15176276

Muchie, M., & Bekele, E. (2009). *Promoting micro, small and medium Enterprises (MSMEs) for sustainable rural Livelihood.* https://vbn.aau.dk/files/17023673/DIIPER_wp_11.pdf

Naidoo, P., & Sibanda, M. (2024). Emerging Trends and Future Directions of the Industrial Internet of Things. In Odhiambo, M. O., & Mwashita, W. (Eds.), *From Internet of Things to Internet of Intelligence* (pp. 91–110). Springer Nature Switzerland., DOI: 10.1007/978-3-031-55718-7_5

Nandeeswariah, K., & Ramana, A. V. (2021). Status And Growth Of Micro, Small & Medium Enterprises (Msmes) Post Msmed 2006 Act Implimentation In India. *Turkish Online Journal of Qualitative Inquiry, 12*(6). https://search.ebscohost.com/login.aspx?direct=true&profile=ehost&scope=site&authtype=crawler&jrnl=13096591&AN=160450965&h=MGhWcU20uszmDPKHnmSMigr79bkuhUIJ2mZ0cekf7infNX2lLb4QVL4w5z4W9g2KCqjFOy3ovDncKQJ1yuU2Sw%3D%3D&crl=c

Panigrahi, R. R., Shrivastava, A. K., Qureshi, K. M., Mewada, B. G., Alghamdi, S. Y., Almakayeel, N., Almuflih, A. S., & Qureshi, M. R. N. (2023). AI Chatbot Adoption in SMEs for Sustainable Manufacturing Supply Chain Performance: A Mediational Research in an Emerging Country. *Sustainability (Basel), 15*(18), 13743. DOI: 10.3390/su151813743

Perrotta, C., & Selwyn, N. (2020). Deep learning goes to school: Toward a relational understanding of AI in education. *Learning, Media and Technology, 45*(3), 251–269. DOI: 10.1080/17439884.2020.1686017

Rahaman, M., Putra, K. T., Irawan, B., & Biyanto, T. R. (2025). Industrial Evolution: The Integration of AI in Robotics and Drone Systems. In Gupta, B. B., & Colace, F. (Eds.), (pp. 85–114). Advances in Computational Intelligence and Robotics. IGI Global., DOI: 10.4018/979-8-3693-2707-4.ch005

Rane, N., Paramesha, M., Choudhary, S., & Rane, J. (2024). Artificial Intelligence in Sales and Marketing: Enhancing Customer Satisfaction, Experience and Loyalty. SSRN *Electronic Journal*. DOI: 10.2139/ssrn.4831903

Sahoo, P., & Ashwani, . (2020). COVID-19 and Indian Economy: Impact on Growth, Manufacturing, Trade and MSME Sector. *Global Business Review*, *21*(5), 1159–1183. DOI: 10.1177/0972150920945687

Sahu, C. K., & Panda, R. K. (2024). Evaluating the relationship between entrepreneurial ecosystem, resilience and SME performance in post-pandemic period. *Journal of Entrepreneurship and Public Policy*, *13*(3), 491–506. DOI: 10.1108/JEPP-12-2023-0136

Santos, A. D. M., & Sant'Anna, Â. M. O. (2024). Industry 4.0 technologies for sustainability within small and medium enterprises: A systematic literature review and future directions. *Journal of Cleaner Production*, *467*, 143023. DOI: 10.1016/j.jclepro.2024.143023

Santosa, A. D., & Surgawati, I. (2024). Artificial Intelligence (AI) Adoption as Marketing Tools among Micro, Small, and Medium Enterprises (MSMEs) in Indonesia. *Jurnal Sosial Humaniora*, *17*(1), 91. DOI: 10.12962/j24433527.v17i1.20520

Singh, A. K., Taterh, S., Kaushik, A., & Goswami, A. (2025). The Role of AI in Digital Transformation. In Misra, S., Kaushik, M., Jain, A., & Banerjee, C. (Eds.), (pp. 109–136). Advances in Computational Intelligence and Robotics. IGI Global., DOI: 10.4018/979-8-3693-8009-3.ch006

Singh, D., Khamba, J. S., & Nanda, T. (2018). Problems and prospects of Indian MSMEs: A literature review. *International Journal of Business Excellence*, *15*(2), 129. DOI: 10.1504/IJBEX.2018.091923

Singh, P. (2025). AI and Financial Risk Management Revolutionizing Risk Assessment and Mitigation. In Derbali, A. M. S. (Ed.), (pp. 373–404). Advances in Computational Intelligence and Robotics. IGI Global., DOI: 10.4018/979-8-3373-1200-2.ch019

Van Der Vlist, F., Helmond, A., & Ferrari, F. (2024). Big AI: Cloud infrastructure dependence and the industrialisation of artificial intelligence. *Big Data & Society*, *11*(1), 20539517241232630. DOI: 10.1177/20539517241232630

Wamba-Taguimdje, S.-L., Fosso Wamba, S., Kala Kamdjoug, J. R., & Tchatchouang Wanko, C. E. (2020). Influence of artificial intelligence (AI) on firm performance: The business value of AI-based transformation projects. *Business Process Management Journal, 26*(7), 1893–1924. DOI: 10.1108/BPMJ-10-2019-0411

## KEY TERMS AND DEFINITION

**Artificial Intelligence (AI):** Artificial Intelligence (AI) is a computer science field that enhances human intelligence by developing systems capable of learning, reasoning, problem-solving, and decision-making. It significantly improves operational efficiency, automates repetitive processes, enhances quality control, and enables predictive maintenance in various industrial sectors.

**AI based Models:** AI-based models, using machine learning, deep learning, and natural language processing, are computational systems designed to perform tasks by learning from data. They identify patterns, predict outcomes, and support complex decision-making processes in industrial applications, enhancing efficiency, reducing costs, and gaining a competitive edge.

**Business Management:** Business management involves planning, organizing, directing, and controlling an organization's resources to achieve defined objectives efficiently. It covers areas like operations, finance, marketing, and human resources, aiming for smooth performance, strategic decision-making, and long-term growth, enabling firms to respond to market demands and maintain competitive advantage.

**Decision Making:** Decision making is the cognitive and analytical process of selecting the best course of action to achieve organizational goals. It involves identifying problems, evaluating solutions, and choosing actions based on data, experience, and strategic priorities. Effective decision making is crucial for resource allocation, risk management, operational efficiency, and long-term success.

**Digital Transformation:** Digital Transformation is the strategic integration of digital technologies into an organization, transforming operations, customer value, and market dynamics. It uses technologies like cloud computing, AI, big data, and IoT to improve processes, enhance customer experiences, and drive innovation, especially in industrial settings.

**Industry 4.0:** Industry 4.0 is the fourth industrial revolution, integrating digital technologies into industrial processes. It combines cyber-physical systems, IoT, AI, big data analytics, and cloud computing to create smart, autonomous production environments, enhancing operational efficiency, real-time monitoring, and predictive maintenance.

**Industry 5.0:** Industry 5.0 is the next industrial development focusing on human-computer collaboration to create personalized, sustainable, and human-centric production systems. It integrates human creativity with advanced technologies like artificial intelligence, robotics, and IoT, aiming to improve customization, social responsibility, and resilience in manufacturing environments.

**MSMEs:** Micro, Small, and Medium Enterprises (MSMEs) are businesses with significant investment in plant and machinery, and annual turnover. They contribute significantly to economic development by generating employment, fostering innovation, and industrial output. Recognized for their flexibility, MSMEs operate in various sectors, particularly in developing countries, driving inclusive and sustainable growth.

Chapter 6

# AI-Powered Growth: Unlocking Opportunities and Navigating Challenges for Micro, Small, and Medium Enterprises


**Usha Prabhu**
http://orcid.org/0000-0001-6219-5358
*Jain University, India*

**Varanasi Rahul**
http://orcid.org/0000-0003-2407-7654
*Jain University, India*

**G. Srividhya**
http://orcid.org/0000-0002-5216-546X
*Jain University, India*

**Y. Fathima**
http://orcid.org/0000-0002-0045-1421
*Jain University, India*

**G. Laxmana Rao**
http://orcid.org/0000-0002-7911-7927
*Dayananda Sagar University, India*



## ABSTRACT

*AI in MSMEs is transforming worldwide business by boosting operational efficiency, creativity, and inclusive economic growth. AI technologies, including machine learning, natural language processing, and predictive analytics, assist MSMEs in automating processes, simplifying value chains, customising customer interactions, and leveraging alternative financing. AIaaS, subscription-based, and data-driven*



DOI: 10.4018/979-8-3373-2817-1.ch006

*business models are developed to enable resource-constrained MSMEs to compete in the digital economy. The chapter notes budget constraints, lack of digital infrastructure, human resource skill gaps, and organisational aversion to technology despite its revolutionary promise. Theories like TOE and DOI identify leadership, policy support, and innovation ecosystems as AI preparedness success factors. Case studies in India, Indonesia, and Jordan recommend digital literacy, localised AI technologies, ethical data governance, and cooperative tactics to boost MSME AI deployments.*

## 1 INTRODUCTION

Micro, Small, and Medium-sized Enterprises (MSMEs) are crucial for economic growth, as they enable innovation, create employment opportunities, and contribute to the rise of the gross domestic product. These businesses contribute to the industrialisation of the nation, reduce regional inequalities, and enhance entrepreneurial activities, particularly in developing economies (Kumar et al., 2024). Distributors and suppliers are Micro, Small, and Medium-sized Enterprises (MSMEs), and therefore, enable large industries to become more flexible in response to various economic influences and shocks (Shakya et al., 2023). The gaps can be addressed by Micro, Small, and Medium-sized Enterprises (MSMEs), which can provide access to financial inclusion and skill development for socially marginalised groups, fostering inclusive economic growth (Patil et al., 2023). Economic growth is also sustained by small, medium, and micro enterprises (MSMEs).

Micro, small, and medium-sized enterprises (MSMEs) are significant contributors to the overall economic development, as they generate employment, promote innovation, and help increase the country's gross domestic product. MSMEs industrialise, reduce spatial inequalities, and enhance entrepreneurial activity, especially in economies that have not been fully developed (Kumar et al., 2024). In this manner, micro, small, and medium-sized enterprises need to gain long-term growth and stability.

The AI can revolutionise the MSME sector by automating company processes, increasing customer interactions, and making data-driven decisions. As an illustration, AI chatbots will be very beneficial in facilitating sales and business operations through automating customer care and promotional activities. It is well established that the use of AI enhances sales and ensures business sustainability by optimising information analysis and automating customer interactions (Khaq et al., 2024). Additionally, AI can help MSMEs incorporate sustainable practices into their operations, such as AI-driven marketing and ethical branding, which will positively impact the process of building consumer confidence and loyalty (Waruwu et al., 2023). However, insufficiency of resources is one of the challenges that hinder the adoption of AI in the manufacturing MSMEs in India. Nevertheless, AI is also being viewed as an engine of growth in the textile, machinery, and food products industries (Kumar et al., 2024).

Industries are changing through Artificial Intelligence (AI), which maximises efficiency, automation, and decision-making. Medical AI, along with AI in banking, production, and retail, is transforming businesses by utilising technologies such as machine learning, natural language processing, and robotics. Artificial Intelligence (AI) is transforming the operations of businesses through the optimisation of efficiency, decision-making, and consumer contact. The use of AI is unavoidable in terms of digital market competitiveness for Micro, Small, and Medium Enterprises (MSMEs) (Abaddi, 2025). Given that AI-based solutions, including chat systems, predictive analytics, and automation, maximise efficiencies, reduce costs, and improve customer interactions, they are maximised (Khaq et al., 2024). The evolution of AI at all levels will drive economic growth, revolutionise the employment market, and enhance global connectivity through its applications in various industries.

The adoption of AI requires institutional and governmental support. Manufacturers and governments should implement economic incentives, educational systems, and information systems to enhance the use of AI by MSMEs (Khaq et al., 2024). Secondly, MSMEs should become more AI literate in order to use the technology and optimise their processes and competitiveness (Ilham & Muawwal, 2024).

## 2 EVOLUTION OF AI-DRIVEN MSME ECOSYSTEMS

Micro, Small, and Medium-sized Enterprises (MSMEs) are integral to global economies, making significant contributions to employment, innovation, and GDP in developing nations. Artificial Intelligence (AI) adoption by MSMEs has catalysed transformation, altering their operations, competitive strategies, and growth trajectories. As AI ecosystems mature, MSMEs are equipped with robust tools that were once the monopoly of large-scale corporations. These tools help automate processes, drive data-driven decisions, and provide customised services.

### 2.1 Stages in the Evolution of AI-Driven MSME Ecosystems

1. **Early Adoption and Technological Foundations:** The early wave of AI adoption in MSMEs revolved primarily around fundamental automation and operational tools like chatbots, CRM solutions, and predictive analytics. These were used to enhance customer interaction and internal process efficiencies, but tended to get implemented in a siloed, ad hoc manner because digital infrastructure development and capabilities were limited. The availability of affordable cloud

computing and SaaS services marked a watershed moment, enabling AI for smaller businesses (Basole & Accenture, 2021). Governments and NGOs in nations such as Indonesia and India have begun to support MSMEs by providing AI-based training and financing to enhance AI preparedness across all sectors (Budiraharjo et al., 2024).

2. **Integrating Open Innovation into Business Models:** AI was integrated into core business models as MSMEs became more digitally advanced. AI-powered systems now facilitate real-time inventory management, consumer segmentation, fraud protection, and cash flow forecasting. The innovation ecosystem also began to encompass multiple parties, including platform providers, fintech start-ups, and local tech partners. In China's fashion industry, MSMEs are adopting AI to facilitate open innovation, utilising knowledge assimilation and collaborative approaches, which significantly enhances sustainability and productivity (Qu & Kim, 2025). Jordanian MSMEs demonstrate a strong relationship between AI autonomy, perceived usefulness, and innovativeness, highlighting the strategic value of AI in competitive markets (Abaddi, 2025).
3. **Human-AI Collaboration and Financial Management:** The evolution has shifted from automation to collaboration between human intelligence and machine learning. This entails optimising decision-making in financial management, increasing transparency, and redefining workforce roles. AI tools optimise budgeting, financial planning, and real-time analytics, with human efforts dedicated to strategic oversight (Tarwiyah et al., 2023). The AI-based Accounting Information System (AIS) has provided greater transparency in decision-making, enhancing performance and compliance within MSMEs (Musdalifah & Hariyanto, 2024).
4. **Technological Problems:** Disadvantages are insufficient digital infrastructure and digital illiteracy, coupled with the shortage of a skilled workforce (Budiraharjo et al., 2024).
5. **Data Privacy and Ethics:** The ethical consideration of the processing of separate consumer or financial data by AI networks is an issue that raises concerns in relation to the ethical aspect, requiring more stringent governance measures (Shvetsova, 2024). Expenses and Extensibility: The installation remains expensive, and alternatives are not available, which makes it less scalable, especially for MSMEs with limited financial means in rural or underdeveloped regions (Khaq et al., 2024). MSMEs ecosystems are not isolated, but they co-evolve with individuals, institutions and technology. Through effective support systems, MSME ecosystems can foster new growth, innovation, and resilience among MSMEs worldwide.

## 3 THEORETICAL FRAMEWORK: AI ADOPTION LIFECYCLE IN MSMES

The introduction of artificial intelligence (AI) in micro, small, and medium enterprises (MSMEs) has transformed how enterprises utilise AI to deliver organisational outputs, improve competitiveness, and drive growth. Some of the impacts of deploying artificial intelligence (AI) technology will include automating processes, improving decision-making, and optimising resource utilisation.

Organisational preparedness, technical infrastructure, and external support should be in place to implement artificial intelligence in the micro, small, and medium enterprise industry. The Technology-Organisation-Environment (TOE) framework (Figure 1) by Tornatzky and Fleischer (1990) and the Diffusion of Innovations theory by Rogers (2003) make good theoretical foundations for research on the adoption of artificial intelligence.

Here are several phases making up the lifecycle of micro, small, and medium-sized enterprises (MSMEs). Their phases are based on three factors: organisational (firm size, leadership commitment, workforce skills), technical (perceived usefulness, ease of integration), and environmental (government support, industry competitiveness, vendor partnerships). Micro, Small, and Medium-sized Enterprises (MSMEs) typically become aware of the capabilities of artificial intelligence (AI) and try out a comparatively small range of applications, gradually implementing AI technology to achieve their strategic objectives. Specifically, Goyal et al. (2018) and Gupta & Sharma (2020) state that the lifespan is iterative and developed in response to the changing requirements of the enterprise and the evolution of ecosystems. An illustration of the theory is presented in the following figure.

*Figure 1. Technology-Organisation-Environment (TOE) framework*

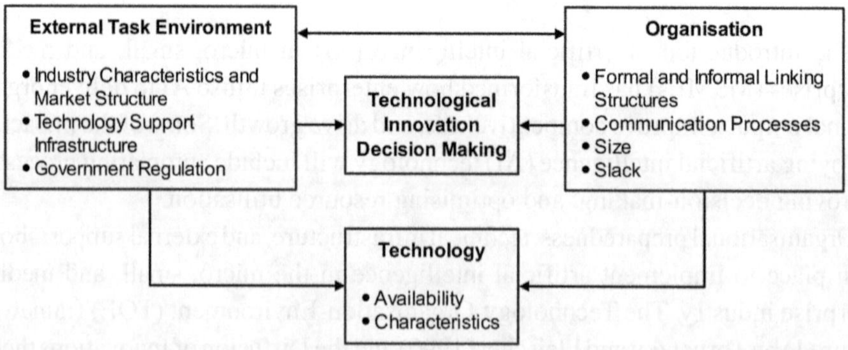


*Source: https://www.researchgate.net/publication/226145805_The_Technology-Organization-Environment_Framework*

Micro, small, and medium-sized enterprises (MSMEs) often lack access to basic capital, human resources, and office space. Therefore, resources accessible to large companies are available to many people (Goyal et al., 2018). According to recent research, the ability of small and medium-sized enterprises (SMEs) to improve financial inclusivity, customer interaction and internal operations by embracing AI practices has been confirmed. Technology powered by Artificial Intelligence can assist small and medium-sized enterprises (SMEs) in cutting costs and enhancing efficiency in inventory management, predictive maintenance and targeted marketing. Additionally, systems based on Artificial Intelligence and credit analysis are expanding capital access to small businesses with poor credit histories (Jain et al., 2021). Although these advantages are present, several obstacles hinder the widespread adoption of artificial intelligence. Part of these issues is the problem of data privacy, a shortage of labour with appropriate skills, and other implementation expenses. According to NASCOM (2023) and Deloitte (2023), the industry is expected to undergo a radical digitisation revolution, facilitated by legislators and the broader availability of artificial intelligence technologies.

## 4 OPPORTUNITIES OF AI FOR MSMES: UNLOCKING POTENTIAL FOR GROWTH AND COMPETITIVENESS

Artificial Intelligence (AI) does not require big companies with significant budgets. Rather, it is beginning to transform its use in Micro, Small, and Medium Enterprises (MSMEs). AI continues to transform industries by driving automation, providing practical insights, enhancing resource optimisation, and providing business opportunities to explore. As MSMEs continue to face rising pressures of competition and changing consumer demands, they have a chance to realise innovations, strengthen operational efficiencies, and succeed in the digital era (Patil et al., 2023).

1. **Repetitive Workloads:** AI significantly decreases the routine and monotony workload of MSMES, enhancing production and efficiency by automating repetitive tasks. The examples of tasks that AI solutions, such as chatbots, intelligent data systems, and document management, handle daily are not the only examples of daily activities that AI solutions manage (Banerjee, B., 2023). As Shakya et al. (2023) and Khaq et al. (2024) note, the technologies can help streamline work, decrease the time it takes to respond to customers, and minimise the occurrence of human error. Incidentally, human resource continuity is achieved (such as by sorting invoice data and automating payroll using AI-assisted software) (Sharma et al., 2022). Khaq et al. (2024) state that AI is used to enable small businesses to grow, offering twenty-four-hour customer service and automated operations.
2. **Supply Chain Optimisation:** AI optimises supply chains to MSMEs by automating the supply chain, such as demand forecasting, inventory management, and logistics planning. AI models study the sales of the past and the history of the market to predict the demand accordingly and, therefore, reduce the cases of stockouts and overstocking, as well as assist companies to ensure the optimal level of inventory (Daraojimba, R. E., & Igbokwe, J. C., 2024; Kumar & Shukla, 2024). These efficiencies lower operational costs and enhance client satisfaction. Furthermore, AI assists in enhancing logistics by analysing traffic and delivery routes, providing MSMEs with opportunities to design more cost-effective and efficient delivery routes. Utilising AI in supply chains will enable them to be more responsive and sustainable, allowing MSMEs to meet their needs more quickly, with fewer delays and a reduced environmental footprint (Joel et al., 2024).
3. **Business Process Reengineering (BPR):** Business Process Reengineering attempts to remodel and re-imagine business processes in order to achieve better performance. This is because AI-driven Business Process Reengineering has the potential to benefit MSMEs greatly by automating and simplifying labour-intensive processes (Banerjee, B., 2023). The AI will be able to identify processes, pinpoint inefficiencies, and suggest optimisation methods. Invoicing, stock management, and data management can be automated, which will contribute to increased efficiency and redirect funds toward corporate growth (Guillen & Lim, 2023).

4. **Predictive AI-based Decision-Making Augmented:** AI will improve the decision-making process of MSMEs, including the delivery of data-driven insights and predictive analytics. In small businesses, it is common to struggle with making informed decisions due to a lack of reliable and credible data and market insights. AI applications combine data from various sources, such as customer behaviour, market trends, and financials and process it to deliver actionable information. As an illustration, AI-driven technologies are capable of identifying patterns in consumer behaviour, and therefore, companies can identify which products or services are trending and which are not. Upon receiving such information, MSMEs can formulate data-driven plans for product development, marketing, and pricing strategies (Udeogu, U. et al., 2024). AI-powered analytics

In addition to risk management, forecasting potential challenges and disruptions is essential. It can identify trends that indicate possible problems, including delays in the supply chain, fluctuating demand in the market, or altered customer behaviour. Therefore, businesses would be able to foresee risks before they occur. Using AI to inform decision-making can help MSMEs develop strategic plans, make more accurate forecasts, and make more informed decisions that have long-term consequences.

5. **Tailored Customer interaction:** Customer interaction is the most important activity to be carried out by MSMEs, especially in competitive industries. This can be enhanced with the help of AI, which will provide a personalised experience through chatbots, recommendations, and sentiment analysis, leading to a higher level of happiness and loyalty (Banerjee, 2023). Conversations between AI-based chatbots and their customers are based on natural language; therefore, they help to understand the questions and provide relevant and individualised answers, thereby improving the quality of the services. Recommendation tools review the history of customer records, such as purchases and browsing history, to offer customised recommendations based on individual preferences, enhancing customer engagement and sales (Banerjee, 2023).
6. **Financial Inclusion and Fraud Mitigation:** Financial access by MSMEs continues to be a challenge, and to a greater extent, those operating in the developing economies. By employing alternative forms of evaluation that diverge from traditional past approaches, AI can be leveraged to drive financial inclusivity (Dwivedi et al., 2020). AI systems utilise additional data, such as transaction history, social media usage, and utility bill payments, to assess creditworthiness and provide more MSMEs with access to formal financial services that were previously unavailable (Dwivedi et al., 2020). AI also accelerates the process of detecting fraud in real-time by establishing an overarching perspective on

financial transactions to identify suspicious transactions, protect assets, and secure transactions (Dwivedi et al., 2020).

7. **Developing the culture of Innovation in Business Models:** AI can assist MSMEs to embrace business models that previously were impossible to implement. A good example is the application of AI to create subscriptions that enable organisations to provide services over the long term, thereby generating a steady stream of revenue. It is frequently applied in software, Internet and entertainment transactions (Hariyanti, S., & Kristanti, D., 2024).

## 5 CHALLENGES AND BARRIERS TO AI ADOPTION IN MSME

Artificial intelligence (AI) is transforming the industry to become more productive, make informed decisions, enhance customer relationships, and achieve cost-effectiveness. The economies of most countries, especially those of developing nations, are comprised of Micro, Small, and Medium-sized Enterprises (MSMEs), which have enormous potential to leverage artificial intelligence. Micro, small, and medium enterprises can be assisted by artificial intelligence to automate their business processes, customise their interaction with consumers, streamline their supply chain and make more predictions. The adoption of AI within MSMEs has been slow, despite its high potential.

Financial constraints are one of the significant issues of MSMEs. In comparison to large organisations with established capital and revenue bases, MSMEs typically possess constrained operating funds and tend to focus on meeting immediate functional demands rather than undertaking long-range strategic initiatives, including AI. The fact that AI tools are costly to purchase, require consultants, and necessitate system maintenance constitutes a significant demerit. Another issue is that Indian manufacturing MSMEs have minimal financial resources, which do not allow them to invest in more modern technologies like AI and Machine Learning (ML), despite understanding the benefits they are missing in terms of productivity and cost reduction (Kumar, S., 2024). According to Indonesian MSMEs, high set-up costs have been the leading discouraging factor, despite over 70 per cent of AI adopters experiencing a rise in operating performance and improved sales performance (Khaq et al., 2024). High setup costs as the primary deterrent, despite more than 70% of AI adopters perceiving increased operating efficiency and improvements in sales performance (Khaq et al., 2024).

Cost is a prevalent deficiency in the technological infrastructure of most MSME-dominated areas. Access to sufficient internet connectivity, cloud computing, and data-processing capacity is often lacking, especially in rural or semi-urban areas, which are home to the majority of MSMEs. This digital disconnect exacerbates the challenge of integrating AI systems that rely on near-instant data processing, cloud computing, and seamless system integration. In Jordan, enabling conditions such as access to stable digital infrastructure had a significant impact on MSMEs' willingness to adopt AI, with companies citing infrastructure deficiencies as a central challenge (Abaddi, 2025).

Even with infrastructure, MSMEs generally lack the human capital to lead and manage AI deployment. Digital and technical human capital deficiencies among MSMEs are perhaps the most frequently reported hurdles to AI uptake worldwide. AI deployment requires workers with data analysis, machine learning, coding, and algorithmic thinking skills—capabilities that are often unavailable in MSMEs, particularly in emerging markets. Small enterprises struggle to recruit and retain talent due to competition from larger enterprises, which often offer more competitive pay and career development opportunities. Researchers in Malaysia, for example, found that levels of digital skills among workers played a significant moderating role in AI uptake; organisations whose workers were digitally literate had a better chance of adopting AI-related technologies (Wong & Yap, 2024).

Perceptions of AI as complicated, opaque, or high-risk also pose significant obstacles to uptake. Most MSME owners are sceptical about tangible returns from AI, especially if their effects are not transparent or easily measurable. Perceptions of risks in Jordan, such as fear of cybersecurity breaches, misuse of data, and system failures, reduced perceived AI usefulness, discouraging business people from pursuing the use despite appreciating promising returns (Abaddi, 2025). Uncertainty over standardisation and transparency in AI integration channels complicates matters further, with many MSMEs choosing to "wait and watch" rather than take early action.

Another pivotal factor is the absence of strategic vision and support from top management. Leadership within MSMEs tends to focus on day-to-day operations, leaving little time or bandwidth for long-term digital transformation planning. AI initiatives fail to gain internal traction without a strong, innovation-driven vision from the top. The importance of leadership was highlighted in studies from Malaysia and Indonesia, where enterprises with active top management support exhibited higher AI adoption rates (Lim & Seng, 2024; Wulandari & Diko, 2024). Moreover, AI implementation often falters without clear internal champions due to misalignment with organisational goals or a lack of coordination across departments.

A lesser visibility but no less important obstacle is that of data quality and availability. AI works on vast amounts of clean, consistent, and well-organised data. However, MSMEs often have no systematic means of data collection or even digitised records. Poor or patchy information curbs AI model performance and can lead to suboptimal decision-making. Indian manufacturing was mentioned to highlight a lack of access to standardised data systems as a central operating bottleneck that undermines the promise of AI-driven predictive modelling and automation (Kumar,

S., 2024). Data privacy concerns and the fear of non-compliance with privacy laws can also deter enterprises from adopting AI, particularly when it involves customer details or payment information.

Organisational, cultural, and psychological resistance also underlie the sluggish adaptation of AI. Employees of some MSMEs and even owners fear that AI could displace jobs, reduce autonomy, or make them overly dependent on impersonal systems(Eyo-Udo, N. (2024). Resistance to change has been mentioned in various studies as a more significant obstacle than technical feasibility or costs. Even with demonstrated gains by AI in recruitment and process standardisation in Indonesian HR activities, many organisations were apprehensive about entrusting major decision-making to algorithms (Wulandari & Diko, 2024). Likewise, in AI-human collaborative settings, such as robot-assisted production, MSMEs are delayed due to uncertainty regarding workforce retraining, job reassignments, and ethical considerations (Shakya et al., 2023).

Institutional support, or the lack thereof, also plays a significant role in determining the uptake of AI. MSMEs require exposure to policy environments, subsidies, training programs, and incubators to become AI-driven enterprises. Proactive countries with appropriate policies have exhibited better AI adoption in Jordan and Malaysia. Government offerings of incentives and regulations, brought about by clarity, have positively affected AI uptake, with uncertainty regarding ROI or compliance issues being especially relevant for such enterprises (Wong & Yap, 2024; Abaddi, 2025). However, in areas with a lack of support from governments or with poorly targeted support, MSMES are left to figure things out on their own, often resulting in failed or stalled endeavours.

One underappreciated hurdle is a lack of a clearly defined ROI for AI projects in MSMES. Most companies struggle with measuring the economic benefits of adopting AI, particularly since the effects do not manifest immediately or are obscured by the sheer complexity of deployment. With no documented examples of successes that specifically relate to their industry scope and organisation, MSMES are reluctant to commit resources to AI. The limited use of customised AI solutions, focusing just on MSME procedures, also fosters this hesitance. Pre-packaged AI solutions typically cater to large corporations, whereas adapting these for MSME operations is both time-consuming and costly (Amponsah et al., 2025).

## 6 STRATEGIES TO OVERCOME AI ADOPTION CHALLENGES IN MSMES

Artificial Intelligence (AI) could transform Micro, Small, and Medium-sized Enterprises (MSMEs) into highly competitive players by optimising their performance, customer relationships, and profitability. Conversely, there is minimal usage of artificial intelligence within the business because a hurdle has always existed due to a lack of funds, technology capability, infrastructure, and strategy (Eyo-Udo, N., 2024). These barriers have been widely documented for a long time. To implement artificial intelligence technology effectively, there is a need to research viable methods that micro, small, and medium-sized enterprises (MSMEs) may implement.

One of the most effective ways to overcome the barriers hindering the widespread adoption of artificial intelligence is to enhance financial aid programs. High implementation costs form one of the most common barriers that micro, small, and medium-sized enterprises (MSMEs) encounter, particularly when they have limited budgets and few financial options (Eyo-Udo, N. 2024). A substantial probability exists that the entry barrier could be overcome by granting financial incentives, such as grants, subsidies, and low-interest funds, specifically for AI implementation purposes. In Indonesia, for example, government financial support has proven to play a significant role in prompting MSMEs to implement AI-driven marketing instruments, such as chatbots and predictive analytics (Khaq et al., 2024).

One of the significant challenges that MSMEs face is the low level of AI literacy among employees and business owners. Most companies lack employees who can implement or support AI systems, and also lack the funds to employ specialised experts. Hence, sector-specific training sessions, mentorships, and qualification courses on using AI in business can create in-house capacities. In Malaysia, the availability of digital skills development programs was found to have a highly significant increase in the readiness of MSMEs in the accounting sector to adopt AI (Wong & Yap, 2024).

MSMEs often operate in areas with limited or no internet accessibility. Policymaking should, therefore, address investments in upgrading digital infrastructure so that even rural MSMEs can utilise cloud-enabled AI systems. In Indonesia, a readiness framework called the AIRI (AI Readiness Indicator) was created to assist MSMEs in recognising infrastructural deficits and applying targeted measures to address them accordingly. It was revealed in the study that once the MSMEs realised their levels of readiness, they were better placed to adopt AI tools in line with their stage of maturity (Budiraharjo et al., 2024).

Leadership also plays a determinant role in AI uptake. Top management directly contributes to aligning the digital transformation agenda and allocating resources. Encouraging a leadership culture of innovation, flexibility, and strategic thinking is paramount. Jordanian studies have shown that companies with visionary leaders who have incorporated AI as a central component of their business strategy are far more likely to adopt AI, especially when supplemented by a culture of organisational innovation (Abaddi, 2025).

Addressing resistance to change is also crucial. Organisational change management techniques, such as workshops, communications strategies, and employee participation in technology planning, can address fears of job displacement or disruptions to operations (Wong & Yap, 2024). In Jordan, companies that involved employees in the decision-making process around AI in a proactive manner experienced better buy-in and easier transitions (Abaddi, 2025). Learning a culture of experimentation—that small-scale pilot efforts are supported and encouraged—will also likely minimise the likelihood of the program causing an adverse reaction and facilitate incremental incorporation of AI without overwhelming the company.(Eyo-Udo, N. (2024).

Another primary tactic is utilising partnerships and ecosystems. MSMEs typically lack the internal capabilities to deploy AI, but can benefit from partnering with universities, AI vendors, or innovation centres. These alliances can provide MSMEs with something as simple as technology demonstrations, collaborative research, and even mutual talent pools. In India, manufacturing MSMEs that had entered these types of partnerships were more likely to apply AI tools in quality control, processes, and predictive maintenance (Wong & Yap, 2024).

Creating simplified and accessible AI capabilities is another crucial step. MSMEs do not require enterprise-class AI systems, but can benefit more from more manageable, low-cost solutions tailored to their specific needs. AI-driven, cloud-based systems featuring drag-and-drop UIS, automated insights, and scalable pricing can significantly reduce barriers to entry. Promoting the development of localised AI work in areas like retail, logistics, agriculture, or finance provides context and uptake. In one Indonesian case, AI-enabled recruitment and SOP automation tools significantly enhanced the work processes of MSMEs while maintaining cost-effectiveness and ease of navigation (Wulandari & Diko, 2024).

Most MSMEs are reluctant to embrace AI due to the lack of tangible ROI or uncertainty of the outcomes. Promoting real-case studies, success stories, and benchmark reports demystifies AI and emphasises its business utility. India and Malaysia studies highlight the necessity of sectoral case evidence in persuading MSME owner-entrepreneurs to adopt AI. Emphasising measurable outcomes, such as increased sales, productivity, or improved customer retention, can convince reluctant adopters (Patil et al., 2023; Lim & Seng, 2024).

Regulations and policies must also provide support to complement internal measures. Government policies must develop AI roadmaps tailored to MSMEs that incorporate ethical frameworks, data governance, and incentives for innovation. Regulations that facilitate data sharing, cloud usage, and cybersecurity norms will reassure enterprises concerned about data abuse or compliance breaches. MSMEs in Jordan, for instance, had better AI adoption intentions in the presence of explicit policies and regulatory frameworks (Abaddi, 2025).

Another crucial approach is for MSMEs to know their current technological maturity, organisational culture, and available resources. Frameworks such as the AIRI framework in Indonesia help MSMES identify gaps and measure improvements. Hence, the integration of AI is more systematic and outcome-focused (Budiraharjo et al., 2024). Above all, innovation-conducive environments need to be encouraged. MSMES that conceptualise AI not as a mere technology but as an innovation driver are more likely to thrive in the future. Integrating AI into the company's business model—such as leveraging it to create new products, tailor-made services, or forecast market trends—will likely generate enduring competitive advantages. Malaysian research emphasises the mediating role of innovation culture in the effects of AI technologies on business performance (Budiraharjo et al., 2024).

## 6.1 AI Business Models for MSMEs- Empowering Growth in the Digital Economy

Artificial Intelligence (AI) is revolutionising the business operations of Micro, Small, and Medium Enterprises (MSMEs). With minimal resources, these small businesses can utilise AI-based solutions to compete, become more efficient, and innovative, which mass companies could only offer until recently. Artificial intelligence enhances procedures, establishing innovative business methods that promote growth and long-term sustainability. In this section, the paper will discuss various AI business models that are transforming MSMEs, providing them with the tools and techniques necessary to succeed in a digital economy (Sinuhaji, F. G., et al., 2024). The most common examples are:

1. **The AI-as-a-Service (AIaaS) model:** It offers MSMEs AI-based services, such as predictive analytics, natural language processing, and computer vision, on either a pay-per-use or subscription policy. The model also eliminates the need for significant initial investment and infrastructure, making it an option available to companies with limited resources (Goyal et al., 2018). Cloud service providers such as AWS, Microsoft Azure, and Google Cloud are AIaaS providers that provide scalable and flexible options to support MSMEs on their platforms and may be used to predict sales, manage inventory, and provide support to customers.
2. **Subscription-Based AI Models:** Subscription-based models are becoming very popular among MSMEs, particularly those that offer recurring services or products. These models help organisations use AI to customise experiences and interact with clients more effectively. For instance, retailers that operate online could suggest products based on past behaviour. Quite the opposite, the health, lifestyle, recreation, and SaaS industries employ AI to customise and

tailor their services and pricing formulations according to customer intelligence (Abaddi, S., 2025). Customisation enhances customer loyalty and retention. Moreover, the subscription model will help MSMEs create a consistent stream of revenue, which is essential for expansion and scalability. Although MSMEs can continuously generate revenue flows by optimising the customer lifecycle with AI, customer satisfaction and long-term viability are increased (Khaq et al., 2024).

3. **Data-Driven Business Models:** Data-driven business models form one of the effective forms of MSMEs adopting AI. Information and AI have enabled companies to gather and process large volumes of information across various sources, including customer interactions, purchases, site traffic, and social media interactions, and put that data to the pivotal business decision-making. Through AI, MSMEs can process data and monitor the behaviour, tastes, and trends of their customers. This enables businesses to develop more targeted advertising campaigns, prescribe personalised products, and adjust pricing strategies (Guillen, N., 2023). AI-driven insights can help a fashion MSME predict fashion trends, manage product mix, and create more effective marketing campaigns based on customer preferences. Moreover, AI will enable the division of MSME customers into more effective segments, allowing them to tailor services to specific segments. This results in more focused marketing spending and better conversion rates, making data-driven models an essential competitive advantage tool for MSMEs (Affini et al., 2024).
4. **AI-Improved Supply Chain Management:** AI has a tremendous improvement in the supply chain of MSME by optimising demand, inventory and transportation. The AI machines analyse past data, seasonal trends, and market data to forecast demand accurately, allowing businesses to maintain optimum inventories and prevent shortages or excessive stock (Khaq et al., 2024). This will facilitate the timely availability of products and minimise wastage. AI is also applied in transportation, where machine learning approximates the movement of traffic and fuel prices, thereby calculating the most efficient route for delivering goods. This reduces operating expenses and maximises delivery time (Sinuhaji et al., 2024). By adopting AI, MSMEs can increase flexibility, reduce costs, and enhance customer satisfaction in competitive markets.
5. **AI-Oriented Personalisation of Products:** MSMEs use product personalisation, which relies on AI, to provide personalised products and services to create value in fashion, home interior, and technology (Legowo & Sorongan, 2022). The customer data, including purchase history and preferences, is input into the AI algorithms, which generate tailored recommendations. Fashion can extend to bespoke sizes and designs, incorporating technology, and can be tailored into custom bundles or environments (Legowo & Sorongan, 2022). This customisa-

tion increases consumer satisfaction and allows MSMEs to set premium prices, distinguishing and fostering closer relationships with consumers (Legowo & Sorongan, 2022).

6. **Artificial Intelligence in Financial Services-Fraud Mitigation and Risk Management:** Artificial intelligence is also gaining significant ground in the financial industry, particularly in the case of MSMEs, to improve access to credit and reduce fraudulent risks. Businesses can assess their creditworthiness more accurately with the help of AI analysis of financial accounts to access capital and other financial products. Conventional methods for measuring credit often depend on incomplete data and omit companies with short or nonexistent credit histories (Guillen, N., 2023). AI-based financial models utilise more data points—such as transaction history, payment behaviour, and social media usage—to present a more comprehensive and accurate picture of a business's financial health. MSMEs can receive the funds needed to develop their business even if banks cannot verify their conventional credit history (Zahra, F. P., Suharto, Y., 2024).
7. **Embedded AI model:** MSMEs integrate AI directly into their core products or services to enhance functionality and customer experience. For instance, small retail businesses use AI-powered recommendation engines to personalise online shopping experiences, while manufacturing MSMEs adopt AI for predictive maintenance within machinery (Sinha et al., 2022)
8. **Platform-based AI models:** Platform-based AI models are becoming increasingly popular, especially in industries such as agriculture, fintech, and logistics. MSMEs serve as the connecting link between end-users and service providers, utilising AI-driven decision-making capabilities (Sinha et al., 2022). These models accrue revenue through commissions, subscriptions, or data monetisation efforts, enabling even small firms to create AI-driven ecosystems.
9. **Freemium and licensing mechanisms:** Freemium and licensing mechanisms are being repurposed for AI solutions aimed at MSMEs, under which companies can use limited AI capabilities free of cost and switch to higher-end versions. Smooth onboarding, thus, builds trust and adoption among price-conscious firms (Guillen, N., 2023). MSMEs are also starting to establish data cooperatives, with several firms sharing anonymised data to train collective AI models, thereby cutting costs and enhancing accuracy. Such collective models not only mitigate the data shortage but also facilitate the ethical use of AI within the MSME community (Gupta & Sharma, 2020). As digitalisation picks up speed, the adaptability and range of AI business models shall play a key role in supporting sustainable growth in the MSME community.

## 7 IMPLICATIONS OF AI ON THE MSME SECTOR

MSMEs use artificial intelligence to work, compete, and innovate, an evolving concept. Artificial intelligence technologies, such as computational vision, natural language processing, and machine learning, can help automate processes, enhance decision-making, and optimise the use of resources by small and medium-sized enterprise businesses with limited human, physical, and financial resources (Affini et al., 2024). Such innovations are crucial for MSMEs, as many lack access to funds, human capital, and physical capital. Artificial intelligence has levelled the ground by bridging resource accessibility even to the smallest companies that initially remained open to large companies (Affini et al., 2024)

Studies have shown that small and medium-sized enterprises (SMEs) that apply artificial intelligence (AI) experience significant increases in access to finance, customer engagement, and productivity. Artificial intelligence-facilitated technology, for example, can help small and medium-sized enterprises (SMEs) reduce costs and enhance productivity in inventory management, proactive maintenance, and customer-targeted marketing. Artificial intelligence-based credit scoring platforms enable small enterprises with no formal credit histories to obtain the required funding (Jain et al., 2021).

### 7.1 Key Implications of AI on MSMEs

1. **Operational Efficiency and Process Automation:** AI-driven systems that contain Robotic Process Automation (RPA)- and Machine Learning (ML)-based algorithms are part of the technology that streamlines inventory management, optimises the supply chain, and minimises the volume of work that needs to be done manually. Artificial intelligence has led to a 17% improvement in production efficiency, according to Sinha et al. (2022), for manufacturing micro, small, and medium-sized enterprises in India.
2. **Increasing Customer Engagement:** MSMEs may enhance customer service with artificial intelligence-based chatbots, customer sentiment analysis, and special campaign promotions. Artificial intelligence-based CRM software provides real-time feedback to increase sales conversions and win clients' loyalty.
3. **Financial Forecasting and Risk Management:** Fintech tools could help micro, small, and medium-sized enterprises (MSMEs) with credit risk assessment, cash flow projections, and strategic business decisions (Jain et al., 2021) state that the application of artificial intelligence to credit assessment has made lending to small and medium-sized enterprises (SMEs) possible even when there is no proven credit record.

4. **AI and Ethical Practices in Business:** AI may help improve ethical business practices and sustainability for micro, small, and medium enterprises or MSMEs. Literature suggests that MSMEs can utilise AI-based marketing tools to develop ethical brands, thereby enhancing customer loyalty and trust. These may help ensure business continuity and the success of sustainable development measures. Micro, Small, and Medium Enterprises (MSMEs) may utilise artificial intelligence for tailor-made marketing strategies and effective customer engagement, thereby improving the ethical appeal of their firm's brand (Waruwu et al., 2023).
5. **Effect on Human Resources and SOP Development:** AI influences HR practices within MSMEs. Adopting AI in Indonesia has increased efficiency in creating Standard Operating Procedures (SOPs) and recruitment. AI enhances HR functions, making them more efficient and saving time and resources. However, bias within the AI system and the need for human-AI collaboration to ensure fairness and effectiveness must be dealt with carefully (Wulandari & Diko, 2024).
6. **AI Readiness and Technological Infrastructure:** The preparedness of the organisation to embrace new technologies is a critical factor influencing the success of AI implementation in MSMEs. Studies have noted that MSMEs in economies such as Indonesia and India tend to be hindered by challenges of inadequate infrastructure and an unskilled workforce. According to research, enhancing MSME AI readiness by utilising guidelines such as the AIRI framework can help MSMEs determine their levels of readiness and effectively adopt AI (Budiraharjo et al., 2024).

## 8 CASE STUDIES OF COMPANIES ADOPTING AI IN MSME

1. **Aicut Precision Engineers, Tamil Nadu:** Aicut Precision Engineers incorporated AI-based predictive maintenance solutions in their CNC equipment for live performance monitoring and preventive diagnosis of possible component failures. Enabled through the SAMARTH Udyog scheme, the change resulted in a notable 30% decrease in unscheduled downtime and a 25% reduction in maintenance costs. The company's productivity increased without incurring extra infrastructural costs. The case highlights the role that government-backed AI adoption can play in driving operational efficiency in small-scale engineering firms (NASSCOM, 2023).
2. **StitchNest – Fashion MSME, Delhi:** StitchNest, an Indian fashion MSME, used AI-driven trend forecasting based on historical purchase patterns, customer behaviour, and fashion databases worldwide. The strategic move enabled them to design clothing according to consumer needs, significantly reducing overpro-

duction. Within six months, the company experienced a 40% increase in sales through online channels and a 20% reduction in raw materials wastage, thereby validating the use of AI in demand forecasting for design-driven companies (Startup India, 2022).

3. **M2P Fintech:** M2P Fintech's embedded finance solutions benefit MSMEs by utilising credit-risk evaluation using AI-driven credit risk assessment models. Their platform evaluates MSMEs' transactional patterns and alternative data to compute credit scores for MSMEs with lesser financial histories. Consequently, more than 300 MSMEs gained access to formal credit, thereby increasing credit penetration and enabling the scalability of their businesses. The case highlights the use of AI to fill credit gaps by analysing alternative data (Deloitte, 2023).
4. **Hutech Solutions – AI in Recruitment:** Hutech Solutions deployed AI-powered recruitment analytics for MSMEs, using natural language processing (NLP) and resume parsing tools to streamline hiring processes. The solution reduced recruitment cycles by 50% and improved employee fit by better matching roles. MSMEs using Hutech's platform reported increased workforce stability and reduced turnover, proving that AI can democratise talent acquisition for small enterprises (Gupta & Sharma, 2020).
5. **Freshokartz – Agri MSME:** Freshokartz, based in Rajasthan, incorporated artificial intelligence-based soil health and climate monitoring solutions to provide farmers with targeted agronomic recommendations through mobile channels. The data-driven approach translated into efficient irrigation, increased fertiliser use, and pest forecasting. The farmers saw a 22% increase in yield and a 15% reduction in costs. The case highlights the potential of AI to revolutionise precision agriculture for agri-MSMEs in rural areas (Sinha et al., 2022).
6. **LogiNext – Logistics Optimisation:** LogiNext, an MSME in logistics-tech, employed machine learning algorithms to analyse and plan routes, and optimise schedule compliance. Their artificial intelligence-driven route planning solutions reduced fuel consumption and delivery delays by 35%. Automated monitoring of fleets by MSME logistics contributed to increased control over customer service parameters, leading to higher customer retention in marketplaces of last-mile deliveries (World Economic Forum, 2024).
7. **TartanSense – Precision Agriculture:** TartanSense created autonomous mini-robots that incorporated AI for small-scale agricultural operations. The AI-equipped mini-robots were designed to focus on identifying weeds and precision spraying. This technology resulted in a 40% reduction in herbicide use and a 25% decrease in labour costs for smallholding farmers, demonstrating the potential of MSMEs to scale agri-tech by miniaturising AI (FICCI, 2023).
8. **Planys Technologies - Underwater Infrastructure:** Planys Technologies, a deep-tech MSME, implemented AI in underwater drone data interpretation to

inspect marinas and dams. The AI technology translated visual data into maps of the risks, cutting the inspection time by 60%. The application has significantly enhanced security, particularly for ports and water utilities with limited access to conventional underwater inspection technology (Startup India, 2022).

9. **Infilect - AI in Retail Analytics:** Infilect provides AI-based computer vision technology that helps MSME retailers track shelf inventory and SKU availability using visual analytics-based solutions. Their AI-driven dashboard facilitates auto-replenishment recommendations, boosting product exposure by 35% and sell-through rates. The platform enables small-scale retail outlets to compete with large-scale chain stores through data-driven inventory management (Shakya et al., 2023).
10. **Synctactic.ai - Analytics for MSMEs:** Synctactic.ai simplifies data science for MSMEs through low-code platforms offering business dashboards, customer profiling, and sales forecasting. A local Chennai-based bakery used the tool to optimise staffing based on footfall prediction, resulting in a 12% reduction in labour costs. This shows how AI democratises business intelligence for non-tech MSMEs (Shakya et al., 2023).
11. **Uncanny Vision - Surveillance Solutions:** Uncanny Vision provides real-time AI surveillance, detecting intrusions and suspicious activities in manufacturing MSMEs. Integration with existing CCTV networks resulted in a 40% reduction in theft incidents, particularly in warehouses with limited night staffing. The solution enabled the cost-effective automation of security protocols without requiring significant capital investment (Deloitte, 2023).
12. **LimeChat—AI in E-commerce MSMEs:** LimeChat provides MSME online businesses with NLP-based chatbot services, such as automated queries for orders, returns, and product recommendations. Due to reduced resolution times, e-commerce MSMEs experienced a threefold increase in repeat sales and improved customer satisfaction. LimeChat is a case of plug-and-play, scalable AI customer support (Gupta & Sharma, 2020).

## 9 BEST PRACTICES FOR AI INTEGRATION IN MSMES

Micro, Small, or Medium Enterprises (MSMEs) will be the starting point for a gradual and strategic approach to implementing artificial intelligence technologies. Pilot projects to address specific problems beforehand, with the intention of expanding to other departments later, are recommended. Some examples are predictive maintenance and automating customer care. This minimises the possibility of adverse effects and makes it easier to have achievable learning milestones (Shakya et al., 2023).

Micro, Small, and Medium Enterprises (MSMEs) align with the findings (Gupta & Sharma, 2020) and begin to adopt open-source artificial intelligence platforms, such as TensorFlow, KNIME, or Google AutoML, to reduce the use of costly proprietary software and improve adaptability in relation to organisational objectives. To the extent that a lack of awareness concerning artificial intelligence (AI) can hinder its adoption to a considerable degree, workers need to reskill and upskill to acquire the necessary abilities. Technical innovations are promoted, and workers' morale is improved by adopting training programs focusing on data handling, basic AI, ML, and ethics in artificial intelligence. There is the prospect that small and medium-sized enterprises (SMEs) can utilise shared facilities and specialised knowledge to the extent that they cooperate with external entities, such as government innovation centres, colleges, and university institutions, as well as artificial intelligence companies.

Initiatives like SAMARTH Udyog, which support small enterprises in India, have already adopted technologies that comprise the Industry 4.0 era (NASSCOM, 2023). Artificial intelligence adoption by SAMARTH Udyog is designed to make intelligent manufacturing a seamless process. For Micro, Small, and Medium Enterprises (MSMEs), the bottom line is that with the phased adoption of artificial intelligence (AI) through an ecosystem and people-oriented approach to the adopted methodology, problems are expected to be minimal, and maximum benefits are anticipated.

## 10 THE FUTURE OF AI IN MSMES: TRANSFORMING OPERATIONS AND SHAPING GROWTH

The potential of Artificial Intelligence (AI) in Micro, Small, and Medium Enterprises (MSMEs) awaits to redefine how these firms perform, innovate, and expand. As AI technologies continue to develop, MSMEs will benefit from increased efficiency, cost savings, and improved decision-making, ultimately leading to a greater chance of sustained growth. Here, we will discuss the key trends that will shape the future of AI in MSMEs and how these enterprises will leverage new AI technologies to remain competitive in the digital economy.

1. **The Growing Adoption of AI-Based Automation:** MSMEs automate their processes by using AI-based automation in inventory management, customer service, improved supply chains, etc. Organisations adopt AI solutions because the tools result in significant cost savings. AI-based chatbots assist in order processing, responding to recurring requests, and interacting with customers,

thereby decreasing the need for human intervention. Inventory management software utilising artificial intelligence analyses past data to predict future demand, ensuring an optimal level of stock and preventing overstocking. AI is also used to enhance supply-chain capacity, as it enables the prediction of demand and the planning of optimal delivery routes, thereby increasing the efficiency of the delivery service. Automated solutions will help MSMEs lower their operational costs, allowing them to redirect funds to business expansion schemes and improve their products and customer services. When artificial intelligence is used to automate operations in a business, it makes the process more competitive, allowing MSMEs to compete effectively in the digital world.

2. **AI-Improved analytics to improve decision-making:** AI analytics will form a significant force that will transform the decision-making processes of MSMEs. As the technology of artificial intelligence develops, companies will have access to high-quality analytics tools that enable the processing of a tremendous amount of data in real time. Micro, Small, and Medium Enterprises (MSMEs) can leverage the benefits of AI-based analytics to gain practical insights into business performance, customer behaviour, and competitive trends, ultimately determining their profitability. AI-based analytics help organisations foresee customer affinity, detect new market trends, and gauge consumer sentiments more precisely. Data helps businesses narrow down their product scope, pricing mechanisms, and precise advertising schedules. Using AI technology, the assessment of various customer touchpoints, including social media use and website visits, is conducted, and personalised product and marketing strategies are created. The personalised experiences maximise connections with customers and purchase rates, which guarantee the growth of brand loyalty. With the introduction of AI-based predictive analytics, organisations will be able to scale their operations to maximise stock utilisation, develop competitive pricing strategies, and effectively utilise their market reach. By predicting shifts in demand and examining customer trends, small and medium-sized businesses can function successfully, keeping pace with market changes. Real-time analytics will also enable MSMEs to make informed business decisions, allowing them to respond to market changes and adapt their operations to the ever-changing business environment.

3. **Artificial Intelligence in Sustainable and Eco-Friendly Business Operations:** Artificial intelligence has a great role to play in providing the sustainability of MSMEs through energy consumption and increased resource utilisation, reducing resource wastage. Artificial intelligence enhances the efficiency of lighting, heating, and cooling systems by optimising their operation based on occupancy and weather data. AI analytics extrapolates supply chain data to determine areas where consumption levels can be reduced and production

optimised with reduced carbon intensity. Artificial intelligence helps MSMEs achieve sustainable production and delivery through demand forecasting and supply chain optimisation, thereby eliminating overproduction. The use of AI applications in monitoring pollutants and waste, controlling resources, ensuring compliance with environmental regulations, and generating sustainability reports is prevalent. Implementing AI technology to facilitate sustainable operations is likely to help MSMEs improve their green image, thereby gaining access to environmentally conscious consumers, competitive financing, and collaborations with environmentally oriented investors and partners.

4. **Artificial Intelligence-led Innovation and Product Development:** Artificial intelligence is a catalyst for dramatic innovation in the process of product development of micro, small, and medium enterprises by improving the features of the current products and developing new solutions that enter previously unexplored markets. Consumer inputs can be analysed with the help of artificial intelligence, and, hence, innovative product ideas can be prioritised to meet unmet market needs. The design of AI programs is based on consumer inputs and current fashion trends. Companies develop adaptive technology products that change according to the interactions of people with AI products, offering some of the most personalised solutions. Artificial intelligence examines existing market opportunities in a novel and untapped way. MSMEs leverage artificial intelligence to analyse consumer and competitor inputs, identifying gaps that enable the creation of new products or services specifically designed to meet emerging trends and niche markets.

## 11 CONCLUSION

Artificial intelligence provides micro, small, and medium enterprises with solutions that help businesses restructure their operations by automating processes, extracting data, customising products, streamlining supply chains, and increasing access to finance. Artificial intelligence makes MSMEs more competitive than other companies by alleviating the traditional constrained resources. Micro, small, and medium enterprises have also implemented customised solutions across the globe to meet their contextual and unique demands, utilising predictive analytics, AI-based customer engagement applications, machine learning, and precision agriculture. Artificial intelligence enables the automation of processes, allowing MSMEs to transform their operational models. Some of the opportunities and challenges facing micro, small, and medium enterprises include navigating the business environment, automating and extracting information using data, product customisation, supply chain optimisation, and enhanced access to finance. Artificial intelligence can help MSMEs overcome traditional resource limitations, enhancing their competitiveness compared to larger organisations. Micro and small businesses have, at the global level, adopted innovative solutions that meet their contextual demands and are utilising predictive analytics, AI-based applications for customer interaction, machine learning, and precision agriculture. The widespread presence of AI-based technologies, available at affordable prices, enables MSMEs to utilise intelligence more effectively and sustainably, thereby facilitating overall economic development. Ultimately, artificial intelligence is not just a technology; it enables MSMEs to be resilient, innovative, and future-proof in the digital economy.

## REFERENCES


Abaddi, S. (2025). Factors and Moderators Influencing Artificial Intelligence Adoption by Jordanian MSMEs. Management & Sustainability. *An Arab Review*, *4*(1), 47–73. DOI: 10.1108/MSAR-10-2023-0049

Affini, D. N., Shiratina, A., & Setyaningrum, R. P. (2024). Improving the Sustainability of MSMES Businesses Through Digital Business Development in Tegal Parang Urban Village, Mampang Prapatan Sub-District, South Jakarta. Akuntansi dan Humaniora. *Jurnal Pengabdian Masyarakat*, *3*(2), 78–83. DOI: 10.38142/ahjpm.v3i2.1116

Amponsah, B. K., Adanuvor, S. Y., Frimpong, M., Buame, R., & Arhin, E. O. (2025). Investigating the Challenges and Opportunities of Implementing AI and Automation in Small Businesses. *Intelligent Control and Automation*, *16*(2), 35–59. DOI: 10.4236/ica.2025.162003

Banerjee, B. (2023). Challenges and opportunities for micro, small, and medium enterprises: Navigating the business landscape. *The American Journal of Interdisciplinary Innovations and Research*, *5*(05), 13–17. DOI: 10.37547/tajiir/Volume05Issue05-04

Basole, R. C., & Accenture, A. I. (2021, January). Visualizing the Evolution of the AI Ecosystem. In HICSS (Vol. 1). https://www.researchgate.net/profile/Rahul-Basole/publication/345119002_Visualizing_the_Evolution_of_the_AI_Ecosystem/links/5fd355e1a6fdccdcb8b830a4/Visualizing-the-Evolution-of-the-AI-Ecosystem.pdf

Budiraharjo, M. H., Muhammad, A. H., & Kusnawi, . (2024). MSME AI Readiness Analysis Using The AIRI Framework. [JTIULM]. *Jurnal Teknologi Informasi Universitas Lambung Mangkurat*, *9*(2), 33–44. DOI: 10.20527/jtiulm.v9i2.307

. Daraojimba, R. E., & Igbokwe, J. C. (2024). Educational approaches in African social work: Implications for US social work training. DOI: 10.30574/ijsra.2024.11.1.0182

Deloitte. (2023). AI in Indian FinTech: Unlocking MSME potential. Deloitte Insights. https://www2.deloitte.com

. Eyo-Udo, N. (2024). Leveraging artificial intelligence for enhanced supply chain optimization. Open Access Research Journal of Multidisciplinary Studies, 7(2), 001-015.: DOI: 10.53022/oarjms.2024.7.2.0044

Goyal, S., Esposito, M., & Kapoor, A. (2018). Circular economy business models in developing economies: Lessons from India on reduce, recycle, and reuse paradigms. *Thunderbird International Business Review*, *60*(5), 729–740. DOI: 10.1002/tie.21883

Goyal, S., Esposito, M., & Kapoor, A. (2018). Circular economy business models in developing economies: Lessons from India on reduce, recycle, and reuse paradigms. *Thunderbird International Business Review, 60*(5), 729–740. DOI: 10.1002/tie.21883

Guillen, N., & Lim, C. T. (2023). Unlocking growth opportunities for Philippine micro, small, and medium enterprises through Facebook advertising and growth hacking strategies in the post-pandemic era. *International Journal of Multidisciplinary: Applied Business and Education Research, 4*(8), 2884–2893. DOI: 10.11594/ijmaber.04.08.26

Gupta, P., & Sharma, V. (2020). Leveraging Artificial Intelligence for MSMEs: Challenges and Enablers. *International Journal of Emerging Markets, 15*(6), 987–1003. DOI: 10.1108/IJOEM-03-2019-0204

Jain, R., Mehta, A., & Deshpande, N. (2021). Financial inclusion through AI-powered credit assessments. *Journal of Financial Innovation, 3*(1), 45–56. DOI: 10.1016/j.jfi.2021.05.007

Khaq, Z. D., Subroto, V. K., & Susanto, E. (2024). AI-driven Strategies for Enhancing MSME Sales and Business Communication: A Case Study. *Journal of Management and Informatics, 3*(2), 180–194. DOI: 10.51903/jmi.v3i2.28

Kumar, M., Raut, R. D., Mangla, S. K., Ferraris, A., & Choubey, V. K. (2024). Adopting artificial intelligence-powered workforce management for effective revenue growth of micro, small, and medium scale enterprises (MSMEs). *Production Planning and Control, 35*(13), 1639–1655. DOI: 10.1080/09537287.2022.2131620

Kumar, S., & Shukla, T. (2024). Optimizing supply chain management through advanced data mining applications. *International Journal of Sciences and Innovation Engineering, 1*(3), 1–9. DOI: 10.70849/IJSCI27936

Legowo, M. B., & Sorongan, F. A. (2022). Accelerating digital transformation during the COVID-19 Pandemic: A model design for Indonesian MSMEs. *Binus Business Review, 13*(2), 203–211. DOI: 10.21512/bbr.v13i2.8447

Lim, T. K., & Seng, L. W. (2024). Determinants Of Artificial Intelligence Adoption In Accounting Among Malaysian Small And Medium-Sized Enterprises. Journal of Accounting [JABM]. *Business and Management, 32*(1), 244–259. DOI: 10.31966/jabminternational.v32i1.1456

Musdalifah, S., & Hariyanto, W. (2024). *AIS Revolutionizes MSMEs, Enhancing Global Financial Transparency*. Indonesian Journal of Law and Economics Review., DOI: 10.21070/ijler.v19i2.1079

NASSCOM. (2023). AI Adoption Trends in Indian MSMEs. National Association of Software and Service Companies. https://nasscom.in/ai-msme-report

Patil, K. P., Pramod, D., & Bharathi, S. V. (2023, October). MSMEs readiness for adopting artificial intelligence and machine learning. In *2023 International Conference on Advanced Computing Technologies and Applications (ICACTA)* (pp. 1–6). IEEE. DOI: 10.1109/ICACTA58201.2023.10392396

Qu, C., & Kim, E. (2025). Investigating AI Adoption, Knowledge Absorptive Capacity, and Open Innovation in Chinese Apparel MSMEs: An Extended TAM-TOE Model with PLS-SEM Analysis. *Sustainability (Basel)*, *17*(5), 1873. Advance online publication. DOI: 10.3390/su17051873

Shakya, T., Sharma, M., Kathuria, S., Yamsani, N., Singh, R., & Negi, P. (2023, July). Micro, small, and medium enterprises' advancement with artificial intelligence and robots. In *2023 IEEE World Conference on Applied Intelligence and Computing (AIC)* (pp. 783–788). IEEE. DOI: 10.1109/AIC57670.2023.10263845

Sharma, P., Shah, J., & Patel, R. (2022). Artificial intelligence framework for MSME sectors focusing on design and manufacturing industries. *Materials Today: Proceedings*, *62*, 6962–6966. Advance online publication. DOI: 10.1016/j.matpr.2021.12.360

Shvetsova, S. (2024). Increasing the attractiveness of electric vehicles for consumers in cold climates. In *E3S Web of Conferences* (Vol. 471, p. 06014). EDP Sciences., DOI: 10.1051/e3sconf/202447106014

Sinha, A., Banerjee, D., & Rajan, M. (2022). AI in manufacturing: Evidence from MSMEs in India. *Technology in Society*, *68*, 101920. DOI: 10.1016/j.techsoc.2022.101920

Sinuhaji, F. G., Sibarani, H. J., & Pakpahan, V. M. (2024). *MSMEs and the role of technology in achieving business sustainability. Journal of Artificial Intelligence and Engineering Applications*. JAIEA., DOI: 10.59934/jaiea.v4i1.724

Startup India. (2022). Case Compendium: AI for MSMEs. Department for Promotion of Industry and Internal Trade (DPIIT), Government of India. https://www.startupindia.gov.in

. Tarwiyah, B., Cipta, S., &, S. (2023). Understanding Human Potential In The Ai Era: Implications For Financial Management Practices In Micro, Small And Medium Enterprises. Journal of Management and Creative Business. .DOI: 10.30640/jmcbus.v1i4.2399

Udeogu, A. C., & Okoye, I. E. (2024). Artificial intelligence and competitive advantage of micro, small and medium enterprises (MSMEs) in Anambra State. *Cross Current International Journal of Economics Management and Media Studies*, *6*(01), 1–9.

Ulum Ilham, B., & Muawwal, A. (2024). AI Literacy Level in MSMEs Assisted by PLUT South Sulawesi. *Proceeding of Research and Civil Society Desemination*, *2*(1), 369–374. DOI: 10.37476/presed.v2i1.52

. Waruwu, E., & Agustina, S. (2023). Leveraging AI-Driven Marketing For Ethical Branding In MSMES. Sammajiva: Jurnal Penelitian Bisnis dan Manajemen, 1(2), 289-298. DOI: 10.47861/sammajiva.v1i2.946

Wong, J. W., & Yap, K. H. A. (2024). Factors influencing the adoption of artificial intelligence in accounting among micro, small medium enterprises (MSMEs). *Quantum Journal of Social Sciences and Humanities*, *5*(1), 16–28. DOI: 10.55197/qjssh.v5i1.323

World Economic Forum. (2024). The Future of MSMEs: AI and Digital Transformation. https://www.weforum.org/reports

Wulandari, A., & Diko, M. A. I. M. J. (2024). HR Management Transformation in Indonesia MSMEs: The Role of AI in SOP Making and Recruitment. *Journal of Ecohumanism*, *3*(7), 5325–5338. DOI: 10.62754/joe.v3i7.4641

Zahra, F. P., & Suharto, Y. (2024). Innovative Business Models for Design Service Providers: Enhancing MSME Digital Transformation. *Journal of International Management Studies*, *2*(2), 205–210.

# Chapter 7
# Competitiveness and Productivity in SMEs: Guided by AI

**Rismawati Rismawati**
http://orcid.org/0000-0001-8046-6764
*Universitas Muhammadiyah Palopo, Indonesia*

**Vicky Bin Djusmin**
*Universitas Cokroaminoto Palopo, Indonesia*

**Gromyko Bongso**
http://orcid.org/0000-0002-5180-0986
*Bina Nusantara University, Indonesia*

## ABSTRACT

*Artificial Intelligence (AI) is revolutionizing the operational framework of Micro, Small, and Medium-Sized Enterprises (MSMEs) by improving efficiency, fostering innovation, and promoting sustainability. AI adoption in MSMEs encounters considerable obstacles, such as budgetary limitations, skill deficiencies, and regulatory hurdles. This book examines the opportunities and problems associated with AI application in MSMEs, emphasizing AI-enhanced operational efficiency, customer interaction, financial management, and sustainable business practices. Furthermore, it analyzes governmental regulations, AI support initiatives, collaborative approaches, and AI-as-a-Service (AIaaS) solutions that facilitate the surmounting of adoption obstacles. The discourse encompasses the function of AI in green marketing and the circular economy, highlighting AI's impact on sustainable corporate development. By strategically leveraging AI, MSMEs may augment competitiveness, refine decision-making, and promote long-term sustainability in a dynamic digital economy*

DOI: 10.4018/979-8-3373-2817-1.ch007

## INTRODUCTION

### 1.1 Micro, Small, and Medium-Sized Enterprises (MSMEs) and the Dynamics of Artificial Intelligence Adoption

Micro, small, and medium-sized enterprises (MSMEs) are essential for job creation, the dissemination of innovation, and the stability of local economies. Although particular limits vary by jurisdiction, policy benchmarks generally classify micro enterprises as having fewer than 10 employees, small firms as having up to fifty, and medium-sized organizations as having up to 250. Despite their macroeconomic importance, the agility and customer closeness of MSMEs—qualities that enable swift responses to market changes and niche opportunities—are hindered by ongoing issues in finance, digital infrastructure, data preparedness, and human resources. These shortcomings are especially acute in emerging and least-developed economies, where informality limits access to formal financing and advanced technologies (Rosyidiana & Narsa, 2024).

In this setting, Artificial Intelligence (AI) offers transformative potential and implementation complexities. Empirical research indicates that AI adoption is inconsistent and predominantly concentrated within larger or more digitally proficient companies possessing strong data ecosystems (McElheran et al., 2024). Adoption patterns throughout Europe differ by industry and national ecosystem factors, influenced by digital competencies, innovation potential, and technological infrastructure (Segarra-Blasco et al., 2025; Aydin et al., 2024). Nevertheless, particular applications—such as demand forecasting, fraud detection, and process automation—are consistently linked to quantifiable enhancements in productivity and growth, particularly when integrated with complementary technologies like the Internet of Things (IoT) and big data analytics (Ardito et al., 2024).

MSME AI adoption can be understood as the reconfiguration of technological and organizational resources within the Technology–Organization–Environment (TOE) framework (Badghish & Soomro, 2024). The intensity of AI adoption—characterized by its breadth, scale, and sophistication—interacts with data quality, digital infrastructure, and human capabilities to produce mediated effects, including process efficiency, insight quality, market agility, and innovation rate. Moderating variables encompass organizational size, sector classification, and regulatory framework. Developing economies face affordability constraints, skill shortages, and inadequate data systems, which require phased adoption strategies, AI-as-a-Service solutions, and responsible AI practices to convert pilot initiatives into sustainable competitive performance (Carayannis et al., 2024; McElheran et al., 2024; Ardito et al., 2024).

Figure 1 depicts the conceptual framework connecting Artificial Intelligence (AI) adoption to organizational competitiveness and performance within Micro,

Small, and Medium-Sized Enterprises (MSMEs). The framework illustrates that the intensity of AI adoption—measured by the breadth, magnitude, and complexity of use cases—acts as the primary catalyst affecting several mediating capacities, including process efficiency, insight quality, market agility, and innovation rate. These mediators subsequently produce quantifiable performance outcomes such as labor productivity, cost efficiency, punctual delivery, sales growth, and export intensity. The model acknowledges that these correlations are influenced by contextual factors—such as sector characteristics, business size and age, digital maturity, governmental backing, and data quality—which determine the intensity and direction of AI's effect on competitiveness. The image illustrates how the integration of technological, organizational, and environmental elements facilitates AI's contribution to sustainable productivity and resilience in MSMEs within the digital economy.

*Figure 1. AI–Capability–Performance Model for MSMEs*

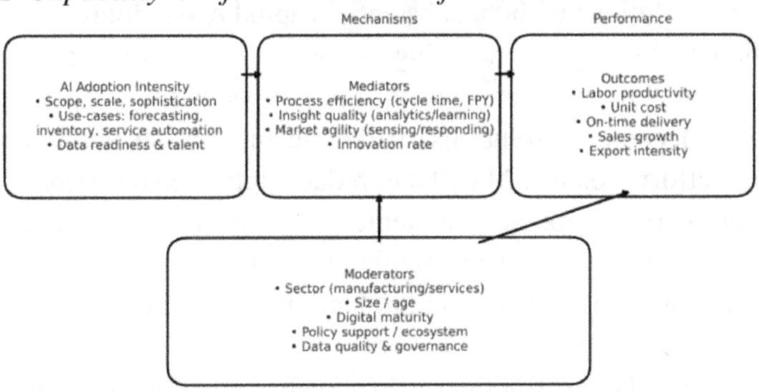


*Source: Adapted from the author's conceptual synthesis based on Carayannis et al. (2024), Ardito et al. (2024), Badghish & Soomro (2024), and Segarra-Blasco et al. (2025).*

## 1.2 Artificial Intelligence Technologies Pertinent to Micro, Small, and Medium Enterprises

Artificial Intelligence (AI) has emerged as a disruptive force, altering organizational structures, workflows, and business models across various sectors. For Micro, Small, and Medium-Sized Enterprises (MSMEs), artificial intelligence signifies both a strategic potential and an operational difficulty. Although resource limitations frequently impede adoption, the growing accessibility of cloud-based and affordable AI solutions has democratized access to advanced technologies. These advancements allow smaller enterprises to utilize AI-driven products for improved efficiency, automation of mundane chores, and enhanced client engagement, hence fortifying their competitive stance in a progressively digital economy (Kumar et al., 2024).

Machine Learning (ML) is a critical AI technology for MSMEs, as it can convert raw data into usable insights. Machine learning algorithms facilitate demand forecasting, fraud detection, credit scoring, and targeted marketing by discerning patterns and trends in extensive datasets (Kumar et al., 2024). For example, machine learning-driven recommendation systems can enhance sales predictions and consumer segmentation, whereas anomaly detection algorithms bolster fraud prevention strategies in e-commerce and finance. Predictive inventory models enhance waste reduction and optimize supply chain coordination. Nonetheless, obstacles to implementation endure—such as restricted access to dependable data, elevated computing expenses, and inadequate expertise. The advent of cloud-based machine learning systems (e.g., Amazon SageMaker, Google AutoML, Microsoft Azure ML) has alleviated these obstacles, enabling micro, small, and medium enterprises to explore scalable solutions without substantial capital expenditures.

Automation technologies, including robotic process automation (RPA) and AI-enhanced workflow tools, are transforming the operational operations of MSMEs. AI-driven accounting solutions, marketing automation, and human resource management platforms enable MSMEs to reduce operational expenses and human error while redirecting workers to strategic and innovative roles. Intelligent automation augments organizational adaptability by enhancing speed, consistency, and compliance, so immediately fostering productivity growth and competitiveness in volatile marketplaces.

The deployment of conversational agents, such as chatbots and virtual assistants, has proliferated swiftly among MSMEs. These solutions improve client engagement, lead creation, and service quality by providing real-time, tailored, and continuous support (Waghambare et al., 2024; Sultana & Rao, 2025). Chatbots like Tidio, ManyChat, and Drift provide economical AI solutions that require minimal technical infrastructure for deployment. In addition to customer service, conversational agents are progressively utilized for internal functions—such as employee onboarding, scheduling, and knowledge management—thereby enhancing operational coherence and alleviating administrative burdens.

Predictive analytics empowers MSMEs to make informed strategic decisions by utilizing historical data to forecast future results. The capacity to predict sales, recognize at-risk consumers, and discern early indicators of operational inefficiencies enables managers to proactively execute corrective measures. Instruments like Google Analytics, IBM Watson Analytics, and Zoho Analytics illustrate that predictive skills, hitherto exclusive to large enterprises, are increasingly attainable for smaller businesses at comparatively low expenses (Ezeife et al., 2024). The increasing amalgamation of predictive analytics with AI-augmented visualization and dashboard tools enables MSMEs to track key performance indicators (KPIs) in real time, hence enhancing their responsiveness to market fluctuations.

The integration of machine learning, automation, conversational agents, and predictive analytics signifies a pivotal transformation in the value creation processes of MSMEs. Collectively, they facilitate capability augmentation across three dimensions:

- Operational efficiency achieved via automation and machine learning-based optimization.
- Quality of decision-making (using predictive analytics), and
- Customer engagement using conversational interfaces.

Notwithstanding persistent obstacles concerning funding, digital literacy, and data infrastructure, the modularity and cost-effectiveness of modern AI systems have enhanced the viability for MSMEs. Strategic and incremental implementation—aligned with company goals and bolstered by ecosystem collaborations—can empower MSMEs to convert AI capabilities into enduring competitiveness and resilience within the digital economy.

A flow diagram illustrating four components (Machine Learning, Automation, Conversational Agents, Predictive Analytics) contributing to three intermediary capabilities—Operational Efficiency, Decision-Making Quality, and Customer Relationship Management—which subsequently lead to Performance Outcomes (Productivity, Innovation, and Competitiveness).

*Table 1. AI Technologies, Applications, and Performance Outcomes for MSMEs*

| AI Technology | Key Applications | Required Inputs | Primary Benefits | Performance Outcomes |
|---|---|---|---|---|
| **Machine Learning** | Forecasting, fraud detection, inventory optimization | Clean datasets, algorithms, cloud computing | Data-driven decision-making | Improved accuracy and productivity |
| **Automation** | Accounting, HR, marketing operations | Workflow data, APIs | Cost reduction, speed, consistency | Operational efficiency |
| **Conversational Agents** | Customer support, lead generation | NLP models, chat platforms | 24/7 interaction, personalization | Customer satisfaction, retention |
| **Predictive Analytics** | Sales forecasting, risk management | Historical data, analytic tools | Anticipatory management, proactive strategies | Sales growth, resilience |

*Source:* Author's synthesis of recent AI–MSME studies (Ardito et al., 2024; Aydin et al., 2024; Badghish & Soomro, 2024; Carayannis et al., 2024; Kumar et al., 2024).

## 1.3 Artificial Intelligence as a Competitive Advantage for Micro, Small, and Medium Enterprises

In the modern digital economy, Artificial Intelligence (AI) has transformed from a technological novelty into a strategic asset that redefines competition across sectors. Although large corporations have historically led in AI adoption via data-driven decision-making and predictive analytics, Micro, Small, and Medium-Sized Enterprises (MSMEs) are progressively incorporating AI to improve operational efficiency, decrease costs, and foster innovation (Kumar et al., 2024; Behl et al., 2023). Notwithstanding financial and technical limitations, data indicates that MSMEs utilizing AI strategically can enhance customer engagement, streamline internal processes, and attain scalable growth in resource-constrained settings.

AI enhances the competitiveness of MSMEs primarily by improving operational efficiency. Automation technologies reduce human involvement in repetitive administrative chores, including bookkeeping, invoicing, and report preparation. Applications such as Microsoft Power Automate and Trello illustrate how MSMEs can diminish processing duration, enhance data precision, and redeploy personnel to more valuable strategic roles. This transition from routine to cognitive labor not only improves productivity but also promotes organizational learning and adaptability—essential precursors to enduring competitive advantage.

In addition to enhancing productivity, AI enables MSMEs to make more informed and proactive decisions. Predictive analytics tools enable companies to forecast market demand, optimize pricing strategies, and synchronize inventory with current trends. AI-augmented customer relationship management (CRM) systems—like Salesforce AI and Zoho CRM—facilitate dynamic customer segmentation and tailored marketing strategies, hence enhancing conversion rates and brand loyalty. Data-driven decision-making changes MSMEs from reactive to proactive entities, enabling rapid responses to environmental unpredictability.

AI technology also transform customer engagement. Chatbots and digital assistants provide ongoing, immediate, and tailored help, allowing MSMEs to sustain high-quality engagement without corresponding increases in personnel expenses. Customized product suggestions and interactive commerce enhance consumer pleasure, retention, and lifetime value (Kumar et al., 2024). The capacity to gather behavioral information from these interactions generates feedback loops that guide future service improvement, enhancing competitiveness through customer intimacy.

Artificial intelligence accelerates innovation by streamlining product development, improving market analysis, and fostering creativity in design and operations. Micro, Small, and Medium Enterprises (MSMEs) can leverage AI-driven research and prototyping technologies to discern market deficiencies, simulate consumer responses, and evaluate product feasibility at a low expense. This expedites innovation cycles, enabling smaller enterprises to compete effectively with established entities and seize niche possibilities through agility and distinction.

Practical instances illustrate AI's concrete impact on the competitiveness of MSMEs. Tars in India facilitated small firms in decreasing customer response times by 40 percent via AI-driven chatbots. TrendyMart in Brazil utilized predictive analytics to reduce inventory overstock by 30 percent, whereas a boutique store in the United Kingdom attained a 25 percent enhancement in repeat sales with AI-optimized marketing. In Indonesia, CraftTech executed predictive maintenance, resulting in a 20 percent reduction in machine downtime and an increase in production output (Bhalla, 2025; Michael, 2025; Behl et al., 2023). These instances demonstrate how strategically integrated AI may yield quantifiable productivity and performance results.

Artificial intelligence is no longer solely the purview of major corporations; it has become a democratized resource that enables micro, small, and medium firms to enhance their competitive standing. By integrating AI into fundamental functions—operations, analytics, marketing, and customer service—MSMEs may surmount structural limitations and develop dynamic capabilities crucial for enduring competitiveness. The intentional and gradual integration of AI, in accordance with company strategy and bolstered by ecosystem collaborations, allows MSMEs to convert technological proficiency into economic stability and sustained competitive advantage.

*Table 2. AI Capability Domains and Competitive Outcomes*

| AI Capability | Representative Technologies | Strategic Function | Competitive Outcomes |
|---|---|---|---|
| Operational Efficiency | Process automation, workflow bots | Cost reduction, productivity | Efficiency advantage |
| Data-Driven Decision-Making | Predictive analytics, CRM AI | Market responsiveness | Agility and precision |
| Customer Engagement | Chatbots, recommender systems | Retention, loyalty, personalization | Relationship advantage |
| Innovation Capability | AI-aided design, R&D analytics | Product and service differentiation | Innovation advantage |

*Source:* Author's synthesis based on Behl et al. (2023); Kumar et al. (2024); Bhalla (2025); Michael (2025).

# BACKGROUND: PROSPECTS FOR AI INTEGRATION IN MSMES

## 2.1 Operational Efficiency and Artificial Intelligence in MSMEs

Operational efficiency is a crucial factor influencing the competitiveness and sustainability of Micro, Small, and Medium-Sized Enterprises (MSMEs). In contrast to major firms, MSMEs frequently contend with resource limitations, insufficient human capital, and technology inadequacies. These limits render efficiency improvement not just a performance goal but a strategic need. Artificial Intelligence (AI) possesses transformative potential in mitigating inefficiencies through the automation of repetitive tasks, enhancement of supply chain coordination, and facilitation of more accurate decision-making. AI improves productivity, lowers operational expenses, and creates a basis for enduring competitiveness through these processes (Bhalla, 2025; Kumar et al., 2024; Michael, 2025; Jain et al., 2025).

AI significantly enhances efficiency in MSMEs through supply chain and inventory management. Smaller firms frequently encounter difficulties including overstocking, stockouts, shipment delays, and inadequate coordination with suppliers. AI-driven forecasting systems may evaluate historical sales trends, seasonal changes, and external market factors to anticipate demand variations with enhanced accuracy. This predictive ability lowers waste and alleviates both inventory excess and deficiencies.

Additionally, AI-driven inventory monitoring systems offer real-time insights into stock levels, automate replenishment procedures, and minimize capital lock-in. In logistics, AI solutions enhance delivery routing, predict potential interruptions, and facilitate supplier collaboration—bolstering both efficiency and robustness throughout the supply chain. These technical advancements illustrate that AI not only facilitates MSME operations but also serves as a strategic catalyst for agility in unpredictable markets.

In addition to logistics, AI enhances efficiency by automating administrative and operational processes. Tasks include accountancy, payroll, document management, and customer inquiries—historically labor-intensive—can be optimized by AI-enabled systems (Lo et al., 2024). Automated accounting systems minimize human mistake and guarantee regulatory compliance, while AI chatbots improve service responsiveness without escalating personnel expenses.

In human resource management, AI algorithms facilitate talent acquisition, payroll administration, and performance assessment, ultimately enhancing worker efficiency and employee contentment. Likewise, AI-assisted workflow management solutions improve coordination, promote inter-departmental communication, and guarantee prompt project execution. Robotic process automation (RPA) minimizes human data-entry inaccuracies and enables MSMEs to reallocate personnel towards innovative and strategic endeavors.

The use of AI into MSME operations signifies both technological and organizational change. The Technology–Organization–Environment (TOE) framework posits that efficiency improvements rely on technology preparedness, organizational capability, and external influences, including market competitiveness and customer demands. From a resource-based view (RBV), AI skills can develop into unique resources that improve productivity and strategic adaptability. In this regard, AI-driven efficiency beyond mere process automation; it embodies a holistic strategic reaction to internal constraints and external ambiguities.

Integrating AI into supply chain systems, administrative processes, and decision-making frameworks allows MSMEs to reallocate limited resources towards innovation and market growth. AI facilitates companies in attaining cost leadership and adaptive resilience, which are fundamental elements of sustainable competitiveness. Despite ongoing challenges concerning financing, skills, and digital infrastructure, the incremental adoption of cost-effective, cloud-based AI solutions offers MSMEs viable avenues to mitigate operational inefficiencies and enhance their market standing (Bhalla, 2025; Michael, 2025; Jain et al., 2025).

*Table 3. AI Applications for Operational Efficiency in MSMEs*

| Operational Area | AI Applications | Efficiency Impact | Strategic Outcome |
|---|---|---|---|
| **Supply Chain & Logistics** | Predictive demand forecasting, route optimization | Reduced inventory waste, faster delivery | Enhanced supply chain resilience |
| **Administration & Finance** | Automated accounting, document processing | Fewer errors, faster processing | Cost and time efficiency |
| **Customer Interaction** | Chatbots, service automation | 24/7 support, faster response | Improved satisfaction and loyalty |
| **Human Resources** | AI-assisted recruitment, performance analytics | Better talent fit, lower turnover | Productivity and morale boost |

*Source:* Author's synthesis based on Bhalla (2025); Kumar et al. (2024); Michael (2025); Jain et al. (2025); and Lo et al. (2024).

## 2.2 Augmenting Customer Experience through Artificial Intelligence in MSMEs

Customer experience (CX) has become a critical factor for the success of Micro, Small, and Medium-Sized Enterprises (MSMEs) in a progressively digital and competitive corporate environment. In contrast to major businesses that can significantly invest in sophisticated customer relationship management (CRM) systems, micro, small, and medium enterprises (MSMEs) frequently have resource limitations that hinder their capacity to provide individualized, high-quality service. Artificial Intelligence (AI) addresses this inequality by providing scalable and cost-effective technologies that enable smaller enterprises to improve service quality, boost engagement, and cultivate lasting brand loyalty (Saad et al., 2022; Kumar et al., 2022).

AI-driven personalization constitutes a highly transformational application for enhancing customer experience. Through the analysis of demographic data, purchasing histories, and behavioral patterns, AI systems facilitate precise client segmentation, enabling MSMEs to create tailored marketing campaigns. Machine learning algorithms embedded in systems like Shopify and WooCommerce may autonomously produce product recommendations according to consumer tastes, thereby enhancing conversion rates and promoting repeat purchases. Furthermore, AI-augmented email and content marketing solutions guarantee timely and pertinent communication, resulting in increased engagement and consumer pleasure. AI converts marketing from a uniform plan into a dynamic, customer-focused model that enhances both retention and revenue.

AI-powered chatbots and virtual assistants have profoundly transformed the manner in which MSMEs engage with clients. For organizations with restricted personnel, these solutions offer a cost-effective means of providing real-time, round-the-clock customer care. Chatbots like Tidio, Drift, and ManyChat automate replies to frequent questions, therefore diminishing response time and improving perceived service dependability. In addition to fundamental support, conversational AI actively facilitates sales by helping clients in their purchasing decisions and providing tailored recommendations. Virtual assistants such as Google Assistant and Alexa for Business augment interactivity, allowing MSMEs to develop responsive and emotionally intelligent client relationships (Michael, 2025; Christopher & Sundjaja, 2024; Jain et al., 2025).

Sentiment analysis is a swiftly evolving application of AI in customer experience management. Platforms like MonkeyLearn and Lexalytics facilitate MSMEs in deriving real-time insights into consumer satisfaction and emerging issues by analyzing online reviews, social media interactions, and feedback surveys. These data enable swift replies, permitting companies to enhance service design, proactively resolve concerns, and augment product offerings. Sentiment analytics consequently shifts customer service from a reactive to a proactive role, allowing MSMEs to foresee client requirements and maintain enduring relationship value.

The incorporation of AI technology into customer experience strongly correlates with the Diffusion of Innovation (DoI) theory, which asserts that early adopters of new technologies achieve competitive distinctiveness by redefining industry standards. MSMEs utilizing AI for customer experience innovation serve as catalysts for digital transformation inside their industries. Through the adoption of customization, conversational intelligence, and sentiment analysis, these organizations augment value co-creation and reinforce emotional connections with customers. The resultant experiences foster not only contentment but also advocacy, transforming customers into proactive brand advocates.

The integration of AI-driven personalization, conversational engagement, and sentiment analytics illustrates how MSMEs can surmount structural constraints to provide enhanced consumer experiences. These technologies facilitate equitable access to advanced CRM functionalities, diminish operational expenses, and improve responsiveness. Thus, AI not only aids MSMEs in sustaining competitiveness but also reconfigures their strategic position within the digital marketplace, facilitating their success through customer intimacy and data-driven innovation (Saad et al., 2022; Kumar et al., 2022; Michael, 2025; Christopher & Sundjaja, 2024; Jain et al., 2025).

## 2.3 AI-Driven Financial Management for MSMEs

Efficient financial management is fundamental to the sustainability and long-term competitiveness of Micro, Small, and Medium-Sized Enterprises (MSMEs). Numerous smaller enterprises encounter persistent difficulties in cash flow management, financial trend forecasts, and risk mitigation due to insufficient experience and limited access to sophisticated analytical tools. In this environment, Artificial Intelligence (AI) serves as a disruptive facilitator—automating intricate financial tasks, producing data-driven insights, and democratizing access to advanced financial intelligence previously exclusive to huge firms. Utilizing predictive analytics and AI-driven fraud detection, MSMEs may improve financial stability, fortify risk management, and facilitate more strategic decision-making (Kumar et al., 2024; Jain et al., 2025).

Predictive analytics has transformed financial planning by moving beyond historical analysis to include real-time market data, consumer behavior, and macroeconomic factors. AI-powered financial platforms—such as Xero, QuickBooks AI, and Zoho Finance—examine historical transactions to discern liquidity cycles, spot abnormalities, and predict cash-flow variations with enhanced accuracy. These tools enable MSMEs to optimize budgets and deploy resources effectively. Similarly, automated expense-monitoring solutions like Expensify and Fyle AI enhance financial oversight by categorizing spending in real time and identifying inefficiencies, hence minimizing manual accounting errors. AI-assisted revenue forecasting allows MSMEs to synchronize investment and expenditure decisions with projected demand cycles, thus enhancing capital efficiency (Kumar et al., 2024; Jain et al., 2025).

AI enhances the defenses of MSMEs against fraud and financial irregularities—risks that are especially pronounced in smaller firms without dedicated compliance teams. Machine-learning detection systems can incessantly monitor transactions to identify suspicious behaviors or unauthorized access. Instruments like PayPal Fraud Protection and IBM Trusteer demonstrate how AI algorithms detect irregularities within extensive transaction datasets, assisting organizations in minimizing losses and preserving consumer trust (Bello et al., 2023; Hasan & Rizvi, 2022). In addition to fraud protection, AI applications also encompass credit risk modeling and loan evaluation. Platforms such as Kabbage and Upstart AI conduct dynamic credit assessments that incorporate alternative data sources, enhancing MSMEs' access to finance and mitigating loan-default risk through more precise credit scoring.

In the digital economy, AI-enhanced cybersecurity has become essential for financial risk management. Advanced protection mechanisms—such as Darktrace and Symantec AI—constantly monitor transactional systems to identify breaches, phishing attempts, or data leaks in real time. For MSMEs with constrained IT skills, these technologies provide proactive protection, safeguarding the confidentiality and integrity of financial information (Thilagavathi et al., 2024). AI-driven monitoring enables small enterprises to alleviate the ripple effects of hacks that frequently result in reputational and financial harm.

From a resource-based view (RBV), AI serves as a dynamic tool that improves the financial acumen and risk management proficiency of MSMEs. By incorporating predictive, diagnostic, and prescriptive analytics into daily operations, companies transition from reactive bookkeeping to proactive strategy development. This transition improves decision-making quality, guarantees sustainable liquidity management, and facilitates responsiveness to external volatility. Thus, AI-driven financial management converts financial control from an administrative task into a strategic asset, associating technology adoption with enduring competitive advantage.

AI-driven financial management systems enable MSMEs to enhance forecasting accuracy, optimize cost management, and improve risk detection. By shifting from manual, reactive methods to data-driven, predictive solutions, MSMEs can enhance financial discipline and strategic vision. The incorporation of AI into financial decision-making functions as more than a technological enhancement; it represents an organizational transformation that empowers small enterprises to prosper in a progressively intricate and unpredictable economic landscape (Kumar et al., 2024; Jain et al., 2025; Bello et al., 2023; Thilagavathi et al., 2024).

## OBSTACLES IMPEDING AI IMPLEMENTATION IN MSMES

### 3.1 Financial Barriers to AI Adoption in MSMEs

Although the promise of Artificial Intelligence (AI) to transform corporate operations is acknowledged, financial constraints persist as a significant obstacle to adoption for Micro, Small, and Medium-Sized Enterprises (MSMEs). In contrast to major firms with significant research and development budgets, MSMEs function under stringent financial limitations that impede their capacity to rationalize the considerable initial expenses and unpredictable returns linked to AI integration. Substantial initial investment demands, unclear cost–benefit evaluations, and limited access to financing foster a risk-laden atmosphere that deters smaller enterprises from pursuing advanced digital transformation (Kar & Kushwaha, 2023; McElheran et al., 2024; Kinkel et al., 2022; Rahman et al., 2023).

A primary problem stems from the substantial capital commitments required for AI implementation. Advanced technologies, including machine learning platforms, process automation tools, and predictive analytics software, frequently necessitate expensive license, hardware, and cloud infrastructure. Advanced applications, such as computer vision and deep learning, require high-performance processing systems that surpass the capabilities of most MSMEs. In addition to acquisition costs, incorporating AI into current operations necessitates further investment in system integration, personnel training, and ongoing maintenance.

These ongoing expenditures intensify uncertainties around return on investment (ROI). Numerous MSMEs find it challenging to assess the immediate advantages of AI implementation, viewing it as a fiscal burden rather than a strategic prospect (Kar & Kushwaha, 2023; McElheran et al., 2024).

Restricted financial access exacerbates the cost barrier. Although governments in advanced economies have implemented grant schemes, tax incentives, and digital transformation funds—such as the European Union's Digital Europe Programme and the U.S. Small Business Innovation Research (SBIR) initiative—numerous MSMEs, especially in developing economies, remain oblivious to these programs or encounter bureaucratic obstacles in accessing them. In environments with weak financial infrastructures, MSMEs frequently lack collateral, credit histories, or the formal documentation necessary to obtain loans.

Despite the recent growth of venture capital and private equity investments, these funding sources remain predominantly focused on urban and high-technology industries, resulting in traditional or rural firms being inadequately supported (Anwar et al., 2025).

Recent breakthroughs underscore novel approaches that can mitigate these financial impediments. Cloud-based AI-as-a-Service (AIaaS) solutions from providers like Google Cloud, Microsoft Azure, and IBM Watson facilitate equitable access to AI for MSMEs by enabling payment on a subscription or consumption model instead of requiring substantial capital investments. AIaaS transitions costs from fixed to variable structures, facilitating experimentation with minimal risk exposure.

Furthermore, collaborations with accelerators, incubators, and innovation hubs can offer MSMEs financial support and chances for technical capacity enhancement.

Nonetheless, disparities in digital literacy and knowledge deficiencies among MSME proprietors persistently hinder the expansion of these activities (Kumar et al., 2024).

In the Technology–Organization–Environment (TOE) framework, financial restrictions signify the interaction among technical expenses, organizational readiness, and environmental support mechanisms. The substantial costs of AI adoption (technological context), inadequate internal preparedness (organizational context), and lack of finance or regulatory incentives (environmental context) together influence MSMEs' capacity to implement AI. Addressing these interconnected problems necessitates a coordinated, multi-stakeholder strategy that amalgamates public-sector incentives, private-sector finance frameworks, and scalable technical advancements.

Financial obstacles continue to be the predominant factor behind the unequal distribution of AI across MSMEs. Surmounting these obstacles requires cooperative engagement among governments, financial entities, and technology suppliers to establish supportive ecosystems. By aligning policies, implementing creative funding, and providing accessible technical models, MSMEs can overcome structural constraints and realize the productivity enhancements that AI offers (Kar & Kushwaha, 2023; McElheran et al., 2024; Kinkel et al., 2022; Rahman et al., 2023; Anwar et al., 2025).

## 3.2 Competency Deficiencies and AI Proficiency Among MSME Proprietors

Although Artificial Intelligence (AI) have the capacity to revolutionize corporate operations, financial limitations are the primary obstacle to AI adoption among Micro, Small, and Medium-Sized Enterprises (MSMEs). In contrast to major firms with significant research and development (R&D) budgets, MSMEs function under stringent financial constraints, rendering it challenging to rationalize the considerable initial expenditures and unpredictable returns linked to AI integration. Substantial implementation costs, unclear cost–benefit analyses, and restricted funding alternatives collectively foster a high-risk milieu that deters smaller enterprises from investing in advanced digital technologies (Kar & Kushwaha, 2023; McElheran et al., 2024; Kinkel et al., 2022; Rahman et al., 2023).

A significant barrier exists in the capital intensity associated with AI implementation. Advanced tools, including machine learning platforms, automation software, and predictive analytics, frequently necessitate expensive licenses and specialized equipment. Complex applications such as deep learning or computer vision necessitate high-performance computing capabilities that surpass the operational budgets of most MSMEs. In addition to acquisition costs, integration and maintenance expenses—such as personnel training, system adaptation, and data management—intensify the financial burden. Numerous MSMEs encounter challenges in measuring short-term returns on AI investments, hence supporting the impression of AI as a financially precarious and nonessential endeavor (Kar & Kushwaha, 2023; McElheran et al., 2024).

The restricted availability of external funding exacerbates these difficulties. Despite the implementation of supportive mechanisms by governments in developed economies—such as the European Union's Digital Europe Programme and the U.S. Small Business Innovation Research (SBIR) grants—numerous MSMEs, especially in developing nations, remain either uninformed or incapable of navigating the bureaucratic application procedures. Moreover, banking institutions frequently demand collateral or formal documentation that small enterprises are unable to furnish, and venture capital and private equity investments predominantly focus on urban high-tech industries, thereby neglecting traditional and rural micro, small, and medium enterprises (Anwar et al., 2025).

Innovative financial solutions present prospective cures. Cloud-based AI-as-a-Service (AIaaS) systems from Google, Microsoft, and IBM facilitate subscription-based access to AI technologies, transforming costs from fixed capital expenditures to predictable operational expenses. This strategy enables MSMEs to incrementally test and expand AI systems, hence minimizing risk exposure. Additionally, partnerships with accelerators, incubators, and innovation hubs can provide both financial support and technical proficiency. Nonetheless, adoption is inconsistent owing to inadequate digital literacy and restricted understanding of AI-driven financial solutions (Kumar et al., 2024).

In the Technology–Organization–Environment (TOE) framework, these financial obstacles signify an intersection of technology expenses, organizational preparedness, and environmental support mechanisms. Addressing these challenges necessitates a collaborative strategy involving regulatory incentives, private-sector finance strategies, and scalable AI technologies to democratize access and promote sustained competitiveness. Through the alignment of policy, finance, and technology, MSMEs may alleviate cost-related obstacles and harness the productivity potential of AI for sustained resilience (Kar & Kushwaha, 2023; McElheran et al., 2024; Kinkel et al., 2022; Rahman et al., 2023; Anwar et al., 2025).

Table 4 delineates a systematic synthesis of the principal financial impediments obstructing the adoption of Artificial Intelligence (AI) by Micro, Small, and Medium-Sized Enterprises (MSMEs), with the relevant enabling mechanisms that can promote effective implementation. Each obstacle—spanning elevated implementation expenses, restricted access to funding, ambiguous return on investment, and inadequate digital literacy—constitutes a significant problem impacting the technological and strategic preparedness of MSMEs. The table also emphasizes potential enabling mechanisms, like AI-as-a-Service (AIaaS), governmental incentives, innovative alliances, and digital inclusion initiatives, which jointly alleviate these hurdles by reducing entry costs and augmenting organizational capability. Situated within the Technology–Organization–Environment (TOE) paradigm, the table highlights the interplay of technological preparedness, organizational competence, and environmental support in influencing MSMEs' financial resilience and adoption trajectory during AI-driven transformation.

*Table 4. Financial Constraints and Enabling Mechanisms for AI Adoption in MSMEs*

| Financial Barrier | Impact on MSMEs | Potential Enabling Mechanism | Supporting Framework Element |
|---|---|---|---|
| **High implementation costs** | Limits technological investment | AI-as-a-Service (AIaaS) | Technological Readiness |
| **Limited financing access** | Restricts scaling capacity | Government incentives, Fintech inclusion | Environmental Support |
| **Uncertain ROI** | Inhibits strategic commitment | Predictive ROI modeling | Organizational Learning |
| **Low digital literacy** | Reduces adoption capability | Incubators, training programs | Organizational Capability |

*Source:* Author's synthesis based on Kar & Kushwaha (2023); McElheran et al. (2024); Kinkel et al. (2022); Rahman et al. (2023); Anwar et al. (2025); Kumar et al. (2024).

## 3.3 Data Privacy, Security, and Ethical Issues

As Micro, Small, and Medium-Sized Enterprises (MSMEs) increasingly adopt Artificial Intelligence (AI) in their operations, issues pertaining to data protection, cybersecurity, and ethical accountability have surfaced as significant barriers to sustainable implementation. In contrast to major organizations that possess specialized compliance teams and sophisticated IT infrastructure, MSMEs frequently lack the financial resources, technical proficiency, and organizational capability necessary for effective data governance. This structural fragility heightens their susceptibility to cyber threats, data breaches, and regulatory non-compliance—risks that may lead to financial losses, reputational harm, and diminished consumer trust (Gupta & Kumar Singh, 2023; Singgalen et al., 2021).

The growing dependence on AI-driven technologies amplifies data vulnerability. Micro, Small, and Medium Enterprises (MSMEs) increasingly handle increasing amounts of sensitive customer and operational data, rendering them attractive targets for hackers. Inadequate protective measures—such as feeble encryption, absence of multi-factor authentication, and insufficient oversight of AI algorithms—result in considerable risks. Cybercriminals are increasingly utilizing AI for nefarious purposes, such as automated phishing, ransomware, and deepfake deception. The lack of structured incident response strategies intensifies these risks, as several MSMEs do not possess defined protocols for risk assessment, data recovery, and crisis management. To address these problems, small firms necessitate economical cybersecurity frameworks, ongoing employee training, and flexible governance structures specifically designed for their resource limitations (Telukdarie et al., 2024).

Adherence to international data protection rules adds a further layer of complication. The General Data Protection Regulation (GDPR) in the European Union and the California Consumer Privacy Act (CCPA) in the United States provide rigorous mandates for data retention, consent, and algorithmic transparency. For MSMEs, meeting these duties can be financially onerous and operationally challenging, especially in the absence of specialist legal experience. Ethical considerations are intertwined with legislative matters, particularly about bias in AI decision-making, algorithmic transparency, and data privacy. Numerous MSMEs encounter difficulties in incorporating ethical safeguards into their systems, despite their necessity for sustaining legitimacy and public trust (Kulkarni et al., 2024).

These concerns underscore the conflict between innovation and governance in the digital transformation of MSMEs. The ethical application of AI should be perceived not merely as a legal obligation, but as a strategic imperative for fostering sustainable growth and consumer trust. The Technology–Organization–Environment (TOE) framework offers a valuable analytical perspective, elucidating the interplay between technology vulnerabilities, organizational shortcomings, and environmental pressures that influence MSMEs' capacity to adopt AI responsibly. Confronting these interconnected concerns necessitates a multi-stakeholder strategy that integrates government-backed cybersecurity initiatives, ethical AI frameworks, and scalable technology protections to guarantee that innovation occurs alongside accountability.

Whereas AI offers MSMEs unparalleled prospects for innovation and efficiency, ongoing concerns around privacy, security, and ethics pose significant obstacles to sustainable implementation. To ensure long-term sustainability, MSMEs must integrate technology safeguards, improve organizational literacy, and adhere to changing ethical and legal standards, thus aligning competitiveness with responsible digital transformation (Bhalla, 2025).

## SURMOUNTING AI ADOPTION OBSTACLES IN MSMES

### 4.1 Government Policies and Artificial Intelligence Support Initiatives

Governments worldwide are rapidly acknowledging the revolutionary capacity of Artificial Intelligence (AI) to drive economic growth, augment productivity, and bolster competitiveness. Nevertheless, Micro, Small, and Medium-Sized Enterprises (MSMEs) persistently encounter financial, technological, and legal obstacles that impede the efficient implementation of AI solutions. Policymakers have implemented various incentive mechanisms, financing schemes, and regulatory frameworks aimed at lowering adoption costs, enhancing technological integration, and enabling smaller enterprises to engage in the digital economy on more equitable terms (Loo et al., 2023).

A primary policy strategy entails providing direct financial support to alleviate the substantial initial expenses linked to AI integration. Governments often provide subsidies, grants, and low-interest loans to incentivize MSMEs to invest in AI and other digital technologies. The European Union's Digital Europe Programme finances innovation initiatives that allow small enterprises to explore AI applications, whereas Singapore's Enterprise Development Grant (EDG) offers monetary assistance to companies involved in digital transformation. Likewise, the U.S. Research & Development (R&D) Tax Credit permits small enterprises to deduct AI-related expenses from taxable revenue, thereby mitigating implementation costs. These financing mechanisms mitigate perceived risk and improve the cost–benefit analysis that frequently discourages MSMEs from digital investment (Saifurrahman & Kassim, 2024).

In addition to financial assistance, numerous governments acknowledge the necessity of improving digital literacy and capacity-building in the MSME sector. Training programs, frequently created in partnership with universities and research organizations, provide business owners and staff with the competencies to discover, integrate, and manage AI systems. The United Kingdom's AI for Small Business Programme provides targeted training and certifications designed to bridge the knowledge gap that limits smaller enterprises. Within the Technology–Organization–Environment (TOE) framework, these activities enhance organizational preparedness, illustrating that human capital and technology competencies are essential factors for effective adoption.

A crucial aspect of public policy is the formulation of regulatory frameworks that harmonize innovation with governance. Robust regulation guarantees that AI deployment adheres to ethical standards of openness, accountability, and data protection, thus protecting customers and maintaining confidence. Singapore's National

AI Strategy exemplifies an integrated policy strategy, amalgamating regulatory sandboxes, financial grants, and governance structures that facilitate experimentation within secure parameters. The European Union's Horizon Europe Programme and its AI regulatory guidelines offer financial and compliance assistance to MSMEs. Canada's Pan-Canadian Artificial Intelligence Strategy integrates funding and ethical oversight via the Canada Digital Adoption Program (CDAP), guaranteeing that innovation is accompanied by accountability (Michael, 2025).

These initiatives highlight the crucial importance of government policy in closing the digital divide between large enterprises and MSMEs. Governments foster an environment conducive to inclusive and sustainable AI deployment by mitigating economic restrictions, augmenting organizational capacity, and offering regulatory clarity. These interventions highlight the environmental aspect of the TOE framework, demonstrating how institutional infrastructure, public policy, and legal systems influence the technological pathways and competitive viability of MSMEs (Loo et al., 2023; Saifurrahman & Kassim, 2024; Michael, 2025).

## 4.2 Collaborative Solutions for AI Adoption in MSMEs

The obstacles encountered by Micro, Small, and Medium-Sized Enterprises (MSMEs) in the adoption of Artificial Intelligence (AI)—such as elevated implementation costs, technological intricacies, and insufficient expertise—can be efficiently alleviated through collaborative strategies. Collaborations with AI startups, technology providers, and research institutes, along with the increasing availability of AI-as-a-Service (AIaaS) platforms, provide MSMEs economical access to sophisticated AI capabilities without the encumbrance of substantial initial expenditures. Collaborative models facilitate gradual AI integration, mitigate risks, and improve competitiveness in progressively digital economies (Sharma et al., 2022).

Partnering with AI startups and technology providers is a viable alternative to expensive in-house development, which is sometimes unfeasible for smaller firms with limited resources. Through collaboration with AI-centric enterprises, MSMEs can obtain tailored, contextually relevant solutions aimed at addressing operational challenges such inventory optimization, service automation, and demand forecasting. AI-driven inventory management systems, such as those created by Shelf Engine, illustrate how collaborative solutions may improve resource efficiency and supply chain accuracy. Furthermore, partnerships with universities and research institutions allow MSMEs to engage in innovation hubs, accelerator initiatives, and government-sponsored pilot projects, granting access to academic knowledge and technical resources while mitigating adoption-related uncertainties. Prominent technology firms, such as Google, Microsoft, and IBM, have strengthened this collaborative environment by providing accelerator programs, mentorship, and AI toolkits specifically tailored for MSMEs, thus democratizing access to digital innovation.

Concurrently, AI-as-a-Service (AIaaS) has arisen as a cost-effective and scalable solution for the digital transformation of MSMEs. AIaaS, offered via cloud platforms, enables small businesses to implement pre-configured AI models for automation, analytics, and customer engagement, utilizing adaptable subscription pricing structures. Platforms like Google Cloud AI, Microsoft Azure AI, and Amazon AI Services reduce infrastructure expenses while offering substantial scalability (Nadi et al., 2024). Moreover, no-code and low-code AI platforms—such as MonkeyLearn, Lobe AI, and Google AutoML—empower non-technical people to intuitively deploy AI applications, thereby broadening accessibility within organizations that lack specialized programming expertise. In the realm of customer relationship management (CRM), AI-as-a-Service (AIaaS) products such as HubSpot AI, Drift, and Zendesk AI automate marketing initiatives, implement conversational agents, and improve personalization, thereby fortifying customer loyalty and stimulating sales growth.

From a theoretical perspective, these collaborative and service-oriented tactics correspond with both the Resource-Based View (RBV) and the Technology–Organization–Environment (TOE) frameworks. The Resource-Based View highlights the limited availability of strategic resources in MSMEs, where partnerships function as means to obtain complementary external resources, so converting collaboration into a competitive advantage. Within the TOE framework, AIaaS illustrates how environmental facilitators, including digital ecosystems and cloud-based infrastructures, can assist MSMEs in surmounting technological and organizational obstacles to adoption.

Collaborative partnerships and AIaaS models offer MSMEs a practical means to overcome financial, technological, and knowledge-related constraints. By utilizing risk-sharing agreements and strategically employing external expertise, MSMEs can effectively integrate AI, improve operational performance, and expedite innovation. These advancements highlight the significance of inter-organizational collaboration and digital ecosystems as catalysts for enabling smaller firms to leverage the revolutionary capabilities of AI (Sharma et al., 2022; Nadi et al., 2024).

## 4.3. Developing a Systematic AI Adoption Plan for MSMEs

The integration of Artificial Intelligence (AI) in Micro, Small, and Medium-Sized Enterprises (MSMEs) necessitates intentional strategic planning to guarantee operational efficiency and long-term sustainability. Notwithstanding the acknowledged benefits of AI—such as increased productivity, superior decision-making, and process automation—numerous MSMEs persist in facing significant obstacles, including elevated initial expenses, restricted technical proficiency, and ambiguity regarding integration strategies. To surmount these limitations, MSMEs must employ a methodical, incremental strategy that facilitates gradual execution, mitigates risks, and connects AI activities with overarching sustainability goals.

The initial phase of this strategic pathway is a thorough evaluation of organizational preparedness and business requirements. MSMEs must pinpoint particular operational inefficiencies—such as in inventory management, customer service, or supply chain operations—where AI might yield quantifiable benefits. This diagnostic evaluation must evaluate the firm's data infrastructure, staff competencies, and technology assets, establishing a baseline for assessing AI viability. By concentrating on high-impact, rapid-result applications—such as AI-powered chatbots for consumer engagement or AI-enhanced accounting tools—companies can attain initial successes that illustrate value and warrant ongoing investment.

The choice of economical platforms is equally essential. AI-as-a-Service (AIaaS) offerings from providers like Google Cloud, Microsoft Azure, and IBM Watson enable MSMEs to utilize AI functionalities without incurring substantial infrastructure expenses. Simultaneously, no-code and low-code AI solutions enhance accessibility, allowing enterprises lacking specialized knowledge to create viable applications. This gradual adoption method mitigates technological and financial risk while promoting innovation. Simultaneously, investment in human capital is essential. By means of training programs, academic collaborations, and partnerships with AI startups, MSME leaders can attain the managerial and technical skills essential for the efficient and responsible application of AI.

A staged implementation framework improves flexibility and knowledge acquisition. Commencing with pilot initiatives, MSMEs can test AI tools, assess efficacy, and enhance applications before comprehensive integration. Key performance indicators (KPIs), such as cost reductions, efficiency improvements, and customer happiness, ought to inform iterative modifications. This evidence-based approach guarantees that AI implementation progresses in accordance with the organization's strategic goals and contextual circumstances.

In addition to operational advantages, the implementation of AI must conform to sustainability standards. AI technology can substantially aid environmental goals by enhancing resource efficiency; for example, predictive maintenance systems can decrease energy consumption, while AI-optimized logistics can lower fuel usage and prevent overproduction. Furthermore, AI-enabled trash monitoring, recycling analysis, and circular economy strategies demonstrate how digital transformation can concurrently improve economic and environmental results.

A systematic AI adoption framework facilitates the cost-effective, scalable, and sustainable integration of technology for MSMEs. This simultaneous emphasis on digital transformation and environmental stewardship enables smaller firms to attain competitiveness while fostering sustainable growth. This framework integrates the ideas of the Technology–Organization–Environment (TOE) and Sustainable Development paradigms, highlighting how MSMEs can attain digital maturity while simultaneously promoting social and environmental responsibility.

## THE PROSPECTS OF ARTIFICIAL INTELLIGENCE IN MICRO, SMALL, AND MEDIUM ENTERPRISES AND SUSTAINABLE MARKETING

### 5.1 AI-Driven Sustainability in Micro, Small, and Medium Enterprises

In a time when sustainability has transitioned from an optional practice to a strategic necessity, Micro, Small, and Medium-Sized Enterprises (MSMEs) have increasing difficulties in reconciling profitability with environmental accountability. Artificial Intelligence (AI) presents significant prospects for MSMEs to concurrently lower expenses and advance global sustainability goals by reducing waste, optimizing energy usage, and integrating eco-efficient practices into their operational frameworks. Through the deliberate incorporation of AI into fundamental business operations, MSMEs can engage in the global shift towards a green economy while enhancing their competitiveness and resilience (Bhalla, 2025; Alabi et al., 2025; Behl et al., 2023; Jain et al., 2025).

An essential method by which AI promotes sustainability is through waste reduction and resource optimization. Predictive analytics allows MSMEs to synchronize production accurately with consumer demand, thereby averting overproduction and reducing surplus inventory. This accuracy not only lowers operational expenses but also decreases material waste and carbon emissions. Similarly, AI-augmented optimization methods in packaging design and raw material usage facilitate optimal resource consumption. Furthermore, AI-enabled trash monitoring and recycling analytics promote circular economy practices by monitoring material flows, recovering recyclable inputs, and prolonging product lifespans. These advancements demonstrate how AI aids MSMEs in transitioning from conventional linear production systems to circular, resource-efficient business models (Michael, 2025; Behl et al., 2023).

In addition to waste management, AI significantly enhances energy efficiency and facilitates intelligent energy management. AI-driven monitoring systems evaluate real-time usage data to identify inefficiencies and propose optimization options. When integrated with Internet of Things (IoT) technologies—such as smart grids and interconnected sensors—AI enables dynamic energy distribution, peak-load prediction, and adaptive control mechanisms. Predictive maintenance promotes sustainability by detecting mechanical flaws before to failures, so extending equipment lifespan, reducing energy waste, and mitigating greenhouse gas emissions.

Moreover, AI models facilitate the incorporation of renewable energy by forecasting meteorological conditions and energy requirements, hence maximizing the utilization of solar, wind, or hybrid systems (Alabi et al., 2025; Kulkarni et al., 2024).

These applications highlight the convergence of AI with global sustainability initiatives, including the United Nations Sustainable Development Goals (SDGs). By implementing intelligent waste reduction, optimizing clean energy, and managing resources circularly, MSMEs reduce their environmental footprint while enhancing legitimacy, stakeholder trust, and market positioning. According to the Resource-Based View (RBV), AI-driven sustainability practices are strategic intangible assets that provide a lasting competitive advantage, especially in markets increasingly influenced by environmental consciousness and eco-friendly customer behavior.

AI enables MSMEs to attain two goals—economic efficiency and environmental responsibility—by integrating sustainability into their technical advancement. The use of AI into waste management, energy efficiency, and circular economy initiatives allows smaller firms to decrease expenses, foster innovation, and support global sustainability objectives. Thus, MSMEs using AI-driven sustainability strategies become not only competitive market entities but also essential contributors to the global green transformation (Bhalla, 2025; Alabi et al., 2025; Kulkarni et al., 2024).

Table 5 delineates the various applications of Artificial Intelligence (AI) in promoting sustainable growth within Micro, Small, and Medium-Sized Enterprises (MSMEs), highlighting essential operational functions and their associated sustainability outcomes. The table illustrates how AI technologies, including predictive analytics, intelligent energy management systems, and circular economy tools, facilitate MSMEs in minimizing resource use, enhancing efficiency, and conforming to global sustainability guidelines. Each application domain aligns with particular United Nations Sustainable Development Goals (SDGs), highlighting AI's ability to incorporate environmental accountability into fundamental business practices. The synthesis illustrates the convergence of the Resource-Based View (RBV) and the Technology–Organization–Environment (TOE) frameworks, showcasing how AI-driven capabilities serve as strategic facilitators that improve competitiveness and sustainability performance in smaller enterprises.

*Table 5. AI Applications and Sustainability Outcomes for MSMEs*

| AI Application Area | Key Functions | Sustainability Outcome | Related SDG | Theoretical Lens |
|---|---|---|---|---|
| **Predictive Analytics** | Demand forecasting, production alignment | Waste reduction, resource efficiency | SDG 12 (Responsible Consumption) | RBV – Operational capability |
| **Smart Energy Systems** | IoT-based energy monitoring | Lower energy use, GHG reduction | SDG 7 (Clean Energy), SDG 13 (Climate Action) | TOE – Technological environment |
| **Circular Economy Tools** | Waste tracking, recycling analytics | Material recovery, eco-innovation | SDG 9 (Industry, Innovation) | RBV – Sustainable advantage |

Source: Author's synthesis based on Bhalla (2025); Alabi et al. (2025); Behl et al. (2023); Jain et al. (2025); Kulkarni et al. (2024).

## 5.2 Emerging Trends: Artificial Intelligence for Circular Economy and Green Marketing in MSMEs

The swift progression of Artificial Intelligence (AI) is transforming the operations of Micro, Small, and Medium-Sized Enterprises (MSMEs) in areas like sustainability and marketing. As international markets increasingly emphasize environmental responsibility, AI offers essential capabilities to synchronize company plans with ecological demands. AI facilitates the execution of circular economy frameworks, prioritizing waste minimization, resource efficiency, and material reutilization, while concurrently promoting green marketing strategies that appeal to environmentally aware consumers. By integrating AI into these two domains, MSMEs can enhance their competitiveness and sustainability, establishing themselves as proactive contributors to the shift towards more environmentally friendly business environments (Bapat et al., 2024).

In the circular economy, AI acts as a catalyst for reducing waste and optimizing resources. Machine learning algorithms can detect inefficiencies in production processes, minimizing material waste and enhancing packaging designs to mitigate environmental impacts. Advanced sorting and recycling systems optimize resource recovery, while predictive analytics boost demand forecasting, reducing the hazards of overproduction and wasteful consumption of raw materials. In addition to waste control, AI facilitates sustainable product innovation. Through the simulation of material consequences and the suggestion of alternatives, AI empowers MSMEs to explore biodegradable inputs and low-carbon production techniques that further both environmental and economic goals. In this regard, AI enhances operational efficiency and enables smaller enterprises to integrate sustainability into their value offers.

Artificial intelligence increasingly assumes a strategic role in sustainable marketing. As customer preferences evolve towards sustainability, MSMEs must adapt their marketing methods to attract environmentally concerned consumers. AI-driven analytics enable organizations to categorize consumers according to their sustainability preferences, providing insights into emerging trends in eco-friendly purchasing behavior (Hernandez et al., 2023). Utilizing systems like HubSpot and Salesforce AI, companies can implement hyper-personalized campaigns that emphasize the environmentally friendly characteristics of their products. Chatbots and virtual assistants augment customer involvement by delivering real-time information regarding sustainable alternatives, so reinforcing transparency and trust. Furthermore, AI-driven advertising optimization diminishes energy usage in digital campaigns, therefore connecting marketing practices with environmental goals while concurrently enhancing efficiency (Zeren, 2025).

These emergent applications can be analyzed through the Resource-Based View (RBV) and the Diffusion of Innovation (DoI) paradigm. In the context of RBV, AI-driven sustainability and green marketing capabilities are precious, scarce, and inimitable resources that provide MSMEs a sustainable competitive edge. Through the viewpoint of the DoI, the early adoption of AI for circular economy projects and eco-marketing establishes MSMEs as pioneers in addressing evolving consumer and regulatory demands. By integrating sustainability mandates with technological advancements, MSMEs not only adhere to global sustainability frameworks but also bolster their market legitimacy and differentiation (Mondal et al., 2025).

The future of AI in MSMEs is intrinsically linked to its contribution to enhancing circular economy practices and green marketing methods. By utilizing AI to minimize waste, enhance resource efficiency, and convey sustainability principles effectively, MSMEs can attain both profitability and environmental responsibility—ensuring resilience in a corporate environment that increasingly prioritizes green innovation.

## CONCLUSION

The incorporation of Artificial Intelligence (AI) signifies a pivotal avenue for augmenting the competitiveness, productivity, and sustainability of Micro, Small, and Medium-Sized Enterprises (MSMEs). This chapter demonstrates that AI adoption enables MSMEs to enhance operations, refine decision-making, and stimulate innovation, thus closing the performance gap with larger enterprises. Technologies like machine learning, predictive analytics, and automation optimize administrative and production operations while improving customer interaction and financial management skills. Nonetheless, ongoing obstacles—especially fiscal limitations, inadequate digital literacy, and regulatory intricacies—persist in hindering extensive adoption in developing economies.

To surmount these obstacles, MSMEs must adopt incremental, strategically aligned AI integration bolstered by capacity-building efforts, collaborative collaborations, and cost-effective AI-as-a-Service (AIaaS) models. Government policies and regulatory frameworks are crucial as they provide financial incentives, technical assistance, and ethical principles that promote inclusive and responsible digital transformation. Furthermore, integrating AI use with sustainability objectives—via waste minimization, energy optimization, and circular economy strategies—can yield dual advantages: environmental responsibility and enduring competitive edge.

The competitiveness of MSMEs in the digital age relies not only on technology access but also on the capacity to develop adaptive capabilities and strategic resilience. By cultivating an ecosystem that integrates innovation, policy support, and sustainability, AI can facilitate the transition of MSMEs from mere operational survival to sustainable growth, significantly contributing to equitable economic development and the achievement of the United Nations Sustainable Development Goals (SDGs).

## REFERENCES


Alabi, A. T., Ubandawaki, A. T., & Issa, S. O. (2025). The Role of Digital Technology in the Sustainability Strategies of SMEs. In *The Future of Small Business in Industry 5.0* (pp. 347–378). IGI Global Scientific Publishing. [HTML], DOI: 10.4018/979-8-3693-7362-0.ch014

Anwar, M., Korthaus, A., Bingley, S., & Burgess, S. (2025). AI in Small Businesses: Current and Potential Applications and Issues for Adoption. In Cutting-Edge Technologies for Business Sectors (pp. 29-56). IGI Global. mailto:DOI: [HTML] DOI: 10.4018/979-8-3693-9586-8.ch002

Bapat, G., Mahindru, R., Kumar, A., Rroy, A. D., Bhoyar, S., & Vaz, S. (2024). Leveraging ChatGPT for Empowering MSMEs: A Paradigm Shift in Problem Solving. Engineering Proceedings, 59(1), 197. https://doi.org/ mdpi.comDOI: 10.3390/engproc2023059197

Behl, A., Sampat, B., Pereira, V., & Chiappetta Jabbour, C. J. (2023). The role played by responsible artificial intelligence (RAI) in improving supply chain performance in the MSME sector: An empirical inquiry. [HTML]. *Annals of Operations Research*, •••, 1–30. DOI: 10.1007/s10479-023-05624-8 PMID: 36743350

Bello, O. A., Ogundipe, A., Mohammed, D., Adebola, F., & Alonge, O. A. (2023). AI-Driven Approaches for real-time fraud detection in US financial transactions: challenges and opportunities. European Journal of Computer Science and Information Technology, 11(6), 84-102. DOI: researchgate.netDOI: 10.37745/ejcsit.2013/vol11n684102

Bhalla, N. (2025, January 31). (). Role of AI in MSMEs and Its Impact on Financial Performance and Business Sustainability. [HTML]. *Advances in Finance, Accounting, and Economics*, 323–336. Advance online publication. DOI: 10.4018/979-8-3693-6011-8.ch013

Carayannis, E. G., Dumitrescu, R., Falkowski, T., & Zota, N. R. (2024). EMPOWERING SMES-"HARNESSING THE POTENTIAL OF GEN AI FOR RESILIENCE AND COMPETITIVENESS". [HTML]. *IEEE Transactions on Engineering Management*, *71*, 14754–14774. Advance online publication. DOI: 10.1109/TEM.2024.3456820

Christopher, Y., & Sundjaja, A. M. (2024, November). The Role of AI Chatbots on E-Commerce Platforms: Understanding its Influence on Customer Trust and Dependability. In 2024 9th International Conference on Information Technology and Digital Applications (ICITDA) (pp. 1-8). IEEE. DOI: [HTML]DOI: 10.1109/ICITDA64560.2024.10809919

Ezeife, E., Eyeregba, M. E., Mokogwu, C., & Olorunyomi, T. D. (2024). Integrating predictive analytics into strategic decision-making: A model for boosting profitability and longevity in small businesses across the United States. World Journal of Advanced Research and Reviews, 24(2), 2490-2507. https://doi.org/ researchgate.netDOI: 10.30574/wjarr.2024.24.2.3635

Gupta, A., & Kumar Singh, R. (2023). Managing resilience of micro, small and medium enterprises (MSMEs) during COVID-19: Analysis of barriers. [HTML]. *Benchmarking*, *30*(6), 2062–2084. Advance online publication. DOI: 10.1108/BIJ-11-2021-0700

Hasan, I., & Rizvi, S. A. M. (2022). AI-driven fraud detection and mitigation in e-commerce transactions. In Proceedings of Data Analytics and Management: ICDAM 2021, Volume 1 (pp. 403-414). Springer Singapore. https://doi.org/ [HTML]DOI: 10.1007/978-981-16-6289-8_34

Hernandez, A. A., Caballero, A. R., Albina, E. M., Balmes, I. L., & Niguidula, J. D. (2023, May). Artificial Intelligence for Sustainability: Evidence from select Small and Medium Enterprises in the Philippines. In 2023 8th International Conference on Business and Industrial Research (ICBIR) (pp. 818-823). IEEE. DOI: researchgate.netDOI: 10.1109/ICBIR57571.2023.10147579

Jain, A., Kakade, K. S., & Vispute, S. A. (2025). The Role of Artificial Intelligence (AI) in the Transformation of Small-and Medium-Sized Businesses: Challenges and Opportunities. Artificial Intelligence-Enabled Businesses: How to Develop Strategies for Innovation, 209-226. https://doi.org/[HTML]DOI: 10.1002/9781394234028.ch12

Kar, A. K., & Kushwaha, A. K. (2023). Facilitators and barriers of artificial intelligence adoption in business–insights from opinions using big data analytics. [HTML]. *Information Systems Frontiers*, *25*(4), 1351–1374. Advance online publication. DOI: 10.1007/s10796-021-10219-4

Kinkel, S., Baumgartner, M., & Cherubini, E. (2022). Prerequisites for the adoption of AI technologies in manufacturing–Evidence from a worldwide sample of manufacturing companies. [HTML]. *Technovation*, *110*, 102375. Advance online publication. DOI: 10.1016/j.technovation.2021.102375

Kulkarni, A. V., Joseph, S., & Patil, K. P. (2024). Artificial intelligence technology readiness for social sustainability and business ethics: Evidence from MSMEs in developing nations. … Journal of Information Management Data …. https://doi.org/ sciencedirect.comDOI: 10.1016/j.jjimei.2024.100250

Kumar, P., Kushwaha, A. K., Kar, A. K., Dwivedi, Y. K., & Rana, N. P. (2022). Managing buyer experience in a buyer–supplier relationship in MSMEs and SMEs. Annals of Operations Research, 1-28. https://doi.org/ springer.comDOI: 10.1007/ s10479-022-04954-3

Lo, W., Yang, C. M., Zhang, Q., & Li, M. (2024). Increased productivity and reduced waste with robotic process automation and generative AI-powered IoE services. Journal of Web Engineering. ieee.orgDOI: 10.13052/jwe1540-9589.2313

McElheran, K., Li, J. F., Brynjolfsson, E., Kroff, Z., Dinlersoz, E., Foster, L., & Zolas, N. (2024). AI adoption in America: Who, what, and where. Journal of Economics & Management Strategy, 33(2), 375-415. DOI: wiley.comDOI: 10.1111/jems.12576

Michael, O. (2025). Maximising the Potentials of Small and Medium Scale Business Enterprises in Developing Nations Through the Use of Artificial Intelligence: AI Adoption by SMEs in …. The Future of Small Business in Industry 5.0. DOI: [HTML]DOI: 10.4018/979-8-3693-7362-0.ch009

Mondal, S., Singh, S., & Gupta, H. (2025). Exploring barriers to innovative marketing in MSMES: An analysis using a BWM-ISM multi-criteria decision-making framework. [HTML]. *Journal of Multi-Criteria Decision Analysis*, *32*(1), e70005. DOI: 10.1002/mcda.70005

Nadi, A. H., Ahshan, K. A., Rahman, S., & Sofin, M. R. (2024). The role of artificial intelligence in business management: The future of small and medium-sized enterprise. In *Utilizing AI and Smart Technology to Improve Sustainability in Entrepreneurship* (pp. 117–133). IGI Global. [HTML], DOI: 10.4018/979-8-3693-1842-3.ch008

Rahman, M., Ming, T. H., Baigh, T. A., & Sarker, M. (2023). Adoption of artificial intelligence in banking services: An empirical analysis. [HTML]. *International Journal of Emerging Markets*, *18*(10), 4270–4300. DOI: 10.1108/IJOEM-06-2020-0724

Rosyidiana, R. N. & Narsa, I. M. (2024). Micro, small, and medium-sized enterprises (MSMEs) during the post-pandemic economic recovery period: digitalization, literation, innovation, and its impact on …. Cogent Business & Management. https:// doi.org/ tandfonline.comDOI: 10.1080/23311975.2024.2342488

Saad, N. A., Elgazzar, S., & Mlaker Kac, S. (2022). Investigating the Impact of resilience, responsiveness, and quality on customer loyalty of MSMEs: Empirical evidence. Sustainability. https://doi.org/ mdpi.comDOI: 10.3390/su14095011

Saifurrahman, A., & Kassim, S. H. (2024). Regulatory issues inhibiting the financial inclusion: a case study among Islamic banks and MSMEs in Indonesia. Qualitative Research in Financial Markets, 16(4), 589-617. DOI iium.edu.myDOI: 10.1108/QRFM-05-2022-0086

Sharma, P., Shah, J., & Patel, R. (2022). Artificial intelligence framework for MSME sectors with focus on design and manufacturing industries. Materials Today: Proceedings. https://doi.org/ pdpu.ac.inDOI: 10.1016/j.matpr.2021.12.360

Singgalen, Y. A., Purnomo, H. D., & Sembiring, I. (2021). Exploring MSMEs Cybersecurity Awareness and Risk Management: Information Security Awareness. IJCCS (Indonesian Journal of Computing and Cybernetics Systems), 15(3), 233-244. https://doi.org/ ugm.ac.idDOI: 10.22146/ijccs.67010

Sultana, S. T., & Rao, T. V. N. (2025). Role of ai-powered crm in business. In *Managing Customer-Centric Strategies in the Digital Landscape* (pp. 223–254). IGI Global. [HTML], DOI: 10.4018/979-8-3693-5668-5.ch009

Telukdarie, A., Dube, T., Munsamy, M., Murulane, K., & Mongwe, R. (2024). Navigating digital challenges for SMEs: a two-tier approach to risks mitigation and sustainability. Sustainability, 16(14), 5857. https://doi.org/ mdpi.comDOI: 10.3390/su16145857

Waghambare, M. A., Prabhu, S., & Ashok, P. (2024). Artificial Intelligence (AI)-Powered Chatbots for Marketing and Online Shopping. In Digital Technologies in Modeling and Management: Insights in Education and Industry (pp. 21-39). IGI Global. DOI: [HTML]DOI: 10.4018/978-1-6684-9576-6.ch002

Zeren, S. K. (2025). From Vision to Reality: Digital Transformation for Sustainable Tourism in Dubai's Megaprojects. In Achieving Business Excellence Through Triple Transformation (pp. 79-120). IGI Global Scientific Publishing. DOI: [HTML]DOI: 10.4018/979-8-3693-9435-9.ch004

Chapter 8

# Does AI Innovation Improve Competitive Advantage of SMEs Through Human Capital in Ethiopia?

**Tafese Niguse**
http://orcid.org/0009-0008-6536-6392
*Bule Hora University, Ethiopia*

**Kenesa Kebede**
http://orcid.org/0009-0004-1860-2752
*Bule Hora Universtity, Ethiopia*

**Lemma Gudissa Angessa**
*Ethiopian Civil Service University, Ethiopia*

**Shashi Kant**
http://orcid.org/0000-0003-4722-5736
*DMI-St. Eugene University, Zambia*

**Zerihun Kinde Alemu**
http://orcid.org/0000-0002-8546-2882
*Ethiopian Civil Service University, Ethiopia*

**Challa Amdissa Jiru**
http://orcid.org/0000-0002-6092-6644
*Independent Researcher, Ethiopia*

## ABSTRACT

*This study investigates the intricate relationship between AI innovations, human capital development, and competitive advantage within Ethiopian small and medium-sized enterprises (SMEs). Utilizing a mixed-methods approach, the research reveals that AI technologies significantly enhance competitive advantage by improving operational efficiencies and decision-making processes. Furthermore, the findings underscore the mediating role of human capital, indicating that organizations that invest in employee training and skills development can better leverage AI tools.*

DOI: 10.4018/979-8-3373-2817-1.ch008

*This dual focus on technological advancement and workforce development is essential for SMEs striving to thrive in an increasingly competitive landscape. The study emphasizes the importance of fostering a culture of continuous learning and collaboration between technology and human resource departments.*

## INTRODUCTION

In Ethiopia, SMEs represent a critical segment of the economy but often struggle with challenges such as limited access to technology, insufficient infrastructure, and inadequate training. These barriers hinder their ability to adopt AI innovations, which could enhance efficiency and competitiveness. Human capital is vital; however, many SMEs lack skilled personnel capable of leveraging AI effectively. Thus, while AI has the potential to improve competitive advantage, the realization of this potential is contingent on addressing human capital deficiencies and fostering a supportive innovation environment (Iyelolu et al., 2024).

The use of artificial intelligence (AI) to boost the competitive edge of small and medium-sized businesses (SMEs) has attracted a lot of interest worldwide in an era characterized by fast technological improvement (Magableh et al., 2024). AI innovation has the potential to be revolutionary, especially in developing nations like Ethiopia where SMEs are essential for innovation, job creation, and economic progress. The idea of using AI to gain a competitive edge has its roots in the growing incorporation of technology into company operations, which is motivated by the need for flexibility and efficiency in a market that is always changing (Niguse& Borji, 2025).

Adoption of AI is positively correlated with increased operational effectiveness, consumer engagement, and decision-making skills, according to empirical research. According to studies, SMEs may improve their product offers, cut expenses, and streamline operations by implementing AI technology, which will ultimately strengthen their position in the market. The practical difficulties of integrating AI in Ethiopian SMEs remain significant, notwithstanding these encouraging results. These include a lack of competent human resources, restricted access to technology infrastructure, and ignorance of the potential advantages of artificial intelligence (Dinku et al., 2024).

Furthermore, nothing is known about the precise ways in which AI innovation affects Ethiopian SMEs' competitive advantage from a human capital perspective. Few research have examined AI's consequences within Ethiopia's distinct socioeconomic and cultural environment, despite the fact that several studies have examined the technology's effects on enterprises worldwide. This gap is especially important as policymakers and practitioners may find useful insights from knowledge of how AI, human capital, and competitive advantage interact (Borji et al., 2025).

By analyzing how AI is integrated into Ethiopian SMEs and how effective implementation depends on human capital, this chapter seeks to close these gaps. The study will offer a thorough foundation for further research and policy suggestions by emphasizing the potential and difficulties encountered by these businesses. The impact of AI innovation on Ethiopian SMEs may differ from that in other countries due to specific challenges such as limited infrastructure, varying levels of human capital, and unique market dynamics. These factors shape how AI can be effectively integrated and utilized. This study's main inquiry is: How does AI innovation enhance Ethiopian SMEs' competitive advantage through the creation and use of human capital? The answer to this issue is crucial for developing policies that improve SMEs' capacities and, eventually, support the region's sustainable economic growth.

## BACKGROUND

Ethiopia's small and medium-sized business (SME) landscape is defined by a vibrant yet difficult setting. These businesses are essential to the country's economy since they greatly foster innovation and the development of jobs. However, several obstacles, such as restricted access to capital, poor infrastructure, and a lack of trained workers, make it difficult for many SMEs to effectively compete despite their potential. One viable way to increase these businesses' competitiveness is through the incorporation of artificial intelligence (AI). However, there are several obstacles that prevent Ethiopian SMEs from reaping the full benefits of AI technology adoption.

These significant challenges include limited resources, inadequate training, and an unsupportive corporate culture. A lack of physical and financial assets, along with insufficient employee skill sets, hinders their ability to innovate and compete effectively. In Ethiopia, the importance of human capital in driving strategic innovation remains underappreciated, making it difficult for SMEs to leverage their workforce effectively (Gebremichael et al., 2020).

A local textile SME in Addis Ababa serves as a real-world case study that demonstrates these difficulties. This business aimed to optimize its supply chain by putting AI-driven inventory management solutions into place. Despite technology's promise to save waste and boost productivity, managers had to overcome many challenges. First, because the local workforce had little exposure to cutting-edge technical tools, there was a shortage of skilled workers who could operate and maintain the AI systems. Furthermore, the initial outlay needed to install AI was exorbitant, particularly in a market with restricted financing options. Despite the initial excitement, the corporation eventually had trouble incorporating the technology into its current procedures, which resulted in disappointing outcomes (Niguse & Borji, 2025).

An agricultural SME in rural Ethiopia made an effort to implement AI technologies for precision farming in another instance. The goal of this project was to maximize agricultural production by analyzing soil health using AI algorithms. However, the real-time data collecting required for AI to work effectively was hampered by rural areas' unreliable internet access. Furthermore, a lot of farmers were reluctant to embrace new technology, favoring tried-and-true, and conventional techniques. This example demonstrates how infrastructure constraints and cultural considerations can seriously impede the effective use of AI advancements (Borji et al., 2025).

These illustrations highlight the various obstacles Ethiopian SMEs have when attempting to use AI technology. Beyond technical obstacles, the situation is made more difficult by problems including budgetary limitations, insufficient training programs, and cultural opposition to change. Gaining an understanding of these contextual elements is essential to creating focused strategies that can help SMEs in Ethiopia successfully incorporate AI into their operational frameworks. In order to facilitate the adoption of AI in the SME sector, this study intends to explore these issues in further detail and offer insights that can guide future research and policy activities (Dinku et al., 2024).

## Related Theories

Numerous theoretical frameworks offer insightful perspectives on the dynamics of AI adoption and how it affects competitive advantage, especially for small and medium-sized businesses (SMEs).

One well-known idea is the Technology Acceptance Model (TAM), which holds that consumers' decisions to embrace and employ new technologies are greatly influenced by their perceptions of their utility and simplicity of use. TAM can assist in elucidating the elements that influence employees' and entrepreneurs' readiness to adopt AI technology in the context of Ethiopian SMEs. Determining adoption obstacles and creating plans to increase acceptance require an understanding of these perspectives (Borji et al., 2025).

The Resource-Based View (RBV), which highlights the significance of internal resources and skills in attaining competitive advantage, is another pertinent perspective. According to this hypothesis, businesses that own distinctive assets—like highly qualified personnel and cutting-edge technologies—are more likely to surpass their rivals. The RBV emphasizes the value of human capital in utilizing AI's potential to boost innovation and operational efficiency. It implies that Ethiopian SMEs should spend money on training and development to acquire the skills required for successful AI deployment (Mebratie et al., 2025).

The Diffusion of Innovations Theory, which examines how, why, and how quickly new concepts and technologies proliferate throughout a culture, is also relevant. This theory can provide light on the obstacles Ethiopian SMEs have while using AI, namely with relation to communication channels, social norms, and the perceived advantages of innovation. By addressing the environmental and cultural elements that affect acceptance, attempts to promote AI adoption may be informed by an understanding of the diffusion process (Dinku et al., 2024).

The Resource-Based View (RBV) is the primary theoretical framework used in this investigation. RBV is especially pertinent since it emphasizes the role of resources in gaining a sustainable competitive advantage in addition to the significance of human capital. This study is to investigate how Ethiopian SMEs may successfully utilize their internal resources to traverse the hurdles of AI implementation by concentrating on the relationship between AI adoption and the growth of human capital. The examination of case studies will be guided by this theoretical framework, which will assist in identifying the skills and assets necessary for effective AI integration in the setting of Ethiopia's SME sector. In the end, the RBV offers a thorough framework for comprehending the intricate dynamics of AI adoption and how they affect Ethiopian SMEs' ability to compete.

## Small and Medium Enterprises in Ethiopia

In 1997, Ethiopia classified businesses as Micro Enterprises if total assets were under 20,000 Birr ($1,200) and Small Enterprises if under 500,000 Birr ($30,000). This definition, based solely on total assets, differed from international standards. In 2011, Ethiopia updated its classification to align with definitions used by other countries and organizations, focusing on Micro and Small Enterprises without distinguishing between Small and Medium Enterprises. The new Small & Micro Enterprises Development Strategy, released by the Ministry of Trade and Industry, defines Micro and Small Enterprises based on labor and capital, establishing similar criteria for medium-sized businesses (Dinku et al., 2024).

## Effect of AI innovation on competitive advantage

Numerous studies have focused on how artificial intelligence (AI) innovation affects competitive advantage, finding a favorable relationship between AI adoption and improved corporate performance. According to research, businesses that use AI technology report increased operational efficiency as a result of data-driven decision-making and automation. AI technologies may lower expenses and streamline procedures, enabling companies to more efficiently utilize resources. For SMEs, this operational efficiency is essential, especially in emerging nations with resource restrictions like Ethiopia. These businesses may level the playing field and outperform competitors that are slower to adopt new technologies by implementing AI (Dinku et al., 2024).

Additionally, it has been demonstrated that AI innovation improves consumer happiness and engagement, giving businesses a competitive edge. Businesses that use AI for personalized marketing and customer care claim improved levels of customer loyalty and retention. For SMEs in Ethiopia, where fostering solid client connections are crucial to viability, this is especially pertinent. These businesses may customize their products to match the unique requirements of their customers by utilizing AI-driven data, which will increase consumer engagement. In addition to improving customer happiness, SMEs' capacity to recognize and cater to consumer preferences sets them apart from rivals and strengthens their position in the market (Abdi et al., 2021).

AI innovation promotes better decision-making procedures in addition to operational effectiveness and client engagement. Artificial intelligence (AI) can analyze enormous volumes of data to find patterns and trends that human analysts would miss. By incorporating AI into decision-making, Ethiopian SMEs may develop better-informed plans that would allow them to more quickly and nimbly overcome market uncertainty. Making decisions based on data improves responsiveness to shifting market conditions, which is essential in an economy that is changing quickly. SMEs that use AI to make decisions are therefore in a better position to take advantage of opportunities and reduce risks, which strengthens their competitive edge (Geru et al., 2025).

Even though AI has many potential advantages, empirical research also reveals obstacles that may prevent its deployment. For example, organizational culture and aversion to change might impede the adoption of AI technology. Overcoming this reluctance is essential to maximizing the promise of AI innovation in Ethiopian SMEs, where conventional methods may predominate. Furthermore, these difficulties may be made worse by restricted access to technology infrastructure and qualified workers, which might lead to disconnect between the potential advantages of AI and the realities that SMEs must deal with (Borji et al., 2025).

H1: AI innovation has significant effect on competitive advantage

## Effect of AI Innovation on Human Capital

Organizational human capital development is significantly impacted by the incorporation of artificial intelligence (AI) innovation. Human resources are being diverted towards higher-value pursuits like creativity and strategic thinking as AI technology progressively automate repetitive work. AI can enhance human capabilities, allowing workers to use their talents more effectively. This change offers Ethiopian SMEs the chance to improve job satisfaction and employee engagement by allowing workers to concentrate on jobs that call for critical thinking and problem-solving skills, which will ultimately result in a workforce that is more talented and adaptable (Geru et al., 2025).

Additionally, AI innovation demands that workers constantly retrain and up skills to work with cutting-edge technologies. Organizations that engage in training programs to boost digital skills report increased productivity and creativity. Establishing a culture of lifelong learning is crucial for Ethiopian SMEs to provide staff members the skills they need to collaborate with AI technologies. These businesses can make sure that their workforce is competitive and equipped to take advantage of AI technology by putting a high priority on human capital development through focused training programs (AlQershi et al., 2020).

AI has an impact on hiring and selection procedures in businesses as well, as companies are looking for people who could succeed in an AI-enhanced workplace. Companies are changing their recruiting standards because of the growing need for tech-savvy workers. This change offers Ethiopian SMEs possibilities as well as obstacles. The need for skilled personnel may make it harder to find suitable applicants, but it also pushes schools to adapt their curricula to meet business needs, which will improve the nation's human capital situation overall (Niguse& Borji, 2025).

AI technology adoption may also result in modifications to worker dynamics, such as patterns of cooperation and communication. AI can help teams work together more effectively by offering data-driven insights that guide decision-making. Promoting a collaborative culture around AI technologies in Ethiopian SMEs can improve group creativity and problem-solving. Addressing any issues with job displacement and making sure that workers are assisted during this change are crucial, nevertheless. Ethiopian SMEs can build a robust workforce that can adjust to the changing needs of the market by concentrating on human capital development in tandem with AI innovation (Awode et al., 2025).

H2: AI innovation has significant effect on human capital.

## Effect of human capital on competitive advantage

Human Capital's Impact on Competitive Advantage Organizations' competitive advantage is largely determined by their capital, especially in dynamic marketplaces. An organization's capacity to innovate and adapt to shifting market conditions is directly impacted by the abilities, expertise, and experience of its workforce. Businesses with well-trained personnel are better positioned to increase productivity and spur development. To gain a competitive edge, Ethiopian SMEs must invest in the development of their human resources. These businesses may use their people's resources to outperform competitors, adjust to changes in the market, and seize new possibilities by developing talent and promoting a culture of continuous learning (Borji et al., 2025).

Furthermore, organizational culture is greatly influenced by human capital, and this in turn influences competitive advantage. Employee engagement and loyalty are fostered by a strong culture of dedication, creativity, and cooperation. Organizations with pleasant workplace cultures are more likely to retain top personnel and achieve greater performance levels. Fostering an inclusive and encouraging culture inside Ethiopian SMEs will improve worker satisfaction, which will reduce attrition and increase output. In addition to bolstering the staff, this cultural investment improves the organization's overall efficacy and boosts its position in the market (Gebremichael et al., 2020).

Human capital also affects an organization's capacity to successfully adopt new procedures and technology. Strong skill sets make employees better at incorporating innovations into their everyday work, which is essential in the fast-paced commercial world of today. Companies that place a high priority on developing their human capital are better able to take advantage of technological breakthroughs to obtain a competitive edge. Maintaining success for Ethiopian SMEs requires giving staff members the skills they need to handle technological advancements. These businesses may increase their operational skills and responsiveness to market needs by cultivating an atmosphere that prioritizes learning and continuous development (Niguse& Borji, 2025).

Lastly, gaining a competitive edge depends on strategically matching organizational objectives with human capital. Good leadership and talent management techniques guarantee that workers' abilities and proficiencies complement the organization's goals and vision. In competitive marketplaces, companies that actively manage their human resources to meet strategic goals have a higher chance of success. A more targeted approach to talent development is made possible for Ethiopian SMEs by coordinating human capital activities with business strategy. By highlighting the role that human capital plays in attaining organizational success, these businesses may create a long-lasting competitive edge that propels performance and growth over the long run (Kusumawijaya & Astuti, 2024).

H3: Human capital has significant effect on competitive advantage

## Mediating role of human capital among AI innovations and competitive advantage

Human Capital's Mediating Function in AI Innovations and Competitive Advantage The link between advancements in artificial intelligence (AI) and competitive advantage is significantly mediated by capital. Organizations' workforce's skills and talents have a significant impact on how well AI technologies operate when they are implemented. According to research, a trained staff can more effectively use AI tools to increase efficiency and production. To get the most out of AI deployments, Ethiopian SMEs must invest in the development of their human resources. These businesses may successfully close the gap between AI capabilities and operational performance by making sure that staff members receive the required training, which will eventually result in a long-term competitive advantage (Dinku et al., 2024).

Furthermore, an organization's ability to successfully incorporate AI breakthroughs into its current procedures is influenced by its human resources. Workers that possess excellent technical and analytical abilities are better able to decipher AI-generated insights and use them to inform decisions. Research indicates that companies with a trained workforce are more equipped to adjust their operations to AI-driven data analysis. Employees at Ethiopian SMEs may confidently use AI technology when a culture of continuous learning is fostered. In addition to improving operational effectiveness, this flexibility puts these businesses in a position to take advantage of fresh market possibilities, strengthening their competitive advantage in a business environment that is changing quickly (Farmanesh et al., 2025).

Human capital influences organizational culture, which influences the acceptance of AI advances, in addition to improving operational performance. Employees are encouraged to interact with new technologies and try out their applications when they work in a creative and encouraging environment. According to research, companies that have a strong learning and teamwork culture have a higher chance of implementing AI projects successfully. The potential for using AI to gain a competitive edge increases dramatically when human capital is in line with an innovative corporate culture (Tolossa et al., 2025).

Lastly, to maximize AI efforts' influence on competitive advantage, human capital development and AI activities must be strategically aligned. Businesses may make sure that their workforce is equipped to handle the demands of a technologically advanced market by giving training and development in AI-related skills first priority. According to research, strategic human resource management improves organizational performance by increasing the efficacy of AI advances. Aligning AI deployment with human capital initiatives benefits Ethiopian SMEs by enhancing operational capabilities and encouraging creativity. Building a sustained competitive advantage via this alignment is crucial for these businesses to prosper in a setting that is becoming more and more competitive (Rony & Yahaya, 2021).

H4: Human capital mediates the association among AI innovation and competitive advantage.

# MAIN FOCUS OF THE CHAPTER

## Conceptual framework

Based on theoretical and empirical literature, the researcher developed the following conceptual framework having independent variable (AI innovations), mediating variable (human capital) and dependent variable (competitive advantage).

*Figure 1. Conceptual framework*

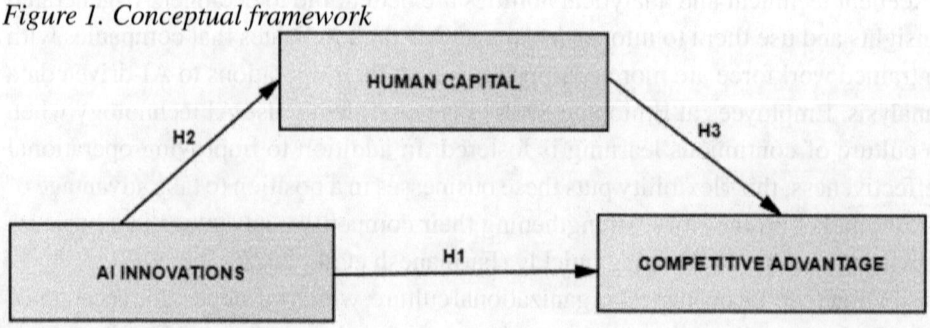


*Source: Authors*

## Statement of the Problem

Artificial intelligence (AI) integration could greatly increase Ethiopian SMEs' competitive edge at this pivotal moment. Adoption of AI technology should ideally enable these businesses to increase operational effectiveness, develop new product offers, and better respond to market demands (Ferede, 2025). The way AI is currently being used in Ethiopian SMEs, however, is far from ideal. The benefits of adopting AI are contradicted by the literature now in publication. While some studies show significant increases in productivity and market competitiveness, others point out enduring obstacles that prevent successful deployment (Iyelolu et al., 2024).

These conflicting results highlight several knowledge gaps regarding AI's contribution to SME development. First, there is a theoretical lack of frameworks that expressly address how AI may be used in Ethiopia to gain a competitive edge. Although international studies shed light on how AI affects companies, they frequently overlook the distinct socioeconomic and cultural elements that influence the Ethiopian market. Furthermore, there are knowledge gaps in the abilities and proficiencies needed for a successful AI deployment. The results of previous studies have been ambiguous since many SMEs lack a clear knowledge of how to successfully employ human capital with AI technology (Niguse & Borji, 2025).

There are also clear contextual gaps because the majority of AI research concentrates on developed economies while ignoring the difficulties encountered by SMEs in developing countries like Ethiopia. The lack of training programs and supporting government regulations exacerbates the practical difficulties of applying AI, which include restricted access to technology, inadequate infrastructure, and a lack of funding. These difficulties provide a complicated environment that prevents AI from being effectively adopted, preventing many SMEs from realizing its full potential (Gebremichael et al., 2020).

By offering a thorough examination of the relationship between AI innovation, human capital, and competitive advantage in Ethiopian SMEs, this research seeks to close these complex gaps. Through examining case studies and using a mixed-methods approach, the study will shed light on the real-world difficulties these businesses confront and offer useful suggestions for practitioners and policymakers. Additionally, by providing a framework that may direct future research endeavors and influence strategic attempts to enhance the competitiveness of SMEs in Ethiopia, this study will advance the theoretical understanding of AI adoption in developing environments. By doing this, it hopes to open the door to a more sophisticated comprehension of how AI may be successfully incorporated into Ethiopia's SME environment, thereby promoting long-term economic growth and development.

## Research Methodology

The mediating function of human capital between AI advances and competitive advantage in Ethiopian SMEs was examined in this study using a quantitative research methodology. 376 individuals in total, selected from a variety of SME landscape sectors, were polled. For this investigation, the researcher used manufacturing SMEs particularly. In addition to this, the target population of current investigation comprised of owners and managers of SMEs. Furthermore, the data for this investigation was collected in the last week of May 2025. Structured questionnaires were intended to assess the concepts of AI advances, human capital, and competitive advantage were used in the data gathering process with five-point Likert scale ranging from strongly disagree to strongly agree.

The Kaiser-Meyer-Olkin (KMO) measure was used to evaluate the sample size prior to the main analysis, and the results showed adequate sampling adequacy. To make sure the data matched the theoretical conceptions, exploration factor analysis (EFA) was then used to find underlying dimensions among the variables. A thorough analysis of both direct and indirect effects was made possible by the use of Structural Equation Modeling (SEM) with AMOS software to analyze the structural relationships between the variables. This analysis shed light on the ways in which human capital mediates the relationship between AI innovations and competitive advantage.

A comprehensive evaluation of relevant literature served as the foundation for the scale development for this investigation. Existing frameworks that highlighted aspects like automation capabilities, data analytics, and innovation adoption served as the basis for the constructions pertaining to AI innovations. Drawing from research that emphasizes the value of training and development in optimizing technological effectiveness, human capital was conceptualized using ideas that place an emphasis on skills, knowledge, and employee engagement. Reflecting the complex nature of competitive positioning, competitive advantage was defined in terms of customer satisfaction, market responsiveness, and operational efficiency.

Each construct's pieces were thoughtfully created to guarantee its clarity and applicability to Ethiopian SMEs. A smaller sample was used for pre-testing to improve validity and reliability and refine the scale items. The constructs assessed were theoretically sound and practically usable because to this meticulous scale creation approach, which also served as a strong basis for the analysis that followed.

## Data Analysis

### KMO and Bartlett's Test Analysis

A high degree of sample adequacy for factor analysis is shown by the Kaiser-Meyer-Olkin (KMO) measure of sampling adequacy findings, which were reported at 0.852. This result indicates that the information gathered from the 376 respondents is appropriate for factor analysis since it is above the generally recognized cutoff of 0.60. The correlations between variables are sufficiently strong when the KMO value is closer to 1, which means that methods like exploratory factor analysis (EFA) may be used. A KMO value of 0.852 in this study indicates that the sample size is sufficient to investigate the underlying structure of the constructs pertaining to competitive advantage, human capital, and AI advances.

The data's suitability for factor analysis is further supported by Bartlett's Test of Sphericity, which produces an estimated chi-square value of 1419.745 with 89 degrees of freedom and a significance level of 0.000. Significant correlations between the variables are confirmed by the significant p-value ($p < 0.001$), which shows that the correlation matrix is not an identity matrix. Because it implies that the variables are sufficiently connected to justify more investigation by EFA, this finding emphasizes the possibility of uncovering underlying causes. When combined, these statistical tests strengthen the dataset's validity and guarantee that the next analysis will offer insightful information about the connections between the dimensions under study (table 1).

*Table 1. KMO and Bartlett's Test*

| **Kaiser-Meyer-Olkin Measure of Sampling Adequacy.** | | **.852** |
|---|---|---|
| Bartlett's Test of Sphericity | Approx. Chi-Square | 1419.745 |
| | Df | 89 |
| | Sig. | .000 |

Source: Authors

The results of the Principal Component Analysis (PCA) of the total variance explained are shown in Table 2, with an emphasis on the eigenvalues and the proportion of variance that each component accounts for. With an initial eigenvalue of 4.51, the first component explains 32.235% of the variation. This noteworthy proportion suggests that a large amount of the data's underlying structure is captured by the first component. At this point, the cumulative percentage of variance is at 32.235%, indicating that the first component by itself offers a significant representation of the components under study.

With an eigenvalue of 1.37, the second component adds 9.787% to the overall variance, increasing the cumulative percentage to 42.022%. With an eigenvalue of 1.27, the third component comes in second, accounting for 9.087% of the variance and contributing to a cumulative total of 51.110%. These results support the existence of discrete underlying elements pertaining to advances AI, human capital, and competitive advantage, as the first three components together explain more than half of the dataset's variation.

With eigenvalues below 1, the fourth, fifth, and sixth components contribute less significantly to the overall structure, demonstrating decreasing benefits in terms of explained variance. Notably, the fifth and sixth components account for 6.223% and 5.519% of the variance, respectively, whereas the fourth component has an eigenvalue of 0.949 and explains 6.782%. The findings imply that although the first components account for most of the variation, further components might not offer significant new information. The idea that concentrating on the first three elements will provide the most pertinent data for comprehending the connections between the constructs under study is supported by this research (table 2).

*Table 2. Total Variance Explained*

| Component | Initial Eigenvalues | | | Extraction Sums of Squared Loadings | | | Rotation Sums of Squared Loadings | | |
|---|---|---|---|---|---|---|---|---|---|
| | Total | % of Variance | Cumulative % | Total | % of Variance | Cumulative % | Total | % of Variance | Cumulative % |
| 1 | 4.51 | 32.235 | 32.235 | 4.51 | 32.235 | 32.235 | 3.00 | 21.451 | 21.451 |
| 2 | 1.37 | 9.787 | 42.022 | 1.37 | 9.787 | 42.022 | 2.16 | 15.491 | 36.942 |
| 3 | 1.27 | 9.087 | 51.110 | 1.27 | 9.087 | 51.110 | 1.98 | 14.168 | 51.110 |
| 4 | .949 | 6.782 | 57.892 | | | | | | |
| 5 | .871 | 6.223 | 64.115 | | | | | | |
| 6 | .773 | 5.519 | 69.634 | | | | | | |

Extraction Method: Principal Component Analysis.
Source: Authors

## Confirmatory Principal Component Examination

The principal component arrangement of a set of guided proxies is verified using a type of statistics known as confirmatory principal component examination. Based on the underlying job frame and correlatives among observed proxies, investigations can evaluate hypotheses utilizing CFA. To evaluate the hypothesis that there is a association among the proxies that are being steered and the latent conceptions that underpin them, the inquiry employed CFA under table 3.

The results of the Principal Component Analysis (PCA) of the total variance explained are shown in Table 2, with an emphasis on the eigenvalues and the proportion of variance that each component accounts for. With an initial eigenvalue of 4.51, the first component explains 32.235% of the variation. This noteworthy proportion suggests that the first with a critical ratio (C.R.) of 8.231 and a standard error of 0.019, the correlation between AI innovations and human capital are 0.240, and it is statistically significant ($p < 0.001$). This high positive correlation suggests that the degree of AI advances in organizations rises in tandem with human capital. The notion that investments in employee knowledge and abilities directly increase the uptake and efficacy of AI technology is supported by the high C.R. value, which indicates a significant link.

This link emphasizes how crucial workforce development is to be optimizing the advantages of AI advances and giving businesses a competitive edge in the context of Ethiopian SMEs.

With a critical ratio of 7.692 and a standard error of 0.028, the correlation between competitive advantage and human capital is 0.300, and it is significant at $p < 0.001$. This shows a strong positive correlation, indicating that gaining a competitive edge is greatly aided by improved human capital. The results are consistent with previous research that highlights how competent workers contribute to the success of organizations. This link emphasizes how important it is for Ethiopian SMEs to put human capital development first as a strategic way to boost market responsiveness and operational efficiency, which will eventually provide a long-lasting competitive advantage.

With a critical ratio of 7.831 and a standard error of 0.240, the correlation between AI innovations and competitive advantage is 0.260, and it is statistically significant ($p < 0.001$). Businesses that successfully use AI technologies have a higher chance of gaining a competitive edge, according to this positive covariance. The idea of using AI technology may result in increased operational efficiency as well as customer happiness is supported by the significant C.R. value. This link is important for Ethiopian SMEs because it shows how AI may be a game-changing tool for increasing competitiveness. These businesses may more effectively negotiate the market's intricacies and set themselves up for long-term success by combining AI technologies with human capital investments.

A significant amount of the data's underlying structure is captured by the t component. At this point, the cumulative percentage of variance is at 32.235%, indicating that the first component by itself offers a significant representation of the components under study.

With an eigenvalue of 1.37, the second component adds 9.787% to the overall variance, increasing the cumulative percentage to 42.022%. With an eigenvalue of 1.27, the third component comes in second, accounting for 9.087% of the variance and contributing to a cumulative total of 51.110%. These results support the existence of discrete underlying elements pertaining to advances AI, human capital, and competitive advantage, as the first three components together explain more than half of the dataset's variation.

With eigenvalues below 1, the fourth, fifth, and sixth components contribute less significantly to the overall structure, demonstrating decreasing benefits in terms of explained variance. Notably, the fifth and sixth components account for 6.223% and 5.519% of the variance, respectively, whereas the fourth component has an eigenvalue of 0.949 and explains 6.782%. The findings imply that although the first components account for most of the variation, further components might not offer significant new information. The idea that concentrating on the first three elements will provide the most pertinent data for comprehending the connections between the constructs under study is supported by this research.

*Table 3. Covariances*

| Covariance | | | Approximation | S.E. | C.R. | P | Hy. |
|---|---|---|---|---|---|---|---|
| **Human capital** | **<-->** | **AI innovations** | **.240** | **.019** | **8.231** | ******* | **H2** |
| Human capital | <--> | Competitive advantage | .300 | .028 | 7.692 | *** | **H3** |
| AI innovations | <--> | Competitive advantage | .260 | .240 | 7.831 | *** | **H1** |

Source: Authors

Table 4 displays the validity metrics for the constructs of AI innovations (AII), human capital (HC), and competitive advantage (CA). All constructions have CR values over the generally recognized cutoff of 0.70, with AII at 0.730, HC at 0.761, and CA at 0.779. The scales' good internal consistency is indicated by these scores, indicating that each construct's items accurately assess the intended notions.

With AII at 0.645, HC at 0.660, and CA at 0.612, the AVE values provide more evidence for the validity of the constructs. The fact that all AVE values are higher than the suggested limit of 0.50 suggests that the constructs account for a substantial amount of the variation in the corresponding indicators. This implies that the measurements are reliable and accurately reflect the constructs' underlying dimensions. With AII at 0.220, HC at 0.132, and CA at 0.274, the MSV values are also comparatively low, reducing the possibility of multicollinearity and demonstrating the constructions' independence from one another.

Finally, with AII at 0.850, HC at 0.763, and CA at 0.787, the MaxR(H) values—which indicate the constructions' maximum reliability—are likewise good. These figures attest to the constructs' continued high validity and reliability. Further evidence that the constructs are connected but still sufficiently different from one another is provided by the inter-construct correlations, which are represented by AII, HC, and CA. All things considered, these validity metrics show that the scales employed in this research are sound and accurately capture the theoretical concepts of competitive advantage, human capital, and AI advances.

*Table 4. Validity Concern*

| | CR | AVE | MSV | MaxR(H) | AII | HC | CA |
|---|---|---|---|---|---|---|---|
| **AII** | 0.730 | 0.645 | 0.220 | 0.850 | **0.648** | | |
| **HC** | 0.761 | 0.660 | 0.132 | 0.763 | 0.170 | **0.659** | |
| **CA** | 0.779 | 0.612 | 0.274 | 0.787 | 0.378 | 0.188 | **0.678** |

Note: AII= AI innovations; HC= Human capital; CA= Competitive advantage
Source: Authors

## Mediating role Examination

*Figure 2. Structural Equation model*

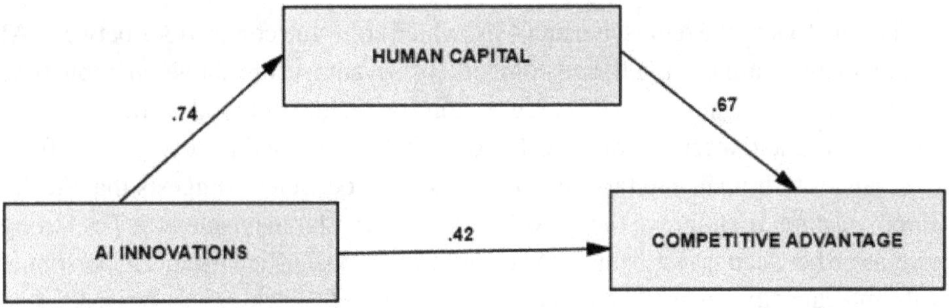


*Source: Authors*

## Model fit indices

The indices for model fit are compiled in Table 5, which provide important information about how well the structural model created in this study works. According to the provided p-value (significant threshold), the model is statistically significant at 0.003. The links between the constructs of AI innovations, human capital, and competitive advantage may be more robustly interpreted when the p-value is low, indicating that the model fits the data well. The general validity of the structural equation modeling technique used in the investigation is supported by its importance. Despite being significant, the Chi-Square value of 1.954 is comparatively low, which is advantageous for evaluations of model fit. Furthermore, a satisfactory fit is shown by the Root Mean Square Residual (RMR), which is given at 0.040. Lower RMR values imply that the model accurately replicates the observed covariance matrix.

With a Confirmatory Fit Index (CFI) of 0.915 and a Goodness of Fit Index (GFI) of 0.927, the goodness-of-fit indices offer further assessment. A high match between the suggested model and the data is shown by both values above the generally recognized cutoff of 0.90. At 0.915, the Tucker-Lewis Index (TLI) likewise shows a strong model fit. The model's strong fit to the data is further confirmed by the Root Mean Square Error of Approximation (RMSEA), which is reported as 0.026, considerably below the acceptable threshold of 0.05. When taken as a whole, these indices imply that the model successfully depicts the connections between the constructs, offering a strong basis for analyzing the research's conclusions.

*Table 5. indices for Model Fit*

| Sig. | Chi-Sq | RMR | Fitness Goodness | Fitness Confirmatory | TLI | RMSEA |
|---|---|---|---|---|---|---|
| 0.003 | 1.954 | .040 | 0.927 | 0.915 | 0.915 | .026 |

Source: Authors

The findings of the regression analysis, which show the connections between AI advancements, human capital, and competitive advantage, are shown in Table 6. A statistically significant ($p < 0.001$) regression coefficient of 0.860, with a standard error of 0.142 and a critical ratio (C.R.) of 7.580, is revealed for the journey from AI advances to human capital. This high positive coefficient suggests that AI developments greatly improve the growth of human capital in businesses. The strong correlation between investments in AI technology and significant gains in personnel skills and capacities is further supported by the high C.R. value.

With a coefficient of 0.330, standard error of 0.129, and a C.R. of 2.851, the second regression line, which looks at how human capital affects competitive advantage, is likewise significant at $p < 0.001$. This research confirms the crucial role that a trained staff plays in attaining organizational success by showing that improved human capital positively adds to competitive advantage. The strong correlation emphasizes how crucial it is for businesses seeking to enhance their operational efficacy and market positioning to make deliberate investments in staff development.

Finally, a statistically significant ($p < 0.001$) coefficient of 0.960, standard error of 0.190, and C.R. of 7.962 are found for the straight path from AI discoveries to competitive advantage. This remarkably high coefficient implies that AI advancements have a strong direct influence on competitive advantage, showing that businesses who successfully use AI can see notable gains in performance indicators. When taken as a whole, these regression findings highlight the complex connections between the categories and show that, in the context of Ethiopian SMEs, both human capital and AI advances are important sources of competitive advantage.

*Table 6. Regression Examination*

| Relative | | | Approx. | S.E. | C.R. | P | Ass. |
|---|---|---|---|---|---|---|---|
| **Human capital** | **<---** | **AI innovation** | **.860** | **.142** | **7.580** | *** | **H2** |
| Competitive advantage | <--- | Human capital | .330 | .129 | 2.851 | *** | H3 |
| Competitive advantage | <--- | AI innovations | .960 | .190 | 7.962 | *** | H1 |

Source: Authors

The investigation of the mediating function of human capital in the connection between competitive advantage and AI advances is shown in Table 7. A considerable direct effect is indicated by the 0.42 quantification of the direct influence of AI advances on competitive advantage. This value highlights the significance of technical improvements in boosting organizational performance by indicating that AI innovations alone significantly improve competitive advantage. This direct influence lays the groundwork for comprehending AI's wider effects on competitive posture.

The chart also emphasizes how advancements in AI indirectly affect competitive advantage through human capital. An indirect influence of 0.48 is obtained by multiplying the impact of AI advances on human capital (0.74) by the impact of human capital on competitive advantage (0.67). According to this research, human capital is essential for mitigating the impact of AI advancements on competitive advantage. It implies that businesses that make investments in training their employees may increase the advantages of using AI, proving that human capital is a crucial resource for utilizing technology breakthroughs.

With both direct and indirect impacts combined, the overall influence is 0.92, suggesting a high correlation between AI advancements and competitive advantage. Although human capital strengthens the link between AI advances and competitive advantage, the term "partial mediation" suggests that AI innovations still have a major direct impact. This research highlights how these dimensions are interrelated and implies that strategic investments in AI technology and human capital development are crucial for Ethiopian SMEs to have a sustained competitive edge in a market that is becoming more complicated.

*Table 7. Mediating role Effect*

| | Influence | Worth | Path Influence |
|---|---|---|---|
| AI innovations → Competitive advantage | Direct Influence | .42 | Direct influence stated |
| AI innovations → Human capital→ Competitive advantage | Indirect Influence | .74*.67=.48 | Indirect Influence Ensued |
| | Whole influence | .92 | Partial mediation |

Source: Authors

## Discussion

The study's conclusions emphasize how crucially AI advancements, human resources, and competitive advantage interact with Ethiopian SMEs. Innovations in AI have a significant direct impact on competitive advantage, which highlights how technology may revolutionize organizational performance. Businesses may improve decision-making, increase operational efficiency, and provide better consumer experience as they use AI technologies increasingly. This is consistent with previous research that highlights the importance of technology in shaping competitive positioning and indicates that SMEs stand to gain a great deal by incorporating AI into their operations.

Nonetheless, a crucial complexity in this connection is shown by the mediating function of human capital. The findings show that while advances in AI directly boost competitive advantage, these benefits are magnified when human capital is improved. Given that a trained staff is essential for utilizing AI technology efficiently; this conclusion emphasizes the need to invest in employee development. Businesses that place a high priority on training and up-skilling their staff will be better able to handle the challenges posed by AI applications and make sure that they are prepared to take full advantage of these advancements. This implies that, in the case of Ethiopian SMEs, maintaining a competitive edge requires a dual emphasis on human capital development and technology investment.

Additionally, the study's findings show that there is a complex and linked relationship between AI advancements, human capital, and competitive advantage. Human capital has a huge indirect impact, which emphasizes how crucial it is for businesses to have an innovative and ever-learning culture. Ethiopian SMEs who adopt this all-encompassing strategy should see improved flexibility and responsiveness to shifts in the market. This realization is especially pertinent in a quickly changing economic environment where survival and expansion depend on adaptability and creativity.

The results highlight the need for Ethiopian SMEs to strategically incorporate AI breakthroughs and make human capital investments if they want to prosper in a competitive market. Organizations may better use technology breakthroughs, propel organizational success, and gain a lasting competitive edge by acknowledging the synergistic link between these components. This study contributes to a more thorough knowledge of competitive advantage in the digital era by laying the foundation for future research into precise tactics that might successfully connect AI deployment with human capital development inside SMEs.

## RECOMMENDATIONS

This study's results suggest several ways that Ethiopian SMEs might improve their competitive edge by using AI advances and building up their human capital. First, companies need to do a full review of their present technology skills and find areas where AI may be used efficiently. This might include pilot projects that look at how AI technologies affect customer engagement and operational efficiency. SMEs should also make sure that their personnel are always getting new training and development so that they have the skills they need to use AI technology. Regular seminars, online courses, and mentoring programs that encourage a culture of learning and creativity might help with this. Finally, encouraging departments to work together, especially IT and human resources, will help create a more unified way to embrace new technologies and manage people, which will lead to long-term progress.

## FUTURE RESEARCH DIRECTIONS

Future study should investigate the enduring effects of AI integration and human capital development in Ethiopian SMEs, especially across various industries. Research might examine the impact of differing levels of technical preparedness on the efficacy of AI advances and the relationship of these characteristics with overall company success. Furthermore, examining the influence of organizational culture on the adoption of AI technology might yield significant insights. Future study can concentrate on the techniques utilized by successful SMEs in using AI and human capital to attain competitive advantage, providing practical frameworks for others to replicate. Furthermore, comparative research across different areas or nations might deepen the knowledge of how cultural and economic settings impact the interaction between technology and human resources, providing to a more complete picture of competitive tactics in the digital age.

## CONCLUSION

This study offers insightful information about the complex connections between competitive advantage, human capital, and AI advances in Ethiopian SMEs. The results show how advancements in AI greatly boost competitive advantage, highlighting the vital role that technology plays in influencing organizational success. However, the data shows that the growth of human capital amplifies the impact of AI, highlighting the need to invest in employee skills and competencies. For

SMEs hoping to prosper in a market that is becoming increasingly competitive, this combined emphasis on worker development and technology innovation is crucial.

Furthermore, the study shows that human capital mediates the link between these variables, indicating that organizations need to promote an innovative and ongoing learning culture. By doing this, businesses may make more use of AI technology and guarantee that staff members are prepared to handle the intricacies of contemporary commercial settings. Achieving a lasting competitive edge requires a comprehensive strategy for integrating AI and building human capital.

The study concludes by highlighting the significance of a strategic framework for Ethiopian SMEs that takes into account both AI advancements and the growth of human capital. Organizations may improve their flexibility and response to market shifts by acknowledging the interconnection of these elements, which will eventually position them for long-term success. The results lay the groundwork for future studies by promoting more investigation into practical methods of trying AI adoption to the development of human capital, which will advance our knowledge of competitive advantage in the digital age.

## Managerial Implications

For executives of Ethiopian SMEs looking to improve their competitive standing, the study's conclusions have several significant management ramifications. The need for managers to give the adoption of cutting-edge technology top priority is highlighted by the notable direct impact of AI developments on competitive advantage. Better decision-making and increased operational efficiency are two benefits of investing in AI tools and systems, both of which are essential in the fast-paced corporate world of today. To stay competitive, managers should aggressively investigate AI solutions that complement their strategic objectives and industry requirements.

The report also emphasizes how important human capital is in moderating the link between competitive advantage and AI advancements. This suggests that managers need to invest in their employees' professional development in addition to technology acquisition. Employees will be more equipped to use AI if training programs are put in place that improves their proficiency with the technology. Companies will be able to adjust to market dynamics and technological advancements more quickly if they cultivate a culture of ongoing learning and innovation.

The results also imply that cooperation between the human resources and technology departments is crucial. To guarantee that AI projects are backed by a knowledgeable workforce, managers should support cross-functional teams that combine technology and personnel management. By doing this, businesses may establish a synergistic setting where human resources and technology collaborate to generate competitive advantage.

The study's management implications, in summary, highlight the significance of a well-rounded strategy that blends investments in AI advancements with a resolute dedication to the development of human capital. Leaders may strategically position their organizations for long-term growth and success in an environment that is becoming more competitive by recognizing how these elements are interrelated. In addition to improving operational performance, this all-encompassing strategy will build an organizational culture that is robust and flexible enough to meet new challenges.

## Practical Implications

The study's conclusions have important applications for Ethiopian SMEs trying to improve their competitiveness and operational efficiency. First off, companies should actively work to integrate AI technology into their operations given the significant association between AI advancements and competitive advantage. This can entail using data analytics, automation, and customer interaction technologies, which help optimize workflows and enhance service quality. To ensure that technology investments result in measurable advantages, SMEs should place a high priority on comprehending their unique demands and choosing AI solutions that complement their corporate goals.

The results emphasized the significance of human capital development as a mediator in the link between AI and competitive advantage, in addition to technical adoption. Practically speaking, this implies that companies must put in place focused training initiatives that provide staff members with the know-how to use AI efficiently. Staff members may fully utilize AI tools by bridging the knowledge gap through workshops, online courses, and practical training. In addition to increasing productivity, empowering staff members via education also promotes engagement and a sense of responsibility.

SMEs should also establish an organizational culture that promotes creativity and ongoing education. This may be accomplished by encouraging teams to collaborate, communicate openly, and try new things. Companies may stimulate innovation and successfully meet changing market needs by creating an atmosphere where workers feel free to exchange ideas and take measured risks. The study's practical implications, in summary, emphasize the necessity for Ethiopian SMEs to take a two-pronged strategy that combines strong human capital strategies with AI advances. By doing this, businesses may improve their operational capacities and develop a workforce that is robust and ready to face the difficulties of a business environment that is changing quickly. In the end, this all-encompassing approach will promote sustainable growth and a competitive edge in the market.

## Theoretical Implications

The results of this study make a big difference in the current research on how technology, human capital, and competitive advantage work together, especially in the context of small and medium-sized businesses (SMEs) in developing countries like Ethiopia. By experimentally establishing the direct effect of AI developments on competitive advantage, this research strengthens the view that technical advancements are essential drivers of organizational performance. This is in line with existing theories that stress the use of technology to improve the efficiency and effectiveness of corporate operations.

Furthermore, the study elucidates a refined comprehension of the mediating function of human capital in this connection. Recognizing human capital as a vital mediator enhances the theoretical dialogue on resource-based perspectives of companies, indicating that the value obtained from technology is considerably increased when integrated with a proficient and informed workforce. This study underscores the necessity for a more cohesive theoretical framework that incorporates both technology and human elements in elucidating competitive advantage, transcending conventional models that may concentrate exclusively on a singular facet.

The research also highlights the necessity for more investigation into the dynamics of technology adoption and human capital development in SMEs across various cultural and economic situations. It proposes that subsequent research should examine the impact of differing degrees of technical readiness and workforce competencies on the efficacy of AI breakthroughs, therefore enhancing the comprehension of competitive tactics across varied contexts. In conclusion, our study not only corroborates existing beliefs about the significance of technology and human capital in securing competitive advantage but also facilitates new theoretical enquiries that examine their interrelationships. By tackling these issues, the research sets the stage for future academic studies on how to manage resources strategically in the age of digital revolution.

## REFERENCES


Abdi, M. D., Dobamo, H. A., & Bayu, K. B. (2021). Exploring current opportunity and threats of artificial intelligence on small and medium enterprises accounting function; evidence from Southwest part of Ethiopia, Oromiya, Jimma and Snnpr, Bonga. *Academy of Accounting and Financial Studies Journal, 25*(2), 1–11.

AlQershi, N. A., Diah, M. L. B. M., Latiffi, A. B. A., & Ahmad, W. N. K. W. (2020). Strategic innovation and competitive advantage of manufacturing SMEs: The mediating role of human capital. *Quality Innovation Prosperity, 24*(3), 70–89. DOI: 10.12776/qip.v24i3.1493

Awode, S. S., & Oduola, M. O. (2025). The interplay between technological innovation and human capital development in driving industrial productivity and competitiveness in Africa. *Journal of Economic Development, 27*(1), 56–71. DOI: 10.1108/JED-03-2024-0079

Borji, B., Niguse, T., & Kant, S. (2025). Effect of Strategic Alignment and Strategic Foresight on Competitive Advantage with Mediating Role of Human Capital a case of SMEs of Sidama Regional State, Ethiopia. *The Ethiopian Journal of Business and Economics, 15*(1), 65–90.

Bortola, G. W., Kero, C. A., & Bali, N. (2024). The Mediating Effect of Competitive Advantage between Innovation Capability and Firm's Competitiveness. [HAJBE]. *Horn of African Journal of Business and Economics, 7*(1), 75–96.

Dinku, A. E., Singh, M., & Singh, S. (2024). Effect of human capital on the performance of small and medium enterprises: A mediating role of innovation practice in Ethiopia. *Cogent Business & Management, 11*(1), 2434729. DOI: 10.1080/23311975.2024.2434729

Farmanesh, P., Solati Dehkordi, N., Vehbi, A., & Chavali, K. (2025). Artificial Intelligence and Green Innovation in Small and Medium-Sized Enterprises and Competitive-Advantage Drive Toward Achieving Sustainable Development Goals. *Sustainability (Basel), 17*(5), 2162. DOI: 10.3390/su17052162

Ferede, D. (2025). Understanding the Artificial Intelligence (AI)-Driven Transformation of the Global South: The Case of Ethiopia.

Gebremichael, H. S., & Tekle, T. G. (2020). Human Capital and Process Innovation Capability for Competitive Advantage: A Study on Manufacturing SMEs in Tigray. [BJET]. *Branna Journal of Engineering and Technology, 2*(1), 78–94.

Geru, A. A., Birbirsa, Z. A., & Dinber, G. N. (2025). The impact of strategic human resource practices on intellectual capital development in Ethiopia: Empirical evidence from Oromia regional public service organizations. *The International Journal of Organizational Analysis*.

Iyelolu, T. V., Agu, E. E., Idemudia, C., & Ijomah, T. I. (2024). Driving SME innovation with AI solutions: overcoming adoption barriers and future growth opportunities. *International Journal of Science and Technology Research Archive, 7*(1), 036-054.

Kusumawijaya, I. K., & Astuti, P. D. (2024). The Impact of Human Capital and Knowledge Creation on Sustaining Competitive Advantage and Innovation in Medium-Sized Companies in Bali. *International Journal of Sustainable Development and Planning*, *19*(6), 2193–2204. DOI: 10.18280/ijsdp.190619

Magableh, I. K., Mahrouq, M. H., Ta'Amnha, M. A., & Riyadh, H. A. (2024). The role of marketing artificial intelligence in enhancing sustainable financial performance of medium-sized enterprises through customer engagement and data-driven decision-making. *Sustainability (Basel)*, *16*(24), 11279. DOI: 10.3390/su162411279

Mebratie, E., Shanbel, B., Awoke, A., & Dessalegne, B. (2025). Knowledge-based human resource management practices and organizational performance in selected universities of Amhara regional state, Ethiopia: The moderating effect of intellectual capital. *Cogent Business & Management*, *12*(1), 2491688. DOI: 10.1080/23311975.2025.2491688

Niguse, T., & Borji, B. (2025). Mediation Effect of Human Capital Among Strategic Innovation and Competitive Advantage: A Case of SMEs in Ethiopia. *International Journal of Global Business and Competitiveness*, *20*(1), 23–32. DOI: 10.1007/s42943-025-00114-z

Rony, P., & Yahaya, N. A. (2021). The role of artificial intelligence (ai) in transforming the human capital management within the smes across the mena region: An empirical investigation. [IJMHRM]. *Int. J. Mark. Hum. Resour. Manage.*, *6*, 6–24.

Tolossa, A. T., Singh, M., & Gautam, R. K. (2025). Bridging Competitive Advantage and Sustainable Development: The Moderating Role of Value Creation for Stakeholders in Ethiopian SMEs. *Business Strategy & Development*, *8*(1), e70066. DOI: 10.1002/bsd2.70066

## KEY TERMS AND DEFINITIONS

**Artificial Intelligence (AI):** Refers to the simulation of human intelligence in machines programmed to think and learn like humans. AI encompasses a range of technologies, including machine learning, natural language processing, and robotics, which enable systems to perform tasks that typically require human intelligence, such as visual perception, speech recognition, and decision-making. The term "artificial intelligence" originated in the 1950s, with pioneers like John McCarthy coining it during the Dartmouth Conference, where the foundational principles of AI research were established (Bortola et al., 2024).

**Competitive Advantage:** Is a strategic position that allows a company to outperform its rivals in the market. It can be achieved through various means, such as cost leadership, differentiation, or niche focus. The concept has its roots in the work of Michael Porter, who introduced the idea in the 1980s through his seminal book "Competitive Advantage." Porter's framework emphasizes the importance of unique resources and capabilities in achieving sustained competitive advantage (Gebremichael et al., 2020).

**Human Capital:** Refers to the economic value of the skills, knowledge, and experience possessed by individuals. It represents the collective abilities that employees bring to an organization, significantly influencing productivity and innovation. The concept of human capital dates back to the early 20th century, with economists like Theodore Schultz emphasizing the importance of investing in education and training to enhance workforce productivity (Niguse& Borji, 2025).

**Small and Medium-sized Enterprises (SMEs):** Are defined as businesses whose personnel numbers fall below certain limits, which vary by country. In Ethiopia, SMEs are typically classified based on their number of employees and annual turnover, playing a crucial role in the economy by contributing to job creation, innovation, and economic growth. The term "SME" gained prominence in the late 20th century as governments and organizations recognized the importance of supporting these businesses for sustainable development and economic diversification (Borji et al., 2025).

# Chapter 9
# Emerging Opportunities and Challenges of MSMEs in Birdwatching: An Approach Based on Artificial Intelligence and Strategic Foresight

**Ivan Vargas**
http://orcid.org/0000-0001-9037-0571
*Quindío Botanical Garden, Colombia*

## ABSTRACT

*Colombia is the most biodiverse country in bird species and one of the top 5 in overall biodiversity in the world. Despite this, its economy has been historically focused on mineral extraction and agricultural products, despising unique and high-demand opportunities in nature-based tourism. Birdwatching offers significant potential for the strongest rural development and community well-being. This chapter applies strategic foresight to project the long-term impact of artificial intelligence (AI) on Micro, Small, and Medium-Sized Enterprises engaged in birdwatching in the Quindío region. Using qualitative methods including indexed literature review, expert interviews, and PESTEL analysis—it identifies emerging challenges and opportunities for sustainable birdwatching supported by AI. The study provides recommendations for each stakeholder involved in a birdwatching governance model, prioritizing the roles of academics, policymakers, MSME leaders, and community actors. The findings offer a replicable framework for aligning AI innovation with conservation and tourism development*

DOI: 10.4018/979-8-3373-2817-1.ch009

## INTRODUCTION

Colombia increased its Gross Domestic Product by 1.7% in 2024 from 2023, reaching USD $418.5 billion (Freixes, 2025). The main historical economic activities are mineral exploitation (petroleum, coal, gold), agricultural products (coffee, rice, bananas, and citrus fruit), and the service sector, according to Colombia's National Administrative Department of Statistics (Hoyos, 2024).

The World Travel and Tourism Council (WTTC, 2025) indicated that tourism in Colombia represents only 1.8% of the national GDP. This is evidenced by the 6.7 million international visitors who traveled to the country, who were attracted by its culture, natural resources, lifestyle, and landscapes.

Despite Colombia having limited sources of data on birdwatching, there are no official numbers on its impact on annual national tourism income, or even in the regions that are characteristic of its large number of bird species. This has left an emergent industry in the hands of some operators, guides, academics, and local communities without any formal governance model. Although some researchers are trying to apport in this gap, for instance, the Quindío Botanical Garden showed that Colombia ranked first globally during the Global Big Day, recording 1,563 bird species across its territory.

Various examples around the world show that the birdwatching industry has grown significantly over the last decade. This has created a new target audience characterized by strong economic capacity and social awareness, with interest in watching birds, experiencing their environment, and interacting with local communities.

Castillo-Aguilar & Roa-Angulo (2021) reported that 278,850 North American birdwatchers were interested in visiting Colombia to interact with birds and their environments. This interest has generated around 7,516 new jobs in rural areas and brought in more than USD 9 million to regions such as Guaviare, Valle del Cauca, and Quindío. The Quindío Botanical Garden hosts approximately 150 native bird species within 15 hectares, becoming a special and interesting place for birdwatchers. On Global Big Day, observers registered 351 bird species in a single day, representing 22% of Colombia's total. In the Quindío department, over 642 bird species can be observed.

However, the main policymakers in the territory recognized the low level of understanding and development of this industry in the region. For instance, they know that 99% of the businesses are MSMEs, but they cannot identify accurate data on the percentage directly involved in birdwatching and how it impacts the department economy (Crónica del Quindío, 2024).

The Quindío Botanical Garden proposed in 2024 a new governance model in this field (Pérez-Uribe et al, 2024) which is used in this chapter to analyze how the stakeholders identified need to rethink and contribute in the coming 15 years to bridging the knowledge gap in this industry, for that it is necessarily have a special consideration to the advancements of artificial intelligence (AI), which is exponentially transforming all bioeconomy sectors. This research chapter proposes a forecasting framework for birdwatching in Quindío over the next 15 years, focusing on the potential impact of AI in improving local economies, community engagement, and sustainable collaboration between residents and MSMEs. To address this, the author applies interviews, the PESTEL method, and a focus group involving experts' input from academics, MSME CEOs, local policymakers, and social leaders. The goal is to explore future scenarios, identify opportunities and challenges, and understand how AI can strengthen the governance of birdwatching ecotourism in this region.

## BACKGROUND

### Birdwatching as Ecotourism

Kutzner (2019) states that birdwatching is part of nature tourism, where people want to admire birds in their local and protected environment. The learning process consists of living this experience and having the opportunity to share it with local communities.

According to Cooper et al., (2020), this industry involves local and international visitors who are looking for recreation, education, and protecting the ecosystems and conserving wildlife with a high engagement and sense of preservation for the next generation.

For Steven et al., (2014), birdwatching is an emergent recreational and educational activity that has been increasing around the world, where their practitioners are promoting a new appreciation of sustainable ecotourism. Examples of this practice are in North America (Point Pelle National Park, Everglades National Park), South America (Pantanal, Mindo Cloud Forest), Europe (Camargue, Hortobágy National Park), Africa (Kruger National Park, Maasai Mara National Reserve), Asia (Bharatpur Bird Sanctuary, Kinabalu Park).

Birdwatchers are generally well-educated individuals who possess high purchasing power and have a high acquisitive power and enjoy spending a long time sharing with the birds in nature between rivers, lakes, mountains, forests, and other places where the birds live (Sekercioglu, 2022).

Kellert (1985) identified that birdwatchers like to interact with the local communities and are more closely associated with those who have green practices and a sustainability economy that really cares about the environment and their social welfare.

The importance of this industry in the bioeconomy system is changing the way tourism services used to operate. In a study conducted in Mingxi County, China, Schwoerer & Dawson (2022 a) concluded that birdwatching has an economic value 3.9 times higher than other ecotourism activities that are considered more rentable.

However, other studies show that when birdwatching companies are run irresponsibly or with little social and governmental oversight, respectively, the impact on nature is enormous, generating overtourism, poor waste management, disruption of the birds' life cycles, and even the promotion of their illegal sale (Kronenberg, 2014).

## MSME Innovation in Rural Economies

According to Purnomo & Purwandari (2025) micro, small, and medium-sized enterprises (MSMEs) are the most prevalent business group in developing countries. These enterprises must be innovation-driven and technology-integrated to deliver high-quality services.

In Colombia, 90% of the tourist sector is composed of MSMEs, which represent 4.7% of Colombian GDP and contribute 1.4 million jobs (World Travel & Tourism Council, 2025). For Randam et al., (2022), the number of MSMEs is growing in their interest in nature tourism that engages citizen science and social responsibility with the ecosystem.

Cooper et al., (2020) emphasize the importance of MSMEs in developing countries with high levels of biodiversity, like Colombia, to look to the natural environment as a business opportunity that is more friendly with the weather change and the future of the coming generations. These organizations can take advantage of the natural competitive advantage that wildlife gives them to achieve their goals and support the welfare of the local region.

In the same way, Sullivan et al., (2014a) indicate the idea to enhance economic viability for these enterprises with local public policies that incentivize their work (tax reduction, flexible schedules, grants), but highlight the role and responsibility of these companies in supporting biodiversity during the development of green strategies to preserve the birds and protect their natural environment from any threat (Rosydiana & Narsa, 2024; Palacios et al., 2020).

Moreover, Schwoerer and Dawson (2022b) promoted the precept that any MSMEs in the tourist sector need to work in a governance model with the public administration, academic researchers, other companies, and local communities. This is the right way to generate added value from these services and make a better place for both international and domestic visitors who are seeking relief from urban stress and return to a peaceful place where they can breathe, listen, and watch birds (Peterson et al., 2024).

For Steven et al., (2016), an average birdwatcher consumer spends USD 56.74 per day in a place that allows them to watch in a safe way and share experiences with local people to understand the ecosystem and their culture. Schwoerer and Dawson (2022b) found that 300,000 birdwatchers in Alaska spent over USD 377 million in 2016, creating around 4,000 jobs and generating both economic benefits and stronger conservation outcomes for local communities, becoming an example for other areas that can increase the revenues and the budget to protect their nature.

Finally, in Colombia, there are different regions with a lot of bird species (Valle del Cauca, Cauca, Guajira, Amazonas, Quindío), but now, there are no national or regional official data for analyzing this industry and how it impacts the tourist sector. For instance, Vox News (2025) reported that thousands of tourists have traveled to Colombia in recent years for nature tourism, but it still doesn't have exact numbers and indicators.

## MSME Innovation in Emergent Economies

According to Nursini (2020), MSMEs represent the most prevalent category of enterprises in developing countries. These businesses require innovation-driven strategies and technological integration in order to deliver high-quality services. In Colombia MSMEs constitute 90% of the tourism sector, contributing approximately 1.4 million jobs (Meija, 2008).

Ramdam et al., (2025) observes a growing interest among MSMEs in engaging with nature-based tourism that incorporates citizen science strategies and promotes ecological responsibility. Cooper et al. (2014) emphasize the importance of MSMEs in developing countries with high levels of biodiversity, like Colombia, which can leverage the natural environment as a business opportunity that is more resilient to climate change and aligned with the long-term well-being of future generations. These enterprises can use wildlife as a competitive advantage to achieve goals and support local welfare.

In the same way, Sullivan et al., (2014b) recommend local policy incentives—such as tax cuts, flexible schedules, and grants—while stressing MSMEs' duty to protect biodiversity (Palacios et al., 2020). Hall and Gössling (2021) promoted the precept that any MSMEs in the tourist sector need to work in a governance model with the public administration, academic researchers, other companies, and local communities.

This collaborative approach is essential to generating added value from these services and making a better place for both international and domestic visitors who are seeking relief from urban stress and returning to a peaceful place where they can breathe, listen, and watch birds (Maldonado et al., 2018). For Steven et al., (2016), an average birdwatcher consumer spends USD 56.74 per day in a place that allows them to watch in a safe way and share experiences with local people to understand the ecosystem and their culture.

Despite the insights, scholars have expressed significant criticisms regarding the proliferation and performance of MSMEs in developed countries, emphasizing that outcomes are not consistently favorable in terms of market positioning. In this sense, La Porta & Shleifer (2014) conclude that these economic actors are mostly informal, produce low productivity, and lack continuous innovation processes. Turning them into a kind of "survivalist" instead of progress drivers, as evidenced in the nations of West Africa (Grimm et al., 2012).

Therefore, the contribution of MSMEs is not directly related to the number of companies in these economies, nor to the number of microcredits they receive (Meager, 2019). Cuero-Acosta (2023) demonstrates that this relationship generates relatively low profits in the absence of complementary support mechanisms from public administrative or private sector actors that facilitate business advancement. This is confirmed by the McKinsey Global Institute (2024), which studied 16 emerging countries and found that globalizing public policies led by national governments are inaccurate and attempt to generate the same incentives and opportunities for different sectors, which have characteristics, expectations, and needs.

In this context, Larios-Francia & Ferasso (2023) argues that while MSMEs tend to create new jobs in these countries, not all of them generate added value and contribute to the sophistication of the country's economic processes, resulting over time in high indirect costs for organizations. This is evidenced in Indonesia, where 67% of MSMEs operate informally, producing low yields and inefficient access to the national market.

The final discussion and analysis conducted by the authors, along with the reviewed literature, help identify and highlight the main causes that put ecotourism MSMEs at risk, as well as their potential to enhance birdwatching as a key component of sustainable development in Quindío.

## Digital innovation

Digital innovation is the design and implementation of entirely digital new technologies that enable organizations to generate new forms of value through the transformation of products and services in the market (Nambisan et al., 2017). Connecting sophisticated technologies like the Internet of Things, cloud computing, or AI to a corporation requires not only integration but also active adaptation and authentic interaction between people and the system (Yoo et al., 2010).

Verhoef et al., (2021) determines that digital innovation requires capabilities, strategies, and organizational changes that transform repetitive and inefficient processes into automatic, optimized, and autonomous production lines. Mariani et al.,

(2023) propose that the degree of AI adoption in organizational processes directly correlates with digital innovation. Companies can achieve results that enhance their utility by implementing innovative strategies and generating added value, which can transform into competitive advantages in the sector (Zopounidis & Christos, 2024).

The theory of digital innovation concludes that the incorporation of advanced technologies into business processes enables organizations to transform value creation, customer interaction, and operational efficiency.

## Barriers to Technological Integration in Rural Ecotourism

Olanrewaju et al., (2021) point out that the lack of awareness about digital services and the high costs of their implementation are the main technological barriers to integration with the rural ecotourism industry.

Therefore, communities require efforts from academia to raise awareness and teach new knowledge to the rural community about the importance and use of these types of solutions for sustainable development (Hnatuyk et al., 2024).

Baquero Márquez, et al., (2020) reported in a study of tourism MSMEs in the Magdalena region of Colombia that data science training improved the digital transformation of companies, achieving a higher success rate for those that adopted it in the first two years.

## Economic and Financing Limitations

Digital innovation in birdwatching requires transition processes in which companies use new technological devices and digital platforms that improve the birdwatcher's experience. To this end, Foroozanfar et al., (2025) warn about the high costs required by these companies and communities for their implementation.

For example, the use of the AudioMoth autonomous recorder costs US $86 per unit, and an operator for 25 devices requires an investment of US $2,150 in hardware and software licenses that depend on the type of platform to be used, creating an economic barrier for those MSMEs that do not have a high technological investment capacity for this transition (Lapp et al., 2023).

Another example is evidenced by the camera-trap networks to explore the wildlife of animals that require an investment of US $150 per unit, and for adequate bird watching, at least 400 units are required, which raises the value to US $60,000 (Smirnov & Starov, 2022).

## Tourist Behavior and Market Segmentation

Birdwatching tourists have unique market characteristics and require a detailed understanding so that MSMEs can define their strategies to attract them, build their loyalty, and turn them into advocates for the benefits of their experiences with potential customers. According to Carvache-Franco et al., (2019) this segment of nature tourism has distinct motivations, high spending capacity, and a preference for connecting with local cultures.

Cooper et al., (2014) indicate that eagle watchers prioritize access to locations where they can observe unique species and specialized guiding services. In a department like Quindío, this creates opportunities due to its large number of endemic birds that are resident rather than migratory (Pérez-Uribe et al., 2024).

The development of this sector requires public administrative authorities to allocate resources for identifying bird movement patterns, thereby generating more information for tourism plan developers and informing tourists about the specific times, schedules, seasons, and locations where they can best achieve the experiences they seek in this type of specialized tourism.

Another essential aspect of market segmentation involves establishing meaningful connections between tourists and indigenous knowledge systems, as well as local community narratives concerning ecological perspectives. These interactions enrich birdwatchers' experience by adding cultural context and environmental awareness (Hunt et al., 2023).

## Institutional Fragmentation

Fadli et al., (2022) demonstrates that on the island of Java, Indonesia, the lack of coordination among local actors generates fragmented governance problems that have impeded the sustainable development of ecotourism in Magelan Regency. This is confirmed by Mhlongo & Daya (2023) in a study of MSMEs, who found that the main cause of the failure of the ecotourism industry was the high level of isolation of institutional networks with entrepreneurs and businesspeople in the sector.

For Kauark et al., (2023), the lack of coordination between the political agendas of a territory's governing bodies impairs opportunities for synergy in ecotourism. This leads to the development of short-term activities instead of projects that go beyond the interests of current administrators and even to MSME managers who experience high turnover rates in the face of industry instability.

In summary, Vergara-Romero et al., (2025) argue that the lack of specialized technical guidance among leaders of ecotourism governance models creates institutional bottlenecks that hinder professionalization, optimization, and business growth.

Finally, Rahman et al., (2025) demonstrates the need to engage the community as a strategic agent to reduce institutional fragmentation. His research found that coordination in tourism projects designed with community leaders tends to improve productivity, inclusion, and the adoption of disruptive technologies.

## Artificial Intelligence Applications in Birdwatching

The evolution of the computational system has been growing fast in the last fifty years, reaching artificial intelligence (AI), which is the technology that uses advanced software development to replace different traditional human tasks. This tool is capable of learning, problem-solving, and making decisions in different scenarios; even in some cases, it is autonomous (Knani et al., 2022).

In the birdwatching sector, this advancement is transforming the concept and the entire business, simplifying trip planning, strengthening the identification and knowledge in real time of the birds, and exploring new ways to provide feedback and create networking between the customers and the operators around the world (Pankiv & Kloetzer, 2024).

Wu & Wang (2025) explains that nature tourism is adopting new AI tools to improve the user experience, data accuracy, and conservation information support. Although rural areas have a lot of cultural, economic, and social limitations, these must be addressed to understand and integrate AI at all stages of the birdwatching industry.

Examples of using AI in birdwatching are starting to be shared among researchers, operators, and governments. Yang et al., (2024) created a free, open-source tool that works to identify birds in image recognition. In the same way, Rew et al., (2019) developed an AI-based heatmap system to track bird migration movements in different areas, increasing the knowledge and understanding of researchers in the behavior of these animals. Also, Sastry et al., (2023) designed a new system that combines satellite identification and ground imagery to create responsible and sustainable birdwatching roads.

Cornell University and École Centrale (Leonard, 2023) created an IA application to detect nocturnal birds, helping to understand the new appreciation that local communities need to change to support the conservation efforts. Finally, Wäldchen & Mäder (2018). used machine learning to build a model that improves the collection of ecological data among sensors and digital cameras.

## MAIN FOCUS OF CHAPTER

### Methodology

This research chapter employed a qualitative analysis, examining the perspectives, experiences, and knowledge of birdwatching stakeholders in the Quindío region and the related opportunities and challenges associated with the use of artificial intelligence. The center of their research focuses on people and organizations that have been working closely with the Quindío Botanical Garden, which is the only research center for bioeconomy and birdwatching in Colombia. The strategy was founded on the PESTEL method, which is a business plan tool useful in the studies of management to identify six key external factors (political, economic, social, technological, environmental, and legal). It aims to identify the context of one company or field analyzed, and anticipate future hypothetical scenarios (optimistic, tendentious, and critical). With this process, the researcher interviewed 8 experts distributed equitably in sectors academic, public, and private in birdwatching in Quindío.

Thanks to that, the next step was the developing a focus group of 6 representants who were characterized by their knowledge and influence in the developing of this industry, as a result the created a strategic and actionable recommendations that allowing them to designing a road map for the future of the birdwatching sector, that need of their working in a co-responsibility model between of academics, local communities, private sector and public administration in the next 15 years.

The resume of the process is represented in the table 1.

*Table 1. Methodology phases*

| Phase | Description | Instrument | Quantity |
|---|---|---|---|
| Review of specialized literature. | Compiled of articles, papers, and government documents that are indexed or published by the governments. The period of this research is between 2010 and 2025. | Literature review in Scopus, ResearchGate, and Google Scholar, and official library | 75 academic papers<br>10 government documents |
| PESTEL method | The design and implementation of the PESTEL method in birdwatching with representatives and leaders of the field in the Quindío Region | Interview semi structured | 2 professors, 2 policymakers, 1 CEO of microenterprise, CEO of small businesses, and 2 community leaders. |
| Validation of the findings | With the results of the last phase as the input for a focus group, then refine the outcomes for create the scenarios of birdwatching in 15 years | Focus group | 1 professor, 1. policymakers, 1 CEO of MSMEs, and 1 community leader in the region. |

Source. Author.

## SOLUTIONS AND RECOMMENDATIONS

The PESTEL method has been applied across multiple fields over the past fifty years and on every continent. It is useful such a management strategic tool that allows organization to understand what it is context and how it will be different futures scenarios than allow them to build a roadmap, goals, strategic, indicators and a vision. For example, Siddiqui (2021) analyzed quality management in the healthcare sector, Timothy & Boyd (2015) applied it to marketing management for trail systems, and Kung (2023) assessed the effectiveness of new digital media strategies.

In the context of ecotourism, this method has also been used effectively. Paul & Roy (2025) explored internal factors influencing the relationship between hospitality and ecotourism, Bezuhla (2020) examined the impact of macroenvironmental elements on ecotourism infrastructure, and Zahin and Shammi (2024) studied sustainable ecotourism development in the Sundarbans Forest of Bangladesh.

The following table 2 presents the primary findings derived from the application of the PESTEL method in the Quindío region's birdwatching sector, thanks to the discussion, experience and expertise of different selected experts in this field. All of them were selected for their knowledge, experience, and the impact of their labor in birdwatching and tourism nature, which serves as the main research focus of this study:

*Table 2. PESTEL analysis for stakeholders*

| Component | Findings | |
|---|---|---|
| | Role | Description |
| Political | Professors | Stability in regional governance (Vargas Ramírez, 2021) and peace consolidation allows continued infrastructure investment. |
| | Policymakers | Bureaucratic obstacles for permits remain high; more inclusive licensing is needed. It is important to promote the region as one of the world's top biodiversity areas, to generate subsidies and tax incentives for local industry. |
| | Community Leader | Local governments impose obstacles for permits; a more community-inclusive process is required. Security protocols and collective protection against major threats and vulnerabilities must be created (Vázquez et al, 2020) |
| | MSMEs | Navigating legal frameworks remains complex; better alignment with tourism realities is needed. Collaboration with the government is necessary to develop new birdwatching infrastructure (routes, observation sites). |

continued on following page

*Table 2. Continued*

| Component | Findings | |
|---|---|---|
| | **Role** | **Description** |
| Economic | Professors | Birdwatching has strong economic potential with high-value, low-impact tourists—ideal for rural diversification. |
| | Policymakers | Seasonality creates income gaps; integrated packages and off-season incentives are needed. Promote exchange rates for international visitors and create economic incentives for national birdwatchers. |
| | Community Leader | Youth employment in tourism is rising, but more training and funding are required for sustained benefit. |
| | MSMEs | Linking birdwatching to coffee and cultural tourism could double revenue streams. Look for strategies to improve the benefits for workers and guarantee their good disposition in the nature tourism sector. |
| Social | Professors | There are not enough birdwatching programs that involve local community groups (Indigenous and Afro-descendants). Limited availability of services for children, adolescents, and adults in bioeconomy. |
| | Policymakers | Visitors seek authentic experiences—more storytelling and culture could differentiate offerings. Create events that increase interest in and marketing of the birdwatching. |
| | Community Leader | Young people are joining bird clubs, but rural depopulation reduces future guide availability (demographic shifts). The media should improve how social media and influencer impact is used positively with the birdwatching industry. |
| | MSMEs | There is a growing domestic interest in nature tourism among educated urban Colombians |
| Technological | Professors | AI and citizen science are underutilized in Quindío; partnerships could boost data and visibility. It is important to support the creation study the creation and implementation of new AI apps for the region such online booking system, smart transportation systems and identification of birds, socialization of experiences in social media with machine learning, and RFID integration (Escobar et al, 2007). |
| | Policymakers | There is insufficient internet coverage in the natural environment, and there are huge gaps between the AI apps and the rural communities. No laws regarding birdwatching and the use of AI in Quindío. |
| | Community Leader | Basic tech access remains uneven, limiting how communities can promote or manage tourism. |
| | MSMEs | Audio guides, e-commerce, and virtual trails are still being piloted tech is becoming a differentiator. Promote the use of AI and Machine Learning that assist on site. Emphasize the use of personal responsibility, ethics, and rules for responsible birdwatching in Quindío. |

continued on following page

*Table 2. Continued*

| Component | Findings | |
|---|---|---|
| | **Role** | **Description** |
| Environmental | Professors | Climate change is shifting altitudinal bird ranges; conservation sustainability practices focused on biodiversity are vital. |
| | Policymakers | Protected areas and the environmental need include restriction that support the regulation of nature and create certification for industry and stakeholders that work for the restoration and conservation of the birds. |
| | Community Leader | Agriculture and poor handling of waste are starting to threaten the bird species and their environment, and there is low engagement of the community in protecting biodiversity. |
| | MSMEs | Business depends on maintaining biodiversity—conservation and tourism go together. Develop programs that face climate change, water scarcity, and energy consumption. |
| Legal | Professors | Current tourism zoning codes do not include birdwatching explicitly—this needs to be revised for sustainability. |
| | Policymakers | Regulatory burdens limit formalization; simplified legal pathways are needed for small operators. Develop health and safety regulation than protect the visitors in their birdwatching experience. Formalize consumer protection laws. |
| | Community Leader | Informal tourism grows due to unclear guide certifications and access rights. |
| | MSMEs | Certification and insurance policies are outdated for ecotourism—modern frameworks are needed. Strong the employment laws that allow an excellent service with high quality |

Source. Author.

The research achieved one of its goals: to understand what the real position of birdwatching is in the Quindío region. In many of the PESTEL components, the experts who represented the professors (academic), policymakers (public administration), community leaders (social), and MSMEs (private sector) agreed with the current situation and the urgent need to design and implement a birdwatching governance model that defines roles, responsibilities, and one vision around the IA and their future to 2040.

This document presents three in-depth future scenarios—Optimistic, Tendential, and Critical—for the development of birdwatching in Quindío, Colombia, with a focus on the integration of artificial intelligence (AI) over the next 15 years. Each scenario is structured using the PESTEL framework (political, economic, social, technological, environmental, and legal) to identify specific opportunities, challenges, and expert insights that contribute to building a sustainable and inclusive ecotourism model.

The optimistic scenario is a collaborative, innovative, and sustainable future where AI technology and birdwatching are positively improved and transform the relationship between local communities, the private sector, public administration, and the academic field. Instead, the tendential scenario represents a fragmented and ineffective evolution between the most advanced technology and this kind of nature tourism. And the last one is the critical scenario that shows the weak governance and bad integration into IA and birdwatching stakeholders, leaving the sector with something useful just for a few organizations and people.

## Optimistic Scenario: AI-Driven Growth & Conservation

The optimistic scenario (Table 3) shows the ideal state that all the stakeholders must achieve in 2040. The policymakers, with the participation of the other stakeholders in their territory, need to create a new public policy on birdwatching from 2025 to 2040 that will be aligned with the National Tourism Public Policies and the Departmental Tourism Public Policies. The experts recommend being more attentive to the international policies promoted by multilateral organizations and commercial agreements.

This public instrument is the master plan with a participatory budget that supports the bioeconomy strategy during the next years, giving a strong opportunity for the students, professionals, managers, and the community to learn, apply, and adapt to a new IA birdwatching governance model. Another important finding in the focus group was the importance of enhancing access to the internet in rural areas, which is an indispensable resource for implementing any IA application in the short and long term.

For the community, it is important to participate actively in training courses that teach them how the workers, entrepreneurs, and any person of the region understand the bird treasure and the importance of adapting new IA applications to recognize, identify, track, and share bird information with the public, social, and private sectors in real time.

*Table 3. Optimistic Scenario: AI-Driven Growth & Conservation*

| PESTEL Component | Expert Insight |
|---|---|
| Political | Government institutions recognize birdwatching as a strategic ecotourism sector. Public-private alliances fuel innovation in birding trails and biodiversity data platforms. New AI governments allow connecting in governance all the stakeholders identifying and sharing tourist information. |
| Economic | AI tools allow MSMEs to optimize operations and increase revenue. Birdwatching becomes a reliable rural income source, and the use of AI provides opportunities to learn about the preferences, expectations, and interests of the watchers. |
| Social | Birding is integrated into education. Youth serve as eco-guides, narrowing the digital divide. The community knows very well their natural resources and the importance of the bird: they have some social programs to create strategies to use IA apps to improve their knowledge and abilities in the birdwatching industry. |
| Technological | High-speed connectivity and AI-powered tools enhance visitor experiences. Co-create IA apps that allow the learning about the characteristics, expectations, and preferences of the national and international visitors to use it to constantly improve the service and promote the Quindío area as a birdwatching paradise. |
| Environmental | AI enables real-time monitoring of bird habitats and supports adaptive trail planning. AI apps could be a controller of bad behaviors of customers and employers and communicate directly with the local authorities. |
| Legal | New regulations enable AI-certified eco-guides and protect biodiversity data rights. Promote the safety and accurate exploitation of the birdwatching industry, then protect the environment and increase the social welfare. |

Source. Author.

## Tendential Scenario: Slow Progress & Partial Adoption

In this tendential scenario, the focus group envisioned a future in the Quindío region marked by weak governance among stakeholders. The frequent turnover of policymakers, every four years, leads to an inconsistent and ambiguous vision of the use of IA in birdwatching, making it difficult to optimize the industry and making rural MSMEs with little probability of accessing the technology.

One critical issue of this vision is about the environmental factor, where without the use of some IA applications that are created to control and preserve the birds' environment, they could become endangered due to the materialization of the risks of the bad use of the environment at this point.

Another recurring factor among the experts is that this scenario showed slow economic progress for the MSMEs, with birdwatchers possibly facing disappointing visitor experiences and damaging the reputation of the Quindío region over the next 15 years. This scenario is shown in Table 4.

*Table 4. Tendential Scenario: Slow Progress & Partial Adoption*

| PESTEL Component | Expert Insight |
|---|---|
| Political | Moderate institutional support exists, but coordination is weak. |
| Economic | Some firms adopt AI tools, but rural MSMEs fall behind. |
| Social | Awareness grows unevenly; rural communities lack engagement. |
| Technological | Basic tools are used, but infrastructure limits effectiveness. |
| Environmental | Inconsistent monitoring allows habitat degradation in some areas. |
| Legal | Tourism laws remain outdated; AI tools operate in legal gray areas. |

Source. Author.

## Critical Scenario: Stagnation & Environmental Decline

The critical scenario (Table 5), as defined by the selected experts, illustrates a deep fragmentation among the private sector, public administration, researchers, and the social community. In this possible future, each actor works for their own interests. Consequently, the implementation and adoption of IA is left solely to the discretion and acquisitive capacity of MSME CEOs and the awareness of individuals.

This scenario will collapse the positioning of the micro and small companies in a region that represents over 90% of the business in the department. That will considerably affect local employment, reduce tourist inflow, and destroy the natural environment. Another example of this disconnection between the public, private, academic, and social actors is the increasing of the threats and risks to directly affect the birdlife, for example, the bad use of the wastes, increasing the effects of the weather change, and the demotivation of the tourist to visit a place that doesn't have the same life as it has today.

On the other hand, the birds may start to be in danger due to the limited land and the overpopulation in close or in the same areas where their habitats are. It is so hard to use the new technologies like AI in the Quindío region, as it will be difficult to connect this place and people with other similar regions, which are working to maintain and increase the experiences of nature tourism around the world.

Increased environmental vulnerability is one of the most urgent effects of this governance gap, despite the lack of government data on birdwatching for 2024. Ineffective waste management, which worsens the consequences of climate change and lessens habitat preservation, is the result of poor coordination. Bird populations are directly threatened by this. Birdwatchers could lose interest in visiting or recommending these places after experiencing the decline of biodiversity, impacting the brand of Quindío as a bird paradise.

Adoption of technology, particularly AI, is very unlikely to be successful in this situation. Quindío misses the chance to work with and learn from other places as it gets disengaged from international efforts to modernize nature-based tourism. It will be challenging to develop the regulations, training programs, and infrastructure required to use AI as a tool for tourism and conservation without a common plan.

*Table 5. Critical Scenario: Stagnation & Environmental Decline*

| PESTEL Component | Expert Insight |
|---|---|
| Political | No public investment in AI tourism; institutional disinterest. |
| Economic | MSMEs collapse; foreign operators dominate AI services. |
| Social | Youth emigrate; communities disconnect from natural heritage. No social awareness about the birdwatching industry and their duty to preserve and conserve the natural environment |
| Technological | Infrastructure collapses: AI tools become obsolete. Not the use of the last IA apps and all their new devices in this field. |
| Environmental | Habitats are lost; bird species decline unnoticed. No tracking and data about the changing climate and the birdlife. |
| Legal | No regulatory clarity on drones, AI, or biodiversity data. No restriction about the protection of birds and their natural places and deregulation in the right way to do sustainable ecotourism |

Source. Author.

The resume of the three scenarios is shown in the next figure 1:

*Figure 1. Scenarios for applying PESTEL to birdwatching with AI in Quindío (2025-2040)*

*Source. Author. Generated using ChatGPT on July 12, 2025.*

## FUTURE RESEARCH DIRECTIONS

This research provides an example of how the PESTEL method can be applied across different sectors and fields by analyzing political, economic, social, technological, legal, and environmental factors. As a result of its implementation, researchers can better understand the framework of this study object in a determinate period but can anticipate different future scenarios that allow them to discuss and define what the strategic actions or the roadmap are that are indispensable to build. It is important that this management tool is focused on the external factors.

In birdwatching, there are a lot of new opportunities to use this method and the results achieved in this chapter to continuously understand the challenges and opportunities that this industry has with different external factors, and how they can shape the way that the policymakers are making their public policies, and how the MSMEs need to invest in technology and collaboration processes to grow their business, and how local communities need to participate directly in the activities that are using their environment to take advantage of it and ensure the co-responsibility to care for and preserve life for future generations. This approach is useful to take to other natural resources that are of interest to tourist trends, like rivers, mountains, or even other wildlife in Colombia and the world.

The next level of research in birdwatching must be in analyzing the impact of the implementation of IA technology in the industry, for example, combining drones, satellite systems, identification platforms, customer fidelity services, integrating RFID and IoT applications, and making a strong IA network at regional, national, and international levels about the birds. The Quindío area is an excellent place to do prototypes because of the high security level, the abundance of life and the incredible biodiversity, and the good relationship between the stakeholders.

Finally, the researcher invites the international and national community to co-create new local IA apps in this region, to be used as an example to take them to other biodiversity in Colombia, and over time in similar territories around the world.

## CONCLUSION

The future of birdwatching in the region of Quindío depends on a great percentage of the efficiency, engagement, cooperation, and co-responsibility of each one of their stakeholders. The use of Artificial Intelligence is not a luxury for this field; the success of this industry must take real actions in the present that use this technological tool to improve each one of the stages of the business. From the way to call and contact the possible visitors, how watchers can improve their identification process of birds, how the guides need to change the routes on time, and how the public administration can learn with real and on-time data, useful to create flexible public policies. Not only do they improve the customer experience and increase the profitability and competitiveness of this business.

In the next 15 years, the progress of artificial intelligence is difficult to anticipate because of exponential speed of their transformation and evolution, even in forecasting the power of the new software and hardware solutions. In conclusion, the expert's agreement doesn't discuss about how it will be the AI technology, instead they are thinking about how must to be flexible the coordination, communication, and adaptation of each one of the birdwatching stakeholders in using, creating, and sharing data, resources and information that enhance to strong this industry and allow the Quindío region becoming in the international top one of the most important places for bird watching.

The progress of using AI in this industry will show the true level of the bioeconomy in the sense of ecological intelligence, preserving the natural environment, conserving the birds, AI ethics in conservation, and developing emergent economies which impact positively to local communities, micro, small, and medium-sized enterprises in the Quindío region.

The following figure presents the primary conclusions of this study. It summarizes a PESTEL analysis exploring the future scenarios anticipated for the experts and is summarized in the opportunities and challenges that has the region of Quindío in the next 15 years considering the impact of AI in this field, how is represented in figure 2.

*Figure 2. Birdwatching with AI in Quindío (2025-2040)*

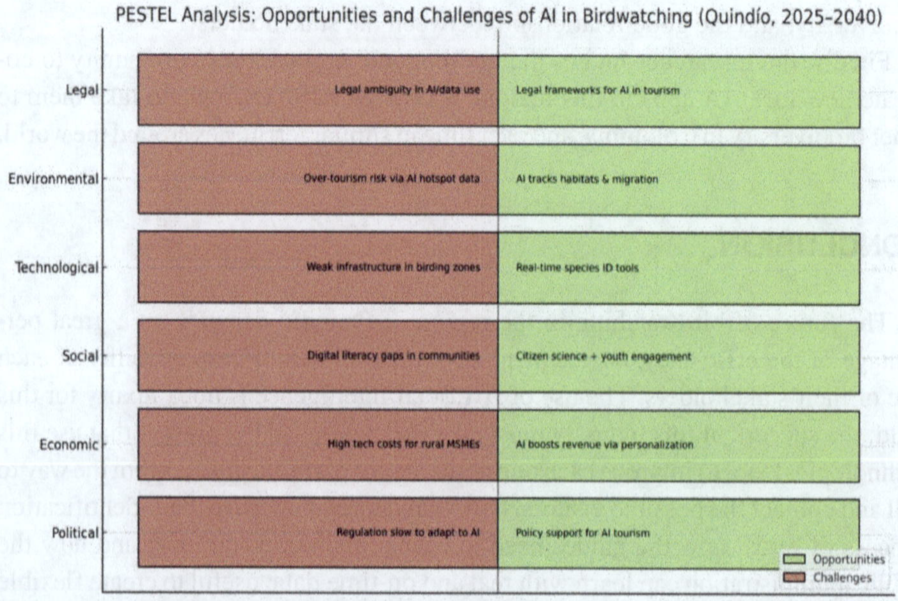


*Source. Author. Generated using ChatGPT on July 12, 2025.*

A governance model proposed by Vargas (2021) shows the multiple relations between the public administration (policymakers), the private sector (CEOs, MSMEs), the community (leaders), and academic researchers to achieve a public goal. In this case, it is around the welfare of the people and organizations in the Quindío area that have the privilege of an extraordinary environment with plenty of life, particularly the huge number of bird species that cohabitate in a small portion of land.

In this sense, the focus group discussed and concluded than each one of the stakeholders need to understand and work from now until 2040 in some strategies than guarantee the adoption constantly of this technology in all the stages of the industry, the author resume this process in the next figure than show what are the main actions that each one of them must to work, and propose that the public administration create one coordination system that allow the participation each six months between them for design this public policy, indicators, responsivities, goals and resource in a participative budget which respond as the necessities and expectations of each one of them, as long as always defend the ecosystem and use a responsible ways to adapt this business in one of the most representatives in their territory and the national country.

Figure 3 shows a proposed birdwatching governance model that resumes the roles and strategies in the next 15 years that the main stakeholders need to develop if they want to become a top tourist destination to watch birds with the aid of IA advantages. This approach, based on the PESTEL method, acts as a forecasting view to promote some strong recommendations to be implemented for policymakers, entrepreneurs, leaders, and researchers in the Quindío region.

The critical scenario, as defined by the selected experts, illustrates a deep fragmentation among the private sector, public administration, researchers, and the social community. In this possible future, each actor works for their own interests. Consequently, the implementation and adoption of IA is left solely to the discretion and acquisitive capacity of MSME CEOs and the awareness of individuals.

The positioning of micro and small businesses in a region that accounts for more than 90% of the department's business will collapse in this scenario. That will have a significant impact on local jobs, decrease tourism, and devastate the ecosystem. The growing threats and risks that directly affect birdlife, such as improper waste management, the intensifying effects of climate change, and the demotivation of tourists to visit a place that doesn't have the same life as it does today, are another illustration of this disconnect between the public, private, academic, and social actors.

However, because of the scarcity of land and the overcrowding in the same or nearby places where their habitats are, the birds may begin to face threats. Using modern technologies like artificial intelligence (AI) in the Quindío region is extremely challenging since it will be hard to connect this area and its inhabitants with other similar locations that are trying to preserve and improve natural tourism experiences globally.

Increased environmental fragility and the erosion of Quindío's reputation as a birdlife paradise are two of the most challenging effects of this government gap, even though official data on birdwatching has been lacking for several years. Ineffective waste management results from a lack of coordination, which worsens climate change's consequences and diminishes ecological protection.

It is quite improbable that technology adoption, especially AI, will be effective in this scenario. As Quindío disengages from international initiatives to modernize nature-based tourism, it loses the opportunity to collaborate with and learn from other locations. Without a shared strategy, it will be difficult to create the laws, educational materials, and infrastructure needed to employ AI as a tool for tourism and conservation.

*Figure 3. Forecasting Quindío Birdwatching governance model 2025-2040.*

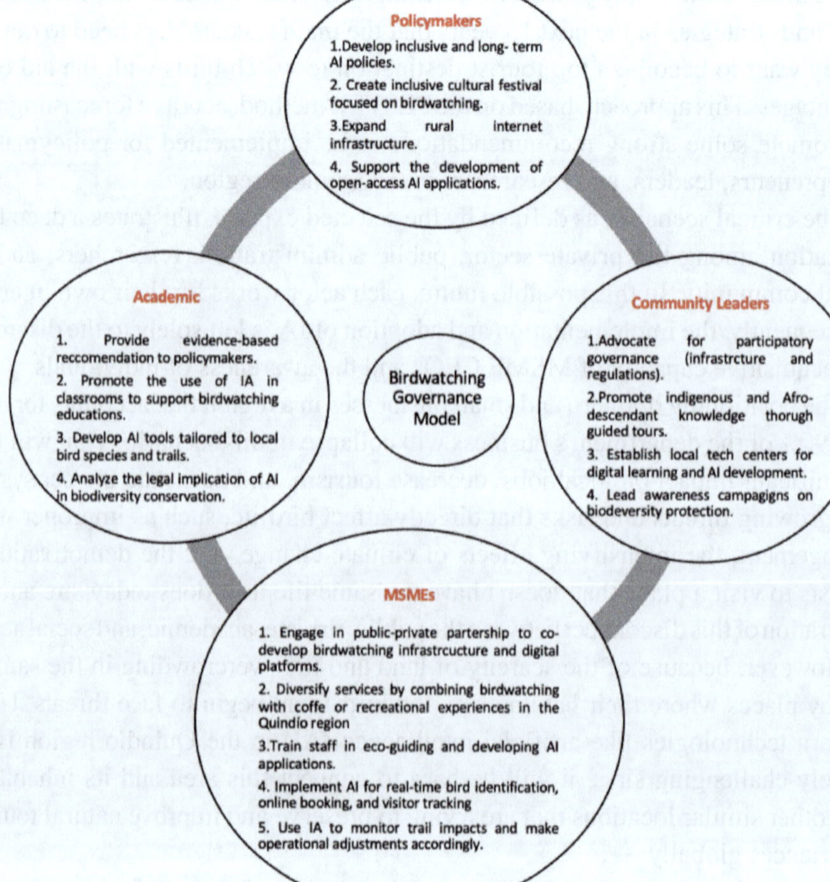


*Source. Author*

One of the main conclusions is the importance of designing and implementing a flexible birdwatching governance model that allows all stakeholders to co-participate, co-work, and co-responsibly care for the welfare of everyone.

All of them will be preserving biodiversity and protecting the environment for the coming generations in a sustainable way. The good use of AI in the next 15 years is one incredible and pertinent opportunity that needs preparation, resources, engagement, and co-working to become the Quindío region in one international model to replicate.

## REFERENCES


Baquero Márquez, V. J., Fandiño Isaza, J. R., Pinzón Varela, M. E., Caraballo Castro, C. M., & Bezuhla, L. (2020). Impact of the macro environment on the ecotourism infrastructure. *Green, Blue & Digital. Economic Journal (London)*, *1*(2), 33–46. DOI: 10.30525/2661-5169/2020-2-6

Carvache-Franco, M., Segarra-Oña, M., & Carrasco-López, C. (2019, January). Motivations analysis in ecotourism through an empirical application: Segmentation, characteristics and motivations of the consumer. *Geo Journal of Tourism and Geosites*, *24*(1), 48–59. DOI: 10.30892/gtg.24106-343

Castillo-Aguilar, M. A., & Roa-Angulo, V. (2021). Birdwatching tourism and environmental education as strategies for the conservation of wetlands in the city of Bogotá, Colombia. *Indian Journal of Science and Technology*, *14*(13), 1036–1043. DOI: 10.17485/IJST/v14i13.1163

Cooper, C. B., Dickinson, J., Phillips, T., & Bonney, R. (2020). Citizen science as a tool for avian conservation and research. *Science Advances*, *6*(23), eabc7287. Advance online publication. DOI: 10.1126/sciadv.abc7287

Cuero-Acosta, Y. A. (2023). *Reputation based on internal capabilities: The case of small enterprises within the Colombian "orange economy"*. https://doi.org/DOI: 10.1371/journal.pone.0285026

Fadli, M., Susilo, E., Puspitwati, D., Liemanto, A., Ridjal, A., & Pawestri, D. (2022, May). Sustainable Tourism as a Development Strategy in Indonesia. *Journal of Indonesian Tourism and Development Studies*, *10*(1), 23–33. DOI: 10.21776/ub.jitode.2022.010.01.04

Foroozanfar, H., Imanipour, N., Mojtaba Sajadi, S., & Habibi, M. R. (2025, April). A sustainability perspective for sharing economy business model and its unintended effects. *Journal of Cleaner Production*, *500*(1), 145177. DOI: 10.1016/j.jclepro.2025.145177

Freixes, J. (2025, February 18). Colombia's economy grew by 1.7% in 2024. ColombiaOne. Retrieved from https://colombiaone.com/2025/02/18/colombia-economy-2024-growth/ bbvaresearch.com+3colombiaone.com+3

Grimm, M., Knorringa, P., & Jann Layc, J. (2012). Constrained Gazelles: High Potentials in West Africa's Informal Economy. https://documents1.worldbank.org/curated/en/468141468337243809/pdf/779260WP0P115100B00PUBLIC00Gazelles.pdf

Hall, C. M., & Gössling, S. (2021). *Tourism and sustainability: Development, globalisation and new tourism in the third world* (5th ed.). Routledge., DOI: 10.4324/9780429276107

Hnatuyk, V., Pshenychna, N., Kara, S., Yaroshchuk, L., and Kolodii, V. (2024). Education's role in fostering environmental awareness and advancing sustainable development within a holistic framework. June 2024. *Multidisciplinary Reviews* 7:2024spe012. DOI: DOI: 10.31893/multirev.2024spe012

Hoyos Sánchez, R. A. (2024). The Crucial Role of Agriculture in the Colombian Economy: Challenges and Opportunities. *Revista Facultad Nacional de Agronomía*, *77*(3), 10795–10796. http://www.scielo.org.co/scielo.php?script=sci_arttext&pid=S0304-28472024000310795&lng=en&tlng=en. DOI: 10.15446/rfnam.v77n3.116117

Hunt, C. A., Barragán-Paladines, M. J., Izurieta, J. C., & Ordóñez, L. A. (2023). Tourism, compounding crises, and struggles for sovereignty. *Journal of Sustainable Tourism*, *31*(10), 2381–2398. DOI: 10.1080/09669582.2022.2108431

Kauark-Fontes, B., Marchetti, L., & Salbitano, F. (2023, June). Integration of nature-based solutions (NBS) in local policy and planning toward transformative change. Evidence from Barcelona, Lisbon, and Turin. *Ecology and Society*, *28*(2), art25. Advance online publication. DOI: 10.5751/ES-14182-280225

Kellert, S. R. (1985). Social and perceptual factors in the preservation of animal species. In Soulé, M. E. (Ed.), *Conservation biology* (pp. 50–69). Sinauer Associates., DOI: 10.1515/9781400857869.50/html

Knani, M., Echchakoui, S., & Ladhari, R. (2022). Artificial intelligence in tourism and hospitality: Bibliometric analysis and research agenda. *International Journal of Hospitality Management*, *107*, 103317. DOI: 10.1016/j.ijhm.2022.103317

Kronenberg, J. (2014). Environmental impacts of the use of ecosystem services: Case study of birdwatching. *Environmental Management*, *54*(3), 617–630. https://link.springer.com/article/10.1007/s00267-014-0317-8. DOI: 10.1007/s00267-014-0317-8 PMID: 24993794

Kung, W. (2023). Using the PESTEL Analysis to Determine the Effectiveness of New Digital Media Strategies. Advances in Economics. *Management and Political Sciences*, *5*(1), 19–25. DOI: 10.54254/2754-1169/5/20220054

Kutzner, D. (2019). Environmental change, resilience, and adaptation in nature-based tourism: Conceptualizing the social-ecological resilience of birdwatching tour operations. *Journal of Sustainable Tourism*, *27*(8), 1142–1166. Advance online publication. DOI: 10.1080/09669582.2019.1601730

La Porta, R., & Shleifer, A. (2014). Informality and Development. 30 Pages Posted: 11 Jun 2014. *NBER Working Paper No. w20205*. https://papers.ssrn.com/sol3/papers.cfm?abstract_id=2448910

Lapp, S., Stahlman, N., & Kitzes, J. A. (2023, June 1). Quantitative Evaluation of the Performance of the Low-Cost AudioMoth Acoustic Recording Unit. *Sensors (Basel)*, *23*(11), 5254. DOI: 10.3390/s23115254 PMID: 37299981

Larios-Francia, R. P., & Ferasso, M. (2023, March). The relationship between innovation and performance in MSMEs: The case of the wearing apparel sector in emerging countries. *Journal of Open Innovation*, *9*(1), 100018. Advance online publication. DOI: 10.1016/j.joitmc.2023.100018

Leonard, P. (2023). AI analyzes bird sightings to help conserve species. Cornell Lab of Ornithology. October 4, 2023. https://news.cornell.edu/stories/2023/10/ai-analyzes-bird-sightings-help-conserve-species

Maldonado, J. H., del Pilar Moreno-Sánchez, R., Espinoza, S., Bruner, A., Garzón, N., & Myers, J. (2018). Peace is much more than doves: The economic benefits of bird-based tourism as a result of the peace treaty in Colombia. *World Development*, *106*, 78–86. DOI: 10.1016/j.worlddev.2018.01.015

Mariani, M., Hashemi, N., & Wirtz, J. (2023). Artificial intelligence empowered conversational agents: A systematic literature review and research agenda. *Journal of Business Research*, *161*, 113838. https://es.scribd.com/document/677103241/Mariani-et-al-2023. DOI: 10.1016/j.jbusres.2023.113838

McKinsey Global Institute. (2024). *A microscope on small businesses: Spotting opportunities to boost productivity*. May 2, 2024 | Report. https://www.mckinsey.com/mgi/our-research/a-microscope-on-small-businesses-spotting-opportunities-to-boost-productivity

Meager, R. (2019, January). Understanding the Average Impact of Microcredit Expansions: A Bayesian Hierarchical Analysis of Seven Randomized Experiments. *American Economic Journal. Applied Economics*, *11*(1), 57–91. https://www.aeaweb.org/articles?id=10.1257/app.20170299. DOI: 10.1257/app.20170299

Meija, J. F. (2008). Tourism as a driver of economic development: The Colombian experience. *Violette Reihe*, *26*, 1–36.

Mhlongo, T., & Daya, P. (2023). Challenges faced by small, medium and micro enterprises in Gauteng: A case for entrepreneurial leadership as an essential tool for success. *Southern African Journal of Entrepreneurship and Small Business Management*, *15*(1), a591. DOI: 10.4102/sajesbm.v15i1.591

Nambisan, S., Wright, M., & Feldman, M. (2017). The digital transformation of innovation and entrepreneurship: Progress, challenges and key themes. *Research Policy*, *46*(3), 333–338. DOI: 10.1016/j.respol.2017.01.003

Nursini, N. (2020). Micro, small, and medium enterprises (MSMEs) and poverty reduction: Empirical evidence from Indonesia. *Development Studies Research*, *7*(1), 153–166. DOI: 10.1080/21665095.2020.1823238

Olanrewaju, G. S., Seun Bunmi Adebayo, S. B., Omotosho, A. Y., & Charles Falajiki Olajide, C. F. (2021). Left behind? The effects of digital gaps on e-learning in rural secondary schools and remote communities across Nigeria during the COVID19 pandemic. *International Journal of Educational Research Open*, *2*, 100092. DOI: 10.1016/j.ijedro.2021.100092 PMID: 35059671

Palacios, F. D., Perez-Uribe, R. I., Ramírez, I. R., & Salcedo-Perez, C. (2020). Orientation to Organizational Learning and Its Effects on Innovation and Performance: The Colombian MSMEs Case. In Masouras, A., Maris, G., & Kavoura, A. (Eds.), *Entrepreneurial Development and Innovation in Family Businesses and SMEs* (pp. 167–186). IGI Global Scientific Publishing., DOI: 10.4018/978-1-7998-3648-3.ch010

Pankiv, K., & Kloetzer, L. (2024). Does Using Artificial Intelligence in Citizen Science Support Volunteers' Learning? An Experimental Study in Ornithology. *Citizen Science: Theory and Practice*, *9*(1), 36. Advance online publication. DOI: 10.5334/cstp.733

Paul, I., & Roy, G. (2025). How eco-service quality affects tourist engagement behaviour in ecotourism: Eco-consciousness and eco activity-based learning and SOR Theory. *Tourism Recreation Research*, *50*(2), 385–401. DOI: 10.1080/02508281.2023.2275240

Pérez-Uribe, R. I., Vargas-Ramírez, I., & Ocampo-Guzmán, D. (2024). *Governance Model from the VUCA Perspective: Proposal for the Department of Quindío*. IGI Global Scientific Publishing., DOI: 10.4018/979-8-3693-0720-5.ch007

Peterson, M. N., Larson, L. R., Hipp, A., Beall, J. M., Lerose, C., Desrochers, H., Lauder, S., Torres, S., Tarr, N. A., Stukes, K., Stevenson, K., & Martin, K. L. (2024). Birdwatching linked to increased psychological well-being on college campuses: A pilot-scale experimental study. *Journal of Environmental Psychology*, *96*, 102306. DOI: 10.1016/j.jenvp.2024.102306

Purnomo, S., & Purwandari, S. (2025). A Comprehensive Micro, Small, and Medium Enterprise Empowerment Model for Developing Sustainable Tourism Villages in Rural Communities: A Perspective. *Sustainability (Basel)*, *17*(4), 1368. DOI: 10.3390/su17041368

Quindío, C. (2024). Economic indicators in birdwatching. *Regional Reports*, *22*(3), 45–50.

Rahman, F., Made, P., Kutanegara, Susilastuti, D.H., and Bachruddin, Z. (2025). Barriers to Local Community Involvement in Community-Based Tourism Development: Evidence from Area Model of Conservation and Education (AMCE) Oro-Oro Ombo Village Batu City Indonesia. *Journal of Tourism Sustainability*, 4(2):133-149. January 2025. DOI: . v4i3.130DOI: 10.35313/jtospolban

Rew, J., Park, S., Cho, Y., Hwang, E., & Jung, S. (2019, October). Animal Movement Prediction Based on Predictive Recurrent Neural Network. *Sensors (Basel)*, *19*(20), 4411. DOI: 10.3390/s19204411 PMID: 31614699

Rosydiana, E., & Narsa, I. M. (2024). Financial sustainability of MSMEs in birdwatching tourism. *Southeast Asian Journal of Tourism*, *8*(2), 89–103.

Sastry, K., Nguyen, T., & Roy, D. (2023). AI and satellite monitoring of avian biodiversity. *Ecological Informatics*, *74*, 101518. DOI: 10.1016/j.ecoinf.2023.101518

Schwoerer, T., & Dawson, C. (2022b). Economic impacts of birdwatching in Alaska. *Ecological Economics*, *190*, 107215. DOI: 10.1016/j.ecolecon.2021.107215

Schwoerer, T., & Dawson, N. G. (2022a). Small sight—Big might: Economic impact of bird tourism shows opportunities for rural communities and biodiversity conservation. *PLoS One*, *17*(7), e0268594. DOI: 10.1371/journal.pone.0268594 PMID: 35793337

Sekercioglu, C. H. (2022). Birdwatchers as conservation allies. *Global Ecology and Conservation*, *34*, e02033. DOI: 10.1016/j.gecco.2022.e02033

Siddiqui, A. (2021). SWOT analysis (or SWOT matrix) tool as a strategic planning and management technique in the health care industry and its advantages. *Biomedical Journal of Scientific & Technical Research*, *40*(2), 32035–32042. DOI: 10.26717/BJSTR.2021.40.006419

Smirnov, A., & Starov, E. (2022, May). Bad News Turned Good: Reversal under Censorship. *American Economic Journal. Microeconomics*, *14*(2), 506–560. DOI: 10.1257/mic.20190379

Steven, R., Morrison, C., & Castley, J. G. (2014). Birdwatching and avitourism: A global review of research and practice. *Journal of Sustainable Tourism*, *22*(6), 850–873. DOI: 10.1080/09669582.2013.862401

Steven, R., Smart, J., Morrison, C., & Castley, G. (2016). Using a choice experiment and birder preferences to guide bird-conservation funding. October 2016. *Conservation Biology*, *31*(4), 818–827. Advance online publication. DOI: 10.1111/cobi.12849 PMID: 27696549

Sullivan, B. L., Aycrigg, J. L., Barry, J. H., Bonney, R. E., Bruns, N., Cooper, C. B., Damoulas, T., Dhondt, A. A., Dietterich, T., Farnsworth, A., Fink, D., Fitzpatrick, J. W., Fredericks, T., Gerbracht, J., Gomes, C., Hochachka, W. M., Iliff, M. J., Lagoze, C., La Sorte, F. A., & Kelling, S. (2014a). The eBird enterprise: An integrated approach to development and application of citizen science. *Biological Conservation*, *169*, 31–40. DOI: 10.1016/j.biocon.2013.11.003

Sullivan, B. L., Wood, C. L., Iliff, M. J., Bonney, R. E., Fink, D., & Kelling, S. (2014b). eBird: A citizen-based bird observation network. *Biological Conservation*, *169*, 31–40. DOI: 10.1016/j.biocon.2013.11.003

Timothy, D. J., & Boyd, S. W. (2015). Tourism and trails: Cultural, ecological and management issues (Vol. 64). Channel View Publications. https://books.google.com/books?hl=es&lr=&id=6PuTBQAAQBAJ&oi=fnd&pg=PP9&dq=Marketing+management+of+trails.&ots=sLOH0JaGl1&sig=dEJ35lgXcyv_wbbDvGiX7xVMDso#v=onepage&q=Marketing%20management%20of%20trails.&f=false

Vargas Ramírez, I. (2021). El estilo de la toma de decisiones de los gobernadores y su relación con los tipos de desempeño de la gestión pública y los nuevos enfoques de gobernanza en Colombia. Disponible en: http://hdl.handle.net/10882/11268

Vergara-Romero, A., Duran, J. L., Jimber-Del Rio, J. A., & Collado-Gonzalez, J. C. (2025, June). Business management of sustainable destinations and its effect on ecotourism entrepreneurship to mitigate overtourism. *Humanities & Social Sciences Communications*, *12*(1), 817. Advance online publication. DOI: 10.1057/s41599-025-05149-4

Vox News Feature (2025, March). *Colombia's* rise as a birdwatching paradise. *Vox Global Travel*, 28–33.

Wäldchen, J., & Mäder, P. (2018). Machine learning for image-based species identification. *Methods in Ecology and Evolution*, *9*(11), 2216–2225. DOI: 10.1111/2041-210X.13075

World Travel & Tourism Council (2025, May 30). *Colombia travel & tourism economic impact factsheet* [PDF]. WTTC Research Hub. WTTC Research Hub website

Wu, S., & Wang, S. (2025). Exploring the impact of AI-enhanced virtual tourism on Tourists' pro-environmental behavior: A stimulus-organism-response model perspective. *Acta Psychologica, 253*, 104773. DOI: 10.1016/j.actpsy.2025.104773 PMID: 39904230

Yang, F., & Sheb, N. (2024, May). Automatic Bird Species Recognition from Images with Feature Enhancement and Contrastive Learning. *Applied Sciences (Basel, Switzerland), 14*(10), 4278. DOI: 10.3390/app14104278

Yoo, Y., Henfridsson, O., & Lyytinen, K. (2010). The new organizing logic of digital innovation: An agenda for information systems research. *Information Systems Research, 21*(4), 724–735. DOI: 10.1287/isre.1100.0322

Zahin, A., & Shammi, M. (2024). Tourism trend in the Bangladesh Sundarbans Mangrove Forest: A PESTEL framework analysis focusing on sustainable ecotourism development. *Journal of Tourism and Heritage Research, 7*(4), 40–63. https://www.jthr.es/index.php/journal/article/view/572

Zopounidis, C., & Christos, C. (2024). The company of the future: Integrating sustainability, growth, and profitability in contemporary business models. *Development and Sustainability in Economics and Finance., 1*(June), 100003. DOI: 10.1016/j.dsef.2024.100003

## KEY TERMS AND DEFINITIONS

**Artificial Intelligence:** The capability of computer systems to perform tasks that normally require human intelligence, such as pattern recognition, decision-making, and language processing. In this context, AI is increasingly used to monitor biodiversity, predict bird behavior, and support MSMEs in tourism (Sastry, Nguyen, & Roy, 2023).

**Avitourism:** A niche form of nature-based tourism focused on birdwatching activities. It contributes to rural development, conservation funding, and environmental awareness, especially in biodiversity-rich countries like Colombia (Maldonado, Ruiz, & Benítez, 2018).

**Birdwatching:** A recreational activity involving the observation and identification of birds in their natural habitats. Birdwatchers often contribute significant economic value through ecotourism and are considered allies in *conservation* (Sekercioglu, 2022).

**Ecotourism:** A sustainable form of tourism that aims to minimize environmental impact while generating economic benefits for local communities. Birdwatching tourism is a typical example. (Steven, Morrison, & Castley, 2014).

**Micro, Small, and Medium-Sized Enterprises (MSMEs):** Businesses that operate on a smaller scale in terms of workforce and capital. In developing countries, MSMEs often lead ecotourism ventures and require support in adopting digital and AI technologies (Rosydiana & Narsa, 2024).

**PESTEL Analysis:** A strategic planning framework used to evaluate the external macro-environmental factors—Political, Economic, Social, Technological, Environmental, and Legal—that can affect an organization or sector (Siddiqui, 2021).

**Strategic Foresight:** A structured and systematic way of using insights about the future to guide present-day decisions. In this study, it is applied to anticipate future scenarios in AI-driven birdwatching ecotourism (Bezuhla, 2020).

# Chapter 10
# Application Cases of Artificial Intelligence (AI) in Micro, Small, and Medium-Sized Enterprises:
## A Critical Analysis of Selected Industries in the Global South

**Chinwe Ebere Nwosu**
http://orcid.org/0009-0001-5664-517X
*Glasgow Caledonian University, UK*

**Ademola Joel Osho**
http://orcid.org/0009-0008-7603-2144
*Glasgow Caledonian University, UK*

**Michael Olaitan Meshioye**
http://orcid.org/0009-0003-6582-4342
*Ahmadu Bello University, Zaria, Nigeria*

**Amarachi Glory Nwosu**
http://orcid.org/0009-0003-9719-7056
*Federal University of Technology, Owerri, Nigeria*

## ABSTRACT

*Artificial Intelligence (AI) offers significant potential for the Micro, Small and Medium Enterprises (MSMEs) that drive economies in the Global South, yet its*

DOI: 10.4018/979-8-3373-2817-1.ch010

*adoption remains low due to systemic barriers. This study explores how AI can be used effectively by these enterprises. Through qualitative analysis of 15 MSMEs across diverse sectors, key adoption strategies, challenges and opportunities were identified. The study's primary contribution is the AI Preparedness and Provision (AIPP) Framework. This model posits that successful adoption hinges on the synergy between two dimensions: a firm's internal AI Preparedness (strategic intent, capacity building, agile adoption, and collaboration) and the Ecosystem Provision of external support (financial, knowledge, contextual, regulations, and infrastructure). The AIPP framework provides a practical guide for both MSMEs and policymakers to bridge the gap between aspiration and action, enabling sustainable AI-driven growth across the Global South.*

## INTRODUCTION

Micro, Small, and Medium Enterprises (MSMEs) are important contributors to economic growth and employment in the Global South (GS). According to Endris & Kassegn (2022), MSMEs contribute more than 50% of gross domestic product (GDP) and provide over 49% of the employment in sub-Saharan African countries like Botswana, Kenya, Malawi, Swaziland and Zimbabwe. In Asia, they represent 96.6% of all enterprises, employ 55.8% of the workforce, and contribute 28.0% to economic output affirming their role in poverty reduction and economic inclusion (Asian Development Bank, 2023). With the accelerating digital technologies such as Artificial Intelligence (AI), MSMEs now have greater opportunities to enhance productivity, innovate, and access new markets.

According to Borines et al. (2025) and Kataria & Mehta (2025), AI technologies enable businesses to streamline operations, improve customer engagement, make data-driven decisions and improve productivity in various industries. For MSMEs in the Global South, Tishtykbayeva et al. (2023) claimed that AI has the potential to address persistent challenges like spotting risk in business finance, optimise supply chains, and personalise marketing strategies, thereby fostering competitiveness and growth. Aderibigbe et al. (2023) noted how MSMEs in Kenya have begun using AI to manage healthcare logistics and customer service, while small businesses in Brazil apply AI for localised environmental services.

Despite these promising prospects, AI adoption among MSMEs in developing regions remains low. Van der Vlist et al. (2024) attributed this disparity to differences in organisational resources, technological infrastructure and internal capacity for AI adoption and scaling. Further insight from surveys conducted by McKinsey (2018) and Lorica & Nathan (2019), identified lack of AI strategy, shortage of skilled talent, inadequate technological infrastructure and limited available data as the major challenges (Figure 1).

*Figure 1. Challenges Associated with AI Adoption*

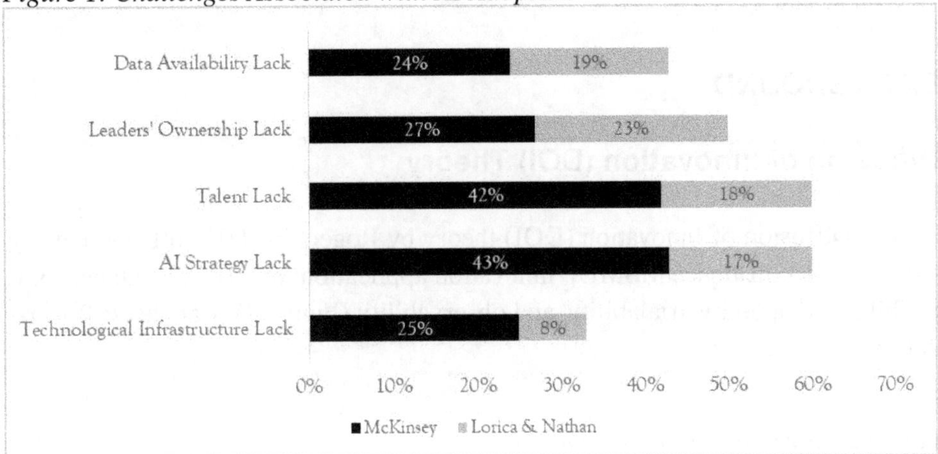


*Source: Adapted from McKinsey (2018) and Lorica & Nathan (2019)*

Moreover, most AI research and development focuses on large enterprises in developed economies, leaving a huge knowledge gap regarding AI application in MSMEs operating within the distinct socio-economic contexts of the Global South. For example, the report by the United Nations Development Programme (UNDP) (2025) revealed that in 2023, the United States alone received $67.2 billion investment in AI, while countries like Kenya and Nigeria received only $15 million and $2.9 million respectively.

This gap is concerning given that studies (Endris & Kassegn, 2022; Dwivedi et al., 2021; McKinsey, 2018) claimed that MSMEs in these regions identify technology adoption as a key barrier to growth. Therefore, understanding how AI can be effectively leveraged by MSMEs is important for promoting inclusive economic development and reducing digital divides. Hence, the aim of this study is to critically analyse the application cases of AI in MSMEs across selected industries in the Global South. By examining current implementations, enablers, and challenges, the research seeks to provide detailed insights to guide policymakers, practitioners, and technology developers in supporting AI adoption tailored to the needs of MSMEs in these regions.

The Objectives of the Study are:

1. To examine the current state of AI application and its impact on MSMEs in the Global South.

2. To identify key barriers faced by MSMEs in application of AI technologies in the Global South.
3. To provide a theoretical and managerial recommendations for AI application among MSMEs in the Global South.

## BACKGROUND

### Diffusion of Innovation (DOI) Theory

The Diffusion of Innovation (DOI) theory by Rogers in 2003 outlines five key attributes that influence MSMEs' innovation application: relative advantage, compatibility, complexity, trialability, and observability (Figure 2) (Lai, 2017; Rogers, 2003).

*Figure 2. Attributes of Innovation Adoption*

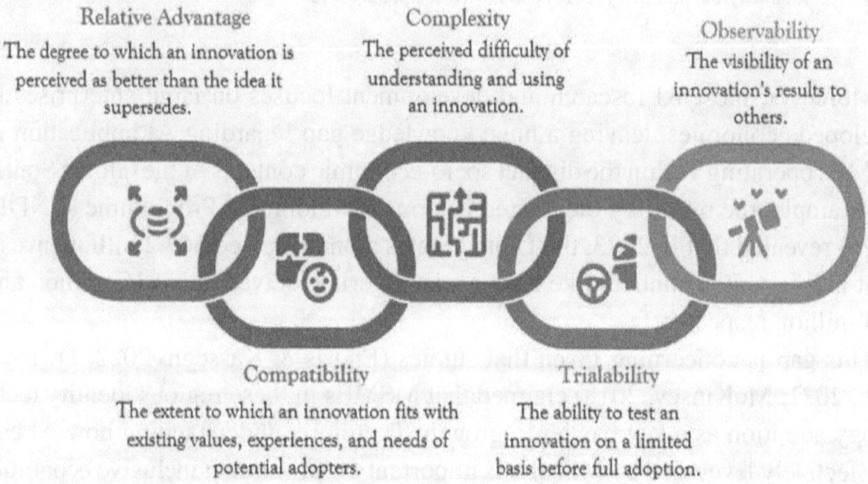


*Source: Adapted from Lai (2017)*

### Relative Advantage

Cahyono et al. (2024) explain that the more an innovation is seen as profitable, efficient, or practically beneficial, the more likely it is to be embraced. For MSMEs operating in resource-constrained environments, AI should demonstrate value beyond traditional practices. Santosa & Surgawati (2024) argued that MSMEs are more likely to adopt AI if it results in measurable gains, such as increased profitability, time savings, reduced workload, or improved business reputation. These benefits are relevant for MSMEs that should balance limited resources with the pressure to remain competitive. Patra (2024) further confirmed that AI and machine learning tools help MSMEs streamline routine operations through automation, allowing business owners to focus on strategic activities that drive growth.

### Compatibility

Compatibility refers to how AI technology fits within an organisation's existing values, needs, and working practices. Gans (2022) found that MSMEs are more likely to adopt AI when it integrates smoothly into current operations without disrupting established workflows. Triandini et al. (2024) emphasise that compatibility also involves alignment with organisational culture and values. The study noted that digital technologies including AI tools should support the work habits of employees and match how the business already operates. In addition, such tool should be compatible with the company's existing infrastructure.

### Complexity

Complexity refers to how difficult a technology is to understand and use. In the case of AI, the more complicated it appears, the less likely MSMEs are to adopt it (Lee et al., 2024). Many MSMEs have limited technical skills and resources, so if AI systems are seen as too complex, they may be avoided altogether. Triandini et al. (2024) suggest that perceived ease of use is closely linked to user acceptance.

### Trialability

Trialability refers to the extent to which a new technology can be tested on a small scale before full adoption. Rogers (2003) explained that when users can try out an innovation temporarily, they are more likely to accept it. In the context of MSMEs, this is important because of financial and infrastructure limitations. Xu et al. (2023) noted that trialability allows MSMEs to assess the benefits and risks of AI without committing significant resources upfront.

### Observability

Observability refers to the extent to which the results of adopting a new technology, such as AI, are visible to others. According to Triandini et al. (2024), when MSMEs can clearly see the benefits experienced by similar businesses, such as improved efficiency, reduced costs, or increased sales, they are more likely to adopt the technology themselves.

## Meaning and Conceptualisation of MSMEs

The definition of MSMEs varies across economies, reflecting local industrial structures and policy priorities. For instance, in India, the distinction is based on investment and turnover. In Cambodia, MSMEs are defined by workforce size and turnover while the investment is not specified, and assets are measured excluding land. In contrast, Nigeria defines MSMEs based on workforce size and assets (Table 1).

*Table 1. Definition of MSMEs across Regions*

| *Region* | *Enterprise Category* | *Workforce Size* | *Turnover* | *Investment* | *Asset* |
|---|---|---|---|---|---|
| *Ministry of MSMEs, India* | Micro | Not specified | 5 crore | 1 crore | Not specified |
| | Small | Not specified | 50 crore | 10 crore | Not specified |
| | Medium | Not specified | 50 crore | 250 crore | Not specified |
| *Cambodia* | Micro | Less than 10 | ≤$5000 | Not specified | Excluding Land |
| | Small | 11 to 50 | $5000 to $250,000 | Not specified | Excluding Land |
| | Medium | 51 to 100 | $250,000 to $500,000 | Not Specified | Excluding land |
| *Small and Medium Enterprise Development Agency of Nigeria (SMEDAN)* | Micro | Less than 10 | Not specified | Not specified | < N5 million |
| | Small | 10 to 49 | Not specified | Not specified | < N50 million |
| | Medium | 50 to 199 | Not specified | Not specified | < N500 million |

**Source:** (SMEDAN & NBS, 2012; Ministry of MSME, 2022; The ASEAN Secretariat, 2025)

## Meaning and Conceptualisation of Artificial Intelligence

The main idea behind AI is that machines can be built to mimic human thought processes and handle complex tasks independently. Rawas (2024) establishes that this idea informs the early development of AI in the 1950s, beginning with symbolic AI, which applied logical rules to perform structured reasoning. However, Gibson (2024) argues that the practical use of AI in businesses began in 1980s when expert systems were introduced in sectors like finance and healthcare to support decision-making processes.

As AI technologies began to expand beyond specialised applications, it became necessary to classify them based on their characteristics and functionality. As such, Rashid & Kausik (2024) noted that that AI systems are often grouped based on two main criteria: their level of intelligence and their capabilities. The study further established that AI is categorised into weak AI, which is designed for specific tasks, and strong AI, which aims to perform any intellectual task a human can do (Figure 3).

*Figure 3. Classification of AI based on Capabilities and Intelligence*

| Characteristic | Strong AI | Weak AI | Notes |
|---|---|---|---|
| Artificial General Intelligence (AGI) | Yes | No | True Strong AI – human-level understanding and reasoning |
| Artificial Super Intelligence (ASI) | Yes | No | Hypothetical future AI surpassing human intelligence |
| Artificial Narrow Intelligence (ANI) | No | Yes | Task-specific intelligence – today's typical AI |
| Rule-based Systems | No | Yes | Rigid logic rules; lacks learning or adaptation |
| Expert Systems | No | Yes | Domain-specific rule-based Weak AI |
| Natural Language Processing (NLP) | Yes | Yes | Present in both; scope depends on depth of understanding |
| Machine Learning System | Yes | Yes | Core AI approach; scale and context determine strength |
| Deep Learning Systems | Yes | Yes | Used in both, but required for Strong AI capability |
| Computer Vision | Yes | Yes | Used for perception in both forms of AI |

*Source: Adapted from Rashid & Kausik (2024).*

## Empirical Review of AI Applications in MSMEs

This section covers four dominant domains of AI deployment in MSMEs:

### AI in Customer Engagement and Marketing

AI-powered Customer Relationship Management (CRM) systems are enabling MSMEs to know and serve their customers better. These systems utilise behavioural data to allow for more precise micro-targeting and dynamic pricing, with the outcome that businesses can tailor offers in ways that more precisely reflect individual needs. For example, Kushwaha et al. (2021) maintain that AI-powered chatbots improve customer response times by automating the standardised interactions and that this is one of the major efficiency gains for small businesses.

Furthermore, Sharma et al. (2025) maintain that natural language processing (NLP) software supports real-time sentiment analysis that allows MSME to tailor messaging according to the emotional tone of the customers and thereby create deeper engagement with different customer segments. These practical applications reflect what Huang & Rust (2021) present as three basic competencies of AI in marketing: Mechanical AI (automating tasks), Thinking AI (data-driven intelligence), and Feeling AI (emotional understanding) (Figure 4). The model demonstrates how MSME with limited resources utilise AI in automating processes, making more informed decisions, and providing emotionally intelligent marketing.

*Figure 4. AI and Strategic Marketing Decisions*

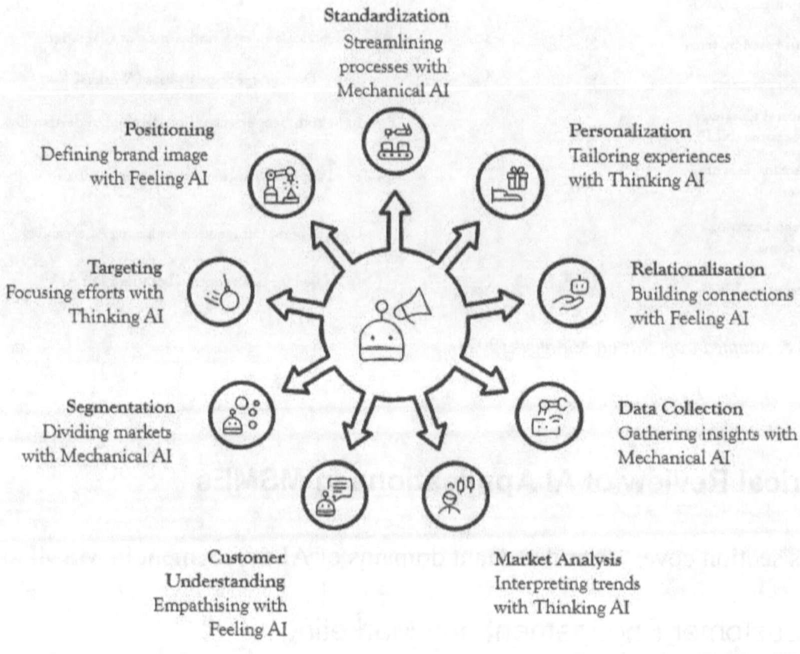


*Source: Adapted from Huang & Rust (2021).*

Nonetheless, Zimmerman et al. (2024) explain that when automation replaces direct human interaction, it can weaken relational capital because trust and personal connections, which are key in business environments, are lost or damaged. In these contexts, customers may feel alienated or less valued. de Marcellis-Warin et al. (2022) argue that opaque algorithmic targeting works by making decisions that are hidden from customers, which can unintentionally reinforce biases or create a ''dark pattern'' which depicts manipulating consumers into decision making by showing selective content without clear explanation.

## AI in Health Care

AI is increasingly being used to address major healthcare challenges in the Global South, where poor infrastructure and shortages in skilled personnel hinder quality care delivery. For example, in India, Hussain et al. (2025) assert that an AI powered platform called the *eSanjeevani* telemedicine service launched in 2019, facilitates both doctor-to-doctor consultations and direct patient-to-doctor outpatient services (*eSanjeevaniOPD*).

According to Hussain et al. (2025), the platform operates across more than 154,000 health centres and had conducted over 276 million consultations by October 2024, saving approximately USD 3 billion in out-of-pocket expenses, primarily by reducing travel burdens and infection risks for underserved rural populations. In diagnostics, Nijiati et al. (2021) report that TB-UNet, developed for tuberculosis detection using chest X-rays in low-resource environments in China, achieved 85% accuracy surpassing radiologists' 62%. Moreover, when used as a decision-support tool, it enhanced radiologist sensitivity by 11.8%.

Beyond diagnostics, AI also optimises healthcare supply chains. Nigerian health technology company LifeBank has applied predictive analytics via platforms such as SkyBank and AirX to improve the delivery of blood and oxygen supplies. Serving over 1,000 hospitals across Nigeria, Kenya, and Ethiopia, LifeBank has delivered more than 45,400 critical units and contributed to saving over 20,000 lives, with about 75% of beneficiaries from low-income communities (Founder Africa, 2023; International Centre of Expertise in Montreal on Artificial Intelligence, 2024). Others in Africa using AI to improve healthcare include Wekebere and MinoHealth AI Labs (Table 2).

*Table 2. AI Solutions in Healthcare by SMEs in Africa*

| *Company* | *Website* | *AI Solutions Adopted* | *Problem Solving* | *Country* |
|---|---|---|---|---|
| *Lifebank* | lifebank.ng | AI-driven algorithms for predicting blood and medical supply demand | Ensures timely delivery of critical medical supplies and optimises delivery routes, reducing delays in transfusions. | Nigeria |
| *Wekebere* | wekebere.com | AI for medical diagnostics and telemedicine | Improves access to healthcare through remote consultations, aiding in timely diagnosis and treatment. | Uganda |
| *MinoHealth AI Labs* | minohealth.com | AI-powered tools for healthcare analytics and disease prediction | Provides early detection and diagnosis of diseases, improving patient outcomes through data-driven insights. | Ghana |

*Source:* Company websites and reports.

## Automation of Routine Tasks and Workflow Optimisation

AI is changing labour-intensive work as adoption gains traction in MSMEs, especially in back-office operations. Kokina & Davenport (2017) posit that organisations are deploying AI for automation of payroll, invoicing, and compliance tasks for cost savings and greater processing efficiency.

Sanka (2025) posits that AI-led automation improves regulatory compliance and reduces human error in document management. However, Srinivasan (2016) emphasise displacement concerns in labour-intensive roles, while Deranty and Corbin (2024) contend that, rather than displacing jobs, AI adoption reconfigures organisational workflow by reallocating human input from routine procedural tasks to more structured and cognitively demanding functions such as exception handling and strategic planning. Keshvarparast et al. (2023) further argue that the integration of AI into workflows challenges the narrative of technological displacement and instead positions AI as a co-productive technology that that fosters new labour dynamics by redistributing task complexity rather than eliminating human roles.

## Risks and Challenges in AI Applications in MSMEs

The prominent challenge in implementing AI is the lack of access to affordable and reliable digital infrastructure. According to Mutasa et al. (2024), countries like Nigeria, India, and Kenya, many MSMEs operate in regions with limited internet connectivity and electricity, which are fundamental for deploying AI solutions. Tishtykbayeva et al. (2023) claimed that high costs associated with AI technologies, including software, hardware, and skilled personnel, are expensive for many small businesses.

In addition, Iyelolu et al. (2024) claimed that AI technologies require specialised knowledge for it development, implementation, and maintenance. However, many MSMEs in the Global South struggle to attract and retain talent with the necessary expertise. Sampath (2021) noted that weak regulatory environment and data privacy concerns in many countries in the Global South creates uncertainty for MSMEs seeking to adopt AI, as regulations are either underdeveloped or overly restrictive. Morley et al. (2025) caution that AI models predominantly trained on Global North data may result in social and ethical problems.

These include the imposition of Western ethical values incompatible with local cultures, exclusion of communities from algorithmic governance and healthcare priorities pertinent to low-resource settings, and perpetuation of bias in systems. Hunter (2024) claimed that decisions made through AI-driven systems, such as automated hiring processes or credit scoring algorithms, may inadvertently discriminate against certain groups.

## MAIN FOCUS OF CHAPTER

### Methodology

This study follows an interpretivist paradigm to explore how MSME owners in the Global South perceive and make sense of AI adoption. Using an inductive, qualitative, cross-sectional approach, data was gathered from 15 purposively selected participants via open-ended questionnaires (Table 3 below) (Saunders, Lewis, & Thornhill, 2019). This purposive sampling strategy was chosen to ensure a rich diversity of perspectives, representing a variety of sectors (including education, healthcare, and technology), firm sizes (from micro to medium), and geographical regions (SSA, MENA, Asia, and LAC).

The goal was to facilitate a comparative understanding of cross-cutting themes rather than to achieve statistical generalisability. Thematic analysis, based on Braun and Clarke's framework, was used to identify emerging patterns (Braun & Clarke, 2022).

*Table 3. Details of Participants*

| *Participants ID* | *Gender* | *Years of Experience (Est)* | *MSME Stage* | *Sector* | *Region* | *Role* |
|---|---|---|---|---|---|---|
| *R-1* | Male | 5-7 years | Small | Education | SSA | Founder / Director |
| *R-2* | Female | 2-4 years | Micro | Creative Art/ Digital Media | SSA | Founder |
| *R-3* | Male | 5-7 years | Small | Agri-Tech | MENA | Founder |
| *R-4* | Male | 5-7 years | Small | Retail / Distribution | LAC | Owner / Manager |
| *R-5* | Female | >7 years | Small | Fashion / Textiles | MENA | Founder / Owner |
| *R-6* | Male | 2-4 years | Micro | Retail | SSA | Owner |
| *R-7* | Male | >7 years | Medium | Food Retail | MENA | Owner |
| *R-8* | Male | 2-4 years | Small | Fintech | SSA | Founder / CEO |
| *R-9* | Female | 2-4 years | Micro | NGO Education | SSA | Director |
| *R-10* | Male | >7 years | Medium | Hospitality / Tourism | Asia | Owner |
| *R-11* | Female | 5-7 years | Small | Social Enterprise | MENA | Co-Founder |
| *R-12* | Female | <2 years | Micro | Food and Beverages | SSA | Founder |
| *R-13* | Male | 2-4 years | Micro | Advisory / Consulting | SSA | Consultant |
| *R-14* | Female | <2 years | Small | Tech Services | SSA | Founder |
| *R-15* | Female | 5-7 years | Small (NGO) | NGO Healthcare | Asia | Director |

Source: (Author's Fieldwork)

## Data Analysis and Interpretation of Findings

This chapter presents the data analysis and interpretation of findings from 15 MSME leaders. Thematic analysis revealed three key themes (figure 5): AI Application Strategies and Value Creation; Barriers and Opportunities for Adoption; and a Participant-driven Roadmap for Practice and Policy.

*Figure 5. Themes and Subthemes (Source: Author's)*

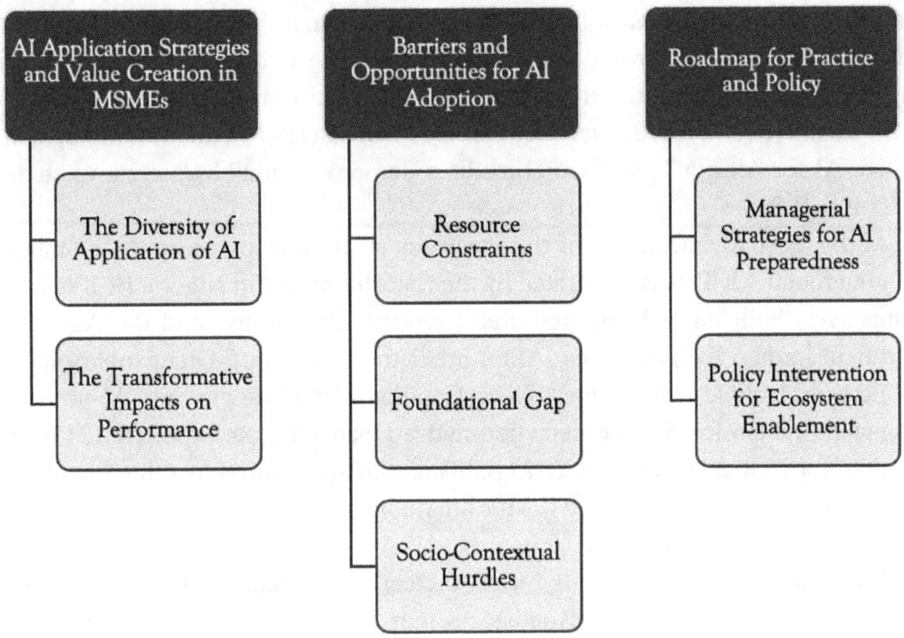


## Theme 1: AI Application Strategies and Value Creation in MSMEs

The study finds that MSMEs are adopting AI in diverse and strategic ways, creating value for their operations. This theme is explored through two sub-themes: the diversity in applications of AI and the transformative impacts resulting from them.

### *Sub-theme 1.1: The Diversity in Application of AI*

The findings reveal that MSMEs in the Global South are not adopting AI uniformly, but rather along a diversity of complexity and integration, pragmatically choosing entry points that match their specific needs and capacities. At the most nascent end of this are businesses in low-resource environments that leverage the principles of automation with basic, often offline-capable tools. The NGO providing education in rural Nigeria (R-9) exemplifies this, using application, which "can recommend lessons based on a child's progress," and automating administrative work with simple "Google Forms."

Following this are most common use cases, where MSMEs apply AI to optimise specific business functions. This typically falls into two areas. Firstly, improving internal operational efficiency, as seen with the education provider (R-1) who uses AI to "auto-grade short answers," the Colombian retailer (R-4) who employs "automated stock management software," and the Tunisian fashion designer (R-5) who utilises 3D software to "prototype designs digitally." Secondly, enhancing customer engagement, which includes the use of chatbots for customer service by a hotelier in Sri Lanka (R-10), a dedicated tech service in Ghana (R-14), and leveraging generative AI for "design" and "social media video production" by a creative studio in Kenya (R-2).

At the most advanced end of the spectrum are businesses whose entire model is built around AI. This is illustrated by the fintech founder in Nigeria (R-8) whose company is built on "AI-powered credit scoring algorithms" and the Agri-tech startup in Jordan (R-3) that uses "AI for predictive irrigation." Other sophisticated applications include a healthcare NGO in Cambodia (R-15) deploying "AI-powered diagnostic tools" for disease detection and a Ghanaian consultant (R-13) using "LLMs" for "critical business decisions." This wide spectrum shows that from basic automation to deep innovation, MSMEs are finding pragmatic and context-specific ways to engage with AI.

These pragmatic entry points reflect a clear assessment by the entrepreneurs of the technology's Relative Advantage, as they consistently select tools that offer immediate and tangible benefits for their specific operational painpoints.

### *Sub-theme 1.2: The Transformative Impacts on Performance*

The various application strategies employed by MSMEs are delivering transformative and multi-faceted impacts, validating their investment in AI. The findings show that these benefits go beyond simple automation, fundamentally enhancing firm performance in four key areas: productivity, cost-efficiency, decision-making, and market competitiveness. The most immediate benefits reported are significant gains in productivity and cost-efficiency. AI tools are allowing these MSMEs to accomplish more in less time and with fewer resources. The Nigerian fintech founder (R-8) described a revolutionary increase in speed, with loan approval times dropping from "72 hours" to "10-15 minutes."

Similarly, a creative director in Kenya (R-2) quantified the gain, noting a "nearly 60%" reduction in project turnaround time, which allows his team to focus on quality rather than deadlines. These productivity gains translate directly into cost savings. A food retailer in Morocco (R-7), for instance, was able to "reduce food waste by approximately 20%" through more accurate, AI-driven demand forecasting. Others, like the education provider in Nigeria (R-1), found they could handle a growing workload without having to "cut costs on hiring extra admin staff," demonstrating how AI enables more efficient scaling.

Beyond operational gains, AI is elevating the strategic capabilities of these entrepreneurs, enabling more sophisticated decision-making and enhancing their competitive edge. The Sri Lankan hotelier (R-10) shared how simple social media analytics led him to create a "very popular and unique selling point" with a cooking demonstration, turning a data insight into a strategic advantage. This shift from intuition to data-driven action is also seen in the Colombian retailer (R-4), who uses system alerts about demand surges to "negotiate better deals with suppliers."

As such, these internal improvements empower MSMEs to compete more effectively in their markets. As the Colombian retailer (R-4) summarised, AI is "starting to level the playing field for MSMEs competing with larger corporations." This sentiment was further echoed by the Kenyan creative director (R-2), who explained that AI has "allowed us to bid for international gigs we'd otherwise never qualify for based on size alone," proving that technology can dismantle traditional barriers of scale and geography.

## Theme 2: Barriers and Opportunities for AI Adoption

Despite the clear benefits and value created by AI, the participants' discussions revealed that the path to adoption is fraught with significant and often prohibitive barriers. This theme explores the interconnected challenges that MSMEs face, which can be grouped into three categories: resource constraints, foundational gaps, and socio-contextual hurdles.

### *Sub-theme 2.1: Resource Constraints*

The most immediate and frequently cited barriers to AI adoption are severe resource constraints, specifically the challenges of prohibitive financial costs and a critical human skills gap. These two issues are often interlinked, creating a difficult cycle where a lack of funds prevents investment in training, and a lack of skills prevents the effective use of affordable tools.

The financial burden was a universal concern. This financial pressure directly inhibits Trialability, a key attribute in innovation diffusion, by preventing MSMEs from experimenting with new tools without incurring significant risk. Entrepreneurs spoke of the high direct costs of software, with a hotelier in Sri Lanka (R-10) noting that one platform's "annual subscription fee was more than the monthly salary of two of our staff members."

For many, AI investment feels like a luxury that could wait. As a food entrepreneur in Ghana (R-12) candidly stated, investing in "advanced AI platforms… often feels secondary" to core production and marketing costs. This challenge is exacerbated by a global market that disadvantages those in the Global South. Participants in Nigeria (R-1, R-8) highlighted the problem of tools being "billed in USD," which creates budgeting uncertainty due to volatile exchange rates. For those operating with minimal profits, like a retailer in Chad (R-6), the reality is that "margins are tight, so investing in AI platforms or training is difficult."

This financial pressure is matched by a profound human capital deficit. Even if a tool is affordable, finding people with the right skills is a major obstacle. This includes the external challenge of attracting expert talent, as an Agri-tech founder in Jordan (R-3) lamented that "talent retention is a problem" due to global competition. A social enterprise leader in the MENA region (R-11) noted the specific difficulty in "finding talent… that combines deep AI expertise with an understanding of the social sector." More commonly, the skills gap is internal. The Sri Lankan hotelier (R-10) articulated this perfectly: "Our team is fantastic at hospitality... But they are not data analysts. The skills gap is enormous." This was summarised by another participant from Ghana (R-14) as a simple but profound "Lack of skills and knowledge of available AI tools."

### *Sub-theme 2.2: Foundational Gaps*

Beyond resource constraints, the participants' discussions revealed that AI adoption is frequently undermined by foundational gaps in both the external digital infrastructure and the internal data quality of the MSMEs. These deficits create a fragile operating environment where even well-funded and well-staffed AI initiatives can fail, forcing entrepreneurs to constantly engineer workarounds to overcome an unstable technical reality.

The most universally cited foundational gap is the poor state of digital infrastructure, particularly unreliable internet connectivity and power. This was a shared frustration across continents, from the educator in Nigeria (R-1) and the retailer in Colombia (R-4) who noted that "Internet connectivity is sometimes unreliable, especially outside major cities,". Moreso, the fashion entrepreneur in Tunisia (R-5) whose use of cloud-based solutions is hampered by "unstable" connections. This directly impacts core business operations.

A food retailer in Morocco (R-7) explained how intermittent access in rural areas complicates "real-time inventory tracking," a critical function for his business. For others, the challenge extends to a lack of appropriate hardware. A creative director in Kenya (R-2), for instance, pointed out that "Some major tools require high-spec devices or stable broadband, which isn't always available." These infrastructural weaknesses force MSMEs to be less ambitious, often choosing simpler or offline-capable tools over more powerful, cloud-dependent AI solutions.

The second critical foundational gap is the quality and availability of data, which serves as the essential fuel for any AI system. Participants described a "garbage in, garbage out" dilemma. The Nigerian fintech founder (R-8), for instance, offered an insight into this challenge, explaining that because his customers operate in the informal sector, the data he collects is often "noisy and inconsistent," making it "hard" to train effective AI models. This problem is particularly acute in sectors handling sensitive or legacy information. The healthcare NGO in Cambodia (R-15) provided an example, finding that in the communities they serve, patient records are frequently "incomplete, inconsistent, or still paper-based." They concluded that this poor data quality directly "reduces the accuracy and effectiveness of AI predictions and recommendations," a fundamental barrier to delivering AI-powered care.

### *Socio-Contextual Hurdles*

Beyond resource and infrastructural gaps, the participants described set of hurdles rooted in social, cultural, and contextual factors. These challenges often proved to be the most complex to overcome, as they involve human trust, cultural identity, and the inherent biases within the technology itself. The findings show that a lack of localisation and a significant "trust deficit" from both employees and customers can stall AI adoption just as effectively as a lack of funding or connectivity.

A primary hurdle is the "context chasm" between generic, globally developed AI tools and the specific local realities of the MSMEs. A creative director in Kenya (R-2) articulated this, stating that "many tools aren't customised for African visual or cultural contexts which limits creativity or causes misrepresentation." This is a stark example of poor Compatibility, which the DOI theory identifies as a major barrier to the diffusion of an innovation.

This lack of localisation extends to language, with an Agri-tech founder in Jordan (R-3) pointing to "Arabic NLP limitations" that affect the accuracy of his services. One significant consequence of this poor contextual fit is the risk of algorithmic bias. The Nigerian fintech founder (R-8) shared an example, admitting that early on, his AI model "unintentionally prioritised male users due to historical data patterns," forcing his team to retrain it to ensure fairness.

This is compounded by a "trust deficit." Internally, employees often resisted AI out of a fear of losing their jobs and professional identity. A fashion entrepreneur in Tunisia (R-5) found that her "Tailors and seamstresses are concerned that digital tools... might replace their artisanal skills." Externally, customers frequently expressed a preference for human connection, with the Jordanian Agri-tech founder (R-3) encountering "Farmer distrust of tech tools," which they viewed as "too foreign." This mistrust is exacerbated when the technology itself is unreliable. As the advisory consultant in Ghana (R-13) noted, a key hurdle is the need for "domain expertise to advise against hallucinations" produced by AI models. This highlights a critical socio-technical barrier: for users to trust AI, its outputs should be reliable, while ensuring this requires human expertise that many MSMEs lack.

## Theme 3: The Path Forward: A Roadmap for Practice and Policy

When asked for way forward, the participants provided a consistent set of suggestions for what is needed to accelerate AI adoption. Their ideas form a comprehensive roadmap, detailing both the "bottom-up" strategies that MSMEs themselves should undertake and the "top-down" interventions required from governments and ecosystem builders.

### *Sub-theme 3.1: Managerial Strategies for AI Preparedness*

The participants consistently emphasised that successful AI adoption begins with internal readiness and a proactive managerial approach. The most critical starting point, according to the leader of a social enterprise (R-11), is for MSMEs to adopt a "'problem-first, not technology-first' mindset," a sentiment highlighted by the hotelier in Sri Lanka (R-10), who wanted a framework to identify which parts of his business could "genuinely benefit from an AI solution." This strategic clarity, they argued, should be supported by an investment in practical skills. Participants called for training focused on real-world application (R-7, R-9, R-13).

Others listed specific competencies like "Design interpretation" and "AI ethics" (R-2), and the need for "basic digital literacy" before advanced tools can be introduced (R-6). Finally, there was a consensus on the need for collaboration to overcome internal limitations. The desire to partner with "local universities" for talent and expertise was a near-universal suggestion, mentioned by entrepreneurs in Colombia (R-4), Morocco (R-7), and Ghana (R-12). The Agri-tech founder in Jordan (R-3) also highlighted the success of partnering with "local agricultural cooperatives," demonstrating the value of leveraging community networks for building trust and driving adoption.

### *Sub-theme 3.2: Policy Interventions for Ecosystem Enablement*

Alongside these internal strategies, the participants articulated a demand for top-down support from governments and institutions to create a more fertile ecosystem for AI adoption. The most urgent and frequently mentioned proposal was for direct financial intervention. Participants from across the Global South suggested policies such as an "AI Subsidy Scheme" in Nigeria (R-1), a "Creative-Tech Fund" in Kenya (R-2), and a "government-supported AI adoption subsidy program" in Tunisia (R-5). Beyond direct funding, there was a strong call for the creation of shared infrastructure for knowledge and experimentation.

This included proposals for a "digital innovation hub" in Chad (R-6) that would offer affordable training and technical support, and a sector-specific "National AI Field Lab for Agriculture" in Jordan (R-3) to allow MSMEs to "test, localise, and scale AI applications." Finally, participants stressed the need for a clearer and more supportive regulatory environment. The founder of a Nigerian fintech firm (R-8) made a specific call for an "AI regulatory sandbox" to allow for safe innovation without ambiguous rules. This desire for clear guidelines on data privacy and ethical use was also highlighted by participants (R-15), who felt that weak policy created uncertainty and delayed progress.

## SOLUTIONS AND RECOMMENDATION

The study's findings on AI adoption, viewed through the Diffusion of Innovations (DOI) theory, highlight the connection between AI's perceived attributes and the unique contexts of MSMEs in the Global South. The decision to adopt AI is often driven by its relative advantage, entrepreneurs adopt tools that offer clear, tangible improvements over current methods (Pillai & Sivathanu, 2020; Bhalerao et al., 2022). For example, in the education sector (R-1), AI's role in reducing teacher workload was key, echoing research linking perceived productivity gains to adoption intention (Gao & Feng, 2023). A Nigerian fintech firm (R-8) reduced loan processing from days to minutes, exemplifying how relative advantage can reshape service delivery (Williams et al., 2015; Dwivedi et al., 2020).

Compatibility with existing workflows also eases adoption (Santosa & Surgawati, 2024). Tools like WhatsApp (R-1) and Google Sheets (R-12) integrate with existing digital habits, reducing barriers (Selamat & Windasari, 2021). Yet, compatibility is not guaranteed. A Kenyan creative director (R-2) found AI tools culturally incompatible with African visual norms, supporting findings that poor cultural and linguistic localisation slows diffusion in non-Western settings (Combi, 2016; Algouzi & Abbas, 2023). Perceived complexity remains the strongest inhibitor, consistent with studies on SME tech barriers (Bhalerao et al., 2022; Sánchez et al., 2025). A Sri Lankan hotelier (R-10) expressed feeling "daunted" by AI integration, largely due to a lack of in-house technical skills (Dwivedi et al., 2021; OECD, 2023). This skills gap means even simple tools may seem inaccessible, preventing adoption (Morandini et al., 2023). Trialability, the option to test AI on a limited scale emerges as a key enabler (Triandini et al., 2024).

Freemium models and low-cost subscriptions, as noted by Okour et al. (2021) and Cai & Spulber (2023), reduce the financial risk of trying AI. The Ghanaian desserts business (R-12) found such models helpful for learning through experimentation, easing entry for resource-constrained firms (Sánchez et al., 2025). Regarding observability, successful AI use can influence peers. While some innovators like the Jordanian agri-tech firm (R-3) set strong examples, the lack of visible, relatable success stories in many regions hinders diffusion (OECD, 2023). For AI to spread, early adopters' results must become more visible to hesitant MSMEs (World Bank, 2023; Al Khalifa, 2025).

This study validates DOI theory in the Global South by showing how negative perceptions of AI's attributes, especially complexity and compatibility, block its spread, as proposed by Dwivedi et al. (2021). Yet, these challenges also create opportunities for innovation and targeted intervention (Naik, 2025). Complexity, most often cited, links directly to a lack of technical skills (Bhalerao et al., 2022; OECD, 2023). The Sri Lankan hotelier (R-10) noted that even their capable team are "not data analysts," revealing a stark skills deficit. Compatibility issues further compound this.

The Chadian retailer (R-6) cited language barriers, AI tools not available in Arabic or Sara, making staff training and customer use more difficult. These gaps offer opportunities for local innovators. The Kenyan creative (R-2) and Nigerian fintech founder (R-8) both pointed to the absence of culturally relevant models and challenges with local data quality (Combi, 2016; Dhokare, 2021; Foka & Griffin, 2024). However, such issues give local entrepreneurs with deep contextual knowledge a unique edge, enabling them to build frugal innovations suited to their environment (Soni & Krishnan, 2014).

High financial risk also restricts trialability, a vital factor in reducing uncertainty (Rogers, 2003). Many MSMEs can't test AI without committing upfront funds, a major deterrent (Coiera, 2019). The Nigerian education provider (R-1) highlighted that most platforms are "billed in USD" and thus unaffordable, making it harder to perceive AI's advantages. High cost undermines net benefit, especially for firms under pressure (Wall et al., 2021). As Kasireddy & Sreenivasu (2025) suggest, these challenges signal demand for tailored financial instruments.

Participants proposed solutions such as "AI Subsidy Schemes" (R-1) and "Creative-Tech Funds" (R-2), directly calling for institutional support. Such policies aim to increase trialability and highlight AI's relative advantage (Sanka, 2025). Studies also show that targeted financial tools and government support are key to enabling firms to adopt and adapt new technologies (Horváth & Szabó, 2019; Mugwagwa et al., 2022). By addressing AI's perceived complexity, lack of compatibility, and limited trialability, local innovators and policymakers can lower adoption barriers and unlock new growth opportunities.

The following are recommended for MSME owners and leaders across the Global South to improve AI Adoption.

## Adopt a "Problem-First, Not Technology-First" Strategic Mindset

The findings reveal that successful adoption begins with clear strategic intent. Therefore, it is recommended that MSME leaders first identify a specific, high-impact business problem before selecting a tool, as articulated by the social enterprise leader (R-11). This approach ensures that the adoption is driven by an understanding of its relative advantage over existing methods (Rogers, 2003). Focusing on a tangible pain point, as suggested by the (R-10), prevents costly investments in misaligned technologies, a common pitfall in SME technology adoption (Gao & Feng, 2023; Kasireddy & Sreenivasu, 2025).

## Invest in practical, context-specific skills to reduce complexity

The study confirms that the perceived complexity of AI is a major barrier, as staff are often not "data analysts" (R-10). To counter this, MSMEs should invest in building internal skills focused on practical application, not abstract theory. This includes developing competence in "Prompt Engineering," as (R-13) advised, and fostering an awareness of "digital ethics," a need identified by the creative director in Kenya (R-2). This aligns with the academic concept of building "absorptive capacity," which argues that firms should have a baseline of internal knowledge to successfully assimilate and apply external innovations (Dwivedi et al., 2020; OECD, 2023).

## Embrace incremental adoption to maximise trialability:

Given the financial constraints, spending heavily to adopt AI is ill-advised. Instead, MSMEs should pursue incremental adoption, a strategy that aligns with the participant from Ghana (R-12) who emphasised a "gradual, low-cost, and user-friendly" approach. This strategy directly enhances trialability (Rogers, 2003). As such, starting with low-cost or freemium tools helps demystify the technology, crucial for MSMEs who are constrained by resources (Bhalerao et al., 2022; Cai & Spulber, 2023).

## Actively cultivate strategic partnerships to access external knowledge:

The findings show a consensus that MSMEs cannot succeed with AI in isolation. It is therefore recommended that leaders proactively seek collaborations, particularly with academic institutions, as desired by entrepreneurs in Sri Lanka (R-10), Colombia

(R-4), and Ghana (R-12). The success of the healthcare NGO in Cambodia (R-15) and the education provider in Nigeria (R-1) with student intern programs provides a proven model. This strategy of tapping into external knowledge networks are vital for SMEs to access cutting-edge talent and research they cannot afford to develop internally (Campion et al., 2020).

## Recommendations for Policymakers and Ecosystem Builders

The following are recommendations for policymakers and ecosystem builders in ensuring effective AI integration and adoption within the Global South.

### Establish direct financial support to increase trialability and access:

The most consistent recommendation from participants was the need to alleviate the direct cost of AI. Policymakers should therefore create targeted financial mechanisms, such as the "AI subsidy schemes" and "Digital adoption vouchers" proposed by participants in Nigeria (R-1) and Sri Lanka (R-10). These interventions are critical because they directly increase the trialability of AI for a wider range of firms (Rogers, 2003). By de-risking the initial investment, such policies make the relative advantage of AI more apparent and accessible, a strategy for accelerating technology diffusion in MSMEs (Bhalerao et al., 2022; OECD, 2023; Al Khalifa, 2025).

### Develop localised capacity-building hubs to reduce complexity:

To address the profound skills gap, it is recommended that governments and development partners invest in physical and regional innovation hubs, as suggested by participants in Chad (R-6) and Jordan (R-3). The detailed proposal for "regional digital business clinics" from the Ghanaian entrepreneur (R-12) offers a practical blueprint. Such intermediary institutions are vital for reducing the perceived complexity of AI by providing hands-on support and increasing the observability of successful applications, which are key drivers of adoption in the DOI framework (Sánchez et al., 2025).

### Fund and incentivise the localisation of AI to ensure compatibility:

The study highlights a critical lack of compatibility between global AI tools and local contexts, a point raised by participants in Kenya (R-2), Jordan (R-3), and Chad (R-6). It is therefore recommended that policy focuses on creating incentives and grants for local tech firms and universities to develop, adapt, and translate AI models for local languages, cultures, and data realities. This will make AI more effective and fosters a sovereign local AI industry, turning a barrier into a source of domestic innovation (Soni & Krishnan, 2014; Triandini et al., 2024).

## Implement clear and supportive "smart regulation":

To foster a safe and predictable environment for innovation, governments should develop clear regulatory frameworks. The call from the Nigerian fintech founder (R-8) for "AI regulatory sandboxes" provides a world-class policy example. Such sandboxes allow for controlled experimentation, which reduces uncertainty for innovators without compromising public safety, thereby encouraging adoption (Didachos & Tambunan, 2024). Moreso, clear guidelines on data protection, as desired by the NGO in Cambodia (R-15), are also essential for building both consumer and investor trust (Mugwagwa et al., 2022).

## Prioritise investment in foundational digital infrastructure:

AI policy cannot succeed without a reliable foundation. The widespread challenges with internet and power, described by participants from Nigeria (R-1), Colombia (R-4), and Cambodia (R-15), represent the ultimate bottleneck. Therefore, any national AI strategy should be preceded or accompanied by significant public and private investment in affordable, reliable digital infrastructure, as this is the fundamental prerequisite upon which all other adoption factors depend.

## The AI Preparedness and Provision (AIPP) Framework

The AI Preparedness and Provision (AIPP) Framework (Figure 6), derived from this research, is proposed as an integrated model to guide AI adoption in MSMEs. It is grounded in DOI theory and posits that AI adoption can be accelerated by systematically improving the key attributes of the technology as perceived by participants. The framework's central hypothesis is that success depends on the synergy between a firm's internal efforts (AI Preparedness) and the external environment's support (Ecosystem Provision).

*Figure 6. AIPP Framework*

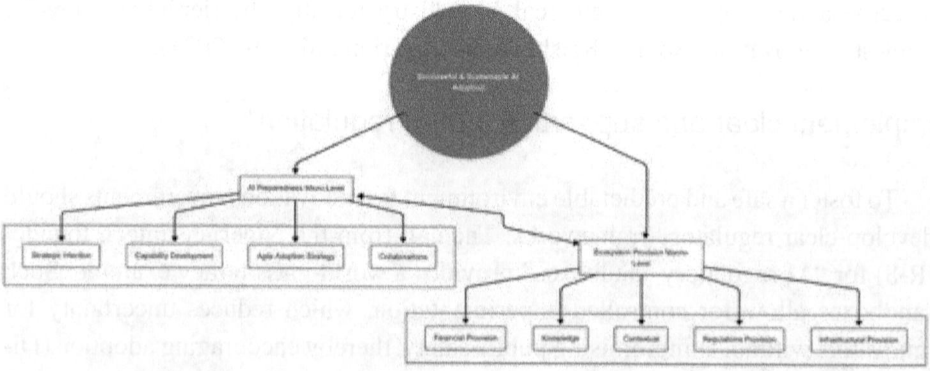

*Source: Author's*

The first dimension, AI Preparedness, represents the firm's proactive strategies to positively shape its engagement with AI. Its pillars include strategic intent, which means moving beyond vague interest to a "problem-first" focus, allowing the firm to clearly define the technology's relative advantage for a specific business need (Kasireddy & Sreenivasu, 2025). It also includes capability development, which refers to building practical internal skills in areas like "prompt engineering" and "digital ethics," as identified by participants. This is the firm's direct effort to reduce AI's perceived complexity (Dwivedi et al., 2020).

Furthermore, an agile adoption strategy, reveals that starting small with low-cost tools, is a direct implementation of the principle of trialability, which is critical for reducing risk in resource-constrained firms (Cai & Spulber, 2023). Finally, a collaborative orientation, or seeking partnerships with universities and peers, enhances the observability of successful applications, a key social driver in the diffusion process (Campion et al., 2020).

The second dimension, Ecosystem Provision, represents the necessary macro-level interventions that make AI more adoptable. This includes financial provision, which refers to targeted mechanisms like the "subsidies" and "vouchers" participants proposed to enable trialability for more firms (OECD, 2023). It also requires knowledge provision, meaning the establishment of innovation "hubs" and "labs" to offer hands-on training that reduces complexity and increases the observability of successful use cases (Sánchez et al., 2025). Crucially, contextual provision, through policies that fund the localisation of AI for regional languages and cultures, is essential for improving its compatibility, a major barrier identified in this study (Triandini et al., 2024). Finally, regulatory provision, further create a stable and predictable environment that reduces the uncertainty inherent in adopting new technologies (Didachos & Tambunan, 2024).

## FUTURE RESEARCH

This study offers insights into AI adoption among MSMEs in the Global South but has limitations. Its qualitative, purposive sample of 15 participants limits statistical generalisability, and the cross-sectional design captures only a moment in time (Saunders et al., 2019). As such, findings reflect specific experiences and not broader trends. Future research should empirically test the proposed AI Preparedness and Provision (AIPP) Framework using quantitative methods to validate and generalise it. Longitudinal case studies are also recommended to track AI adoption over time, offering a richer understanding of evolving challenges, impacts, and the relationship between internal preparedness and external ecosystem support.

## CONCLUSION

This study critically analysed the application, impacts, and barriers of Artificial Intelligence for MSMEs in the Global South. The findings reveal a landscape of potential constrained by significant, systemic challenges. It was found that MSMEs engage with AI across a wide spectrum, from leveraging it for crucial operational efficiencies to, in the most innovative cases, building their entire business model around it. The impacts are transformative, offering profound gains in productivity, cost-efficiency, and the ability to compete on a larger stage. However, these benefits are not easily accessible. The study identified a set of interconnected barriers—including costs, skills gap, inadequate digital infrastructure, and a lack of contextual relevance, hindering widespread adoption. Realising the promise of AI requires a deliberate, two-step strategy, for empowering the firms themselves with the right capabilities, while cultivating a supportive external ecosystem. It is from this conclusion that the following practical recommendations for both MSME leaders and policymakers are derived.

## REFERENCES


Aderibigbe, A. O., Ohenhen, P. E., Nwaobia, N. K., Gidiagba, J. O., & Ani, E. C.Adebayo Olusegun AderibigbePeter Efosa OhenhenNwabueze Kelvin Nwaobia-Joachim Osheyor GidiagbaEmmanuel Chigozie Ani. (2023). Artificial intelligence in developing countries: Bridging the gap between potential and implementation. *Computer Science & IT Research Journal*, *4*(3), 185–199. DOI: 10.51594/csitrj.v4i3.629

Al Khalifa, M. M. (2025). MENA SMEs: Assessing barriers and enablers of technological adoption. *Journal of Ecohumanism*, *4*(4), 108–118. DOI: 10.62754/joe.v4i4.6714

Algouzi, S., & Abbas, A. (2023). The Study of AI-Mediated Communication and Socio-Cultural Language-Related Variables: Gmail Reply Suggestions. *Applied Artificial Intelligence*, *37*(1), 2175114. Advance online publication. DOI: 10.1080/08839514.2023.2175114

Asian Development Bank. (2023). *Asian Development Bank Asia Small and Medium-Sized Enterprise Monitor 2023*. https://www.adb.org/sites/default/files/publication/919641/asia-sme-monitor-2023.pdf

Bhalerao, K., Kumar, A., & Pujari, P. (2022). A Study Of Barriers And Benefits Of Artificial Intelligence Adoption In Small And Medium Enterprise. *Academy of Marketing Studies Journal*, *26*(Sp 1), 1–6. https://www.researchgate.net/publication/360912025_a_study_of_barriers_and_benefits_of_artificial_intelligence_adoption_in_small_and_medium_enterprise

Borines, A., Teckle, P., & Turi, A. N. (2025). Exploring the current AI landscape in global south economies: A systematic literature review and research agenda. In *Tech Transformation and AI Readiness. Future of Business and Finance* (pp. 1–30). Springer Nature Switzerland. DOI: 10.1007/978-3-031-73639-1_1

Braun, V., & Clarke, V. (2022, December 17). *Thematic Analysis: A Practical Guide*. SAGE Publications Inc.

Cahyono, C., Siregar, M., Sutrisna, A., Nurlaili, N., & Susanti, M. (2024). The Role of Artificial Intelligence in Modern Education: Empowering Learning Process through Advanced Learning Technologies. *Doi.org*. DOI: 10.47191/ijsshr/v7-i12-36

Cai, G., & Spulber, D. F. (2023). The Freemium Pricing Strategy and the Opportunity Cost of Time. *Social Science Research Network*, 1–35. DOI: 10.2139/ssrn.4516760

Campion, A., Gasco-Hernandez, M., Jankin Mikhaylov, S., & Esteve, M. (2020). Overcoming the Challenges of Collaboratively Adopting Artificial Intelligence in the Public Sector. *Social Science Computer Review, 40*(2), 462–477. Advance online publication. DOI: 10.1177/0894439320979953

Coiera, E. (2019). The Price of Artificial Intelligence. *Yearbook of Medical Informatics, 28*(01), 014–015. DOI: 10.1055/s-0039-1677892

Combi, M. (2016). Cultures and Technology: An Analysis of Some of the Changes in Progress—Digital, Global and Local Culture. In *Cultural Heritage in a Changing World* (pp. 3–15). DOI: 10.1007/978-3-319-29544-2_1

de Marcellis-Warin, N., Marty, F., Thelisson, E., & Warin, T. (2022). Artificial intelligence and consumer manipulations: From consumer's counter algorithms to firm's self-regulation tools. *AI and Ethics, 2*(2), 259–268. Advance online publication. DOI: 10.1007/s43681-022-00149-5

Deranty, J.-P., & Corbin, T. (2024). Artificial intelligence and work: A critical review of recent research from the social sciences. *AI & Society, 39*(2), 675–691. DOI: 10.1007/s00146-022-01496-x

Dhokare, S. (2021). A Study of Artificial Intelligence Types, Opportunities & Challenges. *Bi-Lingual International Research Journal, 11*(41).

Didachos, M., & Tambunan, T. (2024). *POLICY DISCUSSION PAPER SERIES-AI Adoption in MSMEs and Government Support in Developing Countries.* Global Association for MSMEs and SDGs Research in Developing Countries. DOI: 10.13140/RG.2.2.31908.65923

Dwivedi, Y. K., Hughes, L., Ismagilova, E., Aarts, G., Coombs, C., Crick, T., Duan, Y., Dwivedi, R., Edwards, J., Eirug, A., Galanos, V., Ilavarasan, P. V., Janssen, M., Jones, P., Kar, A. K., Kizgin, H., Kronemann, B., Lal, B., Lucini, B., & Williams, M. D. (2021). Artificial Intelligence (AI): Multidisciplinary perspectives on emerging challenges, opportunities, and agenda for research, practice and policy. *International Journal of Information Management, 57*(101994), 101994. DOI: 10.1016/j.ijinfomgt.2019.08.002

Dwivedi, Y. K., Rana, N. P., Tamilmani, K., & Raman, R. (2020). A meta-analysis based modified unified theory of acceptance and use of technology (meta-UTAUT): A review of emerging literature. *Current Opinion in Psychology, 36*, 13–18. DOI: 10.1016/j.copsyc.2020.03.008

Endris, E., & Kassegn, A. (2022). The role of micro, small and medium enterprises (MSMEs) to the sustainable development of sub-Saharan Africa and its challenges: A systematic review of evidence from Ethiopia. *Journal of Innovation and Entrepreneurship, 11*(1), 20. Advance online publication. DOI: 10.1186/s13731-022-00221-8

Foka, A., & Griffin, G. (2024). AI, cultural heritage, and bias: Some key queries that arise from the use of genAI. *Heritage, 7*(11), 6125–6136. DOI: 10.3390/heritage7110287

Founder Africa. (2023, April 7). *The Journey of LifeBank – Saving Lives, One Blood Bag At A Time*. Where Founders Are Stars. https://founder.africa/founder/the-journey-of-lifebank-profile-funding

Gans, J. (2022). *Internal Disagreement and Disruptive Technologies*. DOI: 10.3386/w30092

Gao, X., & Feng, H. (2023). AI-driven productivity gains: Artificial intelligence and firm productivity. *Sustainability (Basel), 15*(11), 8934–8934. DOI: 10.3390/su15118934

Gibson, K. (2024, September 4). *Leveraging AI in Business: 3 Real-World Examples*. Business Insights Blog. https://online.hbs.edu/blog/post/ai-in-business

Horváth, D., & Szabó, R. Zs. (2019). Driving forces and barriers of Industry 4.0: Do multinational and small and medium-sized companies have equal opportunities? [sciencedirect.]. *Technological Forecasting and Social Change, 146*(1), 119–132. DOI: 10.1016/j.techfore.2019.05.021

Hunter, D. J. (2024). Artificial intelligence & the capacity for discrimination: The imperative need for frameworks, diverse teams & human accountability. *IgMin Research, 2*(10), 801–806. DOI: 10.61927/igmin250

Hussain, S. A., Bresnahan, M., & Zhuang, J. (2025). Can artificial intelligence revolutionize healthcare in the Global South? A scoping review of opportunities and challenges. *Digital Health, 11*, 20552076251348024. Advance online publication. DOI: 10.1177/20552076251348024

International Centre of Expertise in Montreal on Artificial Intelligence (ICEIMIA). (2022). *State of AI in Healthcare in Sub-Saharan Africa. Zenodo*. DOI: 10.5281/zenodo.12635984

Iyelolu, V., Ebele, E., Idemudia, N. C., & Ignatius, T. (2024). Driving SME innovation with ai solutions: overcoming adoption barriers and future growth opportunities. *International Journal of Science and Technology Research Archive, 7*(1), 036–054. DOI: 10.53771/ijstra.2024.7.1.0055

Kasireddy, L. C., & Sreenivasu, M.Lakshmi Chandrakanth Kasireddy. (2025). Overcoming adoption barriers: Strategies for scalable AI transformation in enterprises. *Journal of Informatics Education and Research, 5*(2). Advance online publication. DOI: 10.52783/jier.v5i2.2459

Kataria, J., & Mehta, D. (2025). AI across industries: A comparative analysis of adoption and impact. *International Journal of Innovations & Research Analysis, 04*(04(I)), 213–222. DOI: 10.62823/IJIRA/4.4(I).7053

Keshvarparast, A., Battini, D., Battaia, O., & Pirayesh, A. (2023). Collaborative robots in manufacturing and assembly systems: Literature review and future research agenda. *Journal of Intelligent Manufacturing, 35*(5), 2065–2118. Advance online publication. DOI: 10.1007/s10845-023-02137-w

Kokina, J., & Davenport, T. H. (2017). The emergence of artificial intelligence: How automation is changing auditing. *Journal of Emerging Technologies in Accounting, 14*(1), 115–122. DOI: 10.2308/jeta-51730

Kushwaha, A. K., Kumar, P., & Kar, A. K. (2021). What impacts customer experience for B2B enterprises on using AI-enabled chatbots? Insights from Big data analytics. *Industrial Marketing Management, 98*(1), 207–221. DOI: 10.1016/j.indmarman.2021.08.011

Lai, P. (2017). The Literature Review of Technology Adoption Models and Theories for the Novelty Technology. *Journal of Information Systems and Technology Management, 14*(1), 21–38. DOI: 10.4301/S1807-17752017000100002

Lee, C.-L., Orton, G., & Lu, P. (2024). Global Meta-Analysis of Innovation Attributes Influencing Climate-Smart Agriculture Adoption for Sustainable Development. *Climate (Basel), 12*(11), 192. DOI: 10.3390/cli12110192

Lorica, B., & Nathan, P. (2019). *AI Adoption in the Enterprise*. O'Reilly Online Learning. https://www.oreilly.com/library/view/ai-adoption-in/9781492051800/

McKinsey. (2018). *AI adoption advances, but foundational barriers remain*. McKinsey & Company. https://www.mckinsey.com/featured-insights/artificial-intelligence/ai-adoption-advances-but-foundational-barriers-remain

Ministry of MSME. (2022). *What is the definition of MSME? | Ministry of Micro, Small & Medium Enterprises*. Msme.gov.in. https://msme.gov.in/faqs/q1-what-definition-msme

Morandini, S., Fraboni, F., De Angelis, M., Puzzo, G., Giusino, D., & Pietrantoni, L. (2023). The Impact of Artificial Intelligence on Workers' skills: Upskilling and Reskilling in Organisations. *Informing Science, 26*(1), 39–68. DOI: 10.28945/5078

Morley, J., Hine, E., Roberts, H., Sirbu, R., Ashrafian, H., Blease, C., Boyd, M., Chen, J. L., Filho, A. C., Coiera, E., Cohen, G. I., Fiske, A., Jayakumar, N., Kerasidou, A., Mandreoli, F., McCradden, M. D., Namuganza, S., Nsoesie, E. O., Parikh, R. B., & Floridi, L. (2025). Global Health in the Age of AI: Charting a Course for Ethical Implementation and Societal Benefit. *Minds and Machines*, *35*(3), 31. Advance online publication. DOI: 10.1007/s11023-025-09730-3

Mugwagwa, J., Banda, G., Ozor, N., Bolo, M., & Oriama, R. (2022). Optimising governance capabilities for science, research and innovation in Africa. *Technology in Society*, *68*, 101804. DOI: 10.1016/j.techsoc.2021.101804

Mutasa, E. T., Dhiwwale, C., & Gopal, A. (2024). Artificial Intelligence in Developing Economies: Unpacking Business Innovations, Prospects, and Challenges. *International Journal of Academic Research in Business & Social Sciences*, *14*(11), 586–601. DOI: 10.6007/IJARBSS/v14-i11/23529

Naik, P. (2025, June 5). *The Future of AI in the Global South: Trends, Challenges, and Opportunities*. Geojuristoday. https://www.geojuristoday.in/post/the-future-of-ai-in-the-global-south-trends-challenges-and-opportunities

Nijiati, M., Zhang, Z., Abulizi, A., Miao, H., Tuluhong, A., Quan, S., Guo, L., Xu, T., & Zou, X. (2021). Deep learning assistance for tuberculosis diagnosis with chest radiography in low-resource settings. *Journal of X-Ray Science and Technology*, *29*(5), 785–796. DOI: 10.3233/XST-210894

Okour, M. K., Chong, C. W., & Fattah, F. A. M. (2021). Knowledge management systems usage: Application of diffusion of innovation theory. *Global Knowledge, Memory and Communication*, *70*(8/9), 756–776. DOI: 10.1108/GKMC-08-2020-0117

Organisation for Economic Co-operation and Development (OECD). (2023). *Skill needs and policies in the age of artificial intelligence*. OECD Publishing., DOI: 10.1787/08785bba-e

Patra, S. (2024). AI Implementation. In *MSME Industrial Sectors*. Educational Administration Theory and Practices., DOI: 10.53555/kuey.v30i5.3725

Pillai, R., & Sivathanu, B. (2020). Adoption of AI-based chatbots for hospitality and tourism. *International Journal of Contemporary Hospitality Management*, *32*(10), 3199–3226. DOI: 10.1108/IJCHM-04-2020-0259

Rashid, A. B., & Kausik, A. K. (2024). AI Revolutionizing Industries Worldwide: A Comprehensive Overview of Its Diverse Applications. *Hybrid Advances*, *7*(100277), 100277–100277. DOI: 10.1016/j.hybadv.2024.100277

Rawas, S. (2024). AI: The future of humanity. *Discover Artificial Intelligence*, *4*(1), 1–14. DOI: 10.1007/s44163-024-00118-3

Rogers, E. M. (2003). *Diffusion of innovations* (5th ed.). Free Press.

Sampath, P. G. (2021). Governing Artificial Intelligence in an Age of Inequality. *Global Policy*, *12*(S6), 21–31. Advance online publication. DOI: 10.1111/1758-5899.12940

Sánchez, E., Calderón, R., & Herrera, F. (2025). Artificial intelligence adoption in SMES: Survey based on TOE–DOI framework, primary methodology and challenges. *Applied Sciences (Basel, Switzerland)*, *15*(12), 6465. Advance online publication. DOI: 10.3390/app15126465

Sanka, N. V. (2025). Conversational AI for Enterprise Data Analytics and Governance: A Comprehensive Framework for Natural Language-Driven Business Intelligence. *International Journal of Scientific Research in Computer Science Engineering and Information Technology*, *11*(2), 3922–3928. DOI: 10.32628/CSEIT25111329

Santosa, A. D., & Surgawati, I. (2024). Artificial Intelligence (AI) Adoption as Marketing Tools among Micro, Small, and Medium Enterprises (MSMEs) in Indonesia. *Jurnal Sosial Humaniora*, *17*(1), 91–91. DOI: 10.12962/j24433527.v17i1.20520

Saunders, M. N., Lewis, P., & Thornhill, A. (2019). *Research methods for business students* (8th ed.). Pearson.

Selamat, M. A., & Windasari, N. A. (2021). Chatbot for SMEs: Integrating customer and business owner perspectives. *Technology in Society*, *66*, 101685. DOI: 10.1016/j.techsoc.2021.101685

SMEDAN, & NBS. (2012). Preliminary report of micro, small and medium enterprises in Nigeria. In www.nigerianstat.gov.ng(pp. 1–171). https://www.nigerianstat.gov.ng/pdfuploads/MSMES.pdf

Soni, P., & Krishnan, T., R. (. (2014). Frugal innovation: Aligning theory, practice, and public policy. *Journal of Indian Business Research*, *6*(1), 29–47. DOI: 10.1108/JIBR-03-2013-0025

Srinivasan, V. (2016). Will Financial Auditors Become Extinct? In *Intelligent Enterprise in the Era of Big Data, The* (pp. 171–186). Wiley., DOI: 10.1002/9781118834725.ch7

The ASEAN Secretariat. (2025). *Definitions of MSME in ASEAN Member States*. https://asean.org/wp-content/uploads/2025/02/Definition-of-MSME-in-ASEAN-Member-States.pdf

Tishtykbayeva, A. Z., Gelashvili, N. N., & Turusbekov, A. E. (2023). Artificial Intelligence Implementation in Small Businesses. *BULLETIN of the KARAGANDA UNIVERSITY ECONOMY SERIES*, *111*(3), 125–132. DOI: 10.31489/2023ec3/125-132

Triandini, E., Wijaya, S. N., & Suniantara, P. K. (2024). Analysis of The Digital Technology Adoption by MSMEs Using Diffusion of Innovation. *Journal of System and Management Sciences*, *14*(4). Advance online publication. DOI: 10.33168/JSMS.2024.0415

United Nations Development Programme (UNDP). (2025). *Bending the AI arc towards equity - United Nations Development Programme | UNDP*. Exposure. https://stories.undp.org/bending-the-ai-arc-towards-equity

van der Vlist, F., Helmond, A., & Ferrari, F. (2024). Big AI: Cloud Infrastructure Dependence and the Industrialisation of Artificial Intelligence. *Big Data & Society*, *11*(1), 20539517241232630. Advance online publication. DOI: 10.1177/20539517241232630

Wall, P. J., Saxena, D., & Brown, S. (2021). Artificial Intelligence in the Global South (AI4D): Potential and Risks. *ArXiv (Cornell University)*. https://doi.org//arxiv.2108.10093DOI: 10.48550

Williams, M. D., Rana, N. P., & Dwivedi, Y. K. (2015). The unified theory of acceptance and use of technology (UTAUT): A literature review. *Journal of Enterprise Information Management*, *28*(3), 443–488. DOI: 10.1108/JEIM-09-2014-0088

World Bank. (2023). *Digital Progress and Trends Report*. Www.worldbank.org. https://www.worldbank.org/en/publication/digital-progress-and-trends-report

Xu, S., Kee, K. F., Li, W., Yamamoto, M., & Riggs, R. E. (2023). Examining the Diffusion of Innovations from a Dynamic, Differential-Effects Perspective: A Longitudinal Study on AI Adoption Among Employees. *Communication Research*, *51*(7), 843–866. Advance online publication. DOI: 10.1177/00936502231191832

Zimmerman, A., Janhonen, J., & Beer, E. (2024). Human/AI relationships: Challenges, downsides, and impacts on human/human relationships. *AI and Ethics*, *4*(4), 1555–1567. DOI: 10.1007/s43681-023-00348-8

Zohuri, B. (2023). Artificial Super Intelligence (ASI) The Evolution of AI Beyond Human Capacity. *Current Trends in Engineering Science*, *3*(7), 1–5. DOI: 10.54026/CTES/1049

## KEY TERMS AND DEFINITIONS

**AIPP Framework:** The AI Preparedness and Provision (AIPP) Framework is an integrated model to guide AI adoption in MSMEs. The framework's central hypothesis is that success depends on the synergy between a firm's internal efforts (AI Preparedness) and the external environment's support (Ecosystem Provision).

**Artificial Intelligence (AI):** AI refers to computer systems designed to perform tasks that normally require human intelligence, such as problem-solving, learning, decision-making, and language processing.

**Global South (GS):** The Global South refers to low- and middle-income countries, primarily located in regions such as sub-Saharan Africa, Asia, the Middle East, Latin America, and the Caribbean. It is often used to highlight shared economic and developmental challenges across these regions.

**Gross Domestic Product (GDP):** GDP is the total monetary value of all finished goods and services produced within a country's borders in a specific time period. It is commonly used to measure the size, performance, and health of an economy.

**Micro, Small, and Medium Enterprises (MSMEs):** MSMEs are businesses with limited numbers of employees and annual revenue. They vary by country but are generally defined as having fewer than 250 employees. MSMEs are vital to economic growth, job creation, and innovation, especially in developing economies.

# Chapter 11
# Leveraging AI to Scale SMEs:
## Opportunities for Sustainable Local Economic Development in South Africa

**Mpho Gift Makgamatha**
http://orcid.org/0000-0001-6799-4554
*University of Limpopo, South Africa*

## ABSTRACT

*The study explored the use of Artificial Intelligence (AI) in South Africa to scale Small, Medium and Micro Enterprises (SMMEs) and promote sustainable local economic development. It used a qualitative research approach, analyzing AI integration, challenges, and outcomes. The results indicated that AI improved business efficiency, customer engagement, and market access, especially in urban and semi-urban areas. However, barriers such as limited digital infrastructure, skills shortages, and inadequate policy support persisted. To fully benefit from AI-driven growth, SMMEs require inclusive strategies and targeted interventions.*

## INTRODUCTION

Artificial Intelligence (AI) presents an unprecedented opportunity to transform the landscape of Small, Medium, and Micro Enterprises (SMMEs) in South Africa (Makgamatha & Makgato-Khunou, 2021). As engines of job creation and community-level development, SMMEs play a vital role in the country's economy, accounting for more than 60% of employment and contributing around 34% to GDP, according to

DOI: 10.4018/979-8-3373-2817-1.ch011

the Department of Small Business Development (Enaifoghe & Vezi-Magigaba, 2022; Malatji & Makgamatha, 2024). However, most of these enterprises face significant challenges, including limited access to markets, poor infrastructure, low levels of digitisation, and operational inefficiencies. AI tools such as predictive analytics, customer relationship management systems, and automated supply chain solutions can help overcome these hurdles by enhancing productivity, reducing costs, and expanding market reach (Ismaeil & Lalla, 2024).

One of the most immediate applications of AI for SMMEs lies in automating repetitive administrative tasks, freeing up time and resources for business owners to focus on strategy and growth (Ikpe, 2024). For instance, AI-powered accounting software like Xero and QuickBooks uses machine learning to automate bookkeeping and financial reporting. Similarly, customer service chatbots can provide 24/7 support, improving client satisfaction and retention (Majeed, 2024). In township-based retail businesses or small online stores, these tools can reduce the reliance on expensive personnel and increase responsiveness to customer needs. Moreover, natural language processing tools can assist with generating marketing content and local language translations, helping rural businesses connect with a wider audience (Stojčić et al., 2024).

AI also opens new avenues for market insights and decision-making (Ikpe, 2024). Through data-driven strategies, SMMEs can now identify consumer behaviour patterns, forecast demand, and manage inventory more effectively. A practical example is the use of AI in agriculture-based enterprises where tools like drone imagery and machine learning models predict crop yields and detect disease early (Javaid et al., 2023). For a small farmer's cooperative in Limpopo, such technologies could significantly enhance productivity and reduce losses, thereby improving income stability. Moreover, platforms like Google Market Finder, when combined with AI analytics, can help export-ready SMMEs identify new international markets and compliance requirements, opening paths to global value chains (Stojčić et al., 2024).

Realising these benefits at scale requires addressing the digital divide that still exists in South Africa, especially in rural and peri-urban areas. Limited broadband access, low digital literacy, and high data costs continue to exclude many potential entrepreneurs from the AI revolution (Lethoko, 2024). Government and private sector partnerships will be crucial in developing inclusive digital infrastructure, offering training in AI literacy, and promoting affordable access to tools and platforms. Initiatives such as the Small Enterprise Development Agency's (SEDA) tech incubation programmes and the Council for Scientific and Industrial Research's AI for Development project are promising steps (Rens, 2021). If scaled and integrated into national economic development strategies, AI could empower SMMEs not only to survive but to thrive, ultimately contributing to more inclusive, sustainable local economic development across South Africa.

The chapter aimed to investigate how artificial intelligence (AI) could be leveraged to scale small, medium, and micro enterprises (SMMEs) and contribute to sustainable local economic development in South Africa. The research objectives are:

- To explore the current state of AI adoption among SMMEs in South Africa.
- To identify the opportunities that AI technologies present for scaling SMMEs.
- To examine the challenges faced by SMMEs in adopting and implementing AI solutions.
- To assess the contributions of AI-driven SMMEs to sustainable local economic development.
- To propose policy and strategic recommendations to enhance AI integration in SMMEs.

The Research Questions are:

What is the current level of AI adoption among SMMEs in South Africa?
What opportunities does AI present for scaling SMMEs in the South African context?
What are the main barriers that hinder AI integration within SMMEs?
In what ways can AI-driven SMMEs contribute to sustainable local economic development?
What policy measures and support mechanisms are needed to facilitate AI adoption in SMMEs?

## BACKGROUND

Small, Medium, and Micro Enterprises (SMMEs) constitute the cornerstone of South Africa's economic fabric, contributing an estimated 40% to the national Gross Domestic Product (GDP) and accounting for more than 60% of employment within the private sector (Makgamatha, 2025). These enterprises, often rooted in local communities, serve as vital engines for job creation, poverty alleviation, and inclusive economic participation. Yet, despite their strategic importance, SMMEs across the country continue to grapple with a range of systemic challenges that impede their development. Key among these is limited access to finance, persistent skills shortages, bureaucratic red tape, and the lack of adequate infrastructure, especially in rural and township settings (Vuyokazi, 2022). These constraints not only restrict the growth potential of SMMEs but also undermine their ability to contribute effectively to local economic development efforts. In many cases, the inability of small enterprises to scale operations or adopt modern business practices has resulted in high failure rates and stunted entrepreneurial ecosystems. Therefore, this reality underscores the urgent need for innovative and scalable solutions that can empower SMMEs to overcome barriers, become more competitive, and actively participate in shaping a resilient and inclusive local economy (Makgamatha, 2025).

In recent years, the rapid advancement and proliferation of Artificial Intelligence (AI) technologies have opened new avenues for the transformation and scaling of SMMEs (Makgamatha & Makgato-Khunou, 2021). AI, encompassing tools such as machine learning, natural language processing, and automation systems, has the potential to dramatically enhance business efficiency, streamline operations, and enable data-driven decision-making (Badmus et al., 2024). These technologies can significantly reduce operational costs, improve customer service delivery, and facilitate smarter inventory and supply chain management. For instance, AI-powered chatbots and virtual assistants are increasingly being deployed by service-oriented SMMEs to handle customer queries, appointments, and routine communication, freeing up human resources for more strategic tasks (Iyelolu et al., 2024). Small retailers, often constrained by capital and labour, can benefit from AI-enabled inventory management systems that help prevent overstocking or understocking, while simultaneously optimizing cash flow. In the agricultural sector, AI innovations such as drone-assisted crop monitoring, precision farming techniques, and predictive analytics for weather and soil conditions are revolutionizing small-scale farming practices (Guebsi et al., 2024). These technological interventions not only boost productivity and profitability but also enable SMMEs to offer higher-value goods and services, thereby expanding their market reach and competitiveness in both local and global markets (Javaid et al., 2023).

Beyond operational enhancements, the integration of AI into SMME ecosystems has broader implications for sustainable local economic development (Javaid et al., 2023). By equipping enterprises with tools that improve their adaptability and resilience, AI contributes to the creation of more robust local economies that can withstand market fluctuations and external shocks (Rane et al., 2024). In township and informal economies often marginalized from mainstream financial and commercial systems AI applications are proving particularly transformative. Digital platforms supported by AI, including mobile banking, e-commerce marketplaces, and fintech services, are increasing financial inclusion and enabling micro-entrepreneurs to access new customer bases and revenue streams (Kshetri, 2021). The World Bank (2022) reports that SMMEs adopting AI-backed digital platforms in South Africa have experienced revenue growth of up to 25% within just one year of implementation (Bengu & Beharry-Ramraj, 2025). These findings highlight the transformative potential of AI for even the smallest and most resource-constrained businesses. By democratizing access to technology and data, AI can bridge socio-economic divides and ensure that the benefits of digital transformation extend beyond urban centres into rural and peri-urban areas.

The adoption and diffusion of AI among SMMEs in South Africa remain limited, constrained by several structural and contextual barriers. Digital illiteracy, particularly among older entrepreneurs and those operating in informal sectors, remains a significant challenge (Makgamatha, 2025). Most business owners lack the technical knowledge or confidence required to implement and maintain AI solutions. Moreover, the high cost of digital infrastructure and limited access to affordable internet services in underserved areas further hinder technological adoption. Policy and institutional support, while emerging, has yet to fully address the unique needs of SMMEs on the ground. Although government-led initiatives such as the Department of Small Business Development's digital transformation programme signal progress, these efforts often suffer from poor coordination, insufficient funding, and a lack of alignment with the realities of grassroots entrepreneurs (Malatji & Makgamatha, 2024). To unlock the full potential of AI as a tool for inclusive economic development, South Africa must pursue a coordinated strategy that includes strengthening public-private partnerships, expanding digital skills training, improving digital infrastructure, and offering targeted financial incentives for technology adoption.

Ultimately, leveraging AI for the benefit of SMMEs requires more than just technological solutions it demands an inclusive, collaborative, and context-sensitive approach (Bengu & Beharry-Ramraj, 2025). By investing in human capital, fostering innovation hubs, and designing policies that cater to the needs of both formal and informal enterprises, South Africa can create an enabling environment in which SMMEs thrive (Nkontwana, 2022). Such an ecosystem not only supports enterprise growth but also contributes meaningfully to sustainable local economic development, job creation, and socio-economic transformation. As the country seeks to build a future-proof economy, the strategic use of AI to empower SMMEs offers a promising pathway toward achieving inclusive and resilient development outcomes.

## Conceptualizing Artificial Intelligence in Business

Artificial Intelligence (AI) in business refers to the deployment of intelligent systems that mimic human cognitive functions such as learning, reasoning, and self-correction to improve decision-making and automate complex tasks (Kaushik, 2022). These systems are embedded in software and hardware capable of processing vast amounts of data to identify patterns, make predictions, and execute decisions with minimal human intervention. AI technologies include machine learning, natural language processing (NLP), computer vision, robotics, and expert systems each serving different business functions and sectors. In the contemporary business environment, AI is not merely a technical enhancement but a strategic imperative

(Chinnaiyan et al., 2025). It enables firms to streamline operations, reduce costs, and improve customer experiences. For instance, chatbots powered by AI handle millions of customer interactions daily, providing instant support while reducing the need for large customer service teams (Majeed, 2024). In data-driven sectors such as finance and retail, AI models assist in detecting fraud, assessing credit risk, and delivering personalized marketing, thereby increasing operational efficiency and profitability.

Globally, AI has become a linchpin of competitive advantage (George, 2024). Leading companies in the United States, such as IBM, Microsoft, and Google, are at the forefront of AI innovation, investing in advanced machine learning algorithms, cloud-based AI services, and cognitive computing platforms (Rehan, 2024). In China, corporations like Alibaba and Baidu apply AI to optimize e-commerce logistics, power autonomous vehicles, and facilitate urban planning through smart city infrastructure (Smart et al., 2023). These advancements highlight the centrality of AI in enhancing global value chains and enabling rapid, data-driven decision-making at scale. Moreover, sector-specific applications illustrate the flexibility of AI technologies. In manufacturing, AI-driven robotics and predictive maintenance reduce downtime and boost production output. In agriculture, AI tools analyse soil conditions, weather patterns, and crop health to optimize farming practices (Balai et al., 2025). In healthcare, AI is used for diagnostics, treatment planning, and health monitoring, thereby improving patient outcomes. These applications underscore AI's potential to address systemic inefficiencies and unlock innovation across industries.

Despite its transformative potential, the adoption of AI raises several challenges. Ethical concerns include algorithmic bias, surveillance, and the lack of transparency in decision-making processes (Balai et al., 2025). Data privacy is another pressing issue, particularly as businesses collect and analyse large datasets involving sensitive personal information. Moreover, AI poses a risk of job displacement, particularly for routine and manual occupations, necessitating proactive strategies for workforce reskilling and inclusion (George, 2024). In response, global institutions and governments are developing frameworks for responsible AI governance, emphasizing fairness, accountability, and transparency (Dinker, 2024). The digital divide further complicates the equitable integration of AI. Developed nations benefit from robust infrastructure, high-speed internet, and a large pool of AI talent, while many developing economies, including those in Africa, face systemic constraints such as limited data infrastructure, inadequate funding, and skill shortages (Makgamatha, 2025). This disparity threatens to exacerbate existing economic inequalities if not addressed through inclusive policies and capacity-building initiatives.

In the South African context, AI adoption is gradually advancing, particularly in high-value sectors (Makgamatha, 2025). The banking sector, for example, utilizes AI for customer service, fraud detection, and credit scoring, with Standard Bank and First National Bank being early adopters of intelligent digital solutions (Kaluarachchi & Sedera, 2024). The telecommunications industry leverages AI to manage network traffic and improve service reliability. Most, startups SMMEs are deploying AI tools to support their day to day operation (Makgamatha, 2024). However, the path to widespread AI integration in South Africa is impeded by several challenges. These include a lack of digital infrastructure in rural areas, insufficient investment in research and development, limited access to quality data, and a shortage of skilled professionals in AI and data science (Mhlanga, 2021). To unlock the transformative power of AI for SMMEs and broader local economic development, South Africa must prioritize coordinated multi-stakeholder strategies. These should include investments in digital infrastructure, curriculum reform in tertiary institutions, public-private partnerships, and the establishment of ethical AI frameworks that safeguard against misuse and exclusion (Molina-Carmona & García-Peñalvo, 2024). Conceptualizing AI in business involves understanding it as a multifaceted technological enabler that, when responsibly deployed, can enhance productivity, foster innovation, and support sustainable development. For South Africa, and particularly for its SMME sector, AI offers a unique opportunity to leapfrog development constraints, provided the adoption is inclusive, ethical, and aligned with national development priorities.

## The Legal Landscape of AI in South Africa

While Artificial Intelligence (AI) offers significant opportunities to scale SMMEs and enhance LED in South Africa, its adoption must be viewed within the country's evolving legal and regulatory framework. South Africa currently lacks a dedicated AI-specific regulatory framework, though existing laws such as the Protection of Personal Information Act (POPIA) and the Cybercrimes Act provide important safeguards on data protection, privacy, and cyber ethics (Chitimira & Motlogeloa, 2024). The absence of comprehensive AI legislation raises questions about accountability, intellectual property rights, algorithmic transparency, and ethical use issues that are critical for ensuring responsible AI deployment. Scholars such as Lescrauwaet et al., (2022) argue that a robust legal framework is necessary to balance innovation with societal protection. For SMMEs, this means that legal clarity will be essential to foster trust, ensure compliance, and support sustainable integration of AI into business models. Consequently, any strategy for leveraging AI for LED must include policy development that addresses ethical governance, data security, and equitable access to AI technologies.

## MAIN FOCUS OF THE CHAPTER

### Theoretical Framework

This chapter is grounded in two key theories: Endogenous Growth Theory and the Technology Acceptance Model (TAM), both of which offer essential perspectives for understanding how leveraging Artificial Intelligence (AI) can enhance the growth of SMMEs and contribute to sustainable local economic development in South Africa (Mdingi, 2024). The Endogenous Growth Theory, advanced by economists such as Paul Romer, posits that economic growth is primarily driven by internal factors rather than external influences (Chandra, 2022). Central to this theory is the role of innovation, knowledge spillovers, and human capital in promoting long-term economic development. In the context of South Africa's SMMEs, this theory supports the idea that integrating AI technologies into business operations can enhance productivity, stimulate innovation, and build the capacity of local entrepreneurs. By fostering a knowledge-based economy, AI-enabled SMMEs can become self-sustaining engines of growth that contribute meaningfully to local development without over-reliance on external interventions.

The Technology Acceptance Model (TAM), developed by Davis (1989), provides a framework for understanding how users come to accept and use new technologies (Katebi et al., 2022). TAM focuses on two primary determinants: perceived usefulness and perceived ease of use (Katebi et al., 2022). When applied to AI adoption by SMMEs, this theory helps explain the behavioural intention of entrepreneurs and business managers to integrate AI tools into their operations. The model suggests that for AI to be successfully adopted by SMMEs, stakeholders must believe that AI will enhance their business performance and that it is user-friendly and accessible, especially in resource-constrained environments like those found in many South African localities.

Together, these theories provide a comprehensive lens through which to examine the role of AI in scaling SMMEs for sustainable local economic development. Endogenous Growth Theory situates AI integration as a driver of internal innovation and productivity growth, while TAM highlights the individual and organizational readiness required to adopt such technologies effectively (Chandra, 2022; Katebi et al., 2022). By synthesizing these perspectives, the study underscores the importance of both systemic support for innovation and individual-level adoption dynamics. This dual theoretical foundation informs a holistic approach to policy, capacity building, and technology deployment that can unlock the full potential of SMMEs as catalysts for inclusive and sustainable local economic development in South Africa.

## Research Methodology

This study adopted a qualitative research approach to explore the opportunities for sustainable local economic development in South Africa. Qualitative research was chosen for its ability to provide rich, in-depth insights into complex social and economic phenomena, particularly within diverse and dynamic local contexts (Lim, 2025). This approach enabled the researcher to critically examine and interpret the meanings, experiences, and strategies associated with local economic development initiatives, focusing on sustainability, inclusiveness, and community-driven outcomes. The research relied primarily on secondary data sources, including peer-reviewed academic literature, government policy documents, industry reports, and relevant case studies. The selection of articles and documents was guided by their relevance, credibility, and alignment with the study's objectives. Priority was given to recent peer-reviewed academic sources, official government policy documents, and reputable industry reports that focused on Artificial Intelligence (AI), SMMEs, and LED in South Africa. The criteria also included the reliability of data, methodological rigor, and the extent to which each source contributed to understanding how AI can be leveraged to promote sustainable economic growth and job creation through SMMEs (Kgakatsi et al., 2024). These sources were systematically reviewed and analysed to identify trends, patterns, and gaps in current local economic development practices. Special attention was given to documents that highlight innovative and sustainable approaches within South Africa, as well as comparative international experiences that offer transferable lessons or cautionary insights.

The analysis was conducted through thematic content analysis, which involved categorizing the data into key themes such as local entrepreneurship, green economy initiatives, digital inclusion, and policy frameworks (Hasan et al., 2024). This method facilitated the identification of both enabling and constraining factors influencing sustainable local economic development. By drawing on diverse and credible secondary sources, the study ensured a comprehensive understanding of the current landscape, potential opportunities, and strategic directions for fostering sustainable growth at the local level in South Africa.

## The Current Level of AI Adoption among SMMES in South Africa

The current level of artificial intelligence (AI) adoption among SMMEs in South Africa is steadily increasing, reflecting global trends in digital transformation (Lethoko, 2024). Most SMMEs are beginning to recognise the value of AI tools in streamlining operations, improving customer engagement, and enhancing decision-making processes. For example, small retail businesses are increasingly using AI-powered chatbots for customer service, enabling them to provide 24/7 support without incurring the cost of additional staff. This shift is particularly notable in urban centres like Johannesburg, Cape Town, and Durban, where digital infrastructure is more developed and internet penetration is higher (Majeed, 2024).

In the financial services sector, AI adoption among SMMEs is becoming more pronounced (Hasan et al., 2024). Fintech startups and micro-lenders are leveraging AI for credit scoring, fraud detection, and personalized financial services (Gupta & Xia, 2018). For instance, companies such as Yoco and Lula (formerly Lulalend) utilize AI algorithms to assess the creditworthiness of small businesses and offer tailored financial products, allowing SMMEs faster access to funding (Omokhoa et al., 2024). These technologies not only improve efficiency but also empower entrepreneurs to make informed financial decisions based on real-time insights. AI is also making inroads in the marketing and sales strategies of South African SMMEs. Most small businesses now use AI-driven tools for digital advertising, social media management, and consumer behaviour analysis (Lethoko, 2024). AI platforms like Zoho and HubSpot are being employed to automate marketing campaigns, segment customer data, and optimize lead conversion (Lian, 2023). This shift enables SMMEs to compete more effectively with larger enterprises by providing a personalized customer experience and data-driven marketing strategies that would otherwise require extensive resources.

In the agricultural sector, smallholder farmers and agri-businesses are beginning to adopt AI for smart farming practices (Javaid et al., 2023). Applications range from crop health monitoring using drone imagery analysed by AI to predictive analytics for weather and yield forecasting (Javaid et al., 2023). These tools are being supported by initiatives from both the private sector and government-linked entities such as the Agricultural Research Council. By integrating AI into their operations, even smaller farms in provinces like Limpopo and Mpumalanga can increase productivity and reduce waste, contributing to food security and sustainable rural development.

## The Opportunities of AI for Scaling Small, Medium and Micro Enterprises (SMMES) in South Africa

Artificial Intelligence (AI) presents transformative opportunities for scaling SMMEs in South Africa, particularly by enhancing operational efficiency (Enaifoghe & Vezi-Magigaba, 2023). AI-powered tools such as inventory management systems and automated accounting software help SMMEs streamline routine processes, saving both time and costs (Iyelolu et al., 2024). For instance, a small retail store in Botlokwa Village can deploy AI to manage its stock levels in real time, reducing waste and ensuring that popular products are always available. This level of efficiency allows business owners to focus more on strategic growth rather than day-to-day administration (Makgamatha, 2025). Another key opportunity lies in AI's ability to improve customer engagement and marketing. South African SMMEs can harness machine learning algorithms to analyse customer behaviour, segment their audience, and deliver personalised marketing messages through platforms like WhatsApp and social media (Makgamatha, 2025). A local fashion brand in Durban, for example, can use AI-driven insights to understand which styles are trending among its customers and tailor its product offerings accordingly. This enhances customer satisfaction and encourages repeat business, which is vital for growth and sustainability.

AI also opens doors for smarter decision-making through predictive analytics (Enaifoghe & Vezi-Magigaba, 2023). With access to historical data, SMMEs can use AI to forecast trends, anticipate market shifts, and make data-driven decisions (Jain et al., 2025). South Africa, as a developing country, the agricultural sector might use AI to predict crop yields based on weather patterns and soil conditions, allowing for better planning and resource allocation (Ikudayisi et al., 2022). These insights can improve productivity and profitability, enabling small businesses to compete more effectively in larger markets. AI enables access to broader markets through digital platforms and e-commerce solutions. South African entrepreneurs can use AI to optimise their online presence, recommend products to potential buyers, and even translate content to reach non-native speakers. For example, a handmade crafts business in Limpopo could expand its reach beyond local communities by using AI-driven platforms to connect with buyers across Africa and globally. This capacity for digital expansion can help SMMEs scale rapidly, create jobs, and contribute meaningfully to South Africa's economic development (Enaifoghe & Vezi-Magigaba, 2023).

## The Barriers that hinder AI Integration within SMMES

The AI within SMMEs in South Africa faces several significant barriers. One of the primary challenges is limited financial resources (Botha et al., 2021). Most SMMEs operate on tight budgets, making it difficult for them to invest in expensive AI technologies or to hire skilled personnel to manage and maintain these systems (Makgamatha, 2025). For example, a small logistics company in Limpopo may struggle to afford AI-powered route optimization software, even though it could greatly enhance delivery efficiency and reduce fuel costs (Marwala, 2022). This financial constraint often results in SMMEs relying on traditional methods that are less efficient and more labour-intensive.

Another critical barrier is the lack of digital infrastructure and access to reliable internet connectivity, particularly in rural and peri-urban areas (Mbinda, 2024). AI technologies typically rely on robust digital infrastructure, including cloud computing and data analytics platforms, which are not always readily available or affordable to

SMMEs in underdeveloped regions. For instance, a rural agricultural cooperative in Limpopo Province, like Botlokwa (Matoks) may find it difficult to adopt AI-based crop monitoring systems due to poor network coverage or limited access to smart devices and sensors (Makgamatha, 2025). This digital divide creates a significant disadvantage for these businesses in terms of competitiveness and innovation. Skills shortages remain one of the most significant barriers to the successful integration of Artificial Intelligence (AI) in Small, Medium and Micro Enterprises (SMMEs). Many of these enterprises simply do not have employees with the necessary technical expertise to implement, manage, or even understand AI systems (Kumar, Raut, Mangla, Ferraris & Choubey, 2024). Without staff who can oversee AI projects or interpret AI-generated insights, businesses are unable to fully harness the potential of AI-driven tools. As a result, they risk falling behind competitors who are more technologically equipped, both locally and globally.

In the South African context, this problem is further exacerbated by an education and training system that is still struggling to keep up with rapid technological advancements (Ndabeni-Abrahams, 2024). Formal qualifications and vocational training programs often lag current industry needs, leaving graduates and employees underprepared for the demands of the digital economy (Didier, 2022). This has led to a noticeable gap in AI literacy not just among workers, but also among small business owners themselves. Many are unaware of how AI can streamline operations, improve customer engagement, or increase efficiency, which in turn stifles innovation and growth within the SMME sector.

To illustrate, consider a small retail business operating in Soweto (Scholtz et al, 2023). Despite having access to customer transaction data, such a business might lack staff capable of analyzing that data using AI tools or understanding the value of predictive analytics (Ramya et al., 2024). Without such capabilities, the enterprise misses out on opportunities to personalize services or improve inventory management using AI-driven customer relationship management (CRM) systems (Makgamatha & Makgato-Khunou, 2021). This example underscores the critical need for targeted skills development and accessible AI training programs that are specifically designed to support SMMEs in bridging the digital divide.

Lastly, regulatory uncertainty and lack of awareness about AI's potential benefits also hinder adoption (Makgamatha, 2025). Most SMME owners are unsure about how AI may affect data privacy, cybersecurity, and compliance with laws such as the Protection of Personal Information Act (POPIA) (Ndabeni-Abrahams, 2024). This uncertainty, coupled with limited awareness campaigns or support from government agencies, discourages experimentation and innovation. For example, a home-based fashion business owners might avoid using AI-powered marketing tools because of concerns about handling customer data securely or a general misunderstanding of how the technology works. Addressing these concerns through targeted education, incentives, and supportive policies could help unlock AI's potential for SMMEs across South Africa.

## The Role of AI-Driven SMMES in Advancing Sustainable Local Economic Development

Artificial Intelligence (AI) is revolutionizing the global business landscape, and in South Africa, AI-driven SMMEs are increasingly playing a pivotal role in promoting sustainable local economic development (LED) (Botha et al., 2021; Makgamatha, 2025). These tech-enabled enterprises utilize AI to optimize operations, predict market trends, and deliver personalized services, which enhances their competitiveness and productivity. In a country grappling with high unemployment and inequality, AI-powered SMMEs can serve as catalysts for inclusive economic growth by creating new job categories and upskilling local communities (Otieno & Busili, 2024). One key contribution of AI-driven SMMEs to sustainable LED is their ability to solve local problems with scalable, tech-based solutions. For instance, South African startups like Aerobotics use AI and drone technology to support local farmers with precision agriculture (Habiyaremye et al., 2024). This not only increases agricultural yield but also promotes environmental sustainability by minimizing the overuse of water and pesticides. Similarly, AI-powered fintech companies such as Yoco are improving access to financial services for informal traders, enabling better financial inclusion and empowering micro-entrepreneurs in townships and rural areas (Gupta & Xia, 2018).

AI-driven SMMEs also enhance local economic resilience by diversifying local economies and reducing dependence on traditional sectors like mining and manufacturing (Oyedokun & Ishola, 2025). By operating in emerging industries such as healthtech, edtech, and agritech, these enterprises open new markets and opportunities for youth and women entrepreneurs (Saluja, 2023). In South Africa, there is a growing cluster of AI-based health startups providing affordable diagnostic tools using machine learning algorithms, helping to bridge the healthcare access gap in under-resourced communities (Makgamatha & Makgato-Khunou, 2021). However, for AI-driven SMMEs to fully advance sustainable LED in South Africa, enabling conditions such as digital infrastructure, supportive regulation, and targeted funding must be strengthened (Maleka & Maidi, 2024). Partnerships between government, academia, and the private sector are essential to build AI literacy and incubate innovation hubs in underserved regions. As the country navigates the Fourth Industrial Revolution, fostering a robust ecosystem for AI-enabled SMMEs will be crucial to ensure that technological progress translates into broad-based, inclusive, and sustainable local economic development (Makgamatha & Makgato-Khunou). (Figure1)

*Figure 1. SMME-AI Synergy Model for Local Economic Sustainability*

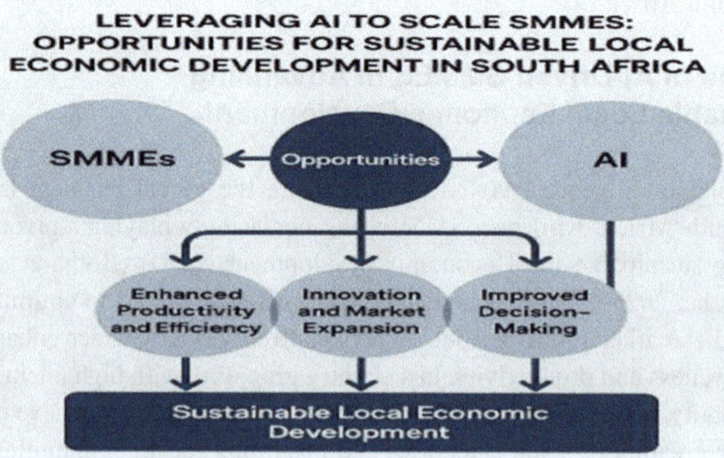


*Source own elaboration*

## RECOMMENDATIONS

### Promote Digital Literacy and AI Awareness Among SMMEs

Most SMMEs in South Africa lack awareness of the potential applications of artificial intelligence. Government agencies, local municipalities, and private sector partners should roll out training programmes that demystify AI and its practical benefits. Digital literacy campaigns targeting township and rural entrepreneurs can empower local businesses to adopt AI-driven solutions for productivity and growth.

### Establish Public-Private Innovation Hubs Focused on AI for SMMEs

The creation of regional AI innovation hubs or centres of excellence, in collaboration with universities, tech firms, and municipalities, can provide SMMEs with access to AI tools, mentorship, and infrastructure. These hubs should offer technical support, prototyping spaces, and shared computing resources to enable local businesses to test and deploy AI solutions tailored to their operations.

## Incentivise AI Adoption Through Financial and Policy Support

The South African government can stimulate AI uptake by offering targeted grants, tax rebates, and subsidised software licenses for SMMEs investing in AI tools. Policies that support digital transformation, such as simplified procurement for tech-enabled SMMEs or reduced regulatory burdens, can further enhance AI adoption across sectors like agriculture, retail, manufacturing, and services.

## Integrate AI into Enterprise Development Programmes

Existing entrepreneurship and SMME development programmes, such as those run by the Small Enterprise Development Agency (SEDA), National Youth Development Agency (NYDA), and provincial development agencies, should include AI modules. This integration ensures that enterprise support is future-oriented and includes competencies in automation, data analytics, and customer intelligence, crucial for enhancing competitiveness and market reach.

## Foster Inclusive AI Research and Development

AI models and tools used by SMMEs must reflect local languages, business practices, and socio-economic contexts. Funding local research in natural language processing (NLP), voice recognition, and predictive analytics that are designed for South African environments will help ensure the technology is accessible and relevant. Collaboration with universities can drive inclusive innovation.

## Enable Market Access Through AI-Driven Platforms

AI-powered e-commerce platforms and logistics management systems can help SMMEs reach broader markets, improve customer engagement, and reduce operational inefficiencies. Government and private sector players should support the development and scaling of such platforms, with a focus on township and rural economies to unlock new value chains.

## Monitor and Evaluate AI Impact on SMMEs and LED

To ensure effective implementation, local governments must establish frameworks for monitoring the impact of AI on SMME performance and local economic development (LED) indicators. Continuous evaluation will help refine strategies, address unintended consequences, and scale best practices nationally.

## The Legal Landscape of AI in South Africa

It is recommended that South Africa develop a comprehensive and dedicated legal framework for AI that addresses accountability, data protection, algorithmic transparency, intellectual property rights, and ethical use. Such a framework should build on existing legislation, including the Protection of Personal Information Act (POPIA) and the Cybercrimes Act, to create clear guidelines that foster innovation while safeguarding societal interests. For SMMEs, this legal clarity will be critical in building trust, ensuring compliance, and enabling the sustainable integration of AI into business operations. Policymakers should prioritise stakeholder engagement, including industry players, legal experts, and civil society, to ensure that AI regulations support inclusive, ethical, and equitable growth in line with Local Economic Development (LED) goals.

# FUTURE RESEARCH DIRECTIONS

Future research on leveraging AI to scale SMMEs in South Africa should explore how AI-driven technologies can be effectively integrated into local business ecosystems to stimulate sustainable economic development. Given the persistent challenges faced by SMMEs, such as limited access to finance, markets, and technical expertise, research should investigate how AI can address these gaps through predictive analytics, automated operations, intelligent marketing, and customer service enhancement. Particular attention should be paid to sector-specific applications of AI in industries such as agriculture, retail, manufacturing, and services, which dominate the local SMME landscape. Moreover, future studies should examine the enabling policy environment, digital infrastructure, and skills development frameworks necessary to support inclusive AI adoption, especially in underserved and rural areas. Research should also interrogate potential risks, such as digital exclusion and job displacement, and propose strategies for ethical and socially responsible AI use. Ultimately, a multi-disciplinary and context-specific approach will be essential to identify scalable models and practical pathways through which AI can empower SMMEs to become resilient, innovative drivers of local economic growth and sustainable development in South Africa.

# CONCLUSION

The study investigated how AI had been increasingly leveraged to scale SMMEs in South Africa, creating new avenues for sustainable local economic development.

It was evident that AI technologies, including data analytics, machine learning, and automation, had started to transform business operations, enabling SMMEs to increase efficiency, reduce costs, and improve decision-making processes. These advancements provided previously under-resourced entrepreneurs with tools that helped bridge traditional barriers such as limited access to markets, finance, and business intelligence. Furthermore, AI-driven platforms allowed for more precise targeting of customer segments, streamlined supply chain processes, and enhanced customer service delivery, all of which contributed to the competitiveness of SMMEs within both local and global markets.

Moreover, the research revealed that the application of AI in SMMEs was not merely a matter of technological advancement but also a critical component in fostering inclusive and sustainable economic growth. Through the adoption of AI, SMMEs have the potential to become significant drivers of employment and innovation in township and rural economies, where formal employment opportunities were scarce. However, the study also highlighted the importance of supportive policy frameworks, digital skills development, and infrastructural investment to ensure that the benefits of AI adoption were equitably distributed. As such, while AI presented vast opportunities, its successful integration into SMMEs required a coordinated effort among government, the private sector, academic institutions, and civil society to build an enabling ecosystem that empowered small businesses to thrive in the digital economy.

## REFERENCES


Badmus, O., Rajput, S. A., Arogundade, J. B., & Williams, M. (2024). AI-driven business analytics and decision making. *World Journal of Advanced Research and Reviews*, *24*(1), 616–633. DOI: 10.30574/wjarr.2024.24.1.3093

Balai, P. S., Sheikh, A., Rabha, G., Das, S., Kuli, B. K., & Raj, M. (2025). Revolutionizing Agricultural Machinery: The Role of AI, IoT, and Renewable Energy in Enhancing Efficiency and Sustainability. *International Journal of Scientific Research in Science and Technology*, *12*(2), 813–830. DOI: 10.32628/IJSRST251222626

Botha, A., Smulders, S. A., Combrink, H. A., & Meiring, J. (2021). Challenges, barriers and policy development for South African SMMEs–does size matter? *Development Southern Africa*, *38*(2), 153–174. DOI: 10.1080/0376835X.2020.1732872

Chandra, R. (2022). *Endogenous growth in historical perspective: From adam smith to paul romer*. Palgrave Macmillan. DOI: 10.1007/978-3-030-83761-7

Chinnaiyan, B., Balasubaramanian, S., Jeyabalu, M., & Warrier, G. S. (2025). AI Applications–Computer Vision and Natural Language Processing. Model Optimization Methods for Efficient and Edge AI: Federated Learning Architectures, Frameworks and Applications, 25-41.

Chitimira, H., & Motlogeloa, K. (2024). An Analysis of the Regulation and Use of Data Protection Measures in the Context of the Fourth Industrial Revolution in South Africa 1. *Perspectives of Law and Public Administration*, *13*(4), 573–587. DOI: 10.62768/PLPA/2024/13/4/08

Dinker, N. (2024). Artificial Intelligence and Inequality: Examining the Social Divides Created by Technological Advancements. International Journal of Innovations in Science, Engineering And Management, 228-236.

Enaifoghe, A., & Vezi-Magigaba, M. F. (2022). Re-thinking the sustainability of local economic development through entrepreneurship in South Africa. Expert Journal of Business and Management, 10(2).

Enaifoghe, A., & Vezi-Magigaba, M. F. (2023). Conceptualizing the role of entrepreneurship and SME in fostering South Africa's local economic development. *International Journal of Research in Business & Social Science*, *12*(4), 96–105. DOI: 10.20525/ijrbs.v12i4.2444

George, A. S. (2024). Artificial intelligence and the future of work: Job shifting not job loss. *Partners Universal Innovative Research Publication*, *2*(2), 17–37.

Guebsi, R., Mami, S., & Chokmani, K. (2024). Drones in precision agriculture: A comprehensive review of applications, technologies, and challenges. *Drones (Basel), 8*(11), 686. DOI: 10.3390/drones8110686

Gupta, A., & Xia, C. (2018). A Paradigm shift in banking: unfolding Asia's FinTech adventures. In *Banking and finance issues in emerging markets* (Vol. 25, pp. 215–254). Emerald Publishing Limited. DOI: 10.1108/S1571-038620180000025010

Habiyaremye, A., Ncube, P., Sichoongwe, K., & Slater, A. (2024). The Use of Advanced Technology in South African Agriculture: Insights from selected sub-sectors.

Hasan, M., Hoque, A., Abedin, M. Z., & Gasbarro, D. (2024). FinTech and sustainable development: A systematic thematic analysis using human-and machine-generated processing. *International Review of Financial Analysis, 95*, 103473. DOI: 10.1016/j.irfa.2024.103473

Ikpe, E. O. (2024). Adoption and implementation of artificial intelligence in small businesses in selected developing countries. *Journal of Health. Applied Sciences and Management, 8*(1), 26–34.

Ikudayisi, A., Calitz, A., & Abejide, S. (2022). An artificial intelligence approach to manage crop water requirements in South Africa. Online J Eng Sci, 23-34.

Ismaeil, M. K. A., & Lalla, A. F. (2024). The Role and Impact of Artificial Intelligence on Supply Chain Management: Efficiency, Challenges, and Strategic Implementation. *Journal of Ecohumanism, 3*(4), 89–106. DOI: 10.62754/joe.v3i4.3461

Iyelolu, T. V., Agu, E. E., Idemudia, C., & Ijomah, T. I. (2024). Improving customer engagement and crm for smes with ai driven solutions and future enhancements. *International Journal of Engineering Research and Development, 20*(8), 1150–1168.

Jain, A., Kakade, K. S., & Vispute, S. A. (2025). The Role of Artificial Intelligence (AI) in the Transformation of Small-and Medium-Sized Businesses: Challenges and Opportunities. Artificial Intelligence-Enabled Businesses: How to Develop Strategies for Innovation, 209-226.

Javaid, M., Haleem, A., Khan, I. H., & Suman, R. (2023). Understanding the potential applications of Artificial Intelligence in Agriculture Sector. *Advanced Agrochem, 2*(1), 15–30. DOI: 10.1016/j.aac.2022.10.001

Kaluarachchi, B. N., & Sedera, D. (2024). Improving Efficiency Through AI-Powered Customer Engagement by Providing Personalized Solutions in the Banking Industry. In Integrating AI-Driven Technologies into Service Marketing (pp. 299-342). IGI Global.

Katebi, A., Homami, P., & Najmeddin, M. (2022). Acceptance model of precast concrete components in building construction based on technology acceptance model (TAM) and technology, organization, and environment (TOE) framework. *Journal of Building Engineering*, *45*, 103518. DOI: 10.1016/j.jobe.2021.103518

Kaushik, M. (2022). Artificial intelligence (AI). In *Intelligent system algorithms and applications in science and Technology* (pp. 119–133). Apple Academic Press.

Kgakatsi, M., Galeboe, O. P., Molelekwa, K. K., & Thango, B. A. (2024). The impact of big data on SME performance: A systematic review. *Businesses*, *4*(4), 632–695. DOI: 10.3390/businesses4040038

Kshetri, N. (2021). The role of artificial intelligence in promoting financial inclusion in developing countries. *Journal of Global Information Technology Management*, *24*(1), 1–6. DOI: 10.1080/1097198X.2021.1871273

Kumar, M., Raut, R. D., Mangla, S. K., Ferraris, A., & Choubey, V. K. (2024). The adoption of artificial intelligence powered workforce management for effective revenue growth of micro, small, and medium scale enterprises (MSMEs). *Production Planning and Control*, *35*(13), 1639–1655. DOI: 10.1080/09537287.2022.2131620

Le Dinh, T., Vu, M. C., & Tran, G. T. (2025). Artificial Intelligence in SMEs: Enhancing Business Functions Through Technologies and Applications. *Information (Basel)*, *16*(5), 415. DOI: 10.3390/info16050415

Lethoko, M. X. (2024). The Age of Digital Entrepreneurship and Digital Information Processing for Entrepreneurs: Are the Entrepreneurs in the Rural, Limpopo Province, South Africa Ready for This Era?. Acta Universitatis Danubius. Œconomica, 20(5), 78-95.

Lian, S. (2023). Customer Relation Management (CRM) system for Customer Service Management (Doctoral dissertation, UTAR).

Lim, W. M. (2025). What is qualitative research? An overview and guidelines. *Australasian Marketing Journal*, *33*(2), 199–229. DOI: 10.1177/14413582241264619

Lim, W. M. (2025). What is qualitative research? An overview and guidelines. *Australasian Marketing Journal*, *33*(2), 199–229. DOI: 10.1177/14413582241264619

Majeed, M. (2024). *Artificial intelligence in business management*. Bentham Science Publishers. DOI: 10.2174/97898152382111240101

Makgamatha, M. G. (2022). *The effects of small and micro-enterprises (SMES) on Employement creation in Sefene Village, Limpopo Province* (Masters dissertation).

Makgamatha, M. G. (2025). Bridging Heritage and Enterprise to Address Socio-Economic Issues: A Policy Analysis of Indigenous Knowledge System Businesses in South Africa. In Revaluation and Preservation of Indigenous Knowledge Systems in Modern Society (pp. 367-384). IGI Global Scientific Publishing. DOI: 10.4018/979-8-3693-7964-6.ch018

Makgamatha, M. G. (2025). The Role of Government in the Commercialization of Indigenous Knowledge-Based Businesses in South Africa: Opportunities and Challenges. Revaluation and Preservation of Indigenous Knowledge Systems in Modern Society, 407-424.

Makgamatha, M. G., & Makgato-Khunou, P. M. (2021). Coronavirus (COVID-19) A Severe Push to the Fourth Industrial Revolution (4IR) Whether Ready or Not: African Realities. In Conference on Cooperatives and the Solidarity Economy (CCSE).

Malatji, T., & Makgamatha, M. G. (2024). An Assessment on The Effect of Immigrant Entrepreneurship on Local Economic Development in South Africa: A Literature Analysis. [Public Administration Journal]. *Jurnal Administrasi Publik*, *14*(2), 92–103.

Maleka, S., & Maidi, C. (2024). The Societal Implications of Technological Innovations and AI in South Africa.https://www.researchgate.net/profile/Stevens-Maleka-2/publication/379907825_The_Societal_Implications_of_Technological_Innovations_and_AI_in_South_Africa_-15_April_2024_The_Societal_Implications_of_Technological_Innovations_and_AI_in_South_Africa_-15/links/66214a8266ba7e2359e85b53/The-Societal-Implications-of-Technological-Innovations-and-AI-in-South-Africa-15-April-2024-The-Societal-Implications-of-Technological-Innovations-and-AI-in-South-Africa-15.pdf

Marwala, T. (2022). *Closing the gap: The fourth industrial revolution in Africa*. Pan Macmillan South Africa.

Mbinda, B. (2024). Maximizing productivity, harnessing the power of portable gadgets for SMTE business communication in Eastern Cape peri-urban areas. International Journal of Business Ecosystem & Strategy (2687-2293), 6(2), 61-74.

Mdingi, Y. (2024). Adoption of custom artificial intelligence models in South African small and medium-sized enterprises (Master's thesis, University of the Witwatersrand, Johannesburg (South Africa).

Mhlanga, D. (2021). Artificial intelligence in the industry 4.0, and its impact on poverty, innovation, infrastructure development, and the sustainable development goals: Lessons from emerging economies? *Sustainability (Basel)*, *13*(11), 5788. DOI: 10.3390/su13115788

Molina-Carmona, R., & García-Peñalvo, F. J. (2024). Safeguarding Knowledge: Ethical Artificial Intelligence Governance in the University Digital Transformation. In *Advanced Technologies and the University of the Future* (pp. 201–220). Springer Nature Switzerland.

Ndabeni-Abrahams, S. T. (2024). Determinants of a Digital Work System for Financing SMMEs in South Africa (Master's thesis, University of the Witwatersrand, Johannesburg (South Africa).

Nkontwana, P. S. (2022). African entrepreneurship: An exploration of innovation hubs as development institutions (Doctoral dissertation, Stellenbosch: Stellenbosch University).

Omokhoa, H. E., Odionu, C. S., Azubuike, C., & Sule, A. K. (2024). AI-powered fintech innovations for credit scoring, debt recovery, and financial access in microfinance and SMEs. *Gulf Journal of Advance Business Research*, *2*(6), 411–422. DOI: 10.51594/gjabr.v2i6.55

Otieno, P. O., & Busili, P. A. (2024). A Research on Labor, Finance, Technology, and Sustainable Growth. *International Journal of Innovative Science and Research Technology*, *9*(9), 3570–3597.

Oyedokun, T. T., & Ishola, J. A. (2025). Leveraging Artificial Intelligence (AI) for Resilience in Industry 5.0: Strategies for Small Businesses. In Insights Into Digital Business, Human Resource Management, and Competitiveness (pp. 35-68). IGI Global Scientific Publishing.

Ramya, J., Yerraguravagari, S. S., Gaikwad, S., & Gupta, R. K. (2024). AI and Machine Learning in Predictive Analytics: Revolutionizing Business Strategies through Big Data Insights. Library of Progress-Library Science, Information Technology & Computer, 44(3).

Rane, N., Choudhary, S., & Rane, J. (2024). Artificial intelligence for enhancing resilience. *Journal of Applied Artificial Intelligence*, *5*(2), 1–33. DOI: 10.48185/jaai.v5i2.1053

Rens, V. (2021). Entrepreneurial marketing as a tool used by business incubators to effectively support SMEs in South Africa (Doctoral dissertation, Cape Peninsula University of Technology).

Saluja, A. (2023). Public–private partnerships in EdTech for transforming rural India: how start-ups are shaping the post-COVID landscape. In India's technology-led development: managing transitions to a digital future (pp. 105-119). DOI: 10.1142/9789811271786_0006

Scholtz, E., Cronje, L., & Cilliers, J. O. (2023). Quality service SMMEs in South African townships: A comparative study of the Soweto and Diepsloot townships. *Journal of Contemporary Management, 20*(2), 199–235. DOI: 10.35683/jcman1037.220

Smart, A., Zhao, Y., & Curran, D. (2023). *Chinese artificial intelligence governance platforms 2.0: The belt and road edition*. Routledge. DOI: 10.4324/9781003365877-19

Stojčić, N., Dabić, M., & Musteen, M. (2024). With a little help from my friends: Institutional obstacles, networking, and SME exporting in emerging European and Asian economies. *International Business Review, 33*(3), 102258. DOI: 10.1016/j.ibusrev.2024.102258

Vuyokazi, S. B. (2022). *A comparative analysis of the use of e-government services by small businesses*. University of Johannesburg.

## KEY TERMS AND DEFINITIONS

**Artificial Intelligence (AI):** Artificial Intelligence refers to the simulation of human intelligence processes by machines, especially computer systems. In the context of SMMEs, AI encompasses technologies such as machine learning, natural language processing, and automation that enable businesses to analyse data, predict trends, enhance operations, and improve decision-making (Le Dinh, Vu & Tran, 2025).

**Local Economic Development (LED):** Local Economic Development is a process by which local governments, community-based organizations, and private sector partners work together to stimulate economic activity, create jobs, and improve the quality of life within a specific locality (Makgamatha, 2022). It focuses on harnessing local resources, skills, and knowledge to drive inclusive and sustainable development.

**Opportunities:** Opportunities in this context refer to the favourable conditions or chances created by the adoption of AI technologies that enable SMMEs to grow, become more competitive, and contribute to broader development goals (Ikpe, 2024). These may include access to new markets, improved efficiency, innovation, and better customer engagement.

**Small, Medium, and Micro Enterprises (SMMEs):** SMMEs are businesses that fall below certain thresholds in terms of the number of employees, annual turnover, and asset value (Makgamatha, 2022; Malatji & Makgamatha, 2024). In South Africa, these enterprises are recognized as vital to economic development, job creation, and poverty reduction, particularly in underdeveloped and rural areas.

**Sustainability:** Sustainability refers to the ability to maintain or support business growth and development over the long term without depleting natural resources or causing harm to the environment and society (Hariram, Mekha, Suganthan, & Sudhakar, 2023). In the context of local economic development and SMMEs, it involves adopting practices and technologies, such as AI, that promote economic, social, and environmental resilience.

# Compilation of References


Aayog, N. I. T. I. (2025). *Artificial Intelligence revolutionising Agriculture*. https://www.niti.gov.in/artificial-intelligence-revolutionising-agriculture

Abaddi, S. (2024). AI's call: Jordan's MSMEs answer with intent. *Journal of Entrepreneurship in Emerging Economies*. DOI: 10.1108/JEEE-11-2023-0446

Abaddi, S. (2025). Factors and moderators influencing artificial intelligence adoption by Jordanian MSMEs. *Management & Sustainability: An Arab Review*, *4*(1), 47–73. DOI: 10.1108/MSAR-10-2023-0049

Abdi, M. D., Dobamo, H. A., & Bayu, K. B. (2021). Exploring current opportunity and threats of artificial intelligence on small and medium enterprises accounting function; evidence from Southwest part of Ethiopia, Oromiya, Jimma and Snnpr, Bonga. *Academy of Accounting and Financial Studies Journal*, *25*(2), 1–11.

Abdin, M. D. (2016). Role of SMEs in Asian Economies. *Role of SMEs in Asian Economies (December 23, 2016)*. https://papers.ssrn.com/sol3/papers.cfm?abstract_id=2889166

Abhishek Sharma. (2025). *Experts Flag DPDP Rules As Hurdle For MSMEs & Digital-first Businesses - BW Businessworld*. https://www.businessworld.in/article/experts-flag-dpdp-rules-as-hurdle-for-msmes-digital-first-businesses-554002

Abubakar, J. E., Yusuf, S. O., & Yusuf, P. O.Justina Eweala AbubakarSamuel Omokhafe YusufProsper Onagie Yusuf. (2025). From branding to sales conversion: How AI-Powered CRM systems shape the customer journey for African SMEs. *International Journal of Science and Research Archive*, *14*(2), 494–506. DOI: 10.30574/ijsra.2025.14.2.0369

Adel, A., Alani, N. H., & Jan, T. (2024). Factories of the future in industry 5.0—Softwarization, Servitization, and Industrialization. *Internet of Things : Engineering Cyber Physical Human Systems*, *28*, 101431. DOI: 10.1016/j.iot.2024.101431

Aderibigbe, A. O., Ohenhen, P. E., Nwaobia, N. K., Gidiagba, J. O., & Ani, E. C.Adebayo Olusegun AderibigbePeter Efosa OhenhenNwabueze Kelvin NwaobiaJoachim Osheyor GidiagbaEmmanuel Chigozie Ani. (2023). Artificial intelligence in developing countries: Bridging the gap between potential and implementation. *Computer Science & IT Research Journal*, *4*(3), 185–199. DOI: 10.51594/csitrj.v4i3.629

Affini, D. N., Shiratina, A., & Setyaningrum, R. P. (2024). Improving the Sustainability of MSMES Businesses Through Digital Business Development in Tegal Parang Urban Village, Mampang Prapatan Sub-District, South Jakarta. Akuntansi dan Humaniora. *Jurnal Pengabdian Masyarakat*, *3*(2), 78–83. DOI: 10.38142/ahjpm.v3i2.1116

Aguinis, H., Beltran, J. R., & Cope, A. (2024). How to use generative AI as a human resource management assistant. *Organizational Dynamics*, *53*(1), 101029. DOI: 10.1016/j.orgdyn.2024.101029

Ahmed, A. (2017). *Overcoming barriers to inclusive mobility: Experience of disabled people in Tertiary Institutions of Kano*. Nigeria / Ahmed Abubakar.

Ahmed, I., & Haseen, S. (2017). Growth of MSME sector and its contribution to exports of India in post reform period. *ZENITH International Journal of Business Economics & Management Research*, *7*(12), 54–65.

Ahmed, S. R.Syeda Rafina Ahmed. (2025). The Future of Artificial Intelligence in Business Management: Exploring Opportunities, Overcoming Challenges, and Shaping the Next Era of Corporate Leadership. *Journal of Information Systems Engineering & Management*, *10*(30s), 559–566. DOI: 10.52783/jisem.v10i30s.4874

Ahsan, S. M. M., Dhungel, A., Chowdhury, M., Hasan, M. S., & Hoque, T. (2024). Hardware accelerators for artificial intelligence. *arXiv (Cornell University)*. https://doi.org//arxiv.2411.13717DOI: 10.48550

Aísa, R., & Cabeza, J. (2025). Artificial intelligence: Redefining the retirement pattern. *Research in Economics*, *79*(3), 101062. DOI: 10.1016/j.rie.2025.101062

Akter, J., Roy, A., Rahman, S., Mohona, S., & Ara, J. (2025). Artificial intelligence-driven customer lifetime value (CLV) forecasting: Integrating RFM analysis with machine learning for strategic customer retention. *Journal of Computer Science and Technology Studies*, *7*(1), 249–257. DOI: 10.32996/jcsts.2025.7.1.18

Al Khalifa, M. M. (2025). MENA SMEs: Assessing barriers and enablers of technological adoption. *Journal of Ecohumanism*, *4*(4), 108–118. DOI: 10.62754/joe.v4i4.6714

Alabi, A. T., Ubandawaki, A. T., & Issa, S. O. (2025). The Role of Digital Technology in the Sustainability Strategies of SMEs. In *The Future of Small Business in Industry 5.0* (pp. 347–378). IGI Global Scientific Publishing. [HTML], DOI: 10.4018/979-8-3693-7362-0.ch014

Aldoseri, A., Al-Khalifa, K. N., & Hamouda, A. M. (2024). AI-Powered Innovation in Digital Transformation: Key Pillars and Industry Impact. *Sustainability (Basel)*, *16*(5), 1790. DOI: 10.3390/su16051790

Algouzi, S., & Abbas, A. (2023). The Study of AI-Mediated Communication and Socio-Cultural Language-Related Variables: Gmail Reply Suggestions. *Applied Artificial Intelligence*, *37*(1), 2175114. Advance online publication. DOI: 10.1080/08839514.2023.2175114

Al-Hattami, H. M. (2022). Impact of AIS success on decision-making effectiveness among SMEs in less developed countries. *Information Technology for Development*, •••, 1–21. DOI: 10.1080/02681102.2022.2073325

Ali, S. (2023). *Predictive Analytics Solutions: Harnessing Data for Proactive Business Strategies*. Open Science Framework. https://doi.org/DOI: 10.31219/osf.io/gy49q

AlQershi, N. A., Diah, M. L. B. M., Latiffi, A. B. A., & Ahmad, W. N. K. W. (2020). Strategic innovation and competitive advantage of manufacturing SMEs: The mediating role of human capital. *Quality Innovation Prosperity*, *24*(3), 70–89. DOI: 10.12776/qip.v24i3.1493

Alzebda, S., & Matar, M. A. I. (2025). Factors affecting citizen intention toward AI acceptance and adoption: The moderating role of government regulations. *Competitiveness Review*, *35*(2), 434–455. DOI: 10.1108/CR-06-2023-0144

Amjad, A. I., Aslam, S., Tabassum, U., Sial, Z. A., & Shafqat, F. (2024). Digital equity and accessibility in higher education: Reaching the unreached. *European Journal of Education*, *59*(4), e12795. Advance online publication. DOI: 10.1111/ejed.12795

Amponsah, B. K., Adanuvor, S. Y., Frimpong, M., Buame, R., & Arhin, E. O. (2025). Investigating the Challenges and Opportunities of Implementing AI and Automation in Small Businesses. *Intelligent Control and Automation*, *16*(2), 35–59. DOI: 10.4236/ica.2025.162003

Andrianandrianina Johanesa, T. V., Equeter, L., & Mahmoudi, S. A. (2024). Survey on AI Applications for Product Quality Control and Predictive Maintenance in Industry 4.0. *Electronics (Basel)*, *13*(5), 976. DOI: 10.3390/electronics13050976

Anwar, M., Korthaus, A., Bingley, S., & Burgess, S. (2025). AI in Small Businesses: Current and Potential Applications and Issues for Adoption. In Cutting-Edge Technologies for Business Sectors (pp. 29-56). IGI Global. mailto:DOI: [HTML] DOI: 10.4018/979-8-3693-9586-8.ch002

Arroyabe, M. F., Arranz, C. F. A., Fernandez De Arroyabe, I., & Fernandez De Arroyabe, J. C. (2024). Analyzing AI adoption in European SMEs: A study of digital capabilities, innovation, and external environment. *Technology in Society*, *79*, 102733. DOI: 10.1016/j.techsoc.2024.102733

Asian Development Bank. (2023). *Asian Development Bank Asia Small and Medium-Sized Enterprise Monitor 2023*. https://www.adb.org/sites/default/files/publication/919641/asia-sme-monitor-2023.pdf

Association of Southeast Asian Nations [ASEAN]. (2025). *ASEAN Digital Masterplan 2025*. https://asean.org/book/asean-digital-masterplan-2025/

Awode, S. S., & Oduola, M. O. (2025). The interplay between technological innovation and human capital development in driving industrial productivity and competitiveness in Africa. *Journal of Economic Development*, *27*(1), 56–71. DOI: 10.1108/JED-03-2024-0079

Ayinaddis, S. G. (2025). Artificial intelligence adoption dynamics and knowledge in SMEs and large firms: A systematic review and bibliometric analysis. *Journal of Innovation & Knowledge*, *10*(3), 100682. Advance online publication. DOI: 10.1016/j.jik.2025.100682

Azman, N. A., Mohamed, A., & Jamil, A. M. (2021). Artificial intelligence in automated bookkeeping: A value-added function for small and medium enterprises. *JOIV: International Journal on Informatics Visualization*, *5*(3), 224–230. DOI: 10.30630/joiv.5.3.669

Baabdullah, A. M., Alalwan, A. A., Slade, E. L., Raman, R., & Khatatneh, K. F. (2021). SMEs and artificial intelligence (AI): Antecedents and consequences of AI-based B2B practices. *Industrial Marketing Management*, *98*, 255–270. DOI: 10.1016/j.indmarman.2021.09.003

Badmus, O., Rajput, S. A., Arogundade, J. B., & Williams, M. (2024). AI-driven business analytics and decision making. *World Journal of Advanced Research and Reviews*, *24*(1), 616–633. DOI: 10.30574/wjarr.2024.24.1.3093

Balai, P. S., Sheikh, A., Rabha, G., Das, S., Kuli, B. K., & Raj, M. (2025). Revolutionizing Agricultural Machinery: The Role of AI, IoT, and Renewable Energy in Enhancing Efficiency and Sustainability. *International Journal of Scientific Research in Science and Technology*, *12*(2), 813–830. DOI: 10.32628/IJSRST251222626

Banerjee, B. (2023). Challenges and opportunities for micro, small, and medium enterprises: Navigating the business landscape. *The American Journal of Interdisciplinary Innovations and Research*, *5*(05), 13–17. DOI: 10.37547/tajiir/Volume05Issue05-04

Bapat, G., Mahindru, R., Kumar, A., Rroy, A. D., Bhoyar, S., & Vaz, S. (2024). Leveraging ChatGPT for Empowering MSMEs: A Paradigm Shift in Problem Solving. Engineering Proceedings, 59(1), 197. https://doi.org/ mdpi.comDOI: 10.3390/engproc2023059197

Baquero Márquez, V. J., Fandiño Isaza, J. R., Pinzón Varela, M. E., Caraballo Castro, C. M., & Bezuhla, L. (2020). Impact of the macro environment on the ecotourism infrastructure. *Green, Blue & Digital. Economic Journal (London)*, *1*(2), 33–46. DOI: 10.30525/2661-5169/2020-2-6

Basole, R. C., & Accenture, A. I. (2021, January). Visualizing the Evolution of the AI Ecosystem. In HICSS (Vol. 1). https://www.researchgate.net/profile/Rahul-Basole/publication/345119002_Visualizing_the_Evolution_of_the_AI_Ecosystem/links/5fd355e1a6fdccdcb8b830a4/Visualizing-the-Evolution-of-the-AI-Ecosystem.pdf

Behl, A., Sampat, B., Pereira, V., & Chiappetta Jabbour, C. J. (2023). The role played by responsible artificial intelligence (RAI) in improving supply chain performance in the MSME sector: An empirical inquiry. [HTML]. *Annals of Operations Research*, ●●●, 1–30. DOI: 10.1007/s10479-023-05624-8 PMID: 36743350

Bella, G., Borowski, E., & Stathopoulos, A. (2025). Examining healthcare access with physical vs. telehealth options: Promise and peril for socially vulnerable older adults. *Journal of Transport & Health*, *40*, 101940. Advance online publication. DOI: 10.1016/j.jth.2024.101940

Bello, O. A., Ogundipe, A., Mohammed, D., Adebola, F., & Alonge, O. A. (2023). AI-Driven Approaches for real-time fraud detection in US financial transactions: challenges and opportunities. European Journal of Computer Science and Information Technology, 11(6), 84-102. DOI: researchgate.netDOI: 10.37745/ejcsit.2013/vol11n684102

Bhalerao, K., Kumar, A., & Pujari, P. (2022). A Study Of Barriers And Benefits Of Artificial Intelligence Adoption In Small And Medium Enterprise. *Academy of Marketing Studies Journal, 26*(Sp 1), 1–6. https://www.researchgate.net/publication/360912025_a_study_of_barriers_and_benefits_of_artificial_intelligence_adoption_in_small_and_medium_enterprise

Bhalla, N. (2025). Role of AI in MSMEs and Its Impact on Financial Performance and Business Sustainability. In Margaretha Van Der Poll, H., Andrew Van Der Poll, J., & Ngwakwe, C. C. (Eds.), (pp. 323–336). Advances in Finance, Accounting, and Economics. IGI Global., DOI: 10.4018/979-8-3693-6011-8.ch013

Bhattacharyya, S. S., & Kumar, S. (2021). Study of deployment of "low code no code" applications toward improving the digitization of supply chain management. *Journal of Science and Technology Policy Management*, *14*(2), 271–287. DOI: 10.1108/JSTPM-06-2021-0084

Bhavan, U. (2023). *Ministry of Micro, Small and Medium Enterprises*. www.msme.gov.in

Borines, A., Teckle, P., & Turi, A. N. (2025). Exploring the current AI landscape in global south economies: A systematic literature review and research agenda. In *Tech Transformation and AI Readiness. Future of Business and Finance* (pp. 1–30). Springer Nature Switzerland. DOI: 10.1007/978-3-031-73639-1_1

Borji, B., Niguse, T., & Kant, S. (2025). Effect of Strategic Alignment and Strategic Foresight on Competitive Advantage with Mediating Role of Human Capital a case of SMEs of Sidama Regional State, Ethiopia. *The Ethiopian Journal of Business and Economics*, *15*(1), 65–90.

Borsotti, V., Begel, A., & Bjørn, P. (2024). Neurodiversity and the accessible university: Exploring organizational barriers, access labor and opportunities for change. *Proceedings of the ACM on Human-Computer Interaction*, *8*(CSCW1), 1–27. DOI: 10.1145/3641011

Bortola, G. W., Kero, C. A., & Bali, N. (2024). The Mediating Effect of Competitive Advantage between Innovation Capability and Firm's Competitiveness. [HAJBE]. *Horn of African Journal of Business and Economics*, *7*(1), 75–96.

Botha, A., Smulders, S. A., Combrink, H. A., & Meiring, J. (2021). Challenges, barriers and policy development for South African SMMEs–does size matter? *Development Southern Africa*, *38*(2), 153–174. DOI: 10.1080/0376835X.2020.1732872

Bourechak, A., Zedadra, O., Kouahla, M. N., Guerrieri, A., Seridi, H., & Fortino, G. (2023). At the Confluence of Artificial Intelligence and Edge Computing in IoT-Based Applications: A Review and New Perspectives. *Sensors (Basel)*, *23*(3), 1639. DOI: 10.3390/s23031639 PMID: 36772680

Braun, V., & Clarke, V. (2022, December 17). *Thematic Analysis: A Practical Guide*. SAGE Publications Inc.

Brynjolfsson, E., Li, D., & Raymond, L. (2024). Generative AI at Work. November 7, 2024 https://arxiv.org/pdf/2304.11771

Brynjolfsson, E., Li, D., & Raymond, L. (2025). Generative AI at Work. *The Quarterly Journal of Economics*, *140*(2), 889–942. DOI: 10.1093/qje/qjae044

Brynjolfsson, E., & McElheran, K. (2016). The rapid adoption of data-driven decision-making. *The American Economic Review*, *106*(5), 133–139. DOI: 10.1257/aer.p20161016

Budiraharjo, M. H., Muhammad, A. H., & Kusnawi, . (2024). MSME AI Readiness Analysis Using The AIRI Framework. [JTIULM]. *Jurnal Teknologi Informasi Universitas Lambung Mangkurat*, *9*(2), 33–44. DOI: 10.20527/jtiulm.v9i2.307

Bughin, J., Seong, J., Manyika, J., Chui, M., & Joshi, R. (2018). *Notes from the AI frontier: Modeling the impact of AI on the world economy*. McKinsey Global Institute. *4*(1), 2-61. https://www.mckinsey.com/featured-insights/artificial-intelligence/notes-from-the-ai-frontier-modeling-the-impact-of-ai-on-the-world-economy

Bussmann, N., Giudici, P., Marinelli, D., & Papenbrock, J. (2020). Explainable AI in fintech risk management. *Frontiers in Artificial Intelligence*, *3*, 26. Advance online publication. DOI: 10.3389/frai.2020.00026 PMID: 33733145

Cahyono, C., Siregar, M., Sutrisna, A., Nurlaili, N., & Susanti, M. (2024). The Role of Artificial Intelligence in Modern Education: Empowering Learning Process through Advanced Learning Technologies. *Doi.org*. DOI: 10.47191/ijsshr/v7-i12-36

Cai, G., & Spulber, D. F. (2023). The Freemium Pricing Strategy and the Opportunity Cost of Time. *Social Science Research Network*, 1–35. DOI: 10.2139/ssrn.4516760

Campion, A., Gasco-Hernandez, M., Jankin Mikhaylov, S., & Esteve, M. (2020). Overcoming the Challenges of Collaboratively Adopting Artificial Intelligence in the Public Sector. *Social Science Computer Review*, *40*(2), 462–477. Advance online publication. DOI: 10.1177/0894439320979953

Carayannis, E. G., Dumitrescu, R., Falkowski, T., & Zota, N.-R. (2024). Empowering SMEs "Harnessing the Potential of Gen AI for Resilience and Competitiveness.". *IEEE Transactions on Engineering Management*, *71*, 14754–14774. DOI: 10.1109/TEM.2024.3456820

Carvache-Franco, M., Segarra-Oña, M., & Carrasco-López, C. (2019, January). Motivations analysis in ecotourism through an empirical application: Segmentation, characteristics and motivations of the consumer. *Geo Journal of Tourism and Geosites*, *24*(1), 48–59. DOI: 10.30892/gtg.24106-343

Castillo-Aguilar, M. A., & Roa-Angulo, V. (2021). Birdwatching tourism and environmental education as strategies for the conservation of wetlands in the city of Bogotá, Colombia. *Indian Journal of Science and Technology*, *14*(13), 1036–1043. DOI: 10.17485/IJST/v14i13.1163

Chandra, R. (2022). *Endogenous growth in historical perspective: From adam smith to paul romer*. Palgrave Macmillan. DOI: 10.1007/978-3-030-83761-7

Cheng, Y., Yang, Z., Cheng, Y., Ge, Y., & Zhu, H. (2025). Evolutionary modeling reveals that value-oriented knowledge creation behaviors reinvent jobs. *Humanities & Social Sciences Communications*, *12*(1), 385. DOI: 10.1057/s41599-025-04706-1

Chinnaiyan, B., Balasubaramanian, S., Jeyabalu, M., & Warrier, G. S. (2025). AI Applications–Computer Vision and Natural Language Processing. Model Optimization Methods for Efficient and Edge AI: Federated Learning Architectures, Frameworks and Applications, 25-41.

Chitimira, H., & Motlogeloa, K. (2024). An Analysis of the Regulation and Use of Data Protection Measures in the Context of the Fourth Industrial Revolution in South Africa 1. *Perspectives of Law and Public Administration*, *13*(4), 573–587. DOI: 10.62768/PLPA/2024/13/4/08

Chitra, M., Surianarayanan, R., Mahamuni, V. S., Mohammed, S., Keno, M. T., & Boopathi, S. (2024). Study on Cloud Computing-Empowered Small and Medium Enterprises. In Patel, R. K. (Ed.), (pp. 189–220). Advances in Business Information Systems and Analytics. IGI Global., DOI: 10.4018/979-8-3693-4227-5.ch008

Chotisarn, N., & Phuthong, T. (2025). A bibliometric analysis insights into the intellectual dynamics of artificial intelligence for the micro, small, and medium enterprises. *Cogent Business & Management*, *12*(1), 2491684. DOI: 10.1080/23311975.2025.2491684

Christopher, Y., & Sundjaja, A. M. (2024, November). The Role of AI Chatbots on E-Commerce Platforms: Understanding its Influence on Customer Trust and Dependability. In 2024 9th International Conference on Information Technology and Digital Applications (ICITDA) (pp. 1-8). IEEE. DOI: [HTML]DOI: 10.1109/ICITDA64560.2024.10809919

Chui, M., Harryson, M., Manyika, J., Roberts, R., Chung, R., & van Heteren, A. (2018). *Applying artificial intelligence for social good*. McKinsey Global Institute. 1-22. https://www.mckinsey.com/featured-insights/artificial-intelligence/applying-artificial-intelligence-for-social-good

Cleantech Insights. (2024). *From Buzz to Impact_AI's Role in Accelerating the Clean Economy _ Cleantech Group*. https://www.cleantech.com/from-buzz-to-impact-ais-role-in-accelerating-the-clean-economy/

Codingmart. (2024). *StyleDotMe MirrAr_ AR for Jewelry & Fashion - Try On Virtually!* https://codingmart.com/styledotme-mirrar-ar-for-jewelry-fashion-try-on-virtually/

Coiera, E. (2019). The Price of Artificial Intelligence. *Yearbook of Medical Informatics, 28*(01), 014–015. DOI: 10.1055/s-0039-1677892

Combi, M. (2016). Cultures and Technology: An Analysis of Some of the Changes in Progress—Digital, Global and Local Culture. In *Cultural Heritage in a Changing World* (pp. 3–15). DOI: 10.1007/978-3-319-29544-2_1

Cooper, C. B., Dickinson, J., Phillips, T., & Bonney, R. (2020). Citizen science as a tool for avian conservation and research. *Science Advances*, *6*(23), eabc7287. Advance online publication. DOI: 10.1126/sciadv.abc7287

Csaszar, F. A., Ketkar, H., & Kim, H. (2024). Artificial intelligence and strategic decision-making: Evidence from entrepreneurs and investors. *Strategy Science*, *9*(4), 322–345. DOI: 10.1287/stsc.2024.0190

Cuero-Acosta, Y. A. (2023). *Reputation based on internal capabilities: The case of small enterprises within the Colombian "orange economy"*. https://doi.org/DOI: 10.1371/journal.pone.0285026

Davenport, T. H., & Ronanki, R. (2018). Artificial intelligence for the real world. *Harvard Business Review*, *96*(1), 108–116. https://hbr.org/2018/01/artificial-intelligence-for-the-real-world

de Marcellis-Warin, N., Marty, F., Thelisson, E., & Warin, T. (2022). Artificial intelligence and consumer manipulations: From consumer's counter algorithms to firm's self-regulation tools. *AI and Ethics*, *2*(2), 259–268. Advance online publication. DOI: 10.1007/s43681-022-00149-5

Deloitte. (2023). AI in Indian FinTech: Unlocking MSME potential. Deloitte Insights. https://www2.deloitte.com

Deloitte. (2024). *ai-adoption-in-India-driven-by-transformative-potential-balanced-by-cost-sensitivity*. https://www.deloitte.com/mu/en/about/press-room/ai-adoption-in-India-driven-by-transformative-potential-balanced-by-cost-sensitivity.html

Deloitte. (2025). *ai-adoption-in-India-driven-by-transformative-potential-balanced-by-cost-sensitivity*.

Dembitska, S., & Sivert, I. (2024). *Digital accessibility in education: challenges and prospects*. Health and Safety Pedagogy.

Deranty, J.-P., & Corbin, T. (2024). Artificial intelligence and work: A critical review of recent research from the social sciences. *AI & Society*, *39*(2), 675–691. DOI: 10.1007/s00146-022-01496-x

Detesan, O.-A., & Moholea, I. F. (2024). Unimate and Beyond: Exploring the Genesis of Industrial Robotics. In Pisla, D., Carbone, G., Condurache, D., & Vaida, C. (Eds.), *Advances in Service and Industrial Robotics* (Vol. 157, pp. 263–271). Springer Nature Switzerland., DOI: 10.1007/978-3-031-59257-7_27

Dhokare, S. (2021). A Study of Artificial Intelligence Types, Opportunities & Challenges. *Bi-Lingual International Research Journal, 11*(41).

Didachos, M., & Tambunan, T. (2024). *POLICY DISCUSSION PAPER SERIES-AI Adoption in MSMEs and Government Support in Developing Countries*. Global Association for MSMEs and SDGs Research in Developing Countries. DOI: 10.13140/RG.2.2.31908.65923

Dinker, N. (2024). Artificial Intelligence and Inequality: Examining the Social Divides Created by Technological Advancements. International Journal of Innovations in Science, Engineering And Management, 228-236.

Dinku, A. E., Singh, M., & Singh, S. (2024). Effect of human capital on the performance of small and medium enterprises: A mediating role of innovation practice in Ethiopia. *Cogent Business & Management*, *11*(1), 2434729. DOI: 10.1080/23311975.2024.2434729

Dipoatmodjo, T. S. P. (2025). Experiencing Change: A Phenomenological Study of Employee Adaptation to AI-Driven Digital Transformation in a Tech Company. International Journal of Humanity Advance [IJHABS]. *Business & Sciences*, *3*(1), 25–34. DOI: 10.59971/ijhabs.v3i1.448

Dwivedi, Y. K., Hughes, L., Ismagilova, E., Aarts, G., Coombs, C., Crick, T., Duan, Y., Dwivedi, R., Edwards, J., Eirug, A., Galanos, V., Ilavarasan, P. V., Janssen, M., Jones, P., Kar, A. K., Kizgin, H., Kronemann, B., Lal, B., Lucini, B., & Williams, M. D. (2021). Artificial Intelligence (AI): Multidisciplinary perspectives on emerging challenges, opportunities, and agenda for research, practice and policy. *International Journal of Information Management*, *57*(101994), 101994. DOI: 10.1016/j.ijinfomgt.2019.08.002

Dwivedi, Y. K., Rana, N. P., Tamilmani, K., & Raman, R. (2020). A meta-analysis based modified unified theory of acceptance and use of technology (meta-UTAUT): A review of emerging literature. *Current Opinion in Psychology*, *36*, 13–18. DOI: 10.1016/j.copsyc.2020.03.008

Dyson, L., Raban, R., Litchfield, A., & Lawrence, E. (2009). Addressing the cost barriers to mobile learning in higher education. *International Journal of Mobile Learning Organisation*, *3*(4), 381–398. DOI: 10.1504/IJMLO.2009.027455

Ekrokpe, O. P., Jayawickrama, U., & Butun, C. (2025). Exploring the Role of Artificial Intelligence in Small and Medium Enterprises for Improved Decision-Making: A Scoping Review. In Delibašić, B., Radovanović, S., Delias, P., Liu, S., & Duarte, S. P. (Eds.), *Decision Support Systems XIV. Human-Centric Group Decision, Negotiation and Decision Support Systems for Societal Transitions* (Vol. 546, pp. 89–109). Springer Nature Switzerland., DOI: 10.1007/978-3-031-90863-7_7

Elshan, E., Dickhaut, E., & Ebel, P. A. (2023). Offense or defense? Digital Innovation strategy to face competitive position shifting in mobile app platform. *Proceedings of the . . . Annual Hawaii International Conference on System Sciences/Proceedings of the Annual Hawaii International Conference on System Sciences*. https://doi.org/ DOI: 10.24251/HICSS.2023.746

Enaifoghe, A., & Vezi-Magigaba, M. F. (2022). Re-thinking the sustainability of local economic development through entrepreneurship in South Africa. Expert Journal of Business and Management, 10(2).

Enaifoghe, A., & Vezi-Magigaba, M. F. (2023). Conceptualizing the role of entrepreneurship and SME in fostering South Africa's local economic development. *International Journal of Research in Business & Social Science*, *12*(4), 96–105. DOI: 10.20525/ijrbs.v12i4.2444

Endris, E., & Kassegn, A. (2022). The role of micro, small and medium enterprises (MSMEs) to the sustainable development of sub-Saharan Africa and its challenges: A systematic review of evidence from Ethiopia. *Journal of Innovation and Entrepreneurship*, *11*(1), 20. Advance online publication. DOI: 10.1186/s13731-022-00221-8

Engelbrecht, A., Yitmen, I., & Almusaed, A. (2024). *Industry 4.0 Transformation Towards Industry 5.0 Paradigm-Challenges, Opportunities and Practices: Challenges*. Opportunities and Practices.

Entrepreneur India. (2025). *News and Trends*. https://www.entrepreneur.com/en-in/news-and-trends/how-one-entrepreneur-is-shaping-the-ai-narrative-for-a/494394

European Commission. (2024). *Shaping Europe's digital future*. https://digital-strategy.ec.europa.eu/en/activities/digital-programme

European Commission. (2025). *Digital Europe Programme*. https://commission.europa.eu/funding-tenders/find-funding/eu-funding-programmes/digital-europe-programme_en

Ezeife, E., Eyeregba, M. E., Mokogwu, C., & Olorunyomi, T. D. (2024). Integrating predictive analytics into strategic decision-making: A model for boosting profitability and longevity in small businesses across the United States. World Journal of Advanced Research and Reviews, 24(2), 2490-2507. https://doi.org/ researchgate.netDOI: 10.30574/wjarr.2024.24.2.3635

Fadli, M., Susilo, E., Puspitwati, D., Liemanto, A., Ridjal, A., & Pawestri, D. (2022, May). Sustainable Tourism as a Development Strategy in Indonesia. *Journal of Indonesian Tourism and Development Studies*, *10*(1), 23–33. DOI: 10.21776/ub.jitode.2022.010.01.04

Farayola, O. A., Abdul, A. A., Irabor, B. O., & Okeleke, E. C. (2023). Innovative business models driven by AI technologies: A review. *Computer Science & IT Research Journal*, *4*(2), 85–110. DOI: 10.51594/csitrj.v4i2.608

Farmanesh, P., Solati Dehkordi, N., Vehbi, A., & Chavali, K. (2025). Artificial Intelligence and Green Innovation in Small and Medium-Sized Enterprises and Competitive-Advantage Drive Toward Achieving Sustainable Development Goals. *Sustainability (Basel)*, *17*(5), 2162. DOI: 10.3390/su17052162

Farooq, M., Ramzan, M., & Yen, Y. Y. (2024). *Transformative Impacts of AI in Management*. IGI Global., DOI: 10.4018/979-8-3693-4322-7

Fatima, P., Haider, S., Ali, M. A., Abbas, M., Akhtar, I., Rasool, M., Maqbool, H., & Khan, N. (2024). AI Unleashed: Pioneering trends and future directions in artificial intelligence. *Saudi Journal of Engineering and Technology*, *9*(08), 406–418. DOI: 10.36348/sjet.2024.v09i08.005

Ferebee, S. (2025). *AI and accessibility: Breaking barriers for people with disabilities*. Premier Journal of Artificial Intelligence., DOI: 10.70389/PJAI.100011

Ferede, D. (2025). Understanding the Artificial Intelligence (AI)-Driven Transformation of the Global South: The Case of Ethiopia.

Foka, A., & Griffin, G. (2024). AI, cultural heritage, and bias: Some key queries that arise from the use of genAI. *Heritage*, *7*(11), 6125–6136. DOI: 10.3390/heritage7110287

Foroozanfar, H., Imanipour, N., Mojtaba Sajadi, S., & Habibi, M. R. (2025, April). A sustainability perspective for sharing economy business model and its unintended effects. *Journal of Cleaner Production*, *500*(1), 145177. DOI: 10.1016/j.jclepro.2025.145177

Founder Africa. (2023, April 7). *The Journey of LifeBank – Saving Lives, One Blood Bag At A Time*. Where Founders Are Stars. https://founder.africa/founder/the-journey-of-lifebank-profile-funding

Freixes, J. (2025, February 18). Colombia's economy grew by 1.7% in 2024. ColombiaOne. Retrieved from https://colombiaone.com/2025/02/18/colombia-economy-2024-growth/ bbvaresearch.com+3colombiaone.com+3

Fui-Hoon Nah, F., Zheng, R., Cai, J., Siau, K., & Chen, L. (2023). Generative AI and ChatGPT: Applications, challenges, and AI-human collaboration. *Journal of Information Technology Case and Application Research*, *25*(3), 277–304. DOI: 10.1080/15228053.2023.2233814

Gans, J. (2022). *Internal Disagreement and Disruptive Technologies*. DOI: 10.3386/w30092

Gao, X., & Feng, H. (2023). AI-driven productivity gains: Artificial intelligence and firm productivity. *Sustainability (Basel)*, *15*(11), 8934–8934. DOI: 10.3390/su15118934

Gebremichael, H. S., & Tekle, T. G. (2020). Human Capital and Process Innovation Capability for Competitive Advantage: A Study on Manufacturing SMEs in Tigray. [BJET]. *Branna Journal of Engineering and Technology*, *2*(1), 78–94.

George, A. S. (2024). Artificial intelligence and the future of work: Job shifting not job loss. *Partners Universal Innovative Research Publication*, *2*(2), 17–37.

Geru, A. A., Birbirsa, Z. A., & Dinber, G. N. (2025). The impact of strategic human resource practices on intellectual capital development in Ethiopia: Empirical evidence from Oromia regional public service organizations. *The International Journal of Organizational Analysis*.

Ghosh, A. R. (2025). *AI for the masses: Inside Meesho's bold leap with BharatMLStack*. Retrieved from ETCIO. https://cio.economictimes.indiatimes.com/news/artificial-intelligence/revolutionizing-e-commerce-meeshos-bharatmlstack-makes-ai-accessible-for-all/122205234

Gibson, K. (2024, September 4). *Leveraging AI in Business: 3 Real-World Examples*. Business Insights Blog. https://online.hbs.edu/blog/post/ai-in-business

Golovianko, M., Terziyan, V., Branytskyi, V., & Malyk, D. (2023). Industry 4.0 vs. Industry 5.0: Co-existence, Transition, or a Hybrid. *Procedia Computer Science*, *217*, 102–113. DOI: 10.1016/j.procs.2022.12.206

Government of the Republic of Korea. (2020). *AI voucher program to help SMEs adopt artificial intelligence*. Korea.net. https://www.korea.net/Government/Briefing-Room/Press-Releases/view?articleId=4933&type=O

Goyal, S., Esposito, M., & Kapoor, A. (2018). Circular economy business models in developing economies: Lessons from India on reduce, recycle, and reuse paradigms. *Thunderbird International Business Review*, *60*(5), 729–740. DOI: 10.1002/tie.21883

Grimm, M., Knorringa, P., & Jann Layc, J. (2012). Constrained Gazelles: High Potentials in West Africa's Informal Economy. https://documents1.worldbank.org/curated/en/468141468337243809/pdf/779260WP0P115100B00PUBLIC00Gazelles.pdf

Guebsi, R., Mami, S., & Chokmani, K. (2024). Drones in precision agriculture: A comprehensive review of applications, technologies, and challenges. *Drones (Basel)*, *8*(11), 686. DOI: 10.3390/drones8110686

Guillen, N., & Lim, C. T. (2023). Unlocking growth opportunities for Philippine micro, small, and medium enterprises through Facebook advertising and growth hacking strategies in the post-pandemic era. *International Journal of Multidisciplinary: Applied Business and Education Research*, *4*(8), 2884–2893. DOI: 10.11594/ijmaber.04.08.26

Gupta, A., & Kumar Singh, R. (2023). Managing resilience of micro, small and medium enterprises (MSMEs) during COVID-19: Analysis of barriers. [HTML]. *Benchmarking*, *30*(6), 2062–2084. Advance online publication. DOI: 10.1108/BIJ-11-2021-0700

Gupta, A., & Xia, C. (2018). A Paradigm shift in banking: unfolding Asia's FinTech adventures. In *Banking and finance issues in emerging markets* (Vol. 25, pp. 215–254). Emerald Publishing Limited. DOI: 10.1108/S1571-038620180000025010

Gupta, P., & Sharma, V. (2020). Leveraging Artificial Intelligence for MSMEs: Challenges and Enablers. *International Journal of Emerging Markets*, *15*(6), 987–1003. DOI: 10.1108/IJOEM-03-2019-0204

Gupta, U., Agarwal, B., & Nautiyal, N. (2022). Financial technology adoption – A case of Indian MSMEs. *Finance: Theory and Practice*, *26*(6), 192–211. DOI: 10.26794/2587-5671-2022-26-6-192-211

Habiyaremye, A., Ncube, P., Sichoongwe, K., & Slater, A. (2024). The Use of Advanced Technology in South African Agriculture: Insights from selected sub-sectors.

Haji, K. (2021). E-commerce development in rural and remote areas of BRICS countries. *Journal of Integrative Agriculture*, *20*(4), 979–997. DOI: 10.1016/S2095-3119(20)63451-7

Hall, C. M., & Gössling, S. (2021). *Tourism and sustainability: Development, globalisation and new tourism in the third world* (5th ed.). Routledge., DOI: 10.4324/9780429276107

Halvoník, D., & Kapusta, J. (2024). Large Language Models and Rule-Based Approaches in Domain-Specific Communication. *IEEE Access : Practical Innovations, Open Solutions*, *12*, 107046–107058. DOI: 10.1109/ACCESS.2024.3436902

Han, Y., & Huang, Y. (2025). Does artificial intelligence lead to human resource slack? Evidence from China. *Finance Research Letters*, *84*, 107803. DOI: 10.1016/j.frl.2025.107803

Hart, S. (2015). Patient education accessibility. *Medical Writing*, *24*(3), 190–194. DOI: 10.1179/2047480615Z.000000000321

Hasan, I., & Rizvi, S. A. M. (2022). AI-driven fraud detection and mitigation in e-commerce transactions. In Proceedings of Data Analytics and Management: ICDAM 2021, Volume 1 (pp. 403-414). Springer Singapore. https://doi.org/ [HTML]DOI: 10.1007/978-981-16-6289-8_34

Hasan, M., Hoque, A., Abedin, M. Z., & Gasbarro, D. (2024). FinTech and sustainable development: A systematic thematic analysis using human-and machine-generated processing. *International Review of Financial Analysis*, *95*, 103473. DOI: 10.1016/j.irfa.2024.103473

Hernandez, A. A., Caballero, A. R., Albina, E. M., Balmes, I. L., & Niguidula, J. D. (2023, May). Artificial Intelligence for Sustainability: Evidence from select Small and Medium Enterprises in the Philippines. In 2023 8th International Conference on Business and Industrial Research (ICBIR) (pp. 818-823). IEEE. DOI: researchgate.netDOI: 10.1109/ICBIR57571.2023.10147579

Hintze, A. (2016, 14 November). From reactive robots to sentient machines: The four types of AI. Live Science. https://www.livescience.com/56858-4-types-artificial-intelligence.html

Hnatuyk, V., Pshenychna, N., Kara, S., Yaroshchuk, L., and Kolodii, V. (2024). Education's role in fostering environmental awareness and advancing sustainable development within a holistic framework. June 2024. *Multidisciplinary Reviews* 7:2024spe012. DOI: DOI: 10.31893/multirev.2024spe012

Horváth, D., & Szabó, R. Zs. (2019). Driving forces and barriers of Industry 4.0: Do multinational and small and medium-sized companies have equal opportunities? [sciencedirect.]. *Technological Forecasting and Social Change*, *146*(1), 119–132. DOI: 10.1016/j.techfore.2019.05.021

Hoyos Sánchez, R. A. (2024). The Crucial Role of Agriculture in the Colombian Economy: Challenges and Opportunities. *Revista Facultad Nacional de Agronomía*, *77*(3), 10795–10796. http://www.scielo.org.co/scielo.php?script=sci_arttext&pid=S0304-28472024000310795&lng=en&tlng=en. DOI: 10.15446/rfnam.v77n3.116117

Hunt, C. A., Barragán-Paladines, M. J., Izurieta, J. C., & Ordóñez, L. A. (2023). Tourism, compounding crises, and struggles for sovereignty. *Journal of Sustainable Tourism*, *31*(10), 2381–2398. DOI: 10.1080/09669582.2022.2108431

Hunter, D. J. (2024). Artificial intelligence & the capacity for discrimination: The imperative need for frameworks, diverse teams & human accountability. *IgMin Research*, *2*(10), 801–806. DOI: 10.61927/igmin250

Hussain, S. A., Bresnahan, M., & Zhuang, J. (2025). Can artificial intelligence revolutionize healthcare in the Global South? A scoping review of opportunities and challenges. *Digital Health*, *11*, 20552076251348024. Advance online publication. DOI: 10.1177/20552076251348024

IDC global. (2024). *Navigate your next move with confidence*. https://www.idc.com/

Ikpe, E. O. (2024). Adoption and implementation of artificial intelligence in small businesses in selected developing countries. *Journal of Health. Applied Sciences and Management*, *8*(1), 26–34.

Ikudayisi, A., Calitz, A., & Abejide, S. (2022). An artificial intelligence approach to manage crop water requirements in South Africa. Online J Eng Sci, 23-34.

İnce, F. (2021). Opportunities and Challenges of E-Learning in Turkey. In Khan, B., Affouneh, S., Hussein Salha, S., & Najee Khlaif, Z. (Eds.), *Challenges and Opportunities for the Global Implementation of E-Learning Frameworks* (pp. 202–226). IGI Global Scientific Publishing., DOI: 10.4018/978-1-7998-7607-6.ch013

İnce, F. (2023). Comparison of Japan and OECD Countries in Terms of Well-Being Resources. *Problemy Ekorozwoju*, *18*(2), 78–85. DOI: 10.35784/preko.3945

İnce, F. (2024). Comparison of National Well-being of Mediterranean Countries in terms of EU: Turkey, Italy, Spain. *Acta Scientiarum. Health Sciences*, *46*(1), e65161. DOI: 10.4025/actascihealthsci.v46i1.65161

Inter-American Development Bank. (2024). *Responsible artificial intelligence for growth in Latin America and the Caribbean (RAI 4 Growth)* (Project No. RG-T4463). https://www.iadb.org/en/project/RG-T4463

International Centre of Expertise in Montreal on Artificial Intelligence (ICEIMIA). (2022). *State of AI in Healthcare in Sub-Saharan Africa. Zenodo*. DOI: 10.5281/zenodo.12635984

International Labour Organization [ILO]. (2021). *Digitalisation of TVET and skills development: Leveraging technology to support lifelong learning*. International Labour Organization. https://www.skillsforemployment.org/sites/default/files/2024-01/WEB-Digitalisation%20of%20TVET.pdf

Ismaeil, M. K. A., & Lalla, A. F. (2024). The Role and Impact of Artificial Intelligence on Supply Chain Management: Efficiency, Challenges, and Strategic Implementation. *Journal of Ecohumanism*, *3*(4), 89–106. DOI: 10.62754/joe.v3i4.3461

Iyelolu, T. V., Agu, E. E., Idemudia, C., & Ijomah, T. I. (2024). Driving SME innovation with AI solutions: overcoming adoption barriers and future growth opportunities. *International Journal of Science and Technology Research Archive, 7*(1), 036-054.

Iyelolu, V., Ebele, E., Idemudia, N. C., & Ignatius, T. (2024). Driving SME innovation with ai solutions: overcoming adoption barriers and future growth opportunities. *International Journal of Science and Technology Research Archive, 7*(1), 036–054. DOI: 10.53771/ijstra.2024.7.1.0055

Iyelolu, T. V., Agu, E. E., Idemudia, C., & Ijomah, T. I. (2024). Improving customer engagement and crm for smes with ai driven solutions and future enhancements. *International Journal of Engineering Research and Development*, *20*(8), 1150–1168.

Jain, A., Kakade, K. S., & Vispute, S. A. (2025). The Role of Artificial Intelligence (AI) in the Transformation of Small-and Medium-Sized Businesses: Challenges and Opportunities. Artificial Intelligence-Enabled Businesses: How to Develop Strategies for Innovation, 209-226.

Jain, A., Kakade, K. S., & Vispute, S. A. (2025). The role of artificial intelligence (AI) in the transformation of small- and medium-sized businesses: Challenges and opportunities. In Dixit, S., Maurya, M., Jain, V., & Subramaniam, G. (Eds.), *Artificial intelligence-enabled businesses: How to develop strategies for innovation* (pp. 209–226). Wiley., DOI: 10.1002/9781394234028.ch12

Jain, R., Mehta, A., & Deshpande, N. (2021). Financial inclusion through AI-powered credit assessments. *Journal of Financial Innovation*, *3*(1), 45–56. DOI: 10.1016/j.jfi.2021.05.007

Javaid, M., Haleem, A., Khan, I. H., & Suman, R. (2023). Understanding the potential applications of Artificial Intelligence in Agriculture Sector. *Advanced Agrochem*, *2*(1), 15–30. DOI: 10.1016/j.aac.2022.10.001

Jha, S., & Dangwal, R. C. (2025). Actual adoption of Fintech services among micro-entrepreneurs of urban slum area of Uttarakhand. *Journal of Science and Technology Policy Management*. DOI: 10.1108/JSTPM-08-2023-0144

Jin, C.-X., & Yu, J.-Q. (2025). Does the popularization of artificial intelligence increase the risk of corporate digital responsibility? *Finance Research Letters*, *80*, 107375. DOI: 10.1016/j.frl.2025.107375

Kaluarachchi, B. N., & Sedera, D. (2024). Improving Efficiency Through AI-Powered Customer Engagement by Providing Personalized Solutions in the Banking Industry. In Integrating AI-Driven Technologies into Service Marketing (pp. 299-342). IGI Global.

Kamalov, F., Calonge, D. S., Hultberg, P. T., Smail, L., & Jamali, D. (2025). Comparative analysis of leading artificial intelligence chatbots in the context of entrepreneurship. *Journal of Innovation and Entrepreneurship*, *14*(1), 58. DOI: 10.1186/s13731-025-00527-3

Kar, A. K., & Kushwaha, A. K. (2023). Facilitators and barriers of artificial intelligence adoption in business–insights from opinions using big data analytics. [HTML]. *Information Systems Frontiers*, *25*(4), 1351–1374. Advance online publication. DOI: 10.1007/s10796-021-10219-4

Kasireddy, L. C., & Sreenivasu, M.Lakshmi Chandrakanth Kasireddy. (2025). Overcoming adoption barriers: Strategies for scalable AI transformation in enterprises. *Journal of Informatics Education and Research*, *5*(2). Advance online publication. DOI: 10.52783/jier.v5i2.2459

Kataria, J., & Mehta, D. (2025). AI across industries: A comparative analysis of adoption and impact. *International Journal of Innovations & Research Analysis*, *04*(04(I)), 213–222. DOI: 10.62823/IJIRA/4.4(I).7053

Katebi, A., Homami, P., & Najmeddin, M. (2022). Acceptance model of precast concrete components in building construction based on technology acceptance model (TAM) and technology, organization, and environment (TOE) framework. *Journal of Building Engineering*, *45*, 103518. DOI: 10.1016/j.jobe.2021.103518

Katz, Y. (2025). Shaping the future of AI governance in agriculture and related industries. *SunText Review of Economics & Business*, *6*(1), 223. DOI: 10.51737/2766-4775.2025.123

Kauark-Fontes, B., Marchetti, L., & Salbitano, F. (2023, June). Integration of nature-based solutions (NBS) in local policy and planning toward transformative change. Evidence from Barcelona, Lisbon, and Turin. *Ecology and Society*, *28*(2), art25. Advance online publication. DOI: 10.5751/ES-14182-280225

Kaushik, M. (2022). Artificial intelligence (AI). In *Intelligent system algorithms and applications in science and Technology* (pp. 119–133). Apple Academic Press.

Kellert, S. R. (1985). Social and perceptual factors in the preservation of animal species. In Soulé, M. E. (Ed.), *Conservation biology* (pp. 50–69). Sinauer Associates., DOI: 10.1515/9781400857869.50/html

Keshvarparast, A., Battini, D., Battaia, O., & Pirayesh, A. (2023). Collaborative robots in manufacturing and assembly systems: Literature review and future research agenda. *Journal of Intelligent Manufacturing*, *35*(5), 2065–2118. Advance online publication. DOI: 10.1007/s10845-023-02137-w

Kgakatsi, M., Galeboe, O. P., Molelekwa, K. K., & Thango, B. A. (2024). The impact of big data on SME performance: A systematic review. *Businesses*, *4*(4), 632–695. DOI: 10.3390/businesses4040038

Khan, M. A. (2024). Understanding the Impact of Artificial Intelligence (AI) on Traditional Businesses in Indonesia. *Journal of Management Studies and Development, 3*(02), 146–158. DOI: 10.56741/jmsd.v3i02.584

Khaq, Z., Subroto, V. K., & Susanto, E. (2024). AI-Driven Strategies for Enhancing MSME Sales and Business Sustainability in the Digital Era. *Journal of Management and Informatics, 3*(2), 180–194. DOI: 10.51903/jmi.v3i2.28

Kinkel, S., Baumgartner, M., & Cherubini, E. (2022). Prerequisites for the adoption of AI technologies in manufacturing–Evidence from a worldwide sample of manufacturing companies. [HTML]. *Technovation, 110*, 102375. Advance online publication. DOI: 10.1016/j.technovation.2021.102375

Knani, M., Echchakoui, S., & Ladhari, R. (2022). Artificial intelligence in tourism and hospitality: Bibliometric analysis and research agenda. *International Journal of Hospitality Management, 107*, 103317. DOI: 10.1016/j.ijhm.2022.103317

Kok, C. L., Tan, H. R., Ho, C. K., Lee, C., Teo, T. H., & Tang, H. (2024). A comparative study of AI and low-code platforms for SMEs: Insights into Microsoft Power Platform, Google AutoML, and Amazon SageMaker. *2024 IEEE 17th International Symposium on Embedded Multicore/Many-core Systems-on-Chip (MCSoC)*, Kuala Lumpur, Malaysia, 50-53. https://doi.org/DOI: 10.1109/MCSoC64144.2024.00018

Kokilavizhi, S., & Amsaveni, R. (2023). Role of MSME in economic self reliance. *Sustainable developments through MSMES: a pathway to self-reliant India, 25*, 97.

Kokina, J., & Davenport, T. H. (2017). The emergence of artificial intelligence: How automation is changing auditing. *Journal of Emerging Technologies in Accounting, 14*(1), 115–122. DOI: 10.2308/jeta-51730

Koundal, P., Bhalla, M., & Bandna. (2024). The Role of AIS in Enhancing Small Business Agility and Sustainability in Industry 5.0: In T. O. Olubiyi, S. D. Suppiah, & C. Chidoko (Eds.), *Advances in Business Strategy and Competitive Advantage* (pp. 301–330). IGI Global. DOI: 10.4018/979-8-3693-7362-0.ch012

Koundal, P., Bhalla, M., & Kailay, M. (2025). Non-financial information as a mediator in the link between accounting information systems and decision-making outcomes in SMEs: A structural equation modelling study. *International Journal of Business and Systems Research, 1*(1), 10071211. DOI: 10.1504/IJBSR.2025.10071211

Kouroupetroglou, C., Tektonidis, D., Koumpis, A., & Ignatiadis, I. (2012). Exploring Accessibility Scenarios for 2020 in Relation with Future ICT Trends on Assistive Technology and Accessibility. [iJIM]. *International Journal of Interactive Mobile Technologies, 6*(1), 7. DOI: 10.3991/ijim.v6i1.1790

Krishnan, C., Gupta, A., Gupta, A., & Singh, G. (2022). Impact of Artificial Intelligence-Based Chatbots on Customer Engagement and Business Growth. In Hong, T.-P., Serrano-Estrada, L., Saxena, A., & Biswas, A. (Eds.), *Deep Learning for Social Media Data Analytics* (Vol. 113, pp. 195–210). Springer International Publishing., DOI: 10.1007/978-3-031-10869-3_11

Kronenberg, J. (2014). Environmental impacts of the use of ecosystem services: Case study of birdwatching. *Environmental Management*, *54*(3), 617–630. https://link.springer.com/article/10.1007/s00267-014-0317-8. DOI: 10.1007/s00267-014-0317-8 PMID: 24993794

Kshetri, N. (2021). The role of artificial intelligence in promoting financial inclusion in developing countries. *Journal of Global Information Technology Management*, *24*(1), 1–6. DOI: 10.1080/1097198X.2021.1871273

Kulkarni, A. V., Joseph, S., & Patil, K. P. (2024). Artificial intelligence technology readiness for social sustainability and business ethics: Evidence from MSMEs in developing nations. ... Journal of Information Management Data .... https://doi.org/ sciencedirect.comDOI: 10.1016/j.jjimei.2024.100250

Kumar, P., Kushwaha, A. K., Kar, A. K., Dwivedi, Y. K., & Rana, N. P. (2022). Managing buyer experience in a buyer–supplier relationship in MSMEs and SMEs. Annals of Operations Research, 1-28. https://doi.org/ springer.comDOI: 10.1007/s10479-022-04954-3

Kumar, M., Raut, R. D., Mangla, S. K., Ferraris, A., & Choubey, V. K. (2024). The adoption of artificial intelligence powered workforce management for effective revenue growth of micro, small, and medium scale enterprises (MSMEs). *Production Planning and Control*, *35*(13), 1639–1655. DOI: 10.1080/09537287.2022.2131620

Kumar, S., & Shukla, T. (2024). Optimizing supply chain management through advanced data mining applications. *International Journal of Sciences and Innovation Engineering*, *1*(3), 1–9. DOI: 10.70849/IJSCI27936

Kung, W. (2023). Using the PESTEL Analysis to Determine the Effectiveness of New Digital Media Strategies. Advances in Economics. *Management and Political Sciences*, *5*(1), 19–25. DOI: 10.54254/2754-1169/5/20220054

Kushwaha, A. K., Kumar, P., & Kar, A. K. (2021). What impacts customer experience for B2B enterprises on using AI-enabled chatbots? Insights from Big data analytics. *Industrial Marketing Management*, *98*(1), 207–221. DOI: 10.1016/j.indmarman.2021.08.011

Kusumawijaya, I. K., & Astuti, P. D. (2024). The Impact of Human Capital and Knowledge Creation on Sustaining Competitive Advantage and Innovation in Medium-Sized Companies in Bali. *International Journal of Sustainable Development and Planning*, *19*(6), 2193–2204. DOI: 10.18280/ijsdp.190619

Kutzner, D. (2019). Environmental change, resilience, and adaptation in nature-based tourism: Conceptualizing the social-ecological resilience of birdwatching tour operations. *Journal of Sustainable Tourism*, *27*(8), 1142–1166. Advance online publication. DOI: 10.1080/09669582.2019.1601730

La Porta, R., & Shleifer, A. (2014). Informality and Development. 30 Pages Posted: 11 Jun 2014. *NBER Working Paper No. w20205*. https://papers.ssrn.com/sol3/papers.cfm?abstract_id=2448910

Lai, P. (2017). The Literature Review of Technology Adoption Models and Theories for the Novelty Technology. *Journal of Information Systems and Technology Management*, *14*(1), 21–38. DOI: 10.4301/S1807-17752017000100002

Lapp, S., Stahlman, N., & Kitzes, J. A. (2023, June 1). Quantitative Evaluation of the Performance of the Low-Cost AudioMoth Acoustic Recording Unit. *Sensors (Basel)*, *23*(11), 5254. DOI: 10.3390/s23115254 PMID: 37299981

Larios-Francia, R. P., & Ferasso, M. (2023, March). The relationship between innovation and performance in MSMEs: The case of the wearing apparel sector in emerging countries. *Journal of Open Innovation*, *9*(1), 100018. Advance online publication. DOI: 10.1016/j.joitmc.2023.100018

Le Dinh, T., Vu, M.-C., & Tran, G. T. C. (2025). Artificial Intelligence in SMEs: Enhancing Business Functions Through Technologies and Applications. *Information (Basel)*, *16*(5), 415. DOI: 10.3390/info16050415

Lee, C.-L., Orton, G., & Lu, P. (2024). Global Meta-Analysis of Innovation Attributes Influencing Climate-Smart Agriculture Adoption for Sustainable Development. *Climate (Basel)*, *12*(11), 192. DOI: 10.3390/cli12110192

Legowo, M. B., & Sorongan, F. A. (2022). Accelerating digital transformation during the COVID-19 Pandemic: A model design for Indonesian MSMEs. *Binus Business Review*, *13*(2), 203–211. DOI: 10.21512/bbr.v13i2.8447

Leng, J., Sha, W., Wang, B., Zheng, P., Zhuang, C., Liu, Q., Wuest, T., Mourtzis, D., & Wang, L. (2022). Industry 5.0: Prospect and retrospect. *Journal of Manufacturing Systems*, *65*, 279–295. DOI: 10.1016/j.jmsy.2022.09.017

Leonard, P. (2023). AI analyzes bird sightings to help conserve species. Cornell Lab of Ornithology. October 4, 2023. https://news.cornell.edu/stories/2023/10/ai-analyzes-bird-sightings-help-conserve-species

Lethoko, M. X. (2024). The Age of Digital Entrepreneurship and Digital Information Processing for Entrepreneurs: Are the Entrepreneurs in the Rural, Limpopo Province, South Africa Ready for This Era?. Acta Universitatis Danubius. Œconomica, 20(5), 78-95.

Lewandowska, A., Berniak-Woźny, J., & Ahmad, N. (2023). Competitiveness and innovation of small and medium enter-prises under Industry 4.0 and 5.0 challenges: A comprehensive bibliometric analysis. *Equilibrium. Quarterly Journal of Economics and Economic Policy*, *18*(4), 1045–1074. DOI: 10.24136/eq.2023.033

Lian, S. (2023). Customer Relation Management (CRM) system for Customer Service Management (Doctoral dissertation, UTAR).

Lim, T. K., & Seng, L. W. (2024). Determinants Of Artificial Intelligence Adoption In Accounting Among Malaysia Small And Medium-Sized Enterprises. *Journal of Accounting* [JABM]. *Business and Management*, *32*(1), 90. DOI: 10.31966/jabminternational.v32i1.1456

Lim, W. M. (2025). What is qualitative research? An overview and guidelines. *Australasian Marketing Journal*, *33*(2), 199–229. DOI: 10.1177/14413582241264619

Li, X. (2023). Analysis of the designs and applications of AI chip. *Highlights in Science. Engineering and Technology*, *76*, 168–180. DOI: 10.54097/k1p7yk27

Lo, W., Yang, C. M., Zhang, Q., & Li, M. (2024). Increased productivity and reduced waste with robotic process automation and generative AI-powered IoE services. Journal of Web Engineering. ieee.orgDOI: 10.13052/jwe1540-9589.2313

Lomas & Reeta. (2024). "AI-Driven FinTech Solutions for Financial Inclusion: A Study on MSME Sector Empowerment," *2024 1st International Conference on Advances in Computing, Communication and Networking (ICAC2N)*, Greater Noida, India, pp. 1887-1891, DOI: 10.1109/ICAC2N63387.2024.10895674

Lorica, B., & Nathan, P. (2019). *AI Adoption in the Enterprise*. O'Reilly Online Learning. https://www.oreilly.com/library/view/ai-adoption-in/9781492051800/

Luger, G. F. (2025). Computing, Representations, and Definitions of Artificial Intelligence. In G. F. Luger, *Artificial Intelligence: Principles and Practice* (pp. 27–49). Springer Nature Switzerland. DOI: 10.1007/978-3-031-57437-5_2

Lu, X., Wijayaratna, K., Huang, Y., & Qiu, A. (2022). AI-Enabled Opportunities and Transformation Challenges for SMEs in the Post-pandemic Era: A Review and Research Agenda. In *Frontiers in Public Health* (Vol. 10). Frontiers Media S.A., DOI: 10.3389/fpubh.2022.885067

Machucho, R., & Ortiz, D. (2025). The impacts of artificial intelligence on business innovation: A comprehensive review of applications, organizational challenges, and ethical considerations. *Systems*, *13*(4), 264. DOI: 10.3390/systems13040264

Madanchian, M. (2024). The Impact of Artificial Intelligence Marketing on E-Commerce Sales. *Systems*, *12*(10), 429. DOI: 10.3390/systems12100429

Madgavkar, A., Piccitto, M., White, O., Ramírez, M. J., Mischke, J., Chockalingam, K., & Bush, J. (2024). *A microscope on small businesses Spotting opportunities to boost productivity*. McKinsey Global Institute.

Magableh, I. K., Mahrouq, M. H., Ta'Amnha, M. A., & Riyadh, H. A. (2024). The role of marketing artificial intelligence in enhancing sustainable financial performance of medium-sized enterprises through customer engagement and data-driven decision-making. *Sustainability (Basel)*, *16*(24), 11279. DOI: 10.3390/su162411279

Mahmud, D. (2025). Building AI-driven economic resilience systems to support stability during future pandemic lockdowns. *Review of Applied Science and Technology*, *4*(2), 1–32. DOI: 10.63125/adyfcg48

Majeed, M. (2024). *Artificial intelligence in business management*. Bentham Science Publishers. DOI: 10.2174/97898152382111240101

Makgamatha, M. G. (2022). *The effects of small and micro-enterprises (SMES) on Employement creation in Sefene Village, Limpopo Province* (Masters dissertation).

Makgamatha, M. G. (2025). Bridging Heritage and Enterprise to Address Socio-Economic Issues: A Policy Analysis of Indigenous Knowledge System Businesses in South Africa. In Revaluation and Preservation of Indigenous Knowledge Systems in Modern Society (pp. 367-384). IGI Global Scientific Publishing. DOI: 10.4018/979-8-3693-7964-6.ch018

Makgamatha, M. G. (2025). The Role of Government in the Commercialization of Indigenous Knowledge-Based Businesses in South Africa: Opportunities and Challenges. Revaluation and Preservation of Indigenous Knowledge Systems in Modern Society, 407-424.

Makgamatha, M. G., & Makgato-Khunou, P. M. (2021). Coronavirus (COVID-19) A Severe Push to the Fourth Industrial Revolution (4IR) Whether Ready or Not: African Realities. In Conference on Cooperatives and the Solidarity Economy (CCSE).

Malatji, T., & Makgamatha, M. G. (2024). An Assessment on The Effect of Immigrant Entrepreneurship on Local Economic Development in South Africa: A Literature Analysis. [Public Administration Journal]. *Jurnal Administrasi Publik, 14*(2), 92–103.

Maldonado, J. H., del Pilar Moreno-Sánchez, R., Espinoza, S., Bruner, A., Garzón, N., & Myers, J. (2018). Peace is much more than doves: The economic benefits of bird-based tourism as a result of the peace treaty in Colombia. *World Development, 106*, 78–86. DOI: 10.1016/j.worlddev.2018.01.015

Maleka, S., & Maidi, C. (2024). The Societal Implications of Technological Innovations and AI in South Africa.https://www.researchgate.net/profile/Stevens-Maleka-2/publication/379907825_The_Societal_Implications_of_Technological_Innovations_and_AI_in_South_Africa_-15_April_2024_The_Societal_Implications_of_Technological_Innovations_and_AI_in_South_Africa_-15/links/66214a8266ba7e2359e85b53/The-Societal-Implications-of-Technological-Innovations-and-AI-in-South-Africa-15-April-2024-The-Societal-Implications-of-Technological-Innovations-and-AI-in-South-Africa-15.pdf

Mariani, M., Hashemi, N., & Wirtz, J. (2023). Artificial intelligence empowered conversational agents: A systematic literature review and research agenda. *Journal of Business Research, 161*, 113838. https://es.scribd.com/document/677103241/Mariani-et-al-2023. DOI: 10.1016/j.jbusres.2023.113838

Martínez-Peláez, R., Escobar, M. A., Félix, V. G., Ostos, R., Parra-Michel, J., García, V., Ochoa-Brust, A., Velarde-Alvarado, P., Félix, R. A., Olivares-Bautista, S., Flores, V., & Mena, L. J. (2024). Sustainable Digital Transformation for SMEs: A Comprehensive Framework for Informed Decision-Making. *Sustainability (Basel), 16*(11), 4447. DOI: 10.3390/su16114447

Martinravi, C. P., & Krishnasamy, K. (2025). Unleashing the potential of MSMEs in India: A strategic analysis. *Journal of the International Council for Small Business, 6*(1), 123–143. DOI: 10.1080/26437015.2024.2397664

Marwala, T. (2022). *Closing the gap: The fourth industrial revolution in Africa*. Pan Macmillan South Africa.

Mbinda, B. (2024). Maximizing productivity, harnessing the power of portable gadgets for SMTE business communication in Eastern Cape peri-urban areas. International Journal of Business Ecosystem & Strategy (2687-2293), 6(2), 61-74.

McCarthy, J. (1956). Dartmouth Summer Research Project on Artificial Intelligence.

McCarthy, J., Minsky, M. L., Rochester, N., & Shannon, C. E. (1955). *A Proposal for the Dartmouth Summer Research Project on Artificial Intelligence*. Dartmouth College.

McCulloch, W. S., & Pitts, W. (1943). A Logical Calculus of Ideas Immanent in Nervous Activity. *The Bulletin of Mathematical Biophysics*, *5*(4), 115–133. DOI: 10.1007/BF02478259

McElheran, K., Li, J. F., Brynjolfsson, E., Kroff, Z., Dinlersoz, E., Foster, L., & Zolas, N. (2024). AI adoption in America: Who, what, and where. Journal of Economics & Management Strategy, 33(2), 375-415. DOI: wiley.comDOI: 10.1111/jems.12576

McKinsey Global Institute. (2024). *A microscope on small businesses: Spotting opportunities to boost productivity.* May 2, 2024 | Report. https://www.mckinsey.com/mgi/our-research/a-microscope-on-small-businesses-spotting-opportunities-to-boost-productivity

McKinsey. (2018). *AI adoption advances, but foundational barriers remain.* McKinsey & Company. https://www.mckinsey.com/featured-insights/artificial-intelligence/ai-adoption-advances-but-foundational-barriers-remain

McKinsey. (2025). *A.* https://www.mckinsey.com/capabilities/quantumblack/our-insights/the-state-of-ai-in-2022-and-a-half-decade-in-review#/

Mdingi, Y. (2024). Adoption of custom artificial intelligence models in South African small and medium-sized enterprises (Master's thesis, University of the Witwatersrand, Johannesburg (South Africa).

Meager, R. (2019, January). Understanding the Average Impact of Microcredit Expansions: A Bayesian Hierarchical Analysis of Seven Randomized Experiments. *American Economic Journal. Applied Economics*, *11*(1), 57–91. https://www.aeaweb.org/articles?id=10.1257/app.20170299. DOI: 10.1257/app.20170299

Mebratie, E., Shanbel, B., Awoke, A., & Dessalegne, B. (2025). Knowledge-based human resource management practices and organizational performance in selected universities of Amhara regional state, Ethiopia: The moderating effect of intellectual capital. *Cogent Business & Management*, *12*(1), 2491688. DOI: 10.1080/23311975.2025.2491688

Meija, J. F. (2008). Tourism as a driver of economic development: The Colombian experience. *Violette Reihe*, *26*, 1–36.

Meng, X. (2024). Optimization of algorithmic efficiency in AI: Addressing computational complexity and scalability challenges. *Applied and Computational Engineering*, *45*(1), 305–311. DOI: 10.54254/2755-2721/45/20241637

Mhlanga, D. (2021). Artificial intelligence in the industry 4.0, and its impact on poverty, innovation, infrastructure development, and the sustainable development goals: Lessons from emerging economies? *Sustainability (Basel)*, *13*(11), 5788. DOI: 10.3390/su13115788

Mhlongo, T., & Daya, P. (2023). Challenges faced by small, medium and micro enterprises in Gauteng: A case for entrepreneurial leadership as an essential tool for success. *Southern African Journal of Entrepreneurship and Small Business Management*, *15*(1), a591. DOI: 10.4102/sajesbm.v15i1.591

Michael, O. (2025). Maximising the Potentials of Small and Medium Scale Business Enterprises in Developing Nations Through the Use of Artificial Intelligence: AI Adoption by SMEs in …. The Future of Small Business in Industry 5.0. DOI: [HTML]DOI: 10.4018/979-8-3693-7362-0.ch009

Ministry of Electronics and Information Technology [MEIT]. (2024). *10fcadec-462c330211502fed3d24ea83*.

Ministry of MSME. (2022). *What is the definition of MSME? | Ministry of Micro, Small & Medium Enterprises*. Msme.gov.in. https://msme.gov.in/faqs/q1-what-definition-msme

Mohib, M., Khan, F. K., El Burari, E. R., & Ali, S. (2025). The Challenges and Limitations of Artificial Intelligence Adoption in Small and Medium-Sized Enterprises. *Review Journal of Social Psychology & Social Works*, *3*(1), 292–303. DOI: 10.71145/rjsp.v3i1.99

Molina-Carmona, R., & García-Peñalvo, F. J. (2024). Safeguarding Knowledge: Ethical Artificial Intelligence Governance in the University Digital Transformation. In *Advanced Technologies and the University of the Future* (pp. 201–220). Springer Nature Switzerland.

Mondal, S., Singh, S., & Gupta, H. (2025). Exploring barriers to innovative marketing in MSMES: An analysis using a BWM-ISM multi-criteria decision-making framework. [HTML]. *Journal of Multi-Criteria Decision Analysis*, *32*(1), e70005. DOI: 10.1002/mcda.70005

Morandini, S., Fraboni, F., De Angelis, M., Puzzo, G., Giusino, D., & Pietrantoni, L. (2023). The Impact of Artificial Intelligence on Workers' skills: Upskilling and Reskilling in Organisations. *Informing Science*, *26*(1), 39–68. DOI: 10.28945/5078

Morley, J., Hine, E., Roberts, H., Sirbu, R., Ashrafian, H., Blease, C., Boyd, M., Chen, J. L., Filho, A. C., Coiera, E., Cohen, G. I., Fiske, A., Jayakumar, N., Kerasidou, A., Mandreoli, F., McCradden, M. D., Namuganza, S., Nsoesie, E. O., Parikh, R. B., & Floridi, L. (2025). Global Health in the Age of AI: Charting a Course for Ethical Implementation and Societal Benefit. *Minds and Machines*, *35*(3), 31. Advance online publication. DOI: 10.1007/s11023-025-09730-3

Mourtzis, D., Angelopoulos, J., & Panopoulos, N. (2022). A Literature Review of the Challenges and Opportunities of the Transition from Industry 4.0 to Society 5.0. *Energies*, *15*(17), 6276. DOI: 10.3390/en15176276

Muchie, M., & Bekele, E. (2009). *Promoting micro, small and medium Enterprises (MSMEs) for sustainable rural Livelihood*. https://vbn.aau.dk/files/17023673/DIIPER_wp_11.pdf

Mugisha, J., Adyanga, A. F., & Ocan, J. (2025). The Role of Artificial Intelligence (AI) in Transforming Small and Medium Enterprises (SMEs): A Narrative Review. *Applied Data Science and Analysis*, *2025*, 112–117. DOI: 10.58496/ADSA/2025/007

Mugwagwa, J., Banda, G., Ozor, N., Bolo, M., & Oriama, R. (2022). Optimising governance capabilities for science, research and innovation in Africa. *Technology in Society*, *68*, 101804. DOI: 10.1016/j.techsoc.2021.101804

Musdalifah, S., & Hariyanto, W. (2024). *AIS Revolutionizes MSMEs, Enhancing Global Financial Transparency*. Indonesian Journal of Law and Economics Review., DOI: 10.21070/ijler.v19i2.1079

Mutasa, E. T., Dhiwwale, C., & Gopal, A. (2024). Artificial Intelligence in Developing Economies: Unpacking Business Innovations, Prospects, and Challenges. *International Journal of Academic Research in Business & Social Sciences*, *14*(11), 586–601. DOI: 10.6007/IJARBSS/v14-i11/23529

Nadi, A. H., Ahshan, K. A., Rahman, S., & Sofin, M. R. (2024). The role of artificial intelligence in business management: The future of small and medium-sized enterprise. In *Utilizing AI and Smart Technology to Improve Sustainability in Entrepreneurship* (pp. 117–133). IGI Global. [HTML], DOI: 10.4018/979-8-3693-1842-3.ch008

Nagar, S., Afaq, A., & Narula, S. (2025). Shaping the Future of Emerging Economies. In Gaur, L. (Ed.), *Generative Artificial Intelligence and Ethics: Standards, Guidelines, and Best Practices* (pp. 143–168). IGI Global., https://doi.org/, DOI: 10.4018/979-8-3693-3691-5.ch007

Naidoo, P., & Sibanda, M. (2024). Emerging Trends and Future Directions of the Industrial Internet of Things. In Odhiambo, M. O., & Mwashita, W. (Eds.), *From Internet of Things to Internet of Intelligence* (pp. 91–110). Springer Nature Switzerland., DOI: 10.1007/978-3-031-55718-7_5

Naik, P. (2025, June 5). *The Future of AI in the Global South: Trends, Challenges, and Opportunities*. Geojuristoday. https://www.geojuristoday.in/post/the-future-of-ai-in-the-global-south-trends-challenges-and-opportunities

Nambisan, S., Wright, M., & Feldman, M. (2017). The digital transformation of innovation and entrepreneurship: Progress, challenges and key themes. *Research Policy*, *46*(3), 333–338. DOI: 10.1016/j.respol.2017.01.003

Nandeeswariah, K., & Ramana, A. V. (2021). Status And Growth Of Micro, Small & Medium Enterprises (Msmes) Post Msmed 2006 Act Implimentation In India. *Turkish Online Journal of Qualitative Inquiry*, *12*(6). https://search.ebscohost.com/login.aspx?direct=true&profile=ehost&scope=site&authtype=crawler&jrnl=13096591&AN=160450965&h=MGhWcU20uszmDPKHnmSMigr79bkuhUIJ2mZ0cekf7infNX2lLb4QVL4w5z4W9g2KCqjFOy3ovDncKQJ1yuU2Sw%3D%3D&crl=c

NASSCOM. (2023). AI Adoption Trends in Indian MSMEs. National Association of Software and Service Companies. https://nasscom.in/ai-msme-report

National Observatory of Technology and Society (ONTSI)(2024). *Brújula | Indicadores de uso de inteligencia artificial en las empresas españolas 2023*. Red.es

Ndabeni-Abrahams, S. T. (2024). Determinants of a Digital Work System for Financing SMMEs in South Africa (Master's thesis, University of the Witwatersrand, Johannesburg (South Africa).

Nguyen, N., Subhan, F., Williams, K., & Chan, C. B. (2020). Barriers and mitigating strategies to healthcare access in Indigenous communities of Canada: A narrative review. *Health Care*, *8*(2), 112. Advance online publication. DOI: 10.3390/healthcare8020112 PMID: 32357396

Niguse, T., & Borji, B. (2025). Mediation Effect of Human Capital Among Strategic Innovation and Competitive Advantage: A Case of SMEs in Ethiopia. *International Journal of Global Business and Competitiveness*, *20*(1), 23–32. DOI: 10.1007/s42943-025-00114-z

Nijiati, M., Zhang, Z., Abulizi, A., Miao, H., Tuluhong, A., Quan, S., Guo, L., Xu, T., & Zou, X. (2021). Deep learning assistance for tuberculosis diagnosis with chest radiography in low-resource settings. *Journal of X-Ray Science and Technology*, *29*(5), 785–796. DOI: 10.3233/XST-210894

Nkontwana, P. S. (2022). African entrepreneurship: An exploration of innovation hubs as development institutions (Doctoral dissertation, Stellenbosch: Stellenbosch University).

Nursini, N. (2020). Micro, small, and medium enterprises (MSMEs) and poverty reduction: Empirical evidence from Indonesia. *Development Studies Research*, *7*(1), 153–166. DOI: 10.1080/21665095.2020.1823238

O'Sullivan, M., & Kearney, G. (2018). Virtual Reality (VR) Technology: Empowering Managers to Reduce and Eliminate Accessibility Barriers for People with Autism Spectrum Disorders. *Studies in Health Technology and Informatics*, *256*, 253–261. DOI: 10.3233/978-1-61499-923-2-253 PMID: 30371482

Okour, M. K., Chong, C. W., & Fattah, F. A. M. (2021). Knowledge management systems usage: Application of diffusion of innovation theory. *Global Knowledge, Memory and Communication*, *70*(8/9), 756–776. DOI: 10.1108/GKMC-08-2020-0117

Olanrewaju, G. S., Seun Bunmi Adebayo, S. B., Omotosho, A. Y., & Charles Falajiki Olajide, C. F. (2021). Left behind? The effects of digital gaps on e-learning in rural secondary schools and remote communities across Nigeria during the COVID19 pandemic. *International Journal of Educational Research Open*, *2*, 100092. DOI: 10.1016/j.ijedro.2021.100092 PMID: 35059671

Oldemeyer, L., Jede, A., & Teuteberg, F. (2024). *Investigation of artificial intelligence in SMEs: A systematic review of the state of the art and the main implementation challenges*. Management Review Quarterly., DOI: 10.1007/s11301-024-00405-4

Omokhoa, N. H. E., Odionu, N. C. S., Azubuike, N. C., & Sule, N. K. (2024). AI-Powered Fintech innovations for credit scoring, debt recovery, and financial access in Microfinance and SMEs. *Gulf Journal of Advanced Business Research*, *2*(6), 411–422. DOI: 10.51594/gjabr.v2i6.55

Organisation for Economic Co-operation and Development (OECD). (2023). *Skill needs and policies in the age of artificial intelligence*. OECD Publishing., DOI: 10.1787/08785bba-e

Organisation for Economic Co-operation and Development [OECD]. (2021). *The digital transformation of SMEs*. OECD Publishing. https://doi.org/DOI: 10.1787/bdb9256a-en

Organisation for Economic Co-operation and Development [OECD]. (2025). *The Adoption of Artificial Intelligence in Firms: New Evidence for Policymaking*. OECD Publishing. https://doi.org/DOI: 10.1787/f9ef33c3-en

Otieno, P. O., & Busili, P. A. (2024). A Research on Labor, Finance, Technology, and Sustainable Growth. *International Journal of Innovative Science and Research Technology*, *9*(9), 3570–3597.

Oyedokun, T. T., & Ishola, J. A. (2025). Leveraging Artificial Intelligence (AI) for Resilience in Industry 5.0: Strategies for Small Businesses. In Insights Into Digital Business, Human Resource Management, and Competitiveness (pp. 35-68). IGI Global Scientific Publishing.

Palacios, F. D., Perez-Uribe, R. I., Ramírez, I. R., & Salcedo-Perez, C. (2020). Orientation to Organizational Learning and Its Effects on Innovation and Performance: The Colombian MSMEs Case. In Masouras, A., Maris, G., & Kavoura, A. (Eds.), *Entrepreneurial Development and Innovation in Family Businesses and SMEs* (pp. 167–186). IGI Global Scientific Publishing., DOI: 10.4018/978-1-7998-3648-3.ch010

Pandey, A. (2025). *Big Tech has AI, but Indian MSMEs need something more—Desi AI. The Economic Times.* https://economictimes.indiatimes.com/small-biz/sme-sector/big-tech-has-ai-but-indian-msmes-need-something-moredesi-ai/articleshow/122015182.cms

Panigrahi, R. R., Shrivastava, A. K., Qureshi, K. M., Mewada, B. G., Alghamdi, S. Y., Almakayeel, N., Almuflih, A. S., & Qureshi, M. R. N. (2023). AI Chatbot Adoption in SMEs for Sustainable Manufacturing Supply Chain Performance: A Mediational Research in an Emerging Country. *Sustainability (Basel)*, *15*(18), 13743. DOI: 10.3390/su151813743

Pankiv, K., & Kloetzer, L. (2024). Does Using Artificial Intelligence in Citizen Science Support Volunteers' Learning? An Experimental Study in Ornithology. *Citizen Science: Theory and Practice*, *9*(1), 36. Advance online publication. DOI: 10.5334/cstp.733

Patil, K. P., Pramod, D., & Bharathi, S. V. (2023, October). MSMEs readiness for adopting artificial intelligence and machine learning. In *2023 International Conference on Advanced Computing Technologies and Applications (ICACTA)* (pp. 1–6). IEEE. DOI: 10.1109/ICACTA58201.2023.10392396

Patra, S. (2024). AI Implementation. In *MSME Industrial Sectors*. Educational Administration Theory and Practices., DOI: 10.53555/kuey.v30i5.3725

Paul, I., & Roy, G. (2025). How eco-service quality affects tourist engagement behaviour in ecotourism: Eco-consciousness and eco activity-based learning and SOR Theory. *Tourism Recreation Research*, *50*(2), 385–401. DOI: 10.1080/02508281.2023.2275240

Peretz-Andersson, E., Tabares, S., Mikalef, P., & Parida, V. (2024). Artificial intelligence implementation in manufacturing SMEs: A resource orchestration approach. *International Journal of Information Management*, *77*, 102781. DOI: 10.1016/j.ijinfomgt.2024.102781

Pérez-Uribe, R. I., Vargas-Ramírez, I., & Ocampo-Guzmán, D. (2024). *Governance Model from the VUCA Perspective: Proposal for the Department of Quindío*. IGI Global Scientific Publishing., DOI: 10.4018/979-8-3693-0720-5.ch007

Perrotta, C., & Selwyn, N. (2020). Deep learning goes to school: Toward a relational understanding of AI in education. *Learning, Media and Technology*, *45*(3), 251–269. DOI: 10.1080/17439884.2020.1686017

Perspektiven schaffen. (2024). *Förderprogramm "go-digital" bis 2024 verlängert*. Bundesministerium für Bildung, Familie, Senioren, Frauen und Jugend. https://www.perspektiven-schaffen.de/ps-de/unternehmen-arbeitgeber/tipps-fuer-kleine-und-mittlere-unternehmen-kmu-/-foerderprogramm-go-digital-bis-2024-verlaengert-194698

Peterson, M. N., Larson, L. R., Hipp, A., Beall, J. M., Lerose, C., Desrochers, H., Lauder, S., Torres, S., Tarr, N. A., Stukes, K., Stevenson, K., & Martin, K. L. (2024). Birdwatching linked to increased psychological well-being on college campuses: A pilot-scale experimental study. *Journal of Environmental Psychology*, *96*, 102306. DOI: 10.1016/j.jenvp.2024.102306

Pillai, R., & Sivathanu, B. (2020). Adoption of AI-based chatbots for hospitality and tourism. *International Journal of Contemporary Hospitality Management*, *32*(10), 3199–3226. DOI: 10.1108/IJCHM-04-2020-0259

Prasetyo, R. J., & Andrilla, R. (2025). Balikpapan Micro, Small, and Medium Enterprises (MSMEs) and Artificial Intelligence Adoption: TOE Framework. *Jurnal GeoEkonomi*, *16*(1), 11–20. Advance online publication. DOI: 10.36277/geoekonomi.v16i1.540

Purnomo, S., & Purwandari, S. (2025). A Comprehensive Micro, Small, and Medium Enterprise Empowerment Model for Developing Sustainable Tourism Villages in Rural Communities: A Perspective. *Sustainability (Basel)*, *17*(4), 1368. DOI: 10.3390/su17041368

PWC. (2025). 54% of the companies have implemented AI for business_ PwC India survey.

Qu, C., & Kim, E. (2025). Investigating AI Adoption, Knowledge Absorptive Capacity, and Open Innovation in Chinese Apparel MSMEs: An Extended TAM-TOE Model with PLS-SEM Analysis. *Sustainability (Basel)*, *17*(5), 1873. Advance online publication. DOI: 10.3390/su17051873

Quindío, C. (2024). Economic indicators in birdwatching. *Regional Reports*, *22*(3), 45–50.

Radanliev, P. (2025). AI ethics: Integrating transparency, fairness, and privacy in AI development. *Applied Artificial Intelligence*, *39*(1), e2463722. Advance online publication. DOI: 10.1080/08839514.2025.2463722

Rahaman, M., Putra, K. T., Irawan, B., & Biyanto, T. R. (2025). Industrial Evolution: The Integration of AI in Robotics and Drone Systems. In Gupta, B. B., & Colace, F. (Eds.), (pp. 85–114). Advances in Computational Intelligence and Robotics. IGI Global., DOI: 10.4018/979-8-3693-2707-4.ch005

Rahman, F., Made, P., Kutanegara, Susilastuti, D.H., and Bachruddin, Z. (2025). Barriers to Local Community Involvement in Community-Based Tourism Development: Evidence from Area Model of Conservation and Education (AMCE) Oro-Oro Ombo Village Batu City Indonesia. *Journal of Tourism Sustainability*, 4(2):133-149. January 2025. DOI: . v4i3.130DOI: 10.35313/jtospolban

Rahman, M., Ming, T. H., Baigh, T. A., & Sarker, M. (2023). Adoption of artificial intelligence in banking services: An empirical analysis. [HTML]. *International Journal of Emerging Markets*, *18*(10), 4270–4300. DOI: 10.1108/IJOEM-06-2020-0724

Ramya, J., Yerraguravagari, S. S., Gaikwad, S., & Gupta, R. K. (2024). AI and Machine Learning in Predictive Analytics: Revolutionizing Business Strategies through Big Data Insights. Library of Progress-Library Science, Information Technology & Computer, 44(3).

Rane, N., Paramesha, M., Choudhary, S., & Rane, J. (2024). Artificial Intelligence in Sales and Marketing: Enhancing Customer Satisfaction, Experience and Loyalty. SSRN *Electronic Journal*. DOI: 10.2139/ssrn.4831903

Rane, N., Choudhary, S., & Rane, J. (2024). Artificial intelligence for enhancing resilience. *Journal of Applied Artificial Intelligence*, *5*(2), 1–33. DOI: 10.48185/jaai.v5i2.1053

Ransbotham, S., Khodabandeh, S., Kiron, D., LaFountain, B., & Kiron, D. (2022). *The cultural benefits of artificial intelligence in organizations*. MIT Sloan Management Review and Boston Consulting Group. 63270, 1-21. https://web-assets.bcg.com/85/90/95939185404cbd901aba0d54f1d7/the-cultural-benefits-of-artificial-intelligence-in-the-enterprise-r.pdf

Rashid, A. B., & Kausik, A. K. (2024). AI Revolutionizing Industries Worldwide: A Comprehensive Overview of Its Diverse Applications. *Hybrid Advances*, *7*(100277), 100277–100277. DOI: 10.1016/j.hybadv.2024.100277

Rawas, S. (2024). AI: The future of humanity. *Discover Artificial Intelligence*, *4*(1), 1–14. DOI: 10.1007/s44163-024-00118-3

Razorpay. (2024). *MSME Full From & Definition_ Latest MSME Turnover Limit & Classification in 2025*. https://razorpay.com/learn/new-msme-definition-turnover-2020/

Rens, V. (2021). Entrepreneurial marketing as a tool used by business incubators to effectively support SMEs in South Africa (Doctoral dissertation, Cape Peninsula University of Technology).

Rew, J., Park, S., Cho, Y., Hwang, E., & Jung, S. (2019, October). Animal Movement Prediction Based on Predictive Recurrent Neural Network. *Sensors (Basel)*, *19*(20), 4411. DOI: 10.3390/s19204411 PMID: 31614699

Rogers, E. M. (2003). *Diffusion of innovations* (5th ed.). Free Press.

Rony, P., & Yahaya, N. A. (2021). The role of artificial intelligence (ai) in transforming the human capital management within the smes across the mena region: An empirical investigation. [IJMHRM]. *Int. J. Mark. Hum. Resour. Manage.*, *6*, 6–24.

Rosydiana, E., & Narsa, I. M. (2024). Financial sustainability of MSMEs in birdwatching tourism. *Southeast Asian Journal of Tourism*, *8*(2), 89–103.

Rosyidiana, R. N. & Narsa, I. M. (2024). Micro, small, and medium-sized enterprises (MSMEs) during the post-pandemic economic recovery period: digitalization, literation, innovation, and its impact on …. Cogent Business & Management. https://doi.org/ tandfonline.comDOI: 10.1080/23311975.2024.2342488

Saad, N. A., Elgazzar, S., & Mlaker Kac, S. (2022). Investigating the Impact of resilience, responsiveness, and quality on customer loyalty of MSMEs: Empirical evidence. Sustainability. https://doi.org/ mdpi.comDOI: 10.3390/su14095011

Sahoo, P., & Ashwani, . (2020). COVID-19 and Indian Economy: Impact on Growth, Manufacturing, Trade and MSME Sector. *Global Business Review*, *21*(5), 1159–1183. DOI: 10.1177/0972150920945687

Sahu, C. K., & Panda, R. K. (2024). Evaluating the relationship between entrepreneurial ecosystem, resilience and SME performance in post-pandemic period. *Journal of Entrepreneurship and Public Policy*, *13*(3), 491–506. DOI: 10.1108/JEPP-12-2023-0136

Saifurrahman, A., & Kassim, S. H. (2024). Regulatory issues inhibiting the financial inclusion: a case study among Islamic banks and MSMEs in Indonesia. Qualitative Research in Financial Markets, 16(4), 589-617. DOI iium.edu.myDOI: 10.1108/QRFM-05-2022-0086

Salesforce. (2024, December 4). *New research reveals SMBs with AI adoption see stronger revenue growth*. https://www.salesforce.com/news/stories/smbs-ai-trends-2025/

Saluja, A. (2023). Public–private partnerships in EdTech for transforming rural India: how start-ups are shaping the post-COVID landscape. In India's technology-led development: managing transitions to a digital future (pp. 105-119). DOI: 10.1142/9789811271786_0006

Sampath, P. G. (2021). Governing Artificial Intelligence in an Age of Inequality. *Global Policy*, *12*(S6), 21–31. Advance online publication. DOI: 10.1111/1758-5899.12940

Sánchez, E., Calderón, R., & Herrera, F. (2025). Artificial Intelligence Adoption in SMEs: Survey Based on TOE–DOI Framework, Primary Methodology and Challenges. *Applied Sciences (Basel, Switzerland)*, *15*(12), 6465. DOI: 10.3390/app15126465

Sanka, N. V. (2025). Conversational AI for Enterprise Data Analytics and Governance: A Comprehensive Framework for Natural Language-Driven Business Intelligence. *International Journal of Scientific Research in Computer Science Engineering and Information Technology*, *11*(2), 3922–3928. DOI: 10.32628/CSEIT25111329

Santos, A. D. M., & Sant'Anna, Â. M. O. (2024). Industry 4.0 technologies for sustainability within small and medium enterprises: A systematic literature review and future directions. *Journal of Cleaner Production*, *467*, 143023. DOI: 10.1016/j.jclepro.2024.143023

Santosa, A. D., & Surgawati, I. (2024). Artificial Intelligence (AI) Adoption as Marketing Tools among Micro, Small, and Medium Enterprises (MSMEs) in Indonesia. *Jurnal Sosial Humaniora*, *17*(1), 91. DOI: 10.12962/j24433527.v17i1.20520

Saranya, T. S., Babhuti, K., Jyoti, D., Kaur, H., & Kapoor, T. (2025). The Evolving Role of Artificial Intelligence (AI) in Human Resource Management (HRM). In Kapoor, T., Singh, A., Sahay, K., Kaur, H., & Verma, R. (Eds.), *Sustainable Management Practices for Employee Retention and Recruitment* (pp. 301–310). IGI Global Scientific Publishing., DOI: 10.4018/979-8-3693-8679-8.ch015

Sastry, K., Nguyen, T., & Roy, D. (2023). AI and satellite monitoring of avian biodiversity. *Ecological Informatics*, *74*, 101518. DOI: 10.1016/j.ecoinf.2023.101518

Satyam, P., Geetha, K., Shashikala, K. S., & Kumar, N. A. (2023). AI-enabled edge computing models: Trends, developments, and future implications. *2023 2nd International Conference on Edge Computing and Applications (ICECAA)*, Namakkal, India, 63-67. https://doi.org/DOI: 10.1109

Saunders, M. N., Lewis, P., & Thornhill, A. (2019). *Research methods for business students* (8th ed.). Pearson.

Scholtz, E., Cronje, L., & Cilliers, J. O. (2023). Quality service SMMEs in South African townships: A comparative study of the Soweto and Diepsloot townships. *Journal of Contemporary Management*, *20*(2), 199–235. DOI: 10.35683/jcman1037.220

Schwoerer, T., & Dawson, C. (2022b). Economic impacts of birdwatching in Alaska. *Ecological Economics*, *190*, 107215. DOI: 10.1016/j.ecolecon.2021.107215

Schwoerer, T., & Dawson, N. G. (2022a). Small sight—Big might: Economic impact of bird tourism shows opportunities for rural communities and biodiversity conservation. *PLoS One*, *17*(7), e0268594. DOI: 10.1371/journal.pone.0268594 PMID: 35793337

Sekercioglu, C. H. (2022). Birdwatchers as conservation allies. *Global Ecology and Conservation*, *34*, e02033. DOI: 10.1016/j.gecco.2022.e02033

Selamat, M. A., & Windasari, N. A. (2021). Chatbot for SMEs: Integrating customer and business owner perspectives. *Technology in Society*, *66*, 101685. DOI: 10.1016/j.techsoc.2021.101685

Shakya, T., Sharma, M., Kathuria, S., Yamsani, N., Singh, R., & Negi, P. (2023, July). Micro, small, and medium enterprises' advancement with artificial intelligence and robots. In *2023 IEEE World Conference on Applied Intelligence and Computing (AIC)* (pp. 783–788). IEEE. DOI: 10.1109/AIC57670.2023.10263845

Sharma, G., Chopra, P., & Singh, S. (2025). Unveiling Security Vulnerabilities in Generative AI. In Gaur, L. (Ed.), *Generative Artificial Intelligence and Ethics: Standards* (pp. 267–286). Guidelines, and Best Practices., DOI: 10.4018/979-8-3693-3691-5.ch012

Sharma, P., Shah, J., & Patel, R. (2022). Artificial intelligence framework for MSME sectors focusing on design and manufacturing industries. *Materials Today: Proceedings, 62*, 6962–6966. Advance online publication. DOI: 10.1016/j.matpr.2021.12.360

Shetty, A. (n.d.). *What is conversational AI?-Benefits and Examples*. https://yellow.ai/conversational-ai/

Shvetsova, S. (2024). Increasing the attractiveness of electric vehicles for consumers in cold climates. In *E3S Web of Conferences* (Vol. 471, p. 06014). EDP Sciences., DOI: 10.1051/e3sconf/202447106014

Siddiqui, A. (2021). SWOT analysis (or SWOT matrix) tool as a strategic planning and management technique in the health care industry and its advantages. *Biomedical Journal of Scientific & Technical Research, 40*(2), 32035–32042. DOI: 10.26717/BJSTR.2021.40.006419

Singgalen, Y. A., Purnomo, H. D., & Sembiring, I. (2021). Exploring MSMEs Cybersecurity Awareness and Risk Management: Information Security Awareness. IJCCS (Indonesian Journal of Computing and Cybernetics Systems), 15(3), 233-244. https://doi.org/ ugm.ac.idDOI: 10.22146/ijccs.67010

Singh, A. K., Taterh, S., Kaushik, A., & Goswami, A. (2025). The Role of AI in Digital Transformation. In Misra, S., Kaushik, M., Jain, A., & Banerjee, C. (Eds.), (pp. 109–136). Advances in Computational Intelligence and Robotics. IGI Global., DOI: 10.4018/979-8-3693-8009-3.ch006

Singh, D., Khamba, J. S., & Nanda, T. (2018). Problems and prospects of Indian MSMEs: A literature review. *International Journal of Business Excellence, 15*(2), 129. DOI: 10.1504/IJBEX.2018.091923

Singh, P. (2025). AI and Financial Risk Management Revolutionizing Risk Assessment and Mitigation. In Derbali, A. M. S. (Ed.), (pp. 373–404). Advances in Computational Intelligence and Robotics. IGI Global., DOI: 10.4018/979-8-3373-1200-2.ch019

Sinha, A., Banerjee, D., & Rajan, M. (2022). AI in manufacturing: Evidence from MSMEs in India. *Technology in Society, 68*, 101920. DOI: 10.1016/j.techsoc.2022.101920

Sinuhaji, F. G., Sibarani, H. J., & Pakpahan, V. M. (2024). MSMEs and the Role of Technology in Achieving Business Sustainability. [JAIEA]. *Journal of Artificial Intelligence and Engineering Applications*, *4*(1), 588–593. DOI: 10.59934/jaiea.v4i1.724

Smart, A., Zhao, Y., & Curran, D. (2023). *Chinese artificial intelligence governance platforms 2.0: The belt and road edition*. Routledge. DOI: 10.4324/9781003365877-19

SMEDAN, & NBS. (2012). Preliminary report of micro, small and medium enterprises in Nigeria. In www.nigerianstat.gov.ng(pp. 1–171). https://www.nigerianstat.gov.ng/pdfuploads/MSMES.pdf

Smirnov, A., & Starov, E. (2022, May). Bad News Turned Good: Reversal under Censorship. *American Economic Journal. Microeconomics*, *14*(2), 506–560. DOI: 10.1257/mic.20190379

Soni, P., & Krishnan, T., R. (. (2014). Frugal innovation: Aligning theory, practice, and public policy. *Journal of Indian Business Research*, *6*(1), 29–47. DOI: 10.1108/JIBR-03-2013-0025

Srinivasan, V. (2016). Will Financial Auditors Become Extinct? In *Intelligent Enterprise in the Era of Big Data, The* (pp. 171–186). Wiley., DOI: 10.1002/9781118834725.ch7

Startup India. (2022). Case Compendium: AI for MSMEs. Department for Promotion of Industry and Internal Trade (DPIIT), Government of India. https://www.startupindia.gov.in

Steven, R., Morrison, C., & Castley, J. G. (2014). Birdwatching and avitourism: A global review of research and practice. *Journal of Sustainable Tourism*, *22*(6), 850–873. DOI: 10.1080/09669582.2013.862401

Steven, R., Smart, J., Morrison, C., & Castley, G. (2016). Using a choice experiment and birder preferences to guide bird-conservation funding. October 2016. *Conservation Biology*, *31*(4), 818–827. Advance online publication. DOI: 10.1111/cobi.12849 PMID: 27696549

Stojčić, N., Dabić, M., & Musteen, M. (2024). With a little help from my friends: Institutional obstacles, networking, and SME exporting in emerging European and Asian economies. *International Business Review*, *33*(3), 102258. DOI: 10.1016/j.ibusrev.2024.102258

Subramanyam, S. V.Sasikiran Vepanambattu Subramanyam. (2025). Cloud-based enterprise systems: Bridging scalability and security in healthcare and finance. *IJSAT-International Journal on Science and Technology*, *16*(1), 2305. Advance online publication. DOI: 10.71097/IJSAT.v16.i1.2305

Sullivan, B. L., Aycrigg, J. L., Barry, J. H., Bonney, R. E., Bruns, N., Cooper, C. B., Damoulas, T., Dhondt, A. A., Dietterich, T., Farnsworth, A., Fink, D., Fitzpatrick, J. W., Fredericks, T., Gerbracht, J., Gomes, C., Hochachka, W. M., Iliff, M. J., Lagoze, C., La Sorte, F. A., & Kelling, S. (2014a). The eBird enterprise: An integrated approach to development and application of citizen science. *Biological Conservation*, *169*, 31–40. DOI: 10.1016/j.biocon.2013.11.003

Sultana, S. T., & Rao, T. V. N. (2025). Role of ai-powered crm in business. In *Managing Customer-Centric Strategies in the Digital Landscape* (pp. 223–254). IGI Global. [HTML], DOI: 10.4018/979-8-3693-5668-5.ch009

Suryani, I. P., Suri, A. G., & Shafira, Z. (2023). How fintech peer-to-peer lending affected MSMEs' financial Access: Case Study Amartha. *InFestasi*, *19*(2), 166–181. DOI: 10.21107/infestasi.v19i2.22921

Su, X., Zeng, L., Shao, B., & Lin, B. (2025). Data-driven optimization for production planning with multiple demand features. *Kybernetes*, *54*(1), 110–133. DOI: 10.1108/K-04-2023-0690

Syed, N., Anwar, A., Baig, Z., & Zeadally, S. (2025). Artificial intelligence as a service (AIaaS) for cloud, fog and the edge: State-of-the-art practices. *ACM Computing Surveys*, *57*(8), 211. DOI: 10.1145/3712016

Tapp, F. W. (2023). Breaking barriers or widening divides? An examination of survey responses. *Journal of Innovations*. https://doi.org/DOI: 10.62470/4a253027

Technology Review, M. I. T. (2025). Inside India's scramble for AI independence _. *MIT Technology Review*.

Telukdarie, A., Dube, T., Munsamy, M., Murulane, K., & Mongwe, R. (2024). Navigating digital challenges for SMEs: a two-tier approach to risks mitigation and sustainability. Sustainability, 16(14), 5857. https://doi.org/ mdpi.comDOI: 10.3390/su16145857

Teo, J. (2023). Overcoming communication barriers to facilitate healthcare access for people with intellectual disability. *The Singapore Family Physician*, *48*(7), 18–21. Advance online publication. DOI: 10.33591/sfp.48.7.u3

Textile Magazine. (2024). *Tirupur's Journey Towards Becoming a Global Hub for Sustainable Textile and Apparel Manufacturing - The Textile Magazine*. https://www.indiantextilemagazine.in/tirupurs-journey-towards-becoming-a-global-hub-for-sustainable-textile-and-apparel-manufacturing/

The ASEAN Secretariat. (2025). *Definitions of MSME in ASEAN Member States*. https://asean.org/wp-content/uploads/2025/02/Definition-of-MSME-in-ASEAN-Member-States.pdf

The United Nations Conference on Trade and Development [UNCTAD]. (2025a). *Technology and Innovation Report 2025: Inclusive artificial intelligence for development*. United Nations Conference on Trade and Development. https://unctad.org/publication/technology-and-innovation-report-2025

The United Nations Conference on Trade and Development [UNCTAD]. (2025b). *AI market projected to hit $4.8 trillion by 2033*. https://unctad.org/news/ai-market-projected-hit-48-trillion-2033-emerging-dominant-frontier-technology

Timothy, D. J., & Boyd, S. W. (2015). Tourism and trails: Cultural, ecological and management issues (Vol. 64). Channel View Publications. https://books.google.com/books?hl=es&lr=&id=6PuTBQAAQBAJ&oi=fnd&pg=PP9&dq=Marketing+management+of+trails.&ots=sLOH0JaGl1&sig=dEJ35lgXcyv_wbbDvGiX7xVMDso#v=onepage&q=Marketing%20management%20of%20trails.&f=false

Tishtykbayeva, A. Z., Gelashvili, N. N., & Turusbekov, A. E. (2023). Artificial Intelligence Implementation in Small Businesses. *BULLETIN of the KARAGANDA UNIVERSITY ECONOMY SERIES*, *111*(3), 125–132. DOI: 10.31489/2023ec3/125-132

Tolossa, A. T., Singh, M., & Gautam, R. K. (2025). Bridging Competitive Advantage and Sustainable Development: The Moderating Role of Value Creation for Stakeholders in Ethiopian SMEs. *Business Strategy & Development*, *8*(1), e70066. DOI: 10.1002/bsd2.70066

Triandini, E., Wijaya, S. N., & Suniantara, P. K. (2024). Analysis of The Digital Technology Adoption by MSMEs Using Diffusion of Innovation. *Journal of System and Management Sciences*, *14*(4). Advance online publication. DOI: 10.33168/JSMS.2024.0415

Udeogu, A. C., & Okoye, I. E. (2024). Artificial intelligence and competitive advantage of micro, small and medium enterprises (MSMEs) in Anambra State. *Cross Current International Journal of Economics Management and Media Studies*, *6*(01), 1–9.

UK Information Commissioner's Office. (2025). *ICO regulatory sandbox: Enabling innovation in the public interest*. https://ico.org.uk/for-organisations/regulatory-sandbox/

Ulum Ilham, B., & Muawwal, A. (2024). AI Literacy Level in MSMEs Assisted by PLUT South Sulawesi. *Proceeding of Research and Civil Society Desemination*, *2*(1), 369–374. DOI: 10.37476/presed.v2i1.52

United Nations Development Programme (UNDP). (2025). *Bending the AI arc towards equity - United Nations Development Programme | UNDP*. Exposure. https://stories.undp.org/bending-the-ai-arc-towards-equity

Van Der Vlist, F., Helmond, A., & Ferrari, F. (2024). Big AI: Cloud infrastructure dependence and the industrialisation of artificial intelligence. *Big Data & Society*, *11*(1), 20539517241232630. DOI: 10.1177/20539517241232630

Vargas Ramírez, I. (2021). El estilo de la toma de decisiones de los gobernadores y su relación con los tipos de desempeño de la gestión pública y los nuevos enfoques de gobernanza en Colombia. Disponible en: http://hdl.handle.net/10882/11268

Vergara-Romero, A., Duran, J. L., Jimber-Del Rio, J. A., & Collado-Gonzalez, J. C. (2025, June). Business management of sustainable destinations and its effect on ecotourism entrepreneurship to mitigate overtourism. *Humanities & Social Sciences Communications*, *12*(1), 817. Advance online publication. DOI: 10.1057/s41599-025-05149-4

Vox News Feature (2025, March). *Colombia's* rise as a birdwatching paradise. *Vox Global Travel*, 28–33.

Vuyokazi, S. B. (2022). *A comparative analysis of the use of e-government services by small businesses*. University of Johannesburg.

Waghambare, M. A., Prabhu, S., & Ashok, P. (2024). Artificial Intelligence (AI)-Powered Chatbots for Marketing and Online Shopping. In Digital Technologies in Modeling and Management: Insights in Education and Industry (pp. 21-39). IGI Global. DOI: [HTML]DOI: 10.4018/978-1-6684-9576-6.ch002

Wäldchen, J., & Mäder, P. (2018). Machine learning for image-based species identification. *Methods in Ecology and Evolution*, *9*(11), 2216–2225. DOI: 10.1111/2041-210X.13075

Wamba-Taguimdje, S.-L., Fosso Wamba, S., Kala Kamdjoug, J. R., & Tchatchouang Wanko, C. E. (2020). Influence of artificial intelligence (AI) on firm performance: The business value of AI-based transformation projects. *Business Process Management Journal*, *26*(7), 1893–1924. DOI: 10.1108/BPMJ-10-2019-0411

Wang, Y. (2017). On the Mathematical Theories and Cognitive Foundations of Information. In IRMA (Information Resources Management Association)(Ed.) *Artificial Intelligence: Concepts, Methodologies, Tools, and Applications* (pp. 122-144), Hershey, PA (USA): IGI Global. https://doi.org/DOI: 10.4018/978-1-5225-1759-7.ch005

Wieland, A., & Durach, C. F. (2021). Two perspectives on supply chain resilience. *Journal of Business Logistics*, *42*(3), 315–322. DOI: 10.1111/jbl.12271

Williams, M. D., Rana, N. P., & Dwivedi, Y. K. (2015). The unified theory of acceptance and use of technology (UTAUT): A literature review. *Journal of Enterprise Information Management*, *28*(3), 443–488. DOI: 10.1108/JEIM-09-2014-0088

Wong, J. W., & Yap, K. H. A. (2024). Factors influencing the adoption of artificial intelligence in accounting among micro, small medium enterprises (MSMEs). *Quantum Journal of Social Sciences and Humanities*, *5*(1), 16–28. DOI: 10.55197/qjssh.v5i1.323

World Bank. (2023). *Digital Progress and Trends Report*. Www.worldbank.org. https://www.worldbank.org/en/publication/digital-progress-and-trends-report

World Bank. (2023). *SME finance policy guide: Creating an enabling environment for small businesses*. International Finance Corporation. https://www.ifc.org/smefinance

World Bank. (2025). *Financial inclusion overview*. https://www.worldbank.org/en/topic/financialinclusion/overview

World Economic Forum. (2024). The Future of MSMEs: AI and Digital Transformation. https://www.weforum.org/reports

World Economic Forum. (2025). *Global risks report 2025*. World Economic Forum. https://reports.weforum.org/docs/WEF_Global_Risks_Report_2025.pdf

World Travel & Tourism Council (2025, May 30). *Colombia travel & tourism economic impact factsheet* [PDF]. WTTC Research Hub. WTTC Research Hub website

Wulandari, A., & Diko, M. A. I. M. J. (2024). HR Management Transformation in Indonesia MSMEs: The Role of AI in SOP Making and Recruitment. *Journal of Ecohumanism*, *3*(7), 5325–5338. DOI: 10.62754/joe.v3i7.4641

Wu, S., & Wang, S. (2025). Exploring the impact of AI-enhanced virtual tourism on Tourists' pro-environmental behavior: A stimulus-organism-response model perspective. *Acta Psychologica*, *253*, 104773. DOI: 10.1016/j.actpsy.2025.104773 PMID: 39904230

Wüst, M., Maskut, N., Baumann, L., Heitplatz, V. N., Wilkens, L., Dirks, S., & Bühler, C. (2023). Easy reading – Keeping the user at the digital original: Assessment and potential use of Easy Reading for digital accessibility. In *Lecture Notes in Computer Science*. http://dx.doi.org/DOI: 10.1007/978-3-031-35897-5_34

Xu, S., Kee, K. F., Li, W., Yamamoto, M., & Riggs, R. E. (2023). Examining the Diffusion of Innovations from a Dynamic, Differential-Effects Perspective: A Longitudinal Study on AI Adoption Among Employees. *Communication Research*, *51*(7), 843–866. Advance online publication. DOI: 10.1177/00936502231191832

Yang, F., & Sheb, N. (2024, May). Automatic Bird Species Recognition from Images with Feature Enhancement and Contrastive Learning. *Applied Sciences (Basel, Switzerland)*, *14*(10), 4278. DOI: 10.3390/app14104278

Yoo, Y., Henfridsson, O., & Lyytinen, K. (2010). The new organizing logic of digital innovation: An agenda for information systems research. *Information Systems Research*, *21*(4), 724–735. DOI: 10.1287/isre.1100.0322

Zahin, A., & Shammi, M. (2024). Tourism trend in the Bangladesh Sundarbans Mangrove Forest: A PESTEL framework analysis focusing on sustainable ecotourism development. *Journal of Tourism and Heritage Research*, *7*(4), 40–63. https://www.jthr.es/index.php/journal/article/view/572

Zahra, F. P., & Suharto, Y. (2024). Innovative Business Models for Design Service Providers: Enhancing MSME Digital Transformation. *Journal of International Management Studies*, *2*(2), 205–210.

Zeren, S. K. (2025). From Vision to Reality: Digital Transformation for Sustainable Tourism in Dubai's Megaprojects. In Achieving Business Excellence Through Triple Transformation (pp. 79-120). IGI Global Scientific Publishing. DOI: [HTML]DOI: 10.4018/979-8-3693-9435-9.ch004

Zimmerman, A., Janhonen, J., & Beer, E. (2024). Human/AI relationships: Challenges, downsides, and impacts on human/human relationships. *AI and Ethics*, *4*(4), 1555–1567. DOI: 10.1007/s43681-023-00348-8

Zoho Creator. (2025). *AI-powered low-code application development platform _ Zoho Creator*. https://www.zoho.com/creator/ai-software-development-platform/

Zohuri, B. (2023). Artificial Super Intelligence (ASI) The Evolution of AI Beyond Human Capacity. *Current Trends in Engineering Science*, *3*(7), 1–5. DOI: 10.54026/CTES/1049

Zook, A. (2017). Game AGI Beyond Characters. In IRMA (Information Resources Management Association) (Ed.) *Artificial Intelligence: Concepts, Methodologies, Tools, and Applications* (pp. 463-484), Hershey, PA (USA): IGI Global. https://doi.org/DOI: 10.4018/978-1-5225-1759-7.ch020

Zopounidis, C., & Christos, C. (2024). The company of the future: Integrating sustainability, growth, and profitability in contemporary business models. *Development and Sustainability in Economics and Finance.*, *1*(June), 100003. DOI: 10.1016/j.dsef.2024.100003

# About the Contributors

**Gromyko Bongso**, S.E., M.M. was born in Jakarta, October 19, 1990. An entrepreneur with various F&B brands, a private company consultant, and a lecturer at BINUS University, BBS - Business Creation Alam Sutera. Received the 2019 Great Youth award from the Indonesian Ministry of Youth and Sports for his research work. Active as a researcher focusing on the fields of management, entrepreneurship and human resources.

**Vicky Djusmin** is an active author and educator in the field of Information Technology and Computer Science. He has published several reference books widely used in academia, including Web Design: HTML, CSS, and JavaScript, Database Systems, Theory and Practice of Database Systems, and Internet of Things. These works reflect his expertise in web development, database systems, and IoT technologies. In addition to his academic role, Vicky is actively involved in professional organizations. He serves as a board member of APTIKOM Region IX Sulawesi (Association of Higher Education in Informatics and Computers), a collaborative platform for IT and computer science institutions. He is also an active member of the Indonesian Lecturer Association (ADI), which aims to enhance the professionalism and national contribution of lecturers.

**Y. Fathima**, BBA.,MFC.,MBA.,M.Phil.,DGT.,Ph.D.,is a Professor in the Department of Commerce, School of Commerce at Jain (Deemed-to-be University) Bangalore. An accomplished educator with demonstrated ability to teach, motivate, and direct students while maintaining high interest and achievement. Articulate communicator able to effectively interact with diverse population of students at a variety of academic levels. She has 18 years of Teaching Experience and 10 years of Research experience. She has published papers in reputed journal and authored 4 books.

**Laxmana Goranta** is a seasoned academician with over 34 years of extensive teaching experience in both undergraduate (UG) and postgraduate (PG) levels. He is currently serving as an Associate Professor in the School of Commerce and Management Studies at Dayananda Sagar University, Bangalore. With a robust academic background and a strong research profile, Dr. Laxmana Rao has made significant contributions to the fields of Finance and Accounts, He obtained M. Com, M.B.A., M. Phil, and PhD degrees from reputed universities, reflecting his deep academic commitment and scholarly excellence. Throughout his career, Dr. Laxmana Rao G has honed his expertise in teaching and research. With 34 years of experience in higher education, he has taught a wide range of subjects related to finance and management. His teaching journey spans various academic levels, including UG and PG programs, where he has mentored and guided students toward achieving academic success. His ability to effectively communicate complex concepts and foster critical thinking has made him a respected figure in the academic community. In addition to his teaching career, Dr. Laxmana Rao has 15 years of dedicated research experience. His research contributions primarily focus on Finance and Accounts, areas in which he continues to explore emerging trends, analyze financial systems, and contribute to the academic discourse. Dr. Laxmana Rao has authored five books on various topics within his field, which have been widely recognized for their academic rigor and practical relevance. His research papers have been published in over 20 journals, including prestigious publications indexed in Scopus. He received the International Research Award from the Institute of Chartered Accountants of India in 2024 for his paper on International Taxation. His work reflects his commitment to advancing knowledge and addressing contemporary challenges in the financial and accounting domains. Dr. Laxmana Rao's primary areas of specialisation are Finance and Accounts. His expertise spans financial analysis, corporate finance, accounting principles, financial management, and related subjects. Over the years, he has developed a deep understanding of both theoretical and practical aspects of these subjects, which he integrates into his teaching and research.

**Fatma İnce** holds a Ph.D. in Management and Organization and currently serves as the Head of the Health Management Department and Vice Dean at the Faculty of Health Sciences, Mersin University, Türkiye. She is also the Head of the Health Management Master's Program (Thesis Track). She teaches both undergraduate and graduate courses in Organizational Behavior, Entrepreneurship, Leadership, Creative Thinking, and Teamwork, aiming to foster not only managerial skills but also personal growth among her students. Her academic interests include entrepreneurship, leadership, creativity, intergenerational synergy, sustainability, and learning organizations. Beyond her academic responsibilities, she is a Board Member of the Mersin University Career Center, where she contributes to career development initiatives and engages in consultancy activities with various organizations. Additionally, she provides mindfulness-based training to support individuals in cultivating awareness and inner balance, offering a holistic perspective that integrates both academic and personal development.

**Priyanka Koundal** holds a Doctorate in Commerce from the Mittal School of Business, Lovely Professional University, India, where her doctoral research focused on the topic of Accounting Information Systems. She obtained her Bachelor of Commerce (B. Com) and Master of Commerce (M. Com) degrees from Kamla Nehru College for Women, affiliated with Guru Nanak Dev University, Amritsar. She is also a qualified UGC-NET holder in the discipline of Commerce. Dr. Koundal has served as a faculty member in the Department of Commerce at DRV DAV Centenary College, Phillaur, Punjab, India. She has actively contributed to academic discourse by presenting research papers at various national and international conferences organized by prestigious institutions, including the Indian Institute of Management (IIM) Amritsar (2024), IIM Jammu (2023), PSGR Krishnammal College for Women, Coimbatore (2023), and Lovely Professional University, Punjab (2022 and 2023). In addition to her conference engagements, Dr. Koundal has published multiple book chapters and research papers in Scopus-indexed journals and edited volumes, further demonstrating her commitment to scholarly research in the field of commerce and accounting.

**Rohit Koundal** is currently working at Lovely Professional University, where he contributes to the academic and professional development of students in the field of commerce. He holds both a Bachelor's and a Master's degree in Commerce from Guru Nanak College, Sukhchainana Sahib, Phagwara, Punjab, where he laid a strong foundation in business studies, financial systems, and economic theory. In addition to his formal academic qualifications, Mr. Koundal has also completed a Certificate Course in Advanced Accounting and Management (CCAAM) from C-NIT, which has further enhanced his expertise in the areas of financial management, accounting principles, and managerial decision-making. Mr. Rohit Koundal brings over two and a half years of professional experience to his academic role, having worked in various capacities that have enriched his practical understanding of commerce and management. His academic career is complemented by a growing body of scholarly work, with several publications to his credit in national and international journals. These publications reflect his research interests in accounting, business management, and emerging practices in commerce education.

**V Lava Kumar** is an accomplished academician with a diverse educational background and over 13 years of enriching experience in the field of education.

Holding an impressive array of qualifications including an MBA, M. Com, PhD in Management, PGDTTM, along with certifications from APSET in Management and APSET in Commerce. His area of specialization is Finance and Accounting. Currently serving as an Assistant Professor at GITAM School of Business, GITAM Deemed to be University, Bengaluru, Dr. Lava Kumar is dedicated to nurturing the minds of future business leaders. His teaching methodology is grounded in both theoretical knowledge and practical insights, ensuring that students receive a holistic understanding of their subjects. Dr. Lava Kumar's contributions extend beyond the classroom, evident through his prolific research endeavours. He has authored numerous research papers, with 3 publications in prestigious Scopus-indexed and ABDC journals, and an impressive tally of 10 research articles in international and peer-reviewed journals. He co-authored a Book which is published in Surana publications. His research interests primarily revolve around contemporary issues in management and finance, where he strives to contribute to the academic discourse with valuable insights and innovative perspectives.

**Mpho Makgamatha** is a lecturer at the University of Limpopo and a Senior researcher at the South African BRICS Youth Association. Finalising his PhD in Administration in Development Planning, he holds a Master's, honours and a degree in Development Planning and Management. Holds a Geographic Information Systems certificate from the University of Venda, Strategic Management from Open2Study (Australia), Facilitator of Student Training for Entrepreneurial Promotion (STEP) from the University of Luneburg (Germany). He is a member of the South African Planning Institute (SAPI), South African Association for Institutional Research (SAAIR), Black Management Forum and Enactus. Won 2nd Best Doctoral Presenter at the Faculty of Management and Law in 2024. Won the Best Emerging Researcher Award at the South African Association of Public Administration (SAAPAM) conference 2024.

**Michael Meshioye** is a multidisciplinary researcher and analyst whose work connects science, finance, and enterprise. He is a master's student at Ahmadu Bello University, Zaria, an independent researcher and data analyst with Supretec.com. Michael brings a systems-thinking approach to explore how financial inclusion, women's entrepreneurship, and sustainable business can drive development, blending academic insight with real-world application.

**Parvathy Nair** is an accomplished academic and researcher in the field of Finance, with over a decade of experience in teaching, consulting, and scholarly research. She holds a PhD in Finance from Chandigarh University of India, where her doctoral research focused on "Behavioral Finance"

**Amarachi Nwosu** is an Engineering graduate from the Federal University of Technology, Owerri and a certified SEO specialist whose work connects science, entrepreneurship, finance and general business management. As an impact multidisciplinary researcher, Amarachi's core interests span science and engineering, sustainable business models, economic development, artificial intelligence, entrepreneurship and women's empowerment within the context of emerging economies.

**Chinwe Nwosu** is a Doctor of Business Administration (DBA) researcher at Glasgow Caledonian University, UK. Her research explores innovative ways to integrate people, policy, process and technology for the sustainability of educational social enterprises in the Global South. She holds an MBA in Management and a Bachelor's in Industrial Relations and Personnel Management. As an impact researcher, Her core interests span social entrepreneurship, entrepreneurial pedagogy, startup growth strategies, human resource management and workplace digitization, Micro, small and medium enterprise development, women entrepreneurship and information management. She is the author of Revamp: What to Do When You Don't Know What to Do and contributes to impactful business and HRM literature.

**Ademola Joel Osho** is a DBA researcher at Glasgow Caledonian University, UK, where his research focuses on developing a framework for effective digital microfinance to empower women entrepreneurs in the Global South. He holds an MSc in Business Management and a certification in cybersecurity. His research interests include financial inclusion, business finance, women's entrepreneurship, SME development, sustainable business practices, and the role of technology in supporting SME growth.

**Usha Prabhu** holds four Master degrees- MA, M. Phil, MBA, UGC- NET, Ph.D. She has more than 22 Years of teaching experience at the graduate and post-graduate levels. She was one of the member in the syllabus revision committee for the PG- MBA at Bangalore University. She is currently a Faculty at Jain (Deemed-to be University, Bangalore Karnataka, India. She co-authored the book- Organization Behaviour for PG Students.

**Arun R** is an Assistant Professor in the Department of Commerce at Jain (Deemed to be University), Bengaluru. Holding a Master of Commerce (Finance) from Mangalore University, Arun has demonstrated academic excellence through prestigious qualifications, including successful clearances of the UGC NET (Commerce) thrice and KSET once. Dedicated to fostering academic excellence, Arun is passionate about teaching and research, striving to inspire students and contribute valuable insights to the field of commerce and finance.

**Varanasi Rahul** is an Assistant Professor at JAIN University (Bangalore), a semi-qualified Cost Accountant, holding three postgraduate degrees: M.Com (Accounting & Taxation), M.Com (Management), and an MA (History). He has cleared the UGC NET in Commerce twice and has also cleared the AP SET in Commerce, History, and Management, as well as the TS SET in Commerce. With 3 years of experience as an Assistant Professor and 6 months as a Corporate Tax Associate for Australian Taxation at PwC (Big 4), he brings both academic and professional expertise to his field. Additionally, he is a freelance archaeologist, practicing epigraphist in Brahmi script, and a numismatist. His scholarly and creative contributions include over 30 newspaper articles published in Deccan Chronicle, Times of India, and other local newspapers. He has presented and participated in 25 national and international seminars and has published 2 research articles in ABDC Journals, 3 in SCOPUS-indexed journals, 2 in Web of Science and 4 in peer-reviewed journals. As a story writer, 5 of his stories have been published in top magazines of Andhra Pradesh. Furthermore, he has authored 3 books. He has also contributed 13 book chapters to various academic publications. In addition to his extensive achievements, he has applied for 16 patents, of which 2 has been granted in India, 2 in UK and 11 have been published.

**Rismawati Rismawati** is a distinguished academic and consultant with a robust focus on sustainability reporting. She currently holds the position of lecturer and Head of the Quality Assurance Institute at Universitas Muhammadiyah Palopo, where she has been pivotal in ensuring the quality of university processes and outputs since February 2020. Additionally, she serves as an Assurer for Sustainability Reporting at the National Center for Sustainability Reporting in Jakarta, specializing in the evaluation of sustainability reports for mining companies across Indonesia. Her academic qualifications are extensive, comprising a Bachelor's degree in Economics and Accounting, a Master's degree in Accounting Science, and a Doctorate in Accounting from Universitas Brawijaya, Malang. Rismawati is also a certified specialist in sustainability reporting, risk management, and tax planning, holding several prestigious certifications including Certified Sustainability Reporting Specialist (CSRS), Certified Risk Management Practitioner (CRMP), Certified Management Accountant (CMA) and Certified Enterprise Risk Analysis (CERA). In her professional capacity, she has provided consultancy services in financial management and tax compliance for companies such as PT. Reski Barito Timur and PT. Helay Raya. Furthermore, she has authored multiple publications on Social Accounting, Sustainability Accounting, Management Accounting and CSR, contributing significantly to the academic community. Her interests in reading, writing, and travel reflect her commitment to lifelong learning and professional growth in her field.

**José Manuel Saiz-Álvarez**, Ph.D. Eco & Soc received his Ph.D. in Economics and Business Administration, Autonomous University of Madrid (Spain), and Ph.D. in Sociology, Pontifical University of Salamanca (Spain). He is currently a postgraduate professor at the Catholic University of Santiago de Guayaquil (Ecuador) and the Autonomous National University of Honduras (Honduras), an associate professor at the Catholic University of Avila (Spain), and an international researcher at the University of Santiago de Chile. He is a member of the Mexican Academy of Sciences, the Tiberina Academy (Italy), and the Royal Academy of the Sea (Spain). He has also worked as a professor and researcher in Colombia (Autonomous University of Manizales), Mexico (Tecnologico de Monterrey), and Spain (Nebrija University, Pontifical University of Salamanca, Alphonse X University, and Autonomous University of Madrid). He is a speaker in Europe and America, has more than 450 publications, and has supervised 81 doctoral theses in universities in Europe and America—a reviewer of about 20 indexed journals. Through Saiz-Alvarez Microdonations, in collaboration with KIVA, he helps hundreds of micro-entrepreneurs located in 79 countries in the fight against poverty.

**N Sathyanarayana** has over 15 years of teaching experience at both undergraduate and postgraduate levels. He holds a Master of Business Administration degree from VTU and a Master of Commerce degree from Periyar University. He has completed his Ph.D. in Banking and Finance from Dayananda Sagar University. Currently, he serves as an Assistant Professor in the School of Commerce at Jain (Deemed-to-be University), Bangalore. He has published 24 research papers in international journals, including three indexed in Scopus, and seven papers in national journals. Additionally, he has presented 14 research papers at international conferences and 11 at national conferences. He has co-authored two books at the national level and contributed nine Scopus-indexed book chapters.

**G Srividhya**, M.Com, M.Phil, Ph.D., is currently an Assistant Professor in the Department of Commerce at the School of Commerce, Jain (Deemed-to-be University), Bangalore. With a career spanning since 2005, she has accumulated 19 years of teaching experience and 10 years of research experience across various institutions. She has published papers in reputed journals and contributed book chapters to various national and international conferences. She is a life member of professional bodies such as IARA and IAA. She also possesses expertise in accounting and finance.

**Ivan Vargas** is an interdisciplinary researcher with a PhD in management, two M.Sc. degrees, and dual STEAM qualifications, bringing 15+ years' expertise in governance, public administration, security, citizen coexistence, project management, and SDLC. Proven leader of high-impact research with peer-reviewed publications and a postdoctoral fellowship in governance for ecotourism. Skilled at securing funding through science and innovation proposals, mentoring and teaching graduate students, and forging international partnerships. Fluent in English, Spanish, and Italian; proficient in data analysis, and the full software development lifecycle. Passionate about applying research to develop practical solutions that enhance community welfare and regional development.

# Index

## A

## B



## C



## D



## E

# F



# G



# H



# I

## L



## M



## O



## P

## Q



## R



## S



## T

www.ingramcontent.com/pod-product-compliance
Lightning Source LLC
LaVergne TN
LVHW080905300926
849162LV00003B/567